# Meridians feminism, race, transnationalism

VOLUME 23 · NUMBER 1 · APRIL 2024

**SPECIAL ISSUE**
Indigenous Feminisms across the World, Part 1

Basuli Deb and Ginetta E. B. Candelario

..........................................................................

# Indigenous Feminisms across the World, Part 1

...........

> In this sense, we wonder whether universities are also responsible for the epistemicide, for they also have tried to kill our way of knowing.
> —Célia Xakriabá, "Indigenous Women on the Frontlines"

> In a settler colonial context, no clear line can be drawn where colonialism ends and patriarchal violence begins. The fight against patriarchy and sexual oppression is intertwined with the fight against settler-colonialism and capitalism.
> —Al-Qaws in Eman Alasah, "Queer Liberation and Palestine"

> The "Fourth World" model . . . comprises indigenous populations in parts of the world where they are excluded from power and describes a process of decolonisation, which is grounded in revitalisation of indigenous practices that settler-colonialism sought to destroy.
> —Denise Monika Schallenkammer, "The 'Grandmother' of Indigenous Filmmaking"

...........

Several years ago *Meridians* joined many academic organizations and institutions in the United States by acknowledging that our Western Massachusetts–based offices are on Nonotuck land. In this we formed part of a wave of solidarity with Indigenous peoples that necessarily begins with recognition of how settler colonialism is deeply ingrained, embedded, and naturalized in every way, from place-naming conventions to thought structures. Further, as a first step toward moving from acknowledging to acting in the spirit of redress and forum building, *Meridians*

MERIDIANS · feminism, race, transnationalism   23:1 April 2024
DOI: 10.1215/15366936-10935407 © 2024 Smith College

undertook an audit of the content we have published in the twenty-four years of our existence. We found a shocking (if all too common) lack of Indigenous feminists and/or Indigenous feminist work in our oeuvre to date. As a result of this data-driven insight, and by way of beginning to transform our archive, we have endeavored to increase the participation of Indigenous feminist scholars and knowledge producers as peer reviewers and contributors to the *Meridians* project. Editor Candelario's preliminary efforts yielded several publishable submissions focused largely on the Americas. Rather than intersperse these among other issues, we decided to devote an entire issue to Indigenous feminisms across the world.[1]

*Meridians* then invited several Indigenous U.S. scholars with long-standing ties to the journal to guest edit or co–guest edit a special issue with editor Candelario, whose scholarly expertise includes racial formation in the Americas, but none were able to take on this project. However, one of those Indigenous consultants suggested that Basuli Deb, a Bengali scholar who works on materialities of Indigenous and transmigrant lives and who has published in *Meridians*, would be well suited to the role. So it was then that Deb and Candelario began their collaboration as coeditors of this special issue, which we hope will inspire future submissions to *Meridians*, as well as proposals for issues guest edited by Indigenous feminist scholars of feminism, race, and transnationalism.

This new special issue on transnational feminist approaches to Indigeneity intervenes in conversations where "decolonial feminism is often associated with Indigenous scholars and those from the Americas, and postcolonial feminism with scholars from South Asia, Africa, and the Middle East," thereby contesting "the spatial markings of decolonial and postcolonial feminisms" (Ramamurthy and Tambe 2017: 504). Collaboratively harnessing postcolonial and decolonial approaches to strengthen South-South epistemologies, including those in the South spatially marked as the North, this special issue also refuses temporal markings, "the eclipsing of post-colonialism . . . and a setting up of decolonial feminism as always already better *in time*" (Ramamurthy and Tambe 2017: 504). Our issue underscores how Indigenous histories blur the boundaries between franchise colonialism that decolonial scholars associate with nineteenth-century Asia and Africa, and settler colonialism that they attribute to the Columbine Americas. For instance, settler colonialism began on the Indian subcontinent more than sixteen centuries before

Christopher Columbus set foot in the Americas. Other feminist editors such as Priti Ramamurthy and Ashwini Tambe have encouraged us to heed decolonial feminism's emphasis on engaging with settler colonial genocide, its legacies of land dispossession in our times, and transnational gendered racial capitalism. However, the "intellectual incommensurabilities" of postcolonial and decolonial approaches do not elude them, as they highlight that "the emphasis on hybrid identity formation and migration in postcolonial literary studies was difficult to reconcile with the centrality of land and blood in narrations of Indigenous identity in decolonial studies" (Ramamurthy and Tambe 2017: 510). Our issue intervenes to generate a dialogue between such incommensurabilities by bringing migrancy and miscegenation into conversation with land and blood, questioning the segregation of decolonial and postcolonial approaches to Indigeneity. Here we hope to bring together conversations about Indigeneity from across Asia and Africa as well as Australia, Europe, and the Americas. A transnational comparative approach to Indigeneity between the Americas and the "elsewhere" as a philosophical category enables a productive decentering of the Western Hemisphere. Thus, our goal is to explore the praxis-driven possibilities of activist, creative, and epistemic engagements within and across world-wide Indigenous politics, economies, histories, and peoples.

Though several of the contributions in this special issue are framed through the contestations of the nation-state by various Indigenous communities, this in no way suggests that the issue attempts to conceptualize the identity of Indigenous peoples through the Westphalian system. In fact, the editors of this special issue remain critical of the United Nations which, despite its 2007 Declaration on the Rights of Indigenous Peoples, operates through a frame of Westphalian sovereignty. Given that Indigenous peoples are disenfranchised by nation-states across the world, and U.N. officials are representatives of their own nation-states, Indigenous peoples are left in a vulnerable state when transnational justice can only operate at the level of the United Nations through the instrument of the nation-state (Deb 2015). However, our vigilance about Westphalian sovereignty does not imply a homogenization of all Indigenous cultures; rather, it is an attempt to recognize the specificities of Indigenous feminist claims in their geopolitical contexts while forging trans-Indigenous linkages between and among them to validate a Fourth World movement paradigm that shifts perspectives beyond the paradigm of the nation-state. The articles in this special issue offer a range of interventions into conversations about Indigeneity. Though the case of the stateless Palestinian people fighting for Indigenous self-determination problematizes a paradigm that refuses to consider the state as an instrument for social benefits, in the wake of the manifested interdependence of heteropatriarchy and settler colonialism in the region, Palestinian feminist and queer movements are situating local struggles within a transnational context to empower solidarity movements.[1] The Assyrian case offers a powerful intervention into current trends of thinking about Indigenous peoples, particularly in the context of the prominent postcolonial project of Kurdish self-determination and statehood on occupied Assyrian land that geopolitically and discursively renders Assyrian Indigeneity invisible. Ainu feminist artivism makes a counterintuitive intervention into Indigenous epistemologies by insisting on Ainu similarity with rather than difference from the dominant Japanese community, in the process reclaiming liberal notions of the "human" on their own terms as a force of decolonial subversion.

In this moment of history, contributors and editors are in a fraught situation. We walk a tightrope between intervening in the capitalocene and its concomitant epistemological and systemic violence that have resulted in intensifying environmental disasters, and not imposing neoliberal demands on Indigenous peoples to perform their scripted and exotified ontological connections to the ecosystem ethnographically. Elizabeth DeLoughrey warns us that while a generation of "salvage anthropologists" have concentrated on the ruins of Indigenous culture, using "ethnographic allegory" to increase awareness about climate change, it has resulted "in a genre of mourning the loss of both island and nonhuman nature that I term 'salvage environmentalism'" (DeLoughrey 2019: 32). As editors, we would like to problematize not only the binary between Indigenous peoples and metropolitan society, but also the homogenization and romanticizing of Indigenous populations as embodying the ecosystem. For instance, Greenland, which is part of the North American continent, though it has been controlled by Denmark since the 1720s and has subsequently served as a U.S. military base, has gained sovereignty over its natural resources of oil and uranium only recently under the 2009 Self-Government Act. Ulunnguaq Markussen eloquently points to the irony of metropolitan society calling upon Arctic peoples who are not responsible for the climate crisis to "forego economic development and extractive industries" (Markussen 2017: 307). For Markussen, such calls to transform Arctic territories into "a form of World Heritage and present the Arctic as a treasure belonging equally to the world as a whole, are ultimately requests that we who have been so long exploited and so thoroughly dispossessed further sacrifice ourselves for the continued wellbeing of those who have proven unwilling to make sacrifices" (307).

As editors, we could only include contributions that were submitted for consideration, and as such in our editors' introduction we have tried to acknowledge interventions that get short shrift in conversations about Indigeneity. We invited activist, creative, and scholarly submissions, as well as overlaps of these, that both include and decenter the Americas in thinking about Indigeneity. We sought submissions that would create space for voices about gendered Indigenous epistemologies and practices grounded in experiences from other transnational, regional, and local experiences that are regularly marginalized in conversations about Indigeneity in the Americas. Submissions focused on New Zealand, Australia, Kenya, the Democratic Republic of Congo, Somalia, South Africa, Indonesia, India, the Philippines, Palestine, Kashmir, Okinawa, and Ainu were especially of interest to us, as our call for submissions indicated, and we solicited submissions focused on those regions when possible. Ultimately, we received enough submissions that successfully underwent double-blind peer review and offered geographic as well as topical range that we decided to publish a second "Indigenous Feminisms across the World" issue in spring 2025. We hope that these two special issues will encourage other feminist Indigeneity scholars to submit their work to *Meridians* more generally.

As is our practice, we open this issue with the Elizabeth Alexander Creative Writing Award (EACWA) prose winner for 2023, Cece Roth-Eagle's "Mes del viento / Month of Wind." Roth-Eagle's piece was double-anonymized selected from more than one hundred submissions to the 2023 EACWA contest, so we were pleasantly surprised to discover that she was a recent Smith College graduate. That her piece aligned with this issue's "Indigenous Feminisms across the World" theme was equally serendipitous. The *Meridians* Creative Writing Advisory Board called it a "masterful blend of narrative with scholarly power" and "emblematic of the work that *Meridians* strives to publish." Written in three languages—English, Spanish, and Mapundungún—the piece relates Roth-Eagle's experience as an undergraduate student researcher working to understand and learn from a Patagonian Mapuche community leader, Amancay, its first female *longko*, in fall 2022. Amancay and her community shared their history and ongoing efforts to counter the epistemes, policies, and practices that harm their lands and their peoples in the name of "development" and "progress."

Likewise, Elena Ruíz's Counterpoint, "Structural Trauma," offers a philosophical reading of the semantics and logics of the settler colonial epistemic, ontological, and political violence that sustains "settler colonial wealth while simultaneously exonerating White settler culpability" in order to argue for "*a politicized understanding of trauma* that foregrounds . . . lived realities of asymmetric harm" (33). In other words, while all humans can and do experience trauma, BIPOC communities live in "hot zones of traumatological effects" by design in that they suffer "population-level harms" caused by the hegemonic economic, political, social, and cultural orders that sustain settler colonial power. Thus, responding to trauma necessarily entails political as well as psychological, emotional, and spiritual interventions that address cause as much as effect. This is poetically reiterated in "Open Your Mouth," a poem by Yael Valencia Aldana that draws on the Mesoamerican figures of Coatlicue and Jaguar woman as emblematic of Indigenous survivance, rebirth, and regeneration.

An analysis of spirituality's central role in "collective healing, political resistance, and radical social change" is the focus of Ruthann Lee's "Honoring the Spirit and Creator: Indigeneity, Diaspora, and the Politics of Spiritual Relationality in Tannis Nielsen's *A Creation* and Rosa Sungjoo Park's *Forgotten Dreams*." Lee's Media Matters piece argues that what she calls "'pedagogies of the Sacred' help constitute a politics of spiritual relationality that attends to the uneven and contradictory effects of settler colonial capitalism on differently positioned" subjects who must address "questions of complicity, accountability, and the politics of solidarity" across, within, and between BIPOC groups. To illustrate what that might look like, Lee offers an examination of artworks by a diasporic South Korean artist and an Indigenous (Cree/Métis, Anishnawbe, Danish) artist in Canada, both of whom "use digital media art to honor their ancestral traditions and spiritual practices" while also striving toward solidarity and "co-resistance" to settler state inclusion (56).

Moving from the United States to Brazil, the In the Trenches piece for this issue is "Indigenous Women on the Frontlines of Climate Activism: The Battle for Environmental Justice in the Amazon," a public address[2] given by the Amazonian Indigenous activists Sônia Bone Guajajara (Guajajara/Tentehar) and Célia Xakriabá of Minas Gerais during their visit to Smith

College in February 2020, which the professor of Brazilian Studies Malcolm McNee organized and hosted.[3] Guajajara and Xakriabá each spoke of Indigenous organizing against the existential threats that capitalism, colonialism, and repressive extractive regimes pose to the planet and all its peoples. They "fight with the power of spirituality, nourished by [their] territories" and in solidarity with "poor and marginalized women, Black men and women, [who are] all in a [similarly] vulnerable position." Guajajara notes that there are 305 different Indigenous nations living across 26 states and 274 spoken languages in Brazil despite more than half a millennium of settler colonial efforts to destroy, "integrate," and dominate the original peoples of the land. Despite forming just 1 percent of the Brazilian population, they protect 13 percent of the country's territory and biodiversity, "sustain[ing] it through [their] daily fight on the steps of Congress . . . tak[ing] on rubber bullets, pepper spray, police brutality, jail time" (93). At the same time, Indigenous women leaders work against the gendered violence of settler colonial *machista* ideologies mistakenly characterized as Indigenous culture, calling for the interlinked decolonization of minds, spirits, bodies, and territory alike.

Similarly, Eman Alasah's Counterpoint, "The Palestinian Feminist Movement and the Settler Colonial Ordeal: An Intersectional and Interdependent Framework," documents how Palestinian feminist and queer organizations contest both the Israeli state's "racist and discriminatory colonial policies against the Indigenous peoples of the land it occupies" and patriarchal Palestinian conservatives. Alasah argues that in the Palestinian context, patriarchal violence and settler colonialism "collude in oppressing Indigenous women" and LGBTQI folks must respond simultaneously to both. She analyzes two contemporary movements that "target [these] overlapping and complementary structures of oppression," Al-Qaws and the Palestinian Feminist Collective. Both exemplify decolonial, anticolonial, and transnational feminist intersectionality that "seeks to end oppression 'from within, as well as without' " (127).

We turn next to northern Fenno-Scandinavia and the Murmansk peninsula, where the Nordic settler colonial state and transnational capital engaged in iron ore mining have likewise endeavored to dispossess the Sámi people of their land. Ina Knobblock's Essay, "A Rape of the Earth: Sámi Feminists against Mines," draws on conversations with Sámi feminists engaged in anti-mining activism, artivism, and advocacy focused on protecting their "children's and grandchildren's natural environment,

health, land, water, and local primary produce" as well as traditional reindeer herding practices. Knobblock argues that the Sámi relational episteme is rooted in the "interconnectedness between land, nature, and
people" similar to the Abya Yala notion of the body-land/*cuerpo-territorio*
continuum. Accordingly, mining's impact on the earth and on Indigenous
reindeer herding violates the land, its nonhuman and human beings alike,
and forms part of the larger history of settler colonial gendered and sexualized violence against Indigenous peoples. Finally, Knobblock presents Ti/
Mimie Märak's poem "What Local People" as an example of Sámi artivist
response to epistemically and ontologically violent settler colonial "denial
of Indigenous . . . presence, cultures, and histories" (149).

The critical role of artistry and creativity in feminist Indigenous activism
is likewise the focus of our second Media Matters feature by Denise Monika
Schallenkammer, "The 'Grandmother' of Indigenous Filmmaking in New
Zealand: Merata Mita—Film Is Her Patu." Schallenkammer discusses
*Merata: How Mum Decolonised the Screen* (2018), a film about the life and work
of Merata Mita—an internationally renowned Māori activist, prolific documentary filmmaker, and single mother—produced by her youngest son,
Heperi Mita. Merata Mita made films about her and her family's experiences of "colonialism, oppression, misogyny, and sexism" that "(metaphorically speaking) [held] up a mirror" to New Zealand society in the
1970s and 1980s. Schallenkammer also presents Merata Mita's own words
to offer "a kind of portrait in which Merata Mita 'speaks directly' to the
reader" (159). Along the way, we learn about both Mita's filmmaking and
the Māori community's decolonial activism that she documented and
screened internationally.

Our next piece, a stunning Visual Essay by Gina Athena Ulysse, offers a
subtle but powerful example of artmaking as epistemology and ontology.
"Tools of the Trade; or, Women's Works" brings together *kwi* (gourds) made
from the calabash tree—which is native to the Caribbean—and the ocher
gifted to her by "a Wiradjuri artist in Darwin, the capital of Australia's
Northern Territory." For Ulysse, this *rasanblaj* of Indigenous and Caribbean
primary materials was the beginning of "a new conversation" about "the
relationship between the quotidian, gendered labor, and the sacred." Similarly, "Woman Digging Thorns out of Field," our cover art by the Palestinian artist-in-exile Dana Barqawi, transforms another medium historically deployed in the service of colonialism, settler colonialism, and
imperialism—photography—into a collage that "is a commentary on the

politics of land and the colonization of the Indigenous body" (295). In this collage, Barqawi recontextualizes the fetishized object of the colonial gaze into a space that makes visible the subject's general humanity and specificity. This explicitly "challenges institutional invisibility of Indigenous history and experience" and deploys "beauty . . . as a tool" to hoist the colonial gaze on its own petard (Botto 2022).

Mariam Georgis's Essay, "Traversing Disciplinary Boundaries, Globalizing Indigeneities: Visibilizing Assyrians in the Present," also engages with the theme of making Indigenous activism globally visible. Georgis focuses on the Middle East's frequently overlooked Indigenous community, the Assyrians who live in *Bath-Nahrain*/Mesopotamia. An Assyrian international relations scholar, Georgis shows "the commonalities Assyrians share with other Indigenous peoples: invasion, dispossession, domination, and marginalization, and the context of the mythmaking of the invaders, which passes as political and cultural truth of the states founded" on their territory. At the same time, she reflects on her own "complicity" with the Canadian settler colonial society in which she lives and works as an (im)migrant who has been re-racialized as "Brown" and presumptively Muslim/potential terrorist due to her Iraqi citizenship. Her essay seeks "to bring the Assyrian struggle in[to] conversation and in solidarity with decolonial struggles and other intertwined struggles across the globe . . . [that challenge] the fundamental legitimacy of the nation-state structure." Georgis's intervention points to the problematic labeling/framing of (Middle Eastern) states that have emerged out of European colonization as "postcolonial" when, in fact, from the perspective of their territory's Indigenous peoples they more accurately represent a new chapter in an ongoing saga of settler colonialism. Thus, for example, while understandable and even "valid," the Kurdish liberation movement's struggle for self-determination, redress of state-sanctioned violence, and the establishment of a sovereign nation-state of its own runs the risk of "building a state on occupied Assyrian land, resulting in the latter's expulsion and subjugation." In other words, Georgis raises and engages with an important question: "What [happens] when settlers are not White but uphold or emulate their occupation of Indigenous lands on the model of White supremacy?" (197).

Our second Counterpoint, Yurika Tamura's "Rehumanizing Ainu: Performance of Desubjectification and a Politics of Singularity," also takes up the question of how non-Western nation-states adopt and adapt European and American settler colonial ideologies, policies, and practices in order to claim Indigenous lands and dispossess Indigenous people. Specifically, Tamura examines how Ainu performers respond to the Japanese government's formal recognition of Ainu culture by undertaking "a subversive desubjectification, a reformulation of their identity defined on their own terms" as human above all else. This strategy rejects the state's strategy of narrowly defining Ainu culture as language, song, dance, crafts, and festivals, and of strategically eliding the historic and ongoing colonial violence against Ainu. Tamura's own positionality "as a transnational Ainu descendant . . . a reconnector to Ainu heritage . . . and as an Ainu person" who was not "raised as Ainu" nor aware of her heritage when growing up in the context of a family culture that was "Ainu, Japanese, [and] Korean" in the Sapporo/Chitose area of Japan exemplifies the complexity of Ainu subjectivity and self-representation. Her positionality also leads her to reflect on the challenges of undertaking ethnographic research in a community that struggled to be officially recognized at home and internationally, as finally happened in 2008 and 2019 respectively. Tamura argues that Ainu performance artists such as Mayunkiki and Sekine Maya, and the Pirka Kotan cultural center, seek to move beyond official state recognition—which is necessarily premised on colonial interpretive frames for perceiving Ainu subjectivity as "deviant, savage, . . . outsider, . . . equated with colonial stigma"—by insisting that "the Japanese . . . imagine Ainu as regular people in a mundane scene" (220).

Continuing with the political paradox inherent in the pursuit of recognition by nation-states founded on the premise of dispossession, displacement, and disappearance of Indigenous communities, cultures, and histories, "What It Takes to be Counted" is Priti Narayan's Interview of Ruby Hembrom, the founder of adivaani,[4] the first Indigenous-run English-language platform for publishing and documenting Adivasi voices in India. Adivasi (plural Adivasis) is a term used to refer to the Indigenous peoples of Northeast India, and adivaani has published nineteen books since its founding in 2012, including several children's books that "center Adivasi tellings in Adivasi voices, as a way to challenge colonial and mainstream representations" of their peoples and culture, and "to bring attention to Indigenous loss and reclamation." Hembrom explains that she publishes in English because "that's what it takes to be counted" and because although "English is as foreign to us as Hindi," "translation is transmission." She also explains that "Adivasi feminism responds to patriarchy entrenched in both colonialism and coloniality," that Adivasi women's relationship to their ancestral land is central to their feminism, as is "repossession of [Adivasi] knowledges, histories, and identities" (243).

Lori Barkley's transcription and contextualization of Marilyn James's thoughts on Smum'iem "obligation to educate" those outside Indigenous communities and to "engage" with patriarchy within the community—which Barkley titled "The Contemporary Origins of Smum'iem Matriarchy in Sinixt Təmxʷúlaʔxʷ"[5]—likewise offers a powerful example of Indigenous self-representation in the public history and culture realm. An author, storyteller, educator, and community advocate, James was Smum'iem matriarchy's appointed spokesperson in the 1990s and subsequently became a smum'iem matriarch herself. In this piece James reflects on the centrality of matrilineality and matriarchy in the Sinixt Nation's survival, explaining that despite the Canadian government designating it "extinct for the purposes of the Indian Act" in 1956, "a matriarchal war is raging, it's raging alive, it's a firestorm" that is inspiring young women to "be of service" to the cause (260).

Moving from Indigenous matriarchy to motherhood, Esther Oluwashina Ajayi-Lowo's In the Trenches essay, "Safe Motherhood Initiative: Whither African Indigenous Birthing Knowledge?," critiques the coloniality of the World Health Organization's Safe Motherhood Initiative (SMI). The SMI was launched in 1987 to address high maternal mortality rates in low- and middle-income countries, and was quickly adopted by the United Nations and global NGOs. Ajayi-Lowo attests to the program's success in establishing Western/Global North medical paradigms and norms as superior to autochthonous Global South maternal, midwifery, or community knowledge and practices by recounting her own experiences as a forty-something-year-old Nigerian mother of four who devoted her "feminist activism for reproductive health and human rights in Nigeria . . . [to] making Western maternal healthcare available, accessible, and affordable for women" despite having grown up witnessing the Indigenous "birthing wisdom" of women in her community. A miscarriage and near–maternal death experience in 2007 "due to medical negligence" within the SMI-modeled system of Nigeria became a "turning point toward remembering the African Indigenous knowledge and practice" displaced by the SMI's hegemony, and led her to research "the perspectives of Indigenous midwives and birthing women who use their services in Lagos, Nigeria" presented in this piece (266).

Finally, we close by noting that Huanani-Kaye Trask (1949–2021) passed away while this issue was in progress. As *Meridians* readers surely know, Trask was an indomitable Native Hawaiian anticolonial activist, scholar, educator, and poet. A political scientist by training who taught at the University of Hawai'i at Mānoa and was the founder and director of the Kamakūokalani Center for Hawaiian Studies there, Trask was also a leader in the Hawaiian sovereignty movement until her death. Trask's life and work exemplified transnational Indigenous feminism devoted to decolonial political action and anti-imperialist solidarity (Williams 2021). Thus, we dedicate this issue to her legacy and celebrate her example: *a hui hou.*

.........................................................................................

**Basuli Deb** is a professorial research associate at the University of London's SOAS School of Law. She is actively engaged with Columbia's Center for Contemporary Critical Thought and has been a visiting scholar at Columbia's Institute for Comparative Literature and Society and Institute for the Study of Human Rights. She is a lifetime scholar at Rutgers's Institute for Research on Women where she previously held a global scholar position. Deb's publications include a monograph, *Transnational Feminist Perspectives on Terror in Literature and Culture* (2015), multiple peer-reviewed articles, coedited special issues, and anthologies. In another completed book manuscript Deb explores the possibility of a rapprochement between decolonial and postcolonial studies through the connected materialities of Indigenous and transmigrant lives in gendered literary, visual, and media archives from Africa, Asia, and the Americas, and in her third monograph project, Deb is combining a transnational feminist analytic with feminist science studies to forge a conversation between climate change and pandemics. She is on the steering committee of Feminist Publishing Futures—a grant-funded international project run by a collective of feminist and social justice journal editors—and has served in feminist leadership capacities at the Modern Language Association and the National Women's Studies Association. Deb has delivered keynotes at international conferences and offered recommendations to the United Nations for addressing sexual violence in the Rohingya genocide.

**Notes**

1   An inquiry into legal-administrative documents from the British Mandate years in Palestine, such as the Balfour Declaration of 1917, British White Paper of 1922, and the 1938 Macdonald White Paper, together with the diplomatic papers of James MacDonald—the U.S. ambassador to Israel in 1948—is especially useful in understanding Palestinian Indigeneity and earlier imperialist decision making that led to the predicament in the region today. See Columbia Rare Book Manuscript Library, Herbert H. Lehman Collections.

2   Elena Langdon, a Smith College undergraduate majoring in Portuguese, translated from the Portuguese language to English, and we include both the original and translation here.

3   McNee's introduction offers brief biographies of Guajajara and Xakriabá and their leadership in Amazonian Indigenous environmental justice movements.

4   We follow the organization's convention of writing its name entirely in lowercase letters. See https://adivaani.org/about/.

5   This piece is a selection from her "Maps of My World" graphic and digital memoir project; the audio file is available in our website's "On the Line" feature: https://sites.smith.edu/meridians/on-the-line/.

**Works Cited**

Botto, Izabella. 2022. "The Act of Existing." ArcGIS StoryMaps, January 2, 2022. https://storymaps.arcgis.com/stories/c1d9a446d0ea465f9649e09bfc06bd5c.

Deb, Basuli. 2015. *Transnational Feminist Perspectives on Terror in Literature and Culture.* New York: Routledge.

DeLoughrey, Elizabeth. 2019. *Allegories of Anthropocene.* Durham, NC: Duke University Press.

Markussen, Ulunnguaq. 2017. "Towards an Arctic Awakening: Neocolonialism, Sustainable Development, Emancipatory Research, Collective Action, and Arctic Regional Policymaking." In *The Interconnected Arctic*, edited by Kirsi Latola and Hannele Savela, 305–11. Cham, Switzerland: Springer.

Ramamurthy, Priti, and Ashwini Tambe. 2017. Preface to *Feminist Studies* 43, no. 3: 503–11.

Williams, Annabelle. 2021. "Huanani-Kay Trask, Champion of Native Rights in Hawaii, Dies at 71." *New York Times*, July 9. https://www.nytimes.com/2021/07/09/us/haunani-kay-trask-dead.html.

Cece Roth-Eagle

........................................................................................

# Mes del viento
Los Mapuche¹ de la lof Kinxikew a través de la perspectiva de su primera longko mujer

# Month of Wind
The Mapuche lof Kinxikew through the Perspective of Their First Female Longko

**Capítulo I: *La fábula de la Amancay // The Fable of the Amancay***
She takes us to her *camino.*

The land exhales into springtime. The romp of the breeze and cry of the condor. Grasses form muddy puddles below our feet, the melt of snow-capped mountains. It smells of soil.

*I know that I can't be without being here. At the beginning, it cost me to understand this dream. It makes me happy to have had this call to return to the territory.*

Under its rows of poplar trees, Amancay's pathway shimmers while she speaks. She had never seen this path before she started dreaming of it as a girl, where we now stand in a patch of balsamic sunlight. Amancay grew up in a tourist-laden town in Patagonia, but in her *pewmas*, she walked the poplars.

*I had fear of my identity. I used to resist anything new. To know that your life was not what you thought it was, that your history was not what you thought it was.*

At the age of nineteen, Amancay's uncle brought her to the ancestral territory for the first time. On that visit, she walked the *camino* of her dreams.

MERIDIANS · feminism, race, transnationalism   23:1 April 2024
DOI: 10.1215/15366936-10926984 © 2024 Smith College

*Sentir que tenés un lugar en donde podés desarrollar tu vida. Yo pienso en mi hijo. Y así, en todas las futuras generaciones para vivir. Estamos cerca de dejarle un lugar a nuestros hijos.*

To feel that you have a place where you can develop your life. I think of my son, and all the future generations to live. We're closer to leaving a place for our children.

Pewma, in Mapuche culture, is not just a dream. It's a revelation. Her face laces in shadow as the canopies shift above us.

A year and a half ago, at the age of thirty-three, amidst a communal reckoning and the peak of the pandemic, Amancay became the lof[2] Kinxi-kew's youngest and first female *longko*.[3]

*I understand that sometimes, the forces of a territory make one return. It's very clear that I had to be here. I still don't know why. Today I am longko, but I don't know if that's the reason.*

o o o

Flor is telling me a *fábula*. A journalist and researcher specializing in social-environmental issues and my advisor on this project, Flor and I spend our time in the car closing the cultural, contextual, and idiomatic gaps that I have yet to grasp after three months in Argentina. She also tells me Mapuche fables.

We pass between Río Negro and Neuquén on the highway and the coarse Patagonic scenery tumbles beyond the panes of our windows.

When her lover becomes ill, a Mapuche woman mounts the cerro in search of an herbal remedy. Once on the mountain peak, the cóndor tells her that the price for the medicine is her heart.

She agrees, saves her lover's life, and ascends the mountain once more. Soon after, the vulture is seen flying away with her heart in his beak.

Amancays are a yellow *flor del bosque*.[4] According to Mapuche legend, the red drops of its center signify the blood of our heroine's heart.

Es *patriarcal*, Flor says as she pushes on her sunglasses.

o o o

## Ley 26.160

"The execution of sentences, procedural or administrative acts whose purpose is the eviction or vacating of the lands referred to in Article 1 shall be suspended for the term of the declared emergency." (Ley 26.160)

In 2006, the Argentine government declared a state of emergency to halt Indigenous evictions across the country. Provinces were instructed to survey territories with their local native communities and ideally, officially recognize their claims; while the law has been extended three separate times to provide provincial governments time to initiate the process, it never reached politically taut regions like Neuquén (Yanniello 2020).

The Mapuche lof Kinxikew have faced two eviction attempts in the last decade from proprietors who believed they had private ownership of ancestral lands. I visit Amancay and her community on November 14, 2022. In accordance with Ley 26.160, the historic *relevamiento de la tierra* begins.

o o o

As Flor and I pull through the gate and onto the territory, there is an outpour of people from the *proveeduría*, the circular operations building for camping administration. Framed in glass panes, it outlooks *Lago Nahuel Huapi* and *Manke Ruka*, the nearest mountain: *Home of the Vulture*.

Amancay's mother, Nora, greets me as I open the car door.

*La escritora*, she says as she kisses both of my cheeks. *The writer.*

We cross the grass to Amancay's partner as he grapples with a hose. ¡Mucho viento! he yells over the shake of the trees. *Much wind!*

The primary meeting of the land survey has adjourned, so the group mills about and we lap them, kissing both of their cheeks. The *lof Melo*, a smaller and more recently established community, are under the protection of the *lof Kinxikew* and participate in the *relevamiento* to certify their territory. I met with them during a previous visit to Patagonia. *Vientísmo!* they call to me.

In our car ride, Flor had explained to me that November is *el mes de viento*, the month of wind, across Patagonia. The heavy clouds twist on the skyline; the snow-drenched peaks seem to teeter.

Flor offers me her cup of mate as we wait outside of the *proveeduría* for Amancay. *Es demasiado amagro para vos? It's too bitter for you?* she shouts and I shake my head.

As far as I can tell, the cultural and social hub of Argentina is the practice of communal-infusion through "taking mate": sipping the herb through a silver straw, or *bombillo*, after combining it with lukewarm water. The cluster of people pass mate between each other.

Many Argentines claim its conception originated from European settlers in the 1800s. But like most things, taking mate was born within Indigenous populations and previous to the constitution of the State.

We're told that she's ready, so Flor and I push our way through the draught and into the darkened room. A paper map hangs on the wall: the product of today's meeting. Colorful lines and crude drawings identify areas of the territory.

*Lafún y La laguna del toro; Río pedregoso y Piedra de soldados; Arroyo las vueltas; Camping Manke Ruka; avistamiento del cuero; usurpador Ovrun.*

The Lafún and the Lagoon of Offering; Stony River and the Rock of Soldiers; the Returns Creek, Camping Manke Ruka; the sighting of the leather; and the Ovrun usurper.

They have to prove to the State that they were here, long before the State ever existed.

○ ○ ○

A lesson in Mapudungún, the Mapuche language.

*El Wallmapu.* Ancestral territory of the Indigenous nations of the Mapuche which crosses the highlands of the Andes.

*Los mapu-che.* People of the land.

*Mapu-dungún.* Language of the land.

As the Mapuche *longko* and researcher Wenteche José Quidel writes,

"*We are not only referring to material land, because that exists in the concept Puji Mapu. Mapu is a term that implies all the dimensions of life within the universe. That is to say, we can understand the cosmos as Mapu*" (Matías Rendón 2018).

Another word: *winka.*

*Los conquistadores* of the sixteenth century. Originally signifying the white race. It stems from the word *Inka* referring to a different colonizer, a different empire that once arrived to El Wallmapu.

El Wallmapu is a region spanning the base of the Southern Hemisphere, extending through parts of Chile and Argentina long before the first *winkas* invented their territorial delimitations.

El Wallmapu is not a territory, explicitly; its aboriginal people now steward only 6 percent of its terrain. It holds the history of conquest, and the modernity of its material exploitation. Private sectors want to convert its mountains to mines of gold and silver, its biodiversity to monoculture forests. How can we conceptualize of a place that *once was*? That has within it buried an ancient knowledge and collective memory?

Amancay is trying to remember.

○ ○ ○

*Yo sabía que mi destino iba a llegar algún día, pero nunca pensé que iba a ser tan rápido.*

Amancay sits in a chair across the room, the quivering land framed behind her head in the windowpane. She began by giving her formal introduction in Mapudungún, which is how she initiates all meetings. The room is lined with family members who sleepily half-listen; her three-year-old son, Toki, circles her with a plastic gun. The room is cool and dark and cast in the shadow of *Manke Ruka*.

*Authority elections were coming up. I talked to my family first. My dad said, "I'll go with you," and my mom said, "Me too."*

*I believe that to be an authority, or to have such strong authority, you need a solid base, which is family. And that base was always there in the worst moments and continues to be there today.*

*My uncle brought me to the community; he told me, "You have to come with me."*

*My uncle brought me here and made me know my family because I didn't know them, and he made me know my identity.*

*I could see with my eyes a dream I had since I was very young, a dream of the path.*

*I am grateful for everything he gave me and for the place he gave me here in the territory, but I also have to be honest that he hurt me a lot.*

*Because at one point, he felt that I was like him.*

In 2020, her uncle was banished from the community, resulting in Amancay's ascent to the role of *longko*.

o  o  o

From across the room, Amancay's other uncle tells us the fable of the *boleadora*, which was found on the grounds of the territory. A *bola* consists of a cord tethered to rock weights; initially a weapon to entangle the legs of prey, it was a popular tool across Indigenous South America.

When the *winkas* arrived to Bariloche, *boleadoras* became a form of protection and defense. *Fue la última resistencia tuvieron*, Amancay says. *It was the last resistance they had.*

o  o  o

The Conquest of the "Desert," from 1878 to 1885, was an Indigenous genocide by part of the Argentine military, commanded by General Julio A. Roca. The South's native populations were to be exterminated for the betterment of a developing Eurocentric state. Roca's forces conducted concentration camps, torture, assassination, enslavement, and *desparecidos*, or disappeared persons (Melfi 2015). Today, there exists a delegitimization campaign sustained by racist ideals and nationalists with the false premise of *extranjerización* or "foreignization" of Mapuche communities: that is, that they are Chilean usurpers without ancestral claim to El Puelmapu[5] (Crespo et al. 2021).

*It was impossible to remove us completely. And those who resisted were sent to live on top of El Cerro, like my family, because the Nahuel Huapi National Park became criminalized. The park put our family in the category of settlers and gave us a precarious permit to occupy the passages. They gave us a little piece of paper saying that we only had the status of settlers and that we had to pay for the grazing of our animals.*

*We became nothing. And on top of that we had to pay them. We needed to adopt a new way of living, of eating, because here the farmers already had plantations and animals, and suddenly they closed everything with wire fences. They turned us into their own employees. . . . Many of our family ended up being the women who took care of their children, or the men who had to put up the fences in our own territory.*

*Then, on top of that, they had to hide their identity. They spoke Mapudungún. They did ceremonies in places where nobody could see them. It was a loss of cultural history that cut with my grandfather. He taught us everything that has to do with the knowledge of the territory, he knows everything. But never about identity. We never had a lesson of Mapudungún, he never told us anything that they did [in terms of] being Mapuche.*

Children and adults alike learn Mapudungún and practice the spiritual and medicinal traditions of their ancestors as acts of cultural restoration. But much of the knowledge has been generationally lost in an attempt at survival.

o o o

On our drive home, Flor pulls to the lip of the highway which cuts through la *meseta*, or plateau. Its shrubs and sands unfold flatly. All I can hear is the scorch of the wind on this hard place.

Beyond, peaks clot the *fondo*,[6] engulfed in mountainous shadow.

This is where the battles once took place, where *conquistadores* met Mapuche, firearms *en contra de boleadoras*. Mapuche *en contra del Estado.*

*Fue la última resistencia tuvieron.*

*It was the last resistance they had.*

Back in the car, Flor tells me that nothing has changed: the heart of the conflict is still firearms against bolas for Patagonia's disputed frontier.

o o o

"Leaving for future times a bastard progeny, rebellious to the culture, . . .
What future awaits . . . South American states that have alive in their
entrails the wild or barbarian Indigenous races that they absorbed in colonization, and that obstinately preserve their traditions of the forests, their
hatred of civilization, their primitive languages, and their habits of indo-
lence and disdainful reputation against the dress, grooming, and comforts
and uses of civilized life?"
—Domingo Sarmiento, *De la educación popular*. President of Argentina
(1868–74) y "padre" of public education

## Capítulo II: El hogar del cóndor // The Home of the Vulture
The beach rocks shift under our feet.

As we walk the shoreline of the *Lago Nahuel Huapi*, Flor distinguishes
plant species for me. *El sauce*, the willow that mirages in the breeze; *las rosas
mosquetas*, sweetbriars which won't ripen until winter comes. On our drives,
flowering retamas ornate the highway in yellowing buds. But they're not
native to this area, and neither are the pines that engulf the *bosques* or the
poplar trees that lined Amancay's *pewma*.

Planted in the 1970s to quickly reforest the farmlands of the steppe,
Douglas firs and other pine species now burn faster and enhance climate-
induced wildfires (Bilbao 2022). Patagonia's vegetal biodiversity could be
reduced entirely to pine in the next hundred years (Leitch 2017).

○ ○ ○

Argentina's nineties marked the emergence of a new political and financial
strategy: neo-extractivism and agro-exportation. The diffusion of neoliberal
ideology encouraged privatization of land (at the cost of the displacement of
Indigenous communities) and the lack of governmental interference and
publicly funded programs. The growth of an exportation economy matched
rising demand for commodities in the West (Harvey 2005).

With the false promise of financial satiation after prolonged economic
crisis, the Argentine State initiated its expansion into, and exploitation of,
rural lands deemed previously unprosperous: El *Wallmapu* (Svampa 2019).

○ ○ ○

*Another fable.*

*Amancay's abuelo, José, once rested upon the rocky shore of the Lago Nahuel Huapi
and beside the slope of Manke Ruka.*

*The ground began to shift under him and he realized that, rather than perching on the usual gravel, the beachfront was leather. It was alive.*

*Then, it tossed him into the center of the lago.*

○ ○ ○

In Mapuche cosmovision, *ngen* are the spiritual forces of El Wallmapu. They reify in order to communicate. In this case, the *ngen-ko* serves as a sacred reminder. Amidst environmental crisis, Mapuche belief systems propose alternative methods of coexistence (Yanniello 2009).

*Biodiversity is threatened today by large speculators and large political forces that do not care about anything at the cost of being able to generate more money. For us, it is not money: it is life that we remember.*

*There is no love; life is not worth anything to them. The important thing is to have more and more property, more and more money, and above all, they don't care about anything.*

*On the other hand, our proposal is kvme felen.*

*There are other proposals of life, where the first priority is love, caring for others and caring for nature. We see ourselves in a space surrounded by life, and that life is in the lake, the mountains, the forest.*

*We are working for a totally different political project, another form of social construction.*

*Life is not about competing, life is about living and being happy, isn't it? Because that is what we were born for, but no. You see so many injustices, you see so much evil in people.*

○ ○ ○

The Patagonic region of El Wallmapu is in stages of exploration: deposits of gold, silver, and uranium; petrolic exploitation using hydrofracking techniques; deforestation and monoculture forests. But with threats of overexploitation and ecosystemic collapse, communal mobilization has stopped advances of these initiatives in recent years (Rodriguéz Pardo 2011). And yet, still they come.

Twenty kilometers away, in the central and northern zones of the Neuquén province, new petroleum reserves have been found underneath the territories of Mapuche communities.

○ ○ ○

This alternative social construction takes form as the *Manke Ruka* camping site, where the community offers an affordable, educational space; guests receive lessons on Mapuche ways of life and ancestral practices of caring for the land.

They are also planning an outreach program for farming, where agricultural processes will be made accessible, where people can learn *where their dulce de leche comes from,* as Amancay puts it.

*Roca made a map.*

*He decided how he was going to distribute all the territory, but he also decided a place where he was going to create national parks, that is, places protected by an institution.*

*It turns out that when he thought and divided all the territory, we were still here. And still, they continue to replicate that logic in the Mapuche territories.*

*They teach park rangers that we have to conserve the native animals of the place, but when they meet and come to work where we live, they realize that there are people and that, for them, we are an attack against all that biodiversity.*

*We bring our knowledge ancestrally.*

*But it is difficult for them to understand our relationship with the territory. They see us as a great threat and, despite the fact that today there is a relationship between the national parks and the Mapuche people, how can we understand these two logics of protecting the territory?*

*Therefore, it is constantly constructing itself through a dialogue that is exhausting. Sometimes they forget and end up fining us for something that we don't consider valid.*

*I am the one in my community who is always trying to ensure that my people do not have a conflict with park rangers.*

El Consejo Intercultural de Comanejo attempts to incorporate this native knowledge into the stewardship of the land by including Mapuche board members. But in general, conservationists distrust Mapuche means of land stewardship because it falls outside of Western frameworks of knowledge and practice.

At one point as she speaks, she turns to Flor: *La cara. The face.* She laughs, asking if I'm understanding.

*Entiendo todo,* I assure her, even as an outsider with questionable language comprehension. Even if I'm not entirely certain that I'm telling the truth.

○ ○ ○

I wander the sleet-shined streets of Bariloche, which slope downward to *Avenida 12 de Octubre* and the long road paralleling *Lago Nahuel Huapi.* The view sprawls, mountain ranges consumed by the frail blues of a cold sky and the dappling water. I stand listening to the slow lap of waves cresting coastline.

Bariloche self-advertises as the "Little Switzerland" of Patagonia. It's a tourist hub of outdoor sporting gear, gothic-style villas, chocolaterías, and neon hotel signage promising vacancy.

Bariloche-goers seem entirely made up of either the retired or back-packing postgraduates. But the town is surrounded on all sides by poverty, nearly half of which are Mapuche communities.

*Virulofche. La gente del otro lado de la montaña.* The people on the other side of the mountain. The name "Bariloche" toponymies from Mapudungún.

In the town's plaza, tourists gaze out over the bruising skyline. I'm looking for an allusion to the cultural hurt behind "Little Switzerland's" neat image: and then I find, in the center of the plaza, a Roca statue mounted on a horse and drenched in the red graffiti of blood.

**Capítulo III: *La fábula de la vuelta* // The Fable of the Return**
*Anyone want maté-cito?* Flor asks.

We sit at a picnic table outside. *I was told that Bariloche finally decided to give me a beautiful day,* and it's true: we are in short sleeves and sleepy under the sunlight's sweet gaze.

Amancay taps out a heartbeat on her chest: *Toc-toc, toc-toc. The noise of a heartbeat is distinct, isn't it?*

I listen to the thud of her palm and the tap of her tongue against the roof of her mouth—her pulse turned outward to me.

*Our heart beats differently at certain moments. When it is calm, it makes toc-toc, toc-toc.*

*When one is with a lot of emotion, it makes tac-tac-tac.*

Amancay is describing the *kultrún* she plays, a sacred Mapuche percussion instrument that replicates heart sounds. The leather of the drum is painted geographically and seasonally: *norte, oeste, este, y sur; otoño, primavera, invierno y verano.*

*When I was nineteen years old, my uncle brought me here. I was studying tourism at that time. He made me meet the rest of my family.*

Amancay's grandmother died giving birth to Amancay's mother, Nora, so her grandfather, José Quintriqueo, gave her away.

*He [her uncle] always knew me, he always saw in me the possibility that I could accompany him in also generating a change in the territory. And from that moment on, everything changed . . . everything changed.*

Her younger self, the one who existed long before she knew her Mapuche heritage, she affectionately refers to as *Mankey*.[7] I feel that girl here with us, as Amancay describes making music under the hum of the life all around us.

*I was always very fearful as a girl.*

*I realized that those insecurities didn't let me be who I am, so Mankey has to let go of those insecurities because she can do a lot.*

*I am capable of generating well-being for many people; I feel that I can make an impact on many. So I have lost my fear and that loss of fear has made me able to do many things that I would never have believed I was capable of.*

*I had never thought I would be so valued and so loved for having, at least, changed someone's life a little bit. Mankey's going to have to know that in the future.*

*A horse wanders by, picking at the grasses.*

*But Mankey always saw a dream when she fell asleep.*

The *paseo* of her dreams was a point of entrance for the evictors that came for the land. It was also the pathway the community took to reenter the territory upon their return.

o o o

**Pregúntame, Cece.**
Amancay and I sink into the verdancy around us. I ask her if she was named for the fable of the Amancay. But no, no; her mother just liked the flower.

*Es romántica,* she tells me, and she smiles.

She's preoccupied with the idea that no one is documenting this period of great restoration, and histories are disappearing, just as they did with her grandfather.

Can she describe the moment she met her family? Saw her land? But she can't tell me of her homecoming—she's lost it all to memory.

*You recreate it like a fable.*

*What I am proposing to you is that you also give yourself the audacity to interpret it as you would have imagined it. I trust you.*

*Kvme felen,* in Mapuche cosmovision, proposes an alternative way of life to the capitalist system.

It does not contain territorial exploitation, cultural devastation, or spiritual eviction; no hyper-consumption and overproduction and materialism.

This way of life asks for the restoration of equilibrium. It suggests the ability to understand ourselves as inseparable from nature, as well as our own capacity for agricultural self-sustenance. The delicate web of nature is revived; love's gentle balance centralized (Confederación Mapuche del Neuquén 2010).

It feels like home without property, like a great return of environmental consonance. It is how El *Wallmapu* once looked, long before any *winkas*. It is the *toc-toc, toc-toc* of the heartbeat of the world, made tranquil again.

That is how her homecoming felt to me.

o o o

*Our spirit does not always go with this body. Sometimes it leaves and goes places where we like to be. He loved to be here, despite all the damage. He fought a lot for it and so his* pini *keeps coming back.*

Amancay breastfeeds her son while she describes her election to *longko*. It did not follow the cultural trajectory of spiritual appointment: rather, it was a democratic process that came during communal crisis. Her uncle and former *longko* was exposed as having sexually abused eight minors within the community.

*It was done to eight people, boys and girls, some of them are still young and some of them are already adults, but it ruined their lives. What's more, they decided to file a complaint in the middle of the pandemic.*

*It is very difficult for them to be part of our community circles, it is very difficult for them to think about a family project, to think about a productive project.*

*Today, they have been able to recover, that is, they have their partners, they have their children, but nevertheless, I still see a certain pain in them that I don't know how to remedy.*

*We had to expel him from the community and tell him never to come back to the territory. But there is still an open wound.*

*For me it was very painful, the process has been very intense for me as a person, as a niece.*

*Because I loved him a lot.*

The communal response to this was the democratic election of a nearly all female, generationally youthful council of leadership.

*I believe that change comes from the youth, right?*

Both she and Flor seem fixed on telling me that it's me who's just a girl, *solo una chica.* But in moments like these, as she switches her son from one nipple to the other, she seems impossibly young for the cost of the world she is building.

*We want him to go away and leave us alone once and for all. We need that tranquility. We decided to rebuild a community circle that he was in charge of destroying.*

*And for that he has to go, and thank you.*

o o o

Amancay pats it out gently for me against her skin. *Toc-toc, toc-toc*, she's clicking her tongue and the canopies lift in the wind. She knows the sound of a tranquil heart, and she plays the kultún in search of it.

### Capítulo IV: *Todos nuestros pewmas* // All Our Pewmas

On the last day of the *relevamiento*, the community takes lunch outdoors, with *tortas fritas* and mate. Amancay is laughing:

*Yo no estoy cansada, ni estresada, y ni hice nada. I'm not tired, nor stressed, and I didn't do anything.*

She seems relieved to be able to rest placidly with us at our picnic table. We pass our mate and watch the waxen sky. A fire snaps under the grill; people sprawl on the grass with their hats over their eyes.

*This survey is not going to guarantee anything.*

On an outbreath, Amancay confesses that, in just the same way that provincial governments permitted eviction attempts despite the federal law forbidding it, the territory is still under threat until a law of communal property is passed through the State.

This type of law threatens Bariloche, a place rooted in private property and burgeoning real estate.

*Solo un freno. It's only a brake.*

But there's so much joy tossed up into this weatherly pause from the month of wind. We watch her son drag around a fallen branch while the whole landscape seems to undulate.

*The only way is a law of community property that allows us generational continu-*
    *ity, so that it is not cut. Right now, I don't know if I can pass it on to my son.*
*That is the only thing we are asking for. Because if not, the truth is that they are*
    *coming.*
*They are coming for the air; they are coming for the minerals.*

o o o

The group calls together for an *afafan*, and I feel honored to be present.

The afafan is a communal ritual that comes in the face of great celebration, gratitude, loss.

They circle and throw their fists in the air: *Marici Wew! Marici Wew! Marici Wew! Diez veces estamos vivos, diez veces venceremos.* Ten times we are alive, ten times we win.

*When we scream, we understand.*

Before the *relevamiento*, the community had gathered at their *Lëfün*, a sacred ceremonial space that protects from the snow, rain, and wind. Amancay and her young nephew describe to me the slant of the morning light, the sacrificial crescents, the delicate reciprocity with spiritual forces; why they bring *maitén* and *manzano* as offerings. But this sacredity should not be described by me: you'll just have to have the *audacity to interpret it as you would have imagined it.*

*La única lucha que se pierda es la que abandona. The only fight you lose is the one you abandon.*

o o o

It's the month of wind in *El Wallmapu*, and private sectors move in on petroleum deposits; land is sold and bought and sequestered. But there are *boleadoras* to be found, little girls who dream of *paseo*.

And it's spring, so the year's flowers begin their blossom; trailing highways, lost in forests, even sprouting within Bariloche's corners of dirt.

To me, this seems lucky.

Because in El Wallmapu, flowers come with fables.

o o o

*Mari mari pu lamgen, mari mari kom pu ce, ince Amancay Quintriqueo pigen. Ince longko tañi lof Kinxikew, Ka kiñel mapu Consejo Zonal Lafkenche de la Confederación Mapuche del Neuquén.*

*Pewmagele kume nuxan ka kvme kuzaw.*

*Hello, all my brothers and sisters. I am Amancay Quintriqueo. I am the longko of this community, the community that is a part of the Zonal Council of the Lafkenche of the Mapuche Confederation of Neuquén. And I hope that we can have good work here today. That the conversation can be circular.*

..................................................................................................

**Cece Roth-Eagle** is a 2022 graduate of Smith College with special interests in playing with literary forms and in Indigenous rights. For the summer, she is working and living with a Jicarilla Apache community in rural Colorado before moving to Spain to teach English in the fall.

**Notes**

1   The word *Mapuche* in its ancestral language, Mapudungún, does not have plurality like in Spanish (Yanniello 2017).

2    "Community" in Mapudungún.
3    Highest authority.
4    Flower of the forest.
5    The ancestral Mapuche territory on the eastern side of the Andes.
6    "Backdrop" in Spanish.
7    Pronounced MAN-kee.

## Works Cited

Bilbao, Guido. 2022. "An Imported Tree Fuels Patagonia's Terrifying Summer Fires." *National Geographic*, January 4. https://www.nationalgeographic.com/environment /article/how-fear-of-summer-came-to-patagonia.

Confederación Mapuche del Neuquén. 2010. *Propuesta para un Kvme Felen Mapuche*. Neuquén: Confedercación Mapuche del Neuquén.

Crespo, Carolina, Ana Ramos, Mariela Eva Rodríguez, Malena Pell Richards, Florencia Yanniello, and Juana Aigo. 2021. "Vivir bajo sospecha." *Revista Anfibia*, November 26. https://www.revistaanfibia.com/vivir-bajo-sospecha/.

Harvey, David. 2005. *A Brief History of Neoliberalism*. Oxford: Oxford University Press.

Leitch, Scott. 2017. "This National Park in Patagonia Is Being Overrun with Invasive Canadian Trees." *Vice*, November 7. https://www.vice.com/en/article/mb3p9n /invasive-tree-species-patagonia-argentina-douglas-fir.

Ley N 26160, 2006. El Senado y Cámara de Diputados de la Nación Argentina, Buenos Aires, Argentina, 1 de noviembre.

Matías Rendón, Ana. 2018. "Wallmapu: Espacio-tiempo mapuche." *Cuadernos de teoría social* 6, no. 11: 66–94. https://www.aacademica.org/ana.matias.rendon/4.pdf.

Melfi, L. 2015. "Historia del pueblo Mapuche." *Made for SIT Argentina: Social Movements and Human Rights*, 7.

Svampa, Maristella. 2019. *Las fronteras del neoextractivismo en América Latina: Conflictas socioambientales, giro ecoterritorial y nuevas dependencias*. Zapopan, Mexico: CALAS. http://calas.lat/sites/default/files/svampa_neoextractivismo.pdf.

Yanniello, Florencia. 2009. "Cosmovisión mapuche y medioambiente." *Tinta verde*, February 12. http://tintaverde.com.ar/?p=121.

Yanniello, Florencia. 2017. *Descolonizando la palabra: Los medios de comunicación del pueblo Puelmapu*. Buenos Aires: La Plata, 121.

Yaniello, Florencia. 2020. "Neuquén: El Gobierno no cumple las leyes y desconoce los derechos indígenas." *ODHPI*, November 14. http://odhpi.com/neuquen-el -gobierno-no-cumple-las-leyes-y-desconoce-los-derechos-in digenas/.

Elena Ruíz

........................................................................

# Structural Trauma

Abstract: This article addresses the experience of precarity and vulnerability in racialized gender-based violence from a structural perspective. Informed by Indigenous social theory and anticolonial approaches to intergenerational trauma that link settler colonial violence to the modalities of stress-inducing social, institutional, and cultural violences in marginalized women's lives, the article argues that philosophical failures to understand trauma as a functional, organizational tool of settler colonial violence amplify the impact of traumatic experience on specific populations. It is trauma by design. The article explores this through the history of the concept of trauma and its connection to tragedy. The article gives a brief overview of prominent theories of trauma and contrasts these with the work of Dian Million (Tanana Athabascan) (2013), who highlights functional complicity of settler colonial institutions in shaping accounts of trauma in the west. The piece begins with an important illustration of the kinds of lives and experiences that call for a politicized understanding of trauma in anticolonial feminist theory. It ends by offering an expansive notion of structural trauma that is a methodological pivot for conducting trauma-based gender-based violence research in a decolonial context, which calls for an end to narratives of trauma that are severed from the settler colonial project of Native land dispossession and genocide.

............

The abject heart of colonialism and neocolonialism, and their practice of capitalism, is *gendered violence*. . . . I think that such violence is not incidental but common to the stresses that race, gender, and sexuality play in ordering and reordering power in our times.
—Dian Million (Tanana Athabascan), *Therapeutic Nations*

............

MERIDIANS · feminism, race, transnationalism  23:1 April 2024
DOI: 10.1215/15366936-10926944 © 2024 Smith College

On the night of April 24, 2019, which coincided with day 5-Eagle (Cuauhtli, 1-Ozomahtli) in the Aztec solar year 7-Reed (Acatl), the mayor of Mixtla Altamirano was traveling on the Zoologica-Orizaba highway in the state of Veracruz when a speeding vehicle pulled up, hovered, and sprayed her car with bullets. Maricela Vallejo Orea, along with her husband and driver, were killed instantly. Maricela was six months pregnant. Prior to her murder, as mayor she had proposed the creation of an agency across every municipality to address the systemic nature of gender-based violence, particularly against her Indigenous community.

There is a very old narrative in Western culture that frames trauma (from the Greek *trōma*, meaning "wound") as the unavoidable casualty of individual fate, something that is built into the very fabric of being in a gambled trade-off for living self-determined lives. The origin story of this narrative can be traced back to ancient Greek myths of white-robed goddesses—the three Moirai—who moved the mortal spheres of life and death and laid out essential vulnerabilities in the character of every human life. They cast their dice and watched mortals react in self-defining acts. If their fates landed well, it said little of the fated's character: "Bad luck" can *make you who you are*, whereas responses to good fortunes reflect who you already are—we learn this from the actions of Oedipus at Colonus and from Aeschylus's trickster king of Corinth, Sisyphus. The *logic of wounding*, which narrates tragedy as an unforeseeable and unavoidable part of human life, was thus intimately tied to the *logic of individuation*, which detaches people from the sets of social, cultural, and epistemic practices that produce them in order to place their lives within a universalized narrative arc of human existence.[1] Together these logics of wounding and individuation are intimately connected to a normalized conception of *tragedy as inherently blameless*, a game of chance where a person's "bad luck" is disassociated from organized, coordinated efforts structured to bring harm and injury to some people but not others.[2]

For Indigenous women and women of color living in settler colonial societies like the United States, Canada, and the United Mexican States (Estados Unidos Méxicanos), these founding myths have had a lasting and damaging impact through the role they play in maintaining conceptions of trauma that preclude the identification of ongoing structural oppressions and systemic femicidal violence in our communities.[3] The philosophical failure (which is not an accidental failure) to understand trauma as a functional, organizational tool of settler colonial violence amplifies the impact of traumatic experience on specific populations, not by accident, but by design. This is not an epistemic "whoopsie," an unintended consequence of historical trajectories codified as tradition. Rather, it is an organized (and actively maintained) hermeneutic standpoint that recognizes the injuries of some populations and perpetuates the conditions for the non-recognition of others for epistemic profit, accumulating in interpretive value/wealth from one white settler generation to the next.[4] The rise of the legal concept of *Iniuria* in ancient Rome did not come about by accident; it developed to formalize the logic of wounding in terms of grievable harms reserved for specific populations and inapplicable to others, namely slaves.[5] If your injury has social cognates, especially ameliorative ones, you're simply more likely to live—that is a powerful social good, one that has been non-accidentally accumulated by one cultural tradition.

Epistemically, not much has changed since the development of the concept of injury rooted in Roman law. Because the logic of individuation ascribes a disembodied faculty of purely abstract rational thought to the individual, which it values above embodied, situated, contextual, and land-based understanding and knowledge rooted in webs of reciprocal relationships, the logic of wounding tied to individuation remains reserved for those already recognized as subjects in settler colonial culture.[6] The logic of wounding frames Indigenous land dispossession and genocide on Turtle Island as a historic tragedy located in the past that was caused more by the unforeseeable effects of the spread of European diseases in the "New World" than by the deliberate, methodical plotting of settlers and the governments that supported them to slaughter Native peoples and occupy and exploit Native lands in order to secure land and livelihood for future generations of white settler offspring.[7] The logic of wounding has also been tied to what Patrick Wolfe (1999, 2006) calls a *logic of elimination* for Indigenous peoples, which settlers use to portray colonial invasion as a finite "historical event" reducible to "frontier homicide" and the moral pitfalls of a young nation instead of an organized structure with ongoing tactics of spatial containment and violence (Wolfe 2006: 388). For Wolfe, "Elimination refers to more than the summary liquidation of Indigenous peoples, though it includes that," such that colonial violence and destruction can take on a range of physical, spatial, linguistic, epistemic, and political formations to achieve the cultural genocidal ends of white settlement of Indigenous lands—for the colonial settler to become, as it were, the original inhabitants of Indigenous lands (Wolfe 2006: 390).[8] Here we note the importance of his definition of colonialism as a "structure, not an event," that distinguishes settler colonialism from genocide without excluding it (Wolfe 1999: 2).

Thinking of colonialism as a structure is essential to theorizing the complex and dynamic operations of gender-based violence in settler colonial societies. It is also critical to formulate a necessary relationship to the adaptive range of settler colonial logics that target and maldistribute harm to Black, Brown, Asian, immigrant, and internally/externally displaced people of color, disabled people, as well as gender and sexual minorities, as part of the global neoliberal settler colonial project of enduring white dynastic socioeconomic supremacy—logics that work to secure the next thousand years of more of the same harmful nonsense. In this regard, the logic of individuation also underlies and is entangled with colonial ideologies that help carry out the colonial project, such as neoliberal carceral ideologies. It is thus additionally tied to a *logic of containment* for people of color. Like the logic of elimination, the logic of containment is multipronged; it upholds settler colonial structures of oppression and is in turn strengthened by them, creating an endless positive feedback loop. It justifies the hyper-surveillance of communities of color and leads to the removal of people of color from our communities and our absorption into the prison-industrial complex in order to extract our labor while promoting intergenerational harm and trauma to our communities through the destruction of our families. It is also a geopolitical strategy of coordinated restraint in response to extralegal uses of force that enables the systematic production of torture, abuse, and sexual violence through structural impunity; it makes *uncountable* those violences that function to further the goals of settler-capital industrial economies and neoliberal agendas.[9] Whether by sword or shield, the logic of containment produced by the logic of individuation within settler societies thus invariably also leads to elimination for people of color. The logic of elimination and the logic of containment are both rooted in the structural automation and expansive reproduction of fertile avenues of *force*, positive and negative, that promote the production and maintenance of settler colonial wealth while simultaneously exonerating white settler culpability through cultural apparatuses like law, policy, law enforcement, governance, and the concepts that uphold them. I explain this nonaccidental, strategic, and complex settler colonial use of force (*forcis*) further in terms of institutionalized violence and the idea of *structural trauma*.

Before proceeding, and to thwart risks of getting too theoretically abstract—because Maricela's life was not abstract—let me clearly state that what I am arguing for is *a politicized understanding of trauma* that foregrounds our lived realities of asymmetric harm when it comes to traumatic experience. Trauma and its impacts are not evenly distributed across all populations, despite the fact that medical and disciplinary literature often treat them as if they are. In the standard Western picture, trauma is portrayed as a human risk factor to which people are universally vulnerable. Social determinants such as poverty, war, social class, and environmental exposures are presented as predisposing some populations to greater incidence of traumatic harm. These factors, then, create hot zones of traumatological effects. In contrast to this picture, I contend that the primary producers of trauma and its impacts are systems-based phenomena, such as the organizational logics of domination that arise from the self-organizing properties of settler colonialism. It is these organizational logics, as systems-based phenomena, that perpetuate conditions of poverty, war, racism, and sexual violence for some populations but not others—strategically, predictively, and intergenerationally.

One way to understand how the standard medical approach disappears the colonial production of population-level harms is through the distinction in population health science between "causes of cases" and "causes of incidence." As Sean Valles (2018: 116) explains:

> The distinction is between two types of causal explanation for two different types of causal phenomena. . . . For instance, genetic variations make individual people a substantially higher or lower risk of hypertension (Padamanabhan et al. 2015), but these individual-level variations seem to make no causal contributions to the extensively studied massive disparity in hypertension rates between US white and Black populations (Kaufam et al. 2015). Genetics may explain much about sick individuals (causes of cases) but do little to explain why some populations are plagued by hypertension more than other populations (causes of incidence).

Trauma models of care often follow the "causes of cases" model. As such, they fail to address the systemic violence and functionalization of racist sexism and sexual violence in women's lives that a "causes of incidence" approach might help track. Such an approach could better capture, for instance, how settler colonial governments infrastructurally support femicide with impunity through law and policy, as well as how gender has always been a primary tool of settler colonial violence, particularly against Indigenous women and women of color (Deer 2015; Ritchie 2017). Importantly, politicized approaches to trauma do not take away provision models of care for those suffering from the effects of trauma today;[10] they only insist that traumatic effects are being *non-accidentally* glossed over and strategically misrecognized or pathologized when those who suffer the logic of wounding are not white.

Since the term first rose to prominence in sixteenth-century European anatomical treatises and later experienced a resurgence in the developing fields of psychology and neurology, *trauma* has been characterized in a range of domains. These include emotion-based accounts that characterize trauma as "an experience of unbearable affect" (Krystal 1978; Stolorow 2007), socio-ecological models of multiple traumas and clinical disorders such as PTSD, and surgical approaches to wound triage in emergency medicine. Today, while trauma can be used to refer equally well to physical or mental injury, accounts of trauma's cause, duration, and function diverge. Today, while trauma can be used to refer equally well to physical or mental injury, accounts of trauma's cause, duration, and function diverge.[11]

One of the main lines of thought about trauma, whether understood as a physical or mental injury or both, has been its special connection to the idea of tragedy and the emotional life of individuals undergoing pain. In "Tragedy: A Curious Art Form," the classicist Anne Carson (2006: 7) writes, "Why does tragedy exist? Because you are full of rage. Why are you full of rage? Because you are full of grief." This grief comes from an injury, a wound (*trōma*), that bereavement tries to suture closed. What is lost in this *tragedy-rage-grief* causal triad is the direct link from rage to the causes of incidence that perpetuate grief-inducing violence in some communities but not others, strategically, predictively, and from one generation to the next.[12] This triad is no accident. The ancient Greeks were experts at depoliticizing grief and creating a new form of public art to regulate the shifting emotional boundaries between public and private life in the tenuous rise of democratic rule. This was the work of tragic plays.[13] The very meaning of *tragedy* comes from these plays—*tragōidia*, from *tragos*, meaning "goat," as in the human-goat satyrs that performed between acts, and *ōidē*, or public performance of song. Tragedy arose in the West as a public mechanism to contain social forces and resistance to violence through (1) internalizing conflicts and (2) depoliticizing violence by portraying it as a naturally occurring phenomenon. The latter is represented in the tragic hero's inability to foresee the consequences of his actions. More recently, Stephen Diamond's (1996: 9) celebrated work on the psychological genesis of violence reinforces the depoliticized view of trauma by characterizing increased homicide rates in the United States as "senseless violence," something he says we can make sense out of only if we see violence "existentially" as the "naturally occurring, universal, *inescapable* aspects of the human condition" (emphasis added). We can also get a glimpse of the internalizing function of tragedy in Carson's (2006: 7) universalist account of the psychology behind it:

> Grief and rage—you need to contain that, to put a frame around it, where it can play itself out without you or your kin having to die. There is a theory that watching unbearable stories about other people lost in grief and rage is good for you—may cleanse you of your darkness. Do you want to go to the pits of yourself all alone? Not much. What if an actor could do it for you? Isn't that why they are called actors? They act for you. You sacrifice them to action.

Except tragedy has always been a theater of sacrifice that kills the Black actors first, enacts horrific sexual violence on women for endless replay, and systemically degrades the human worth of immigrants of color for the benefit of white audiences and the settler gaze.[14] Who is sacrificing whom in order to visualize pain? The *trauma-pain-tragedy* triad is one of the most strategically depoliticized configurations in settler epistemic systems. It was central to the rise of the model of Native informancy in colonial testimonies of trauma and remains a powerful force today. It manifests most vividly in the silencing of calls for change made in the wake of communally traumatizing targeted violence against racialized peoples, as in the recent mass shooting of Mexicans in El Paso, Texas, by a white nationalist. Let's bury the dead first. Don't politicize tragedy—no one could have predicted this, another official says (Attanasio, Bleiberg, and Weber 2019).[15] Except predictive outcomes are exactly what settler governance schemes are designed to produce. The difference is for whose benefit. The inability to understand trauma as a functional, organizational tool of settler colonial violence amplifies the impact of traumatic experience on specific populations, not by accident, but by design.

Another motif in Western conceptions of trauma has been trauma's redemptive value. Much of psychoanalysis, some of phenomenology, and all of the Western existential tradition find some positive value in trauma, even when it is characterized as unassailable personal despair. This is because trauma is said to be a possible gateway to authentic self-knowledge and personal transformation (again, the logic of individuation at play), and even thought to yield philosophical insights into the very heart of the human condition. Take, for instance, Robert Stolorow's (2007: 15–16) self-analysis of trauma and the subsequent advice he gave a patient:

> I recalled my feeling at the conference dinner as though I were an alien to the normals around me. In Gadamer's terms, I was certain that the horizons of their experience could never encompass mine, and this conviction was the source of my alienation and solitude, of the unbridgeable gulf separating me from their understanding. It is not that the traumatized and the normals live in different worlds; it is that these discrepant worlds are felt to be essentially and ineradicably incommensurable. . . . This is the legacy of your experiences with terrible trauma. You know that any moment those you love can be struck down by a senseless, random event. Most people don't really know that.

The implicit white and abled social location of "most people" and "normals" is important here. Indigenous people and people of color do not, generally, agree that "most people don't really know" that they and their loved ones can be struck down at any moment and for any reason. When I was growing up, one of the first stories my mother taught me—after she taught me a four-digit proof-of-life code and singable emergency phone contact—was a story that her father told her. She said, "He sat me down when I was your age and told me, I do not want to die before you grow up. But it is possible and you and your siblings must prepare. And you may die before me. I would be very sad, but I would go on. You have to understand how to go on." She repeated that last part often. Years later, I told the story to an American therapist when asked to relay my earliest memories. She quickly diagnosed the exchange as child abuse. I wondered for the first time about the range of pathologizing techniques used to contain and erase marginalized people's tactics of survival against colonial violence. If there is something traumatizing in this narrative, it is not the powerful lesson of survival in the name of what Kyle Whyte (2018) calls "collective continuance" and J. Kēhaulani Kauanui calls "enduring Indigeneity." Rather, it is the intergenerational impact of the reliance on colonial deficiency narratives about our powerlessness to change things, a reliance that trades on a logic of woundedness, hurt, and fear whose function is to stunt coordinated action against the systemic violences we face. What is traumatic is the structurally enabled use of trauma discourses to disarm strategies of refusal—our refusal to be systematically disappeared or to accept anything less than the reclamation of what is rightfully ours—our lives, our safety, our well-being in our personhood and our communities, and, in Indigenous contexts, having stolen lands rematriated and uncoerced treaties honored.

This is one way that concepts of trauma that acknowledge the nonaccidental nature of structural violence can be helpful—by normalizing positions of political resistance rather than simply teaching how to cope with and accept *structured* loss in the name of narrative wholeness. This latter strategy, which is an all too common method in Western mental health care and social work, is a normative violence aimed at finishing what colonialism started.[16] As my mother knew intuitively, psychic trust is not deserved in settler colonial contexts.[17] The Native feminist scholar Dian Million (Tanana Athabascan) explains: "Given the history between Indigenous peoples and settler states, *no safe place has been obtainable*. Mistrust *should be* a feature of appropriate mental health in Indian Country" (Million 2013: 90; first emphasis added). For Indigenous peoples and people of color living within landscapes terraformed by settler colonialism, *there is no safety*, and recognizing this fact is necessary to our survival. Yet passing this knowledge on intergenerationally in the name of collective continuance is pathologized within the very mental health frameworks that claim universal application to our trauma while simultaneously delinking it from the structures that produce it consistently, predictively, and by design.

Million's account of therapeutic care frameworks in settler colonial societies is critical to the notion of trauma as a nonaccidental, organized violence. In *Therapeutic Nations: Healing in an Age of Indigenous Human Rights*, Million (2013) questions "the healing industry" in Canada and the United States that functionalizes violence against Indigenous peoples in the name of humanitarianism and human rights advocacy. There are two sides to the settler healing coin, but both license Western intervention in Native people's lives. On the one hand, Indigenous peoples are often portrayed as *terminally* traumatized by the wounds inflicted on them by settler colonialism, as injured beyond repair. When those who suffer the logic of wounding are not white, pathology is typically the first response.[18] On the other hand, Million (2013: 102) points out that when Indigenous peoples are not seen as terminally wounded but rather as possible subjects contained within the logic of individuation, they are treated as "painfully subscribed *subjects for healing*" (emphasis added). In other words, they are identified as sites for legitimate state and cultural intervention, whether in the form of forced state residential schooling or aid for humanitarian development. Trauma is the "preferred language" of international human rights instruments in the aftermath of globalization and the rise of neoliberal market economies, where development metrics and humanitarianism meld into frameworks intended to empower the disenfranchised (Million 2013: 178). On both accounts, the Western legal positioning of victims prevails. The objective is never to disappear the traumatic suffering Indigenous peoples encountered as a result of intersecting violences, but to disappear Native lives altogether. This follows Wolfe's notion of the logic of elimination, which analyzes "what might be called the settler-colonial will, a historical force that ultimately derives from the primal drive to expansion," a "greedy dynamic [that] is internal and self-generating" (Million 2013: 167). Elimination is strategic because it aims to vacate Indian lands and render them available for settlement (Million 2013: 29). On this account, trauma narratives can easily trigger calls for humanitarian emergencies that are coordinated by settler colonial cultures, not unlike the engineered Bengal famines of 1770 and 1943 that killed millions of Bengalese under colonial British administration. This does not mean that marginalized peoples have been passive recipients of structurally violent surroundings (McKittrick 2006), but rather that our surroundings have been shaped to deflect the realities of our experiences with structured trauma.

One thing to take away from this analysis is that simply expanding Western trauma models and provision care to include experiences of injury and colonial violence from Indigenous communities and people of color is not an appropriate response.[19] Such an attempt to make existing understandings of trauma more inclusive would simply constitute what Ezgi Sertler (forthcoming-a) calls a "recognition bluff." A type of administrative violence, according to Sertler, a recognition bluff is a "form of misrecognition where administrative systems enable new categories of legibility promising recognition for certain populations while, at the same time, they limit that category in ways that harm those populations." Consider that none of the mainstream approaches to trauma recognize, as phenomena that can be encompassed under the logic of wounding, the strategic elimination of referential networks of lands, rivers, plants, animal life (Maracle 2015), the intergenerational sexual abuse of children in residential state

schools, the systemic targeting and elimination of antiviolence leaders like
Maricela, or the banality of femicide and normalized impunity over organized disappearances of women. Widening the net of existing Western
understandings of trauma would thus merely "include" more people under
the category of those who have experienced trauma while continuing to
limit the category of trauma in ways that uphold the logics of elimination
and containment. As a normative violence, accounts of traumas to narrative life do not generally account for the history of organized violence
against forms of narrativity that are not Western. It's settler epistemology
all the way down. This does not mean we've been epistemically colonized
and there is nothing left of our cultures (the colonial dream of trauma).
It does mean there are great epistemic labors and untallied epistemic
exploitations (Berenstain 2016) that must be accounted for in discussions
of trauma, including intergenerational trauma.

Perhaps one of the most promising frameworks for addressing the
structured and systemic nature of gender-based violence in our communities arose in the post-Holocaust discourses of historical trauma and intergenerational trauma. The framework produced directly addressed injuri-
ous effects to whole communities across generations rather than just to
individuals. In the *Discourse on Colonialism*, Aimé Césaire ([1955] 2000)
famously connected the logic of colonial violence with fascism, arguing
that the racist logics of elimination perpetrated by Nazi Germany were
first developed and perfected on colonized peoples. His concern was *not*
that global moral horror over the Holocaust was misplaced (he widely
condemned the Nazi's genocidal project), but that the moral outrage of
humanism is "sordidly racist" (Césaire [1955] 2000: 36); it recognized the
pain of subjects *already recognized as subjects* (because of their comparative
proximity to whiteness relative to peoples racialized by european colonialism) while ignoring the pain and suffering of non-white peoples under the
colonial regime and its aftermath. This logic still exists today. Consider
that in an entire contemporary book-length philosophical treatment on
trans-generational trauma (Grand and Salberg 2017) that specifically takes
up "dialogues across history and difference," grapples with the "ghosts of
our forebears" and promotes the idea that "to heal human suffering, we
often need to reclaim our elders," there is not a single reference to Native
Americans. Not one. This isn't laughable, it's consistent.[20]

The logic of wounding even underlies many contemporary accounts
of structural violence. Consider Johan Galtung's (1969) definition of

structural violence as "violence that results in harm but is not caused by a clearly identifiable actor"—a definition that has had a significant impact on international organizations such as UNESCO and WHO and that also influences the CDC and contemporary public health research on inequality. In a study of differential outcomes for patients living in trauma deserts, defined as areas where a Level I or II trauma center is more than one hour away by car, researchers (unsurprisingly) concluded that race was a strong predictor of worse trauma outcomes (Sossenheimer et al. 2018). For the researchers, this constituted structural violence, which they defined as the contingent "social arrangements that put individuals and populations in harm's way" but which have "*no identifiable aggressors,*" "does not involve physical act" and cannot be seen as "intentional" (Sossenheimer et al. 2018: 537–38; emphasis added). Serious genealogical whitewashing work has gone into rendering social structures as arbitrary sets of relations that are as accidental as they are historically contingent. Indigenous social theory and anticolonial approaches to intergenerational trauma (Brave Heart and DeBruyn 1998; Million 2013; Linklater 2014; Fellner 2018; Methot 2019) have addressed this issue by linking settler colonial violence to the modalities of stress-inducing social, institutional, and cultural violences in marginalized people's lives. Trauma, when functionalized through institutions, is designed to finish what violent colonial settlement started—to consolidate the program of colonial techniques of violence that began in brutalizing physical as well as epistemic and hermeneutic violences. The goal is to dispossess Native peoples of lands and resources, exploit racialized labor (including gendered racialized labor) for surplus profit, and contain resistance through gender-based violences and their normalization. Colonial violence contains and pathologizes resistance through institutional violence, so that there is always functional complicity within settler colonial institutions. One way this is done is by instilling fear through the ongoing possibility of retraumatization. Operation Janus, the Trump administration's most recent anti-immigrant policy agenda instrument aimed at broadening the reach of denaturalization (i.e., revoked citizenship), is one example. If an immigrant woman obtains citizenship through marriage legally and suffers intimate partner violence, she is forever wedded to her abuser through the lifelong possibility they could fabricate claims of entering into a false marriage among myriad other possible accusations, extortions, and abuses.

The idea that a racialized woman is able to produce evidence that can be deemed satisfactory under an epistemic economy based on over five

hundred years of Native informancy is weak at best. Tortured asylum seek-
ers have borne their mutilated bodies in U.S. asylum credibility interviews
and U.S. citizens have produced empirical proof such as birth certificates,
social security cards, and biometrics, all to no avail in proving the legitimacy of their claims. This is the reality we face in *settler credibility economies.*
As Emma LaRocque explains in "Here Are Our Voices—Who Will Hear?":
"It was not that they had been silent; it was not that they hadn't spoken.
They were not heard. But 'heard' is a complexity. . . . [First Nation] statements were widely known *but had no weight as any publicly accepted truth*"
(paraphrased in Million 2013: 93; emphasis added). The traumatizing
impact of these hermeneutic practices is not tragic, the result of unforeseeable forces, but structured and strategic to harm some people but not
others. The level of perpetual structural anxiety this supports also makes it
difficult to address issues of past violence, abuse, and survivorship among
women of color immigrants. While one should not forget that this precarity
is *structurally engineered*, through policy and law, this insight also adds a layer
of complexity to discussions of structural trauma by having to recenter
settler colonial configurations of birthright and belonging in racialized
immigrant women's fight against spousal abuse. The function of trauma in
this case is to create conditions of perpetual precarity and vulnerability that
work to disappear those who resist settler formation of social life, thus
centering violence on those who transgress colonial gender binaries, such
as racialized women, and nonbinary, trans, and Two-Spirit people.

Conceptual approaches to practical problems, however promising, can
lose track of the material details central to organizing resistance to violence: the names, dates, causes of death; the families left behind, suspended in life but unable to die without knowing where the bodies are.
The statistics can be given. They have been given, the evidence entered.[21]
In many cases, compelling physical evidence has been used to sentinel
impending violence: Before Maricela was murdered, she had received
numerous death threats. Members of her family also received them before
they, too, were killed. And before Maricela, Gisela Mota Ocampo was
sworn in as the first female mayor of Temixco, only to be slain later that
day—shot at home in front of her family. She too had received numerous
threats. And before Gisela, the Tiquicheo mayor María Santos Gorrostieta
Salazar survived two assassination attempts—one of which claimed her
husband's life—before being tortured and slain in front of her young
daughter. Over a hundred mayors have been murdered in Mexico alone, and
tens of thousands of Indigenous women and women of color have been

murdered or disappeared across Turtle Island in the last few years. If enu-
merating our losses were enough to produce justice, more of us would do
that critical work. But there exists a systemic design-of-distribution to the
way our losses shake out that continues to underlie our attempts to address
systemic violence—why tremendous public resources are often utilized to
address sexual assault, kidnapping, and murder when it happens to some
populations and not others. On paper, Mexico has some of the most progressive policies against gender-based violence (see Secretaría de Relaciones Exteriores 2007). Day-to-day life, however, is quite different than
official policy in settler cultures. New fertile lines of force (*forcis*) are gener-
ated to serve as enforcement mechanisms when older uses of force and
violence become obsolete or illegal within settler legal systems. In a recent
gang-rape case in Veracruz, a girl's rapists were recorded on a Facebook
Live video confessing to the assault they perpetrated, with some claiming
remorse for their actions. Refusing to press charges after watching the
video, the state prosecutor argued that what he saw and heard was not a
confession but an *apology*. It is not incidental that the accused perpetrators
were white or white-adjacent Latino elites, just as it is not incidental that
municipalities with the greatest rates of impunity for these crimes are
places where tourism, natural resources, petrochemical, and extractive
industries are centered. Force and enforcement come together in the logic
of wounding when the protection and regeneration of settler wealth is at
stake. This is because trauma operates within a settler colonial architecture
oriented toward the basic reproduction of social structures for transmit-
ting intergenerational wealth among white settlers and their descendants.
I can't say this enough: it's about profit, wealth, and privilege at the expense
of other's lives and well being, including the lands that bore us into being
and that sustain all life. There is such a thing as enough. But not under
settler capitalism and the dynastic violence it supports as a system.

   This work takes a toll on us, and reframing problems in different lights
can help address our own enraged pain as feminist scholars of violence.
Not theoretical violence. Real violence, harms, and injuries. Reframing the
phenomenological experience of precarity and vulnerability in racialized
gender-based violence from a structural perspective can help in this direction.[22] Such a reframing rejects the idea of tragedy as inherently blameless,
disassociated from organized efforts to enforce colonial relations through
social transformations by structuring the conditions for loss. As Shannon
Speed (2019: 286) notes, "Formulating violence against women as purely

interpersonal phenomena only serves to de-politicize gender violence. Individual or interpersonal gender violence cannot be understood outside of the historical and ideological structures that give rise to it and in which it is enacted." Structural trauma, in this view, is a functional, organizational tool of settler colonial violence that amplifies the impact of traumatic experience on specific populations by design. It calls for an end to narratives of trauma that are severed from the settler colonial project of Native land dispossession and genocide. It also calls for divestment from the logics of traumatology that recenter the founding myths and tacit values of Anglo-European culture. Structural trauma, then, is a methodological pivot for conducting trauma-based gender-based violence research in an anticolonial context. It is not a new approach but a reaffirmation of what Indigenous, Black, and Brown feminisms have contended for centuries about the nonaccidental role of gender-based violence in the consolidation of the colonial project: it is a structural phenomenon.

.......................................................................................

**Elena Ruíz** is director and associate professor of the Research Institute for Structural Change (RISC) at Michigan State University. She is a survivor advocate and served as the principal researcher on gender-based violence for MeToo International, the organization behind the #metoo movement. Her writings on structural justice and system change have focused on race, gender, ethnicity, and colonial occupation in the Americas.

**Notes**

1   This became particularly important for psychoanalysis, which refined the association between wounding and subjectivity in the notions of original trauma and constitutive loss (Beardsworth 2009: 45). The notion of individuation is not exclusive to Western culture, yet in the West it developed through particular epistemological and metaphysical commitments to (a) exclusionary logic (see, for example, Aristotle's laws of thought) and (b) *nonreciprocal* dualisms, and it is these commitments that pillared the rise of the particular model of modern individualism that underlies settler colonial cultures. While the principle of individuation (*principium individuationis*) took on slight variations in ecclesiastic, existential, and post-Renaissance notions of selfhood, they did not uproot the core of these commitments. One important consequence of the metaphysical and epistemological orthodoxies rooted in this view was the conceptual predevelopment of hierarchical binaries that allowed for clear and neat differentiations between alleged "races" opposing one another in form and/ or kind. This is an example of the conceptual schema that organizes social concepts prestructurally.

2   Tragedy and trauma thus entered the *affective* realm of pain, where Euripides's
    *Trojan Women* dwelled, rather than a political realm that worked to directly dis-
    mantle organized violence against women. While affects can be powerfully
    political (see Lorde 1981; Chemaly 2018; Cooper 2018), the Western intellectual
    tradition that encompasses Attic tragedy sought to contain organized resis-
    tance to state violence by internalizing conflicts, linking human agency to this
    internalization, and redirecting affects to this experience. Simultaneously,
    institutions were set up to formalize affects as public goods reserved for certain
    people and to function as sites for regulating the affective behavior of others.
    Delicts in Roman law, for instance, carefully outlined how "outrage" as an
    injury (*Iniuria*) from a perceived insult was a grievable harm by slave owners,
    but not slaves. This pattern continues today and can be found across a range of
    settler social institutions, from systemically racist pushout policies in educa-
    tion that target the behavior of girls of color for punishment, to the disparate
    dispensation of damages awarded for emotional injury in libel, defamation,
    and discrimination suits (cf. *Johnson v. Strive E. Harlem Emp't Grp*, *MacMillan v. Mil-*
    *lennium Broadway Hotel*, *Cosmos Forms, Ltd. v. State Div. of Human Rights*, and *Laboy*
    *v. Office Equip. and Supply Corp* for cases where courts lower original damages
    awards and discuss the "N-word" as a "garden variety" mental harm—a legal
    notion that in these cases is tied to the presumptive limited evidentiary value of
    Black plaintiffs' testimony about their own affective lives).

3   It should be noted that the conceptual shift argued for in this paper is one that
    advocates and depends on a *coalitional* approach to solidarity among Indigenous
    feminisms and women of color feminisms, rather than one that collapses them
    or simplifies their political, geographic, and historical complexity. For more on
    interhemispheric structural feminisms, feminist anticolonial visions of coali-
    tion, and contingent collaborations, see Speed 2017, 2019; Dotson 2017a; and
    Tuck 2012.

4   Well-known challenges to the Nobel Peace Prize recipient Rigoberta Menchú
    Tum's testimony of Indigenous genocide provide one powerful example of this
    process. See also Kristie Dotson's (2017) notion of "epistemic backgrounding"
    for further insight into the mechanisms, processes, and functionalization of set-
    tler colonial violences in epistemic practices, as well as her important discussion
    of "epistemic power" and its cultural accumulation (2018). See also Ezgi Sertler's
    (forthcoming-b) account of *structural epistemic dependence*, in which she theorizes
    how people and communities rely on background structures' practices of manag-
    ing knowledge and ignorance when they come to know something.

5   The institutes of Justinian law, from which we get the term *institution* (from the
    Latin *institutuere*—to set up, establish custom), formalized customs specific to
    *conditions of war*—the taking of live prisoners to extract profit in return for spar-
    ing their lives (from which the term *slave* derives)—into an internal regulative
    social practice. Institutions, in this view, were never value-free social phenom-
    ena or blank-slate structures universal across all cultures, but social formations
    set up to functionalize specific mechanisms of regulative power, like racial and
    gendered violence, for particular ends.

6   This is one way inequality is sustained in democratic societies that depend on settler colonial social structures for the production of wealth: the reliance on prestructural conceptual schemata that uphold the unequal distribution of social goods through the power conferred to public institutions. Legal criteria for the right to sue for an injury (*locus standi*), the rights and immunities in castle doctrines, stand-your-ground laws, and other developments of common law illustrate this.

7   The logic of wounding tied to white settler populations, by contrast, uses the logic of individuation positively to create functional pathways for accessing infrastructural support from settler institutions like the legal system.

8   For important Indigenous feminist receptions of Wolfe's work, refer, for example, to Barker 2017; Kēhaulani Kauanui 2016; Speed 2017.

9   The concept of the "logic of containment" is useful here because it shows how colonial violence traversed various settler conceptual and biocultural strategies (such as the creation of controlling racial taxonomies) to achieve unified goals of providing enduring wealth for white lineages of settlement. It upends the settler conceptual schemata of racialization that controlled Black labor through (among other things) the one-drop rule, exploited Brown labor through reverse one-drop rules of Spanish blood, and dispossessed Native peoples of their lands through genocidal violence, spatial containment, and blood quantum rules. Containment and elimination are thus not mutually exclusive, even in the logic of containment's negative uses of force as noncontainment and impunity for violence. This is illustrated in the staggering rates of sexual violence and forced disappearance Native women face, but also in the structured impunity of non-Native perpetrators who rape Native women on Native lands (as is illustrated by the fact that more than two-thirds of rapes against Native women are perpetrated by non-Native men).

10   This is an example of the "leveling down" settler epistemic concern. See Valles 2018: 171–72.

11   In the humanities, two models have prevailed following the assumptive trends in Cartesian and post-Cartesian traditions: psychoanalysis and narrative theory, the latter of which approaches trauma from the notion of relationality, and both of which include corresponding feminist approaches. Some of these texts, such as Susan Brison's landmark work, *Aftermath*, have been curative in the healing processes of individuals recovering from experiences of violence, especially rape. They have helped some survivors make sense of experiences that were meant to undo us as individuals, to inflict a terror that has both has a bodily object and that proceeds in time without one—a dizzying and dislocating feeling. This account can also be found in Gloria Anzaldúa's work and her idea of "intimate terrorism" in psychic life (1987). The concern is thus not with what these texts do or don't do, it is with a wider structured inattention to how trauma has been used strategically as an institutional technology to consolidate colonial dispossession, whether in feminist theory or elsewhere.

12    Many have fought against this delinking and reconnected the strings between racist sexism, colonial violence, and our pain. Cf. Indigenous Zapatistas' speeches (Marcos 2018) on "dignified rage"; and Cooper 2018.

13    This was a shaky time politically, with renewed calls for oligarchical rule in the aftermath of the Peloponnesian War and the need to contain the Helot uprisings since the second Messenian War.

14    For example, in a recent episode of *Black Mirror*, a twenty-two-year-old Black man is violently kidnapped at gunpoint by a white middle-aged man who killed his own fiancée and the driver of another vehicle while texting and driving, admittedly out of sheer boredom. Unable to accept the outcome of his actions, he brutalizes and psychologically tortures his victim in order to attract the attention of the social media company he blames for addicting him to his phone. The script culminates in a late-stage apology to his victim. What is staged is not the apology, but the response: a hokey, *oh that's OK!* This is emblematic of the staging and restaging of (non)resistance to organized trauma. It has a function. And the mechanism is not just settler cinema (a modern version of tragic plays) and aesthetics, but education as well. Trauma has always been designed to create a pathos of distance from pain for some populations, so that others acquiesce and mirror what Amphitryon says to Lykos in Euripides's play, *Herakles*: "Our death is your decree, we acquiesce. It must be as you say." But we do not acquiesce. This is why it is not accidental that *Birth of a Nation* maintains a near perfect (98 percent) critic score, for as long as there is resistance to the consolidation of the settler colonial project, resistance will be met with wide and ever-expansive nets of interconnected force.

15    One important point of these appeals to tragedy is to avoid broadening the reach of *Iniuria*. The 1989 Exxon Valdez oil spill and other manmade disasters, for example, are similarly portrayed as environmental "tragedies" to prevent Indigenous peoples harmed by structurally foreseeable consequences of human actions from seeking relief in response to injury, especially through settler legal mechanisms.

16    This differs, for example, from calls to politicize deaths from gun violence, particularly on social media outlets. (The #IfIDieInaMassShooting campaign sought to mobilize efforts against the gun lobby and lax regulations of rapid-fire weaponry through the slogan, "If I die in a mass shooting, politicize my death.")

17    Moreover, the elitist idea that most people don't really know about the worldly precarities they face is built on the settler colonial assumption that the world is generally *a safe place* that is worthy of trust until an unexpected, tragic event disrupts that tacit expectation of temporal flow through the fragmenting effects of trauma. This assumption of safeness is not rooted in universal normative grounds, such as in the idea that all children deserve to feel safe and physically secure in the world around them, but in the premise that the spatial and temporal coordinates around one *already belong to one's cultural tradition, giving one*

*pre-reflective access to its interpretive resources.* This is the other side of the hermeneutic violence coin: that settler populations accumulate interpretive wealth for
epistemic profit (See Ruíz forthcoming).

18 Patricia Hill Collins (2017) points out this aspect of Simone de Beauvoir's work
   when Beauvoir portrays Black Americans (and U.S. Black women in particular)
   as pathologically traumatized by slavery, almost irredeemably broken as possible subjects of freedom.

19 A recent study of PTSD in orphaned and homeless Haitian children who "experienced multiple traumas such as neglect, maltreatment, psychological, physical and sexual abuse" failed to obtain scores reaching clinical rates for PTSD for
   any more than 15 percent of the children studied (Cénat et al. 2018). The conclusion: Haitian "street children" are incredibly resilient, wherein "a large majority
   presented a level of resilience between moderate to very high" (Cénat et al.
   2018). While Haitian children are undoubtedly resilient, the discourse of resilience is often applied to structurally traumatized populations to produce what
   Tuck and Yang (2012) call a "settler move to innocence" that attempts to escape
   complicity in creating and maintaining colonial violences that force people to
   become resilient or die. As Williams and Mohammed (2013) have shown, resilience comes with a high cost; it has measurable health effects that contribute
   to population-level health inequities that not all populations face (see also Bassett et al. 2012).

20 In 2015, the geneticist Rachel Yehuda led a team of researchers from Mount
   Sinai in a series of studies that showed descendants of Holocaust survivors
   have altered stress hormones that impact their ability to "bounce back" from
   stress or illness, particularly PTSD (Rodriguez 2015). The Native geneticist
   LeManuel "Lee" Bitsoi (Navajo) aptly notes that epigeneticists' recent findings
   of historical traumas are hardly news to Native Americans, as "Native healers,
   medicine people and elders have always known this and it is common knowledge in Native oral traditions" (quoted in Pember 2016).

21 Rosa-Linda Fregoso, for example, has powerfully laid out the case for asymme-
   try and siege in the torture and killing of Brown and Indigenous women. Her
   work has been critical to feminist efforts to stem the tide of femicide and forced
   disappearances of Mexican women and to linking gender-based violence with
   structural violence. See Fregoso 2003; Fregoso and Bejarano 2010. Victoria San-
   ford's forensic anthropological work documenting mass graves has also been
   important in this regard.

22 Elizabeth Bowen and Nadine Murshid (2016: 223) apply the principles of
   trauma-informed care, "conceptualized as an organizational change process
   centered on principles intended to promote healing and reduce the risk of
   retraumatization for vulnerable individuals," to social policy. Bowen and
   Murshid's proposal can prove helpful in developing examples of incidence
   approaches to trauma if structures are understood as nonaccidental relations
   between elements in settler societies rather than objectively neutral sets of
   social relations.

**Works Cited**

Anzaldúa, Gloria. 1987. *Borderlands / La Frontera*. San Francisco, CA: Aunt Lute Books.

Attanasio, Cedar, Jake Bleiberg, and Paul Weber. 2019. "Police: El Paso Shooting Suspect Said He Targeted Mexicans." Associated Press, August 9.

Bassett, Deborah, Ursula Tsosie, and Sweetwater Nannauck. 2012. "'Our Culture Is Medicine': Perspectives of Native Healers on Post-trauma Recovery among American Indian and Alaska Native Patients." *Permanente Journal* 16, no. 1: 19–27.

Beardsworth, Sara. 2009. "Overcoming the Confusion of Loss and Trauma: The Need of Thinking Historically." In *The Trauma Controversy*, edited by Kristen Brown Golden and Bettina Bergo, 45–70. Albany: State University of New York Press.

Berenstain, Nora. 2016. "Epistemic Exploitation." *Ergo: An Open Access Journal in Philosophy* 3, no. 22. http://dx.doi.org/10.3998/ergo.12405314.0003.022.

Bowen, Elizabeth, and Nadine Murshid. 2016. "Trauma-Informed Social Policy: A Conceptual Framework for Policy Analysis and Advocacy." *American Journal of Public Health*, no. 106: 223–29. https://doi.org/10.2105/AJPH.2015.302970.

Brave Heart, Maria Yellow Horse, and Lemyra DeBruyn. 1998. "The American Indian Holocaust: Healing Historical Unresolved Grief." *American Indian and Alaska Native Mental Health Research* 8, no. 2: 60–82.

Brison, Susan. 2002. *Aftermath: Violence and the Remaking of a Self*. Princeton, NJ: Princeton University Press.

Carson, Anne. 2006. "Tragedy: A Curious Art Form." In *Grief Lessons: Four Plays by Euripides*, 7–9. Translated by Anne Carson. New York: New York Review of Books Classics.

Cénat, Jude Mary, Daniel Derivois, Martine Hébert, Laetitia Mélissande Amédée, and Amira Karray. 2018. "Multiple Traumas and Resilience among Street Children in Haiti: Psychopathology of Survival." *Child Abuse and Neglect*, no. 79: 85–97. http://doi.org/10.1016/j.chiabu.2018.01.024.

Césaire, Aimé. (1955) 2000. *Discourse on Colonialism*. New York: Monthly Review Press.

Chemaly, Soraya. 2018. *Rage Becomes Her: The Power of Women's Anger*. New York: Atria.

Collins, Patricia Hill. 2017. "Simone de Beauvoir, Women's Oppression, and Existential Freedom." In *A Companion to Simone de Beauvoir*, edited by Laura Hengehold and Nancy Bauer, 325–38. Hoboken, NJ: Blackwell.

Cooper, Brittany. 2018. *Eloquent Rage: A Black Feminist Discovers Her Superpower*. New York: St. Martin's Press.

Deer, Sarah. 2015. *The Beginning and End of Rape*. Minneapolis: University of Minnesota Press.

Diamond, Stephen. 1996. *Anger, Madness, and the Daimonic: The Psychological Genesis of Violence, Evil, and Creativity*. Albany: State University of New York Press.

Dotson, Kristie. 2017a. "On the Way to Decolonization in a Settler Colony: Re-introducing Black Feminist Identity Politics." *AlterNative* 14, no. 3: 190–99.

Dotson, Kristie. 2017b. "Theorizing Jane Crow, Theorizing Unknowability." *Social Epistemology* 31, no. 5: 417–30. http://doi.org/10.1080/02691728.2017.1346721.

Fellner, Karlee. 2018. "Therapy as Ceremony: Decolonizing and Indigenizing Our Practice." In *Counselling in Cultural Contexts: Identities and Social Justice*, edited by Nancy Arthur, 181–201. Cham, Switzerland: Springer.

Fregoso, Rosa-Linda. 2003. *MeXicana Encounters: The Making of Social Identities on the Borderlands*. Berkeley: University of California Press.

Fregoso, Rosa-Linda, and Cynthia Bejarano, eds. 2010. *Terrorizing Women: Feminicide in the Américas*. Durham, NC: Duke University Press.

Galtung, Johan. 1969. "Violence, Peace, and Peace Research." *Journal of Peace Research* 6, no. 3: 167–91.

Grand, Sue, and Jill Salberg, eds. 2017. *Trans-generational Trauma and the Other: Dialogues across History and Difference*. London: Routledge.

Kauanui, J. K. 2016. "'A Structure, Not and Event': Settler Colonialism and Enduring Indigeneity." *Lateral* 5, no. 1: https://doi.org/10.25158/L5.1.7.

Krystal, Henry. 1978. "Trauma and Affects." *The Psychoanalytic Study of the Child* 33 no. 1: 81–116.

Linklater, Renee. 2014. *Decolonizing Trauma Work: Indigenous Stories and Strategies*. Vancouver: Fernwood.

Lorde, Audre. 1981. "The Uses of Anger: Women Responding to Racism." *Women's Studies Quarterly* 25, nos. 1–2: 278–85.

Maracle, Lee. 2015. *Memory Serves*. Alberta, BC: NeWest Press.

Marcos, Subcomandate Insurgente. 2018. *The Zapatistas' Dignified Rage: Final Public Speeches of Subcommander Marcos*. Edited by Nick Henck. Translated by Henry Gales. Oakland, CA: AK Press.

McKittrick, Katherine. 2006. *Demonic Grounds: Black Women and the Cartographies of Struggle*. Minneapolis: University of Minnesota Press.

Methot, Suzanne. 2019. *Legacy: Trauma, Story, and Indigenous Healing*. Toronto: ECW Press.

Million, Dian. 2013. *Therapeutic Nations: Healing in an Age of Indigenous Rights*. Tucson: University of Arizona Press.

Moeke-Pickering, Taima. 2019. "Indigenous Worldviews and Pedagogies in Indigenous-Based Programs: Social Work and Counselling." In *Handbook of Research on Indigenous Knowledge and Bi-culturalism in a Global Context*, edited by S. Hameed, S. El-Kafafi, and R. Waretini-Karena, 1–10. IGI Global.

Pember, Mary Annette. 2016. "Intergenerational Trauma: Understanding Natives' Inherited Pain." *Indian Country Today*.

Ritchie, Andrea. 2017. *Invisible No More: Police Violence against Black Women and Women of Color*. Boston: Beacon Press.

Rodriguez, Tori. 2015. "Descendants of Holocaust Survivors Have Altered Stress Hormones." *Scientific American Mind* 26, no. 2: 10.

Ruíz, Elena. Forthcoming. "Cultural Gaslighting." *Hypatia: A Journal of Feminist Philosophy*.

Secretaría de Relaciones Exteriores. 2007. "General Law on Women's Access to a Life Free of Violence." http://www.summit-americas.org/brief/docs/Law_on_access _to_a_life_free_violence.pdf.

Sertler, Ezgi. Forthcoming-a. "Calling Recognition Bluffs: Structural Epistemic Injustice and Administrative Violence." In *Epistemic Injustice and the Philosophy of Recognition*, edited by Paul Giladi and Nicola McMillan. New York: Routledge.

Sertler, Ezgi. Forthcoming-b. "Epistemic Dependence and Oppression: A Telling Relationship." *Episteme*.

Simpson, Audra. 2007. "Ethnographic Refusal: Indigeneity, 'Voice,' and Colonial Citizenship." *Junctures: The Journal for Thematic Dialogue*, no. 9: 67–80.

Sossenheimer, P. H., M. J. Andersen Jr., M. H. Clermont, C. V. Hoppenot, A. A. Palma, and S. O. Rogers Jr. 2018. "Structural Violence and Trauma Outcomes: An Ethical Framework for Practical Solutions." *Journal of the American College of Surgeons* 227, no. 5: 537–42.

Speed, Shannon. 2017. "Structures of Settler Capitalism in Abya Yala." *American Quarterly* 69, no. 4: 783–90.

Speed, Shannon. 2019. *Incarcerated Stories: Indigenous Women Migrants and Violence in the Settler-Capitalist State*. Chapel Hill: University of North Carolina Press.

Stolorow, Robert. 2007. *Trauma and Human Existence: Autobiographical, Psychoanalytic, and Philosophical Reflections*. New York: Routledge.

Tuck, Eve, and K. Wayne Yang. 2012. "Decolonization Is Not a Metaphor." *Decolonization: Indigeneity, Education, and Society* 1, no. 1: 1–40.

Valles, Sean. 2018. *Philosophy of Population Health: Philosophy for a New Public Health Era*. New York: Routledge.

Whyte, Kyle. 2018. "Critical Investigations of Resilience." *Daedalus: Journal of the American Academy of Arts and Sciences* 147, no. 2: 136–47.

Williams, David R., and Selina A. Mohammed. 2013. "Racism and Health I: Pathways and Scientific Evidence." *American Behavioral Scientist* 57, no. 8: 1152–73. http://doi.org/10.1177/0002764213487340.

Wolfe, Patrick. 1999. *Settler Colonialism and the Transformation of Anthropology: The Politics and Poetics of an Ethnographic Event*. London: Cassell.

Wolfe, Patrick. 2006. "Settler Colonialism and the Elimination of the Native." *Journal of Genocide Research* 8, no. 4: 387–409.

Yael Valencia Aldana

· · · · · · · · · · · · · · · · · · · · · · · · · · · · · · · · · · · · · · · · · · · · · · · · · · · · · · · · · · · · · · · · · ·

# Open Your Mouth

Jaguar woman crawls out of the ground,
bone white shells for eyes flashing unseeing
iridescence. Open your mouth, granddaughter
Bring us, we are waiting, your bone-harrowed
ancestors beneath this soil
Coatlicue exhales her fanged breath over my
goosebumped flesh, her two serpent face so ugly
she was buried twice. open your mouth daughter
breathe in my sinewed avian air. breathe
in my feathered muscled coils spun around your neck.
uncover our plowed-over bones. we are waiting,
call our people out of the mountains, out of rubbled
burned ash piles, out of silted, slimy river bottoms
bring us. we will return to our glinting azure edged shores
dip our feet in fine clear water. hold my yellowed skull
in your hands. open your mouth, clean my teeth
make them yours, intertwine your fingers with us
the terrible women from below this sand.

· · · · · · · · · · · · · · · · · · · · · · · · · · · · · · · · · · · · · · · · · · · · · · · · · · · · · · · · · · · · · · · · · ·

**Yael Valencia Aldana** is a Caribbean Afro-Latinx writer and poet. Yael is a descendant of the Indigenous people of Colombia. She earned her MFA in creative writing from Florida International University. Her work has appeared or is upcoming in *Typehouse, Florida Book Review, South Florida Poetry Journal, Scapegoat Review, Antithesis Blog,* and *Slag Glass City,* among others. She lives in South Florida with her son.

MERIDIANS · feminism, race, transnationalism   23:1 April 2024
DOI: 10.1215/15366936-10927008 © 2024 Smith College

Ruthann Lee

......................................................................................

# Honoring the Ancestors and Creator

Indigeneity, Diaspora, and the Politics of Spiritual
Relationality in Tannis Nielsen's A Creation
and Rosa Sungjoo Park's Forgotten Dreams

Abstract: Contemporary feminist scholars problematize the difficulties of creating meaningful political alliances between Indigenous and diasporic communities in settler states such as Canada and the United States. This essay
uses a relational framework to trace how two feminist artists, one Indigenous and one diasporic, creatively resist the ongoing and uneven conditions
of settler colonial capitalism. The essay examines artwork by Tannis Nielsen,
a midcareer Indigenous artist with Métis, Anishnawbe, and Danish ancestry,
and Rosa Sungjoo Park, an emerging diasporic Korean artist with landed status in Canada. Taken together, the artists' works offer fruitful opportunities
to think through difficult questions about power, history, and representation
on Turtle Island. Both Nielsen and Park engage "pedagogies of the Sacred"
to honor ancestral traditions and spiritual practices while disrupting binary
narratives of tradition vs. modernity. I contend that their creative use of digital media draws on lived experience, embodied knowledge, and spirituality
to refuse colonialism's hyper-individualism and imagine alternative worlds.

Black, Indigenous, and women of color feminists have long recognized that
spirituality and activism are deeply intertwined. The Black lesbian feminist
Audre Lorde's ([1978] 1984: 56) concept of "erotic knowledge," for example,
contends that "the dichotomy between the spiritual and the political is
false, resulting from an incomplete attention to our erotic knowledge."
The queer Chicanx/Latinx feminist Gloria Anzaldúa's (2015) writings on

MERIDIANS · feminism, race, transnationalism    23:1 April 2024
DOI: 10.1215/15366936-10926912 © 2024 Smith College

"spiritual activism" likewise draw attention to how women's embodied knowledge and relational connections to land and nonhuman life provide powerful frameworks to dismantle and resist structures of heteropatriarchy, racism, and settler colonial capitalism (Keating 2008). Yet since it is often associated with organized fundamentalism, especially right-wing Christianity, there remains a palpable reluctance to acknowledge the role of spirituality in feminist theory and practice.

In *Pedagogies of Crossing: Meditations on Feminism, Sexual Politics, Memory, and the Sacred*, the transnational feminist scholar M. Jacqui Alexander (2005: 15) recounts that "no self-respecting postmodernist would want to align herself (at least in public) with a category such as the spiritual, which appears so fixed, so unchanging, so redolent of tradition. Many, I suspect, have been forced into a spiritual closet." However, contested religious fundamentalisms indicate that spiritual pedagogies are in fact *necessary* in transnational feminism "because it remains the case that . . . *the majority of women in the world—cannot make sense of themselves without it*" (Alexander 2005: 15; emphasis mine). In other words, transnational feminists have a stake in pursuing spiritual knowledge—pedagogies of the Sacred—as a way to explore the crucial but often disregarded significance of spiritual healing in social justice work. Alexander invokes both Lorde's and Anzaldúa's work to argue that erotic knowledge can be a crucial guiding principle for feminism, urging critical scholars to take seriously aspects of the spiritual despite the risks of dismissal in the purportedly secular academy.

This essay turns attention to the Sacred and the erotic to examine how they might offer radical alternatives to the hyper-individualized pursuit of knowledge in the neoliberal academy. Because questions of spirituality, faith, and healing are different and not always overlapping processes, they can be especially difficult—and perhaps even dangerous—to comprehend solely in terms of queer, Marxist, and liberal theories of power, subjectivity, and identity that privilege the individual human subject. Queer psychoanalytic theory only inconsistently engages Indigenous epistemologies and other decolonial intellectual traditions to theorize embodiment and community formations (Driskill et al. 2011; Smith 2010). By contrast, the relational worldviews espoused by many Indigenous knowledge keepers, especially Indigenous feminists, recognize the profound connections between life, land, and spirit to intimate a radical feminist ethic of community-building. Critical scholarship on spiritual practices is limited by Marxist paradigms that inexorably rely on modern liberal fantasies of human progress and rational development. In her critique of leftist theory, the Indigenous feminist thinker Zainab Amadahy (2011: para. 9) elaborates:

> Marxism, socialism and anarchy do not address relationality, that is, the inter-relatedness and inter-connectedness of life. . . . Such theories still operate under the assumption that we two-leggeds are separate, differentiated individuals. As a species we are still considered to be superior to rather than inherently part of other life forms. . . . Relationality is inadequately understood and still seen as an appendix to existing theory, rather than a legitimate and viable worldview in and of itself.

Current theories of affect and emotion emphasize the complex interactions between bodies, geographies, the repressive state, and colonial institutions. In many discussions, concepts such as "postcolonial haunting" and "postmemory" offer important critical insights about the colonial histories and racism that are collectively experienced by various postcolonial and diasporic "subjects of emotion" (see, for example, Phung 2012). Nevertheless, the roots of affect theory are most often located within Western European ontologies and attributed to continental philosophers and psychoanalytic scholars—what Claudia Garcia-Rojas aptly describes as the institutionalization of "white affect studies." Garcia-Rojas (2016: 259) points out, "In turning away from women of color feminist theory and citing only white thinkers, scholars contributing to white affect studies knowingly disavow theories by lesbian and queer women of color that provide critically distinct notions of affect, and how their understandings of affect influence theories of desire, embodiment, and subjectivity." In other words, feminist women of color, particularly Black lesbian feminists such as M. Jacqui Alexander and Audre Lorde, offered insightful articulations of affect long before the "affective turn," but their contributions have been epistemically erased. My reading of contemporary artwork that enables audiences to experience and acknowledge multidimensional forms of life reveals how Black lesbian and women of color feminists not only offer useful ways to theorize affect and emotion but also meaningful understandings of how practices of spirituality are deeply connected to forms of collective healing, political resistance, and radical social change. These spiritually influenced feminist frameworks invoke non-Western and Indigenous relational epistemologies that exceed historical materialist critiques of knowledge production and the human subject by signaling alternate cosmologies and by honoring ancestors through feminist spiritual practices or "pedagogies of the Sacred."

Correspondingly, I borrow Felicity Amaya Schaeffer's definition of spirituality in her related discussion of Gloria Anzaldúa's writings. According to Schaeffer (2018: 1005), Anzaldúa's "generative explorations of the spiritual" encompass "the idea of relationality as well as the recognition of worlds or realities beyond those immediately visible" to suggest a "decolonizing of the human, of agency, and of justice." Spirituality is thus "deeply embodied yet always tied to the cosmic scale" by queerly disrupting colonial notions of time and space "beyond the limits of a rational and human-centered worldview" (1005). Spirituality, as articulated by Amadahy, Anzaldúa, and Schaeffer, summons non-Western and Indigenous relational epistemologies that both threaten and *exceed* historical materialist critiques of knowledge production and the human subject. In this way, my elucidation of spirituality brings together queer, Black, Indigenous, and women of color feminist paradigms to explore and deepen feminist understandings of embodied knowledge and nonhuman relations. I build on the compelling dialogues initiated by many Black, Indigenous, and women of color feminist scholars to reflect on the importance of spiritual healing in political activism as a way to theorize radical (and not necessarily "new") possibilities for social transformation.[1]

Black, Indigenous, and women of color feminists offer compelling alternatives to historical materialism by articulating how decolonization involves a deep intellectual, emotional, and bodily awareness that connects individuals to larger collectivities and cosmologies. Honoring their radical insights, I maintain that "pedagogies of the Sacred" help constitute a politics of spiritual relationality that attends to the uneven and contradictory effects of settler colonial capitalism on differently positioned groups, in particular, the fraught relationships between Indigenous, Black, and other diasporic subjects. As a diasporic Korean Canadian lesbian feminist scholar, I gratefully acknowledge the wisdom from Black, Indigenous, and women of color feminists within and beyond the academy. I recognize that we are unevenly and contradictorily positioned with respect to our subject locations and corresponding responsibilities on Turtle Island. As a result, my research, teaching, and activism are increasingly preoccupied with questions of complicity, accountability, and the politics of solidarity.[2]

In recent years, through ongoing conversations and the teachings of Indigenous mentors, I am humbled to recognize that, even though I am subject to white racism as an Asian diasporic person, I benefit from my complicity in settler colonialism as a Canadian citizen *in relation* to Indigenous peoples and their lands. As Robinder Sehdev (2011: 266) suggests,

"We belong here not because Canada opened its doors, but because Aboriginal nations permitted settler governance on their lands." In other words, my belonging on this land is made possible by treaty. I join a growing number of non-Indigenous scholars and activists who understand that acknowledging land and place enables us to learn our roles and responsibilities and take direction from Indigenous peoples who often describe themselves as caretakers—and not owners—of the land (Lawrence and Dua 2005; Walia 2014). I want to complicate conventional liberal, Marxist, and queer psychoanalytic theories that evacuate any spiritual connections to other forms of life and evade questions of historical accountability and political complicity in relation to the land. I am interested in naming how Indigenous and women of color feminist theories have consistently recognized spiritual connectedness through ancestral reverence and our relational responsibilities to land and one another. Rita Wong (2012: 528) eloquently explains: "From an imposed settler perspective, land belongs to people. From an older Indigenous perspective, however, people belong to the land." The recognition of land as something that is shared and not owned is one of the most remarkable and useful teachings I have learned since engaging with Indigenous perspectives.[3] For this reason, I want to think deeply about the places I *come to* and how I arrived (Haig-Brown 2012). Acknowledging territory demonstrates respect and recognition for Indigenous peoples (Canadian Association of University Teachers 2017). Although Indigenous land acknowledgments can too often become tokenizing gestures, they can also help establish reciprocal relations if they occur within a larger context of ongoing work to forge meaningful and concrete practices to dismantle settler colonialism (Vowel 2016).

In this regard, I examine two contemporary artworks by Rosa Sungjoo Park, an emerging diasporic South Korean artist with recent landed status in Canada, and Tannis Nielsen, a midcareer Indigenous artist with Cree/ Métis, Anishnabwe, and Danish ancestry. Both Nielsen and Park use digital media art to honor their ancestral traditions and spiritual practices. Ironically, digital media is also a place of symbolic violence where settler colonial capitalism can be reproduced through powerful global infrastructures and racialized female labor that is flexible, cheap, and consistent (Hearne 2017; Nakamura 2014). To resist this trend, I take this opportunity to document contemporary activist interventions of Indigenous and diasporic feminist artists.[4] I suggest that their creative use of digital media technology disrupts a tradition vs. modernity binary that forms the basis of heteropatriarchal, capitalist, and settler colonial rule. By drawing attention to spiritual and

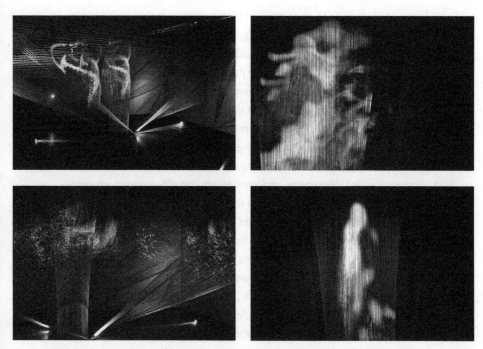

Figures 1a–1d. Stills from *Forgotten Dreams: Meditations on Narrative Space*. Photos courtesy of Rosa Sungjoo Park.

multidimensional forms of life, Nielsen's and Park's artworks imagine radical alternatives to neoliberal multiculturalism while at the same time being subject to appropriation within these increasingly institutionalized logics. Because the distinct colonial experiences of Indigenous and diasporic Korean women cannot be conflated, I draw attention to these spiritually inspired creative practices to build deeper relationships of solidarity and co-resistance among Black, diasporic, and Indigenous groups on Turtle Island—relationships that reject claims for settler state inclusion and are instead based on our sacred responsibilities to land and life.

### Honoring the Ancestors: Korean Diasporic Memory, Feminist Spiritual Recovery, and the *Mudang*

It is the early summer of 2014, and my partner, Anne-Marie, and I are attending an opening MFA exhibition called Forgotten Dreams: Meditations on Narrative Space by the digital media artist Rosa Sungjoo Park, an international student from South Korea (see figs. 1a–1d). Her show is held in the FINA Art Gallery at the University of British Columbia Okanagan where I've worked since 2012. Previously, I've

told Anne-Marie how glad I am to have met Rosa and share our stories of arriving—
uninvited—to the unceded territory of the Syilx peoples as Korean diasporic women
despite our uneven experiences of travel, privilege, and embodiment.

Anne-Marie arrives to meet me, slightly flushed and breathless from her trek across
the courtyard that leads to the exhibition space. She looks perplexed. As she approaches,
she asks, "Was there ever a burial ground in this area? I just got a weird feeling." I reply,
"I don't think so. If there was, I haven't learned about it."

We enter the art gallery along with several other audience members. At first, the
room is completely dark. When the show begins, loud metallic sounds of rapidly clash-
ing cymbals, flashing video images, and bursting patterns of light project onto exqui-
sitely constructed, three-dimensional string screens. I listen to the crashing rhythms
and watch black-and-white photos of Korean women in crescent-sleeved and full-
skirted hanbok flicker hypnotically across the screens. As I listen, my heart starts to
pound and ache. The photos remind me of my recently deceased halmonis. I feel a
hauntingly (un)familiar yearning—a mixture of sorrow, gratitude, and revelation. At
certain moments, I hold my breath. At others, I suppress tears.

The music and video images are looped. Anne-Marie and I exit the art gallery to
congratulate Rosa on her stunningly crafted work. Rosa tells us that the installation is
inspired by her childhood memories of attending a traditional Korean funeral rite. It is a
tribute to her maternal ancestors. Anne-Marie, who has always been more attuned to
ghosts and spiritual forces, glances at me wide-eyed, now understanding her uncanny
sensation of approaching a cemetery.

In her written thesis, Park (2014: 29) explains that she was taken to a
traditional Korean funeral as a child where she was deeply impressed by the
"vivid sounds of dirges, hand-bells, and a large gong that were played while
the procession was moving towards the grave." She describes how the
mourners' emotional outbursts were intensified by traditional Korean
music with diverse tempos that evoked contradictory feelings of grief and
cheerfulness associated with death and a spiritual afterlife. Park (2014: 29–
30, 34) recreates these paradoxical sensations in her exhibition through a
remarkable audiovisual installation that reflects her fragmented recollec-
tions of the event:

> I incorporate personal items such as portraits of my family members
> who passed away and the poems written by my mother for a funeral rite.
> I visualize the movement of the spirit of the deceased with light . . . to
> portray his or her journey to the next world. . . . The music and images
> are juxtaposed to recreate traditional Korean funerals. . . . Sounds and

symbolic visuals help the spectators be aware of a "threshold" between the two worlds, the liminal space of the funeral rite.

I have never been to a traditional Korean funeral, yet as I listened to the *Forgotten Dreams* musical narrative and watched the light-filled images dance on screens across the dim gallery, I felt an intensely "peculiar sensation"—a flood of unexpected memories and pangs of longing to see my grandmothers, two women who embodied vastly different personifications of Korean tradition during my youth.[5] Indeed, I felt momentarily suspended in an intergenerational "liminal space" created through Park's captivating installation whereby my sense of cultural displacement as a diasporic Korean woman in the university art gallery was alternately supplanted by paradoxical feelings of recognition and ancestral healing. I could see and hear representations of my family and homeland—grandmothers that I never quite knew and a place I never really inhabited. Somehow, I connected to my diasporic home in this miraculously constructed space even though I was on Indigenous land.

Park's fragmented use of mother-daughter narratives, autobiography, personal photos, calligraphy, poetry, sound, and video implicitly echoes the nonlinear themes and aesthetics inspired by the late Korean American artist Theresa Hak Kyung Cha's (1982) complex literary work, *Dictée*. Since the early 1990s, Cha's trailblazing work has been reclaimed by Asian North American feminist artists and scholars who celebrate how it problematizes binary and essentialist constructions of gender, ethnicity, race, sexuality, nation, language, and citizenship. It "thematizes the contradiction of an identity logic that privileges a developmental narrative as the mode of the subject's individual formation" through its provocative form and content (Lowe 1994: 37). *Dictée*'s deliberately chaotic narrative offers a searing critique of U.S. anti-immigration sentiments and Third World imperialism by linking Japanese colonialism with America's role in the Korean War and the subsequent division of Korea. As Lisa Lowe (1994: 38) suggests, this piercing historical connection incites alternative epistemic worldviews, especially in regard to identity formation: "While rendering unavoidably explicit the traces of colonial and imperial damage and dislocation on the subject, it articulates a voice in opposition to those dominations that persistently refuses the assimilation of that subject to fictions of identity and development, and writes this 'subject' as a possible site for active cultural and ideological struggle." Like the multidimensional, contradictory, and

Figures 2a–2d. Stills from *Forgotten Dreams: Meditations on Narrative Space*. Photos courtesy of Rosa Sungjoo Park.

hybrid subject of Cha's *Dictée*, Park's *Forgotten Dreams* evokes a Korean diasporic imaginary that defies the human development narrative. Instead, it combines intergenerational memory, historical artifacts, and cultural signifiers, and makes innovative use of digital media to ultimately disrupt a tradition vs. modernity dichotomy (see figs. 2a–2d). The exhibition is at once disorienting, stimulating, and potentially liberating. By presenting the digitized images and sounds in a continuous loop, the audience (re)experiences Korean "tradition" through modern technology. Yet rather than articulating an oppositional Korean diasporic subject position or problematizing a fixed or binary identity formation, *Forgotten Dreams* opens up radical alternatives to heteropatriarchal and colonial racist logics by honoring the spiritual relational knowledge that is transferred through maternal ancestors, specifically the healing practices imparted by Korean shamans, commonly referred to as *mudang*.[6] Park (pers. comm., July 31, 2017) explains, "I think much of the work process and approaches I've done for *Forgotten Dreams* mirror *mudang* practices in terms of healing. Korean *mudangs* are healers in a way, helping people and families who [suffer] from physical and mental illness." The healing and interconnected work of Korean shamans in community mirrors the crucial role of spirituality in transnational feminist activism. *Mudang* are Korean women who have the ability to invoke or be possessed by a spirit who communicates through them.[7] Through the *mudang*, Koreans plead or speak with ancestors or recently deceased loved ones. Many Korean scholars suggest that the rituals conducted by *mudang* can resolve the emotional and spiritual state of being known as *han*, a Korean word that describes a wounded heart caused by excessive hardship, violence, and exploitation instigated by social injustice. According to Jonghyun Lee (2009: 188–89), *han* is resolved only through shamanic ritual, and suffering is a prerequisite to becoming a *mudang*. In other words, on the basis of healing from her own hardship and spiritual anguish or *han*, the *mudang* heals the wounds of others. *Forgotten Dreams* makes creative use of modern technology to elicit the *mudang*'s responsibility for spiritual healing and recovery through ceremony and ancestral recognition. This onto-epistemological space is ornately constructed on Indigenous lands through Park's powerful diasporic feminist imaginings.[8]

In her feminist reading of the South Korean novelist Han Kang's *The Vegetarian*, Sneja Gunew (2016) traces *han*'s distinct meaning to a history of *mudang* practices, Korean anticolonial resistance movements, and liberation theologies. Gunew (2016: 14) discerns that, in translation, *han* appears to emphasize a "personally felt political awareness (both singular and plural)" engendered by the violence of Japanese colonialism. Gunew indicates that the English translation of non-European concepts such as *han* can offer "new taxonomies" that not only illustrate the conceptual limits of Western theories of affect but also draw attention to contemporary questions of geopolitical responsibility. It is the *collective* suffering (as opposed to individual) and pluralized political consciousness associated with *han* that Gunew finds promising because it exceeds affect theory's reliance on universalized and self-serving psychoanalytic frameworks. To imagine a "new materialism," Gunew (2016: 18) claims we can explore *han* as an unconventional affective concept that "provides the unfamiliar singularity of an intensity of suffering and frustration yoked to the plural as well as specific histories of political oppression and inequity currently but not inevitably linked to dense substrata of national groups enduring colonialism and other forms of oppression." Put differently, the Korean shaman's *han* suggests a transnational feminist ethic and collective anticolonial consciousness. Yet shamanism is often rendered deviant because it is a woman-led spiritual practice that contradicts colonial and modernist state ideologies in Korea. It was historically outlawed by Japanese colonial and Korean national governments who deemed *mudang* to be immoral agents of superstition and witchcraft.[9] Despite repeated institutional attempts to eradicate shamanism, however, *mudang* continue to practice their ceremonies, and the misogynistic stigmas surrounding the *mudang* do not prevent other Koreans from soliciting them. Paradoxically, even though the *mudang* and their spiritual practices are largely deemed antithetical to the development of a modern capitalist nation-state, since the early 1960s shamanism has been reappropriated by the South Korean government as a national revival strategy to promote cultural heritage and global tourism.[10] Merose Hwang (2007) suggests that the South Korean state's newfound attempts to celebrate shamanism reflect biopolitical agendas that hypocritically serve to co-opt, manage, and regulate Korean women's bodies and knowledge.

*Mudang* practices are sometimes revealed in Korean postcolonial feminist research on comfort women redress and sex workers' movements where traditional shamanistic rituals are described as empowering forms of collective healing and mourning. For example, Kun Jong Lee (2004) examines how the Korean American novelist Nora Okja Keller's *Comfort Woman* (1998) transforms the protagonist—a former Korean comfort woman—into Princess Pari, "the prominent female deity in the fundamentally women-centered Korean shamanism . . . in order to remember the victims of Japanese military sex slavery and to guide the spirits of comfort women to the next world" (Lee 2004: 432). In a related way, Elizabeth W. Son (2016: 371) studies *The Trojan Women: An Asian Story*, an international Bosnian-Korean theater production that premiered in 2007, featuring an all-Korean female cast that uses the Korean musical style of *pansori* and visual imagery of a shamanic ritual movement to offer "a symbolic reclamation of violated bodies while providing a redressive space for the audience to witness the long history of wartime sexual violence against women." Such investigations uncover the institutionalized sex work of Japanese colonial and U.S. military occupations and relay the painful but resilient narratives of comfort women survivors and military camp town sex workers through personal testimony and forms of visual and performance art, film, video, and creative writing. This work adds to the growing archive of Asian American feminist research on the historical links between forced military sexual slavery in colonial Japan and the U.S.

military camp town sex industry sanctioned in South Korea (Cho 2007; Son 2018; Chuh 2003).

My reading of Park's *Forgotten Dreams* aligns with this crucial body of feminist scholarship, but I am troubled by the risks of theorizing concepts such as "tradition" and "spirituality" and relatively shallow translations of *mudang* and *han*.[11] These terms are especially loaded within a neoliberal academic context that rewards "native informants" for producing discourses of authenticity that demonize or romanticize difference (Ahmed 2012). For example, closely tied to the concept of *han* and a *mudang*'s spiritual calling are specific psychological characteristics classified in the fourth edition of the *Diagnostic and Statistical Manual of Mental Disorders* under the category of *shinbyung*, a "Korean culture-bound syndrome" and "folk label for a syndrome in which the initial phases are characterized by anxiety and somatic complaints (general weakness, dizziness, fear, anorexia, insomnia, gastrointestinal problems), with subsequent dissociation and possession by ancestral spirits" (Lee 2009: 188). Such descriptions of *han* rely on pathologized and essentialist understandings of Koreanness defined by Westernized biomedical standards of mental health and normalcy that also invite romanticized notions of *mudang* and their "traditional" acts of spirituality. Like Christine Kim (2013: 35), "I am forced to recognize the ways in which I, as a second-generation Korean Canadian, produce and reproduce the Asian/non-Asian binary through and within myself in complex, disorienting and infuriating ways."

Although I'm not fluent in the language, I have Korean ancestry. My parents spoke to me in Korean when I was a child, but I lost my fluency in public school because they both encouraged me to assimilate into white Anglo-Canadian culture as fast as possible. I am now tentatively relearning my native tongue as a way to reclaim my ancestral history. Importantly, this process involves ancestral healing and the recognition of Indigenous land and place. I was born and raised on what I've learned to be the traditional lands of the Mississaugas of the Credit River, the Huron-Wendat First Nation, and the Haudenosaunee Confederacy, or the city of Toronto, Ontario (Canadian Association of University Teachers 2017: 18). It is the shared territory where the historic Two Row Wampum Treaty was established between Dutch traders and Haudenosaunee peoples and later extended to relationships with French, British, and American settlers.

The Two Row Wampum belt depicts two boats on a river. According to Indigenous philosophers such as Dale Turner (2006: 49), the Two Row

Wampum provides an important decolonizing framework that connects water, sovereignty, and law. The purple rows represent paths that the boats make as they travel down the river. One boat is the European ship and the other is a Haudenosaunee canoe. The boats travel side by side but do not interfere with one another, which symbolizes respect for autonomy. The white background represents the river of life and a relationship based on peace, respect, and friendship. The fringe indicates that the relationship is unending.

My diasporic journey entails familiarizing myself with Indigenous lands and territorial protocols that are distinguished through treaty. Margaret Kovach (2013: 110) clarifies that treaty is a concept that is often understood in terms of identity; however, "to consider treaties as solely a categorical demarcation of identity demonstrates a limited understanding of Indigenous culture and philosophy." Put differently, a "treaty is not a 'thing.' It is a word that describes an active relational process that includes seeking continuous counsel and dialogue on matters that have bearing on the parties it involves" (Kovach 2013: 212). The understanding of treaty as an enduring relationship of balance, respect, and mutual responsibility is key to my discussion in this essay. As a transnational feminist, I recognize this decolonizing journey to be a challenging responsibility that entails profoundly epistemological spiritual engagements. Spiritual work enables us to think, feel, enact, and understand our obligations to resist colonial oppression collectively. I ask, How do understandings and experiences of spirituality shape and affect feminist practices of solidarity and resistance? What are my responsibilities to, especially, Black and Indigenous women whose work on spirituality I invoke and seek to honor? What are our responsibilities to each other? And how are these responsibilities linked to spirituality and our collective healing?

I turn to the work of Tannis Nielsen, a Cree/Métis/Anishnawbe/Danish midcareer artist, educator, and community activist, whose creative use of digital media similarly disrupts binary narratives of tradition vs. modernity by exploring themes of lived experience, embodied knowledge, and spirituality. Analogous to *Forgotten Dreams*, this exhibit summons the awareness of my responsibilities as a transnational feminist to multiple dimensions of life via spiritual and erotic knowledges. Taken together, Park's and Nielsen's works offer fruitful opportunities to think through the complex asymmetries of power, history, and representation between Indigenous and diasporic groups on Turtle Island.

Figure 3. Virtual sketch for *A Creation*. Image courtesy of Tannis Nielsen.

## Honoring the Creator: Cree Cosmology and Survivance

Two years after I saw *Forgotten Dreams*, I was invited to another digital media installation by a new faculty member, Tannis Nielsen, taking place in the FINA gallery, the same space where Park held her MFA exhibition. Nielsen and I discovered our overlapping histories in Toronto where we helped organize feminist antiviolence initiatives in the early 2000s. In addition to teaching for the visual arts program at the University of British Columbia Okanagan, Nielsen was a featured artist-in-residence at the Indigenous Summer Intensive Program in 2016. During the artists' residency, Nielsen showed her work in progress, a six-channel video and sound installation called *A Creation*.[12] In *A Creation*, Nielsen combines electromagnetic energy with digital video in a stimulating representation of Indigenous creation stories. The six videos are synchronized and projected onto the walls, ceiling, and floor of the darkened gallery where the audience is invited to immerse themselves in this hypnotic loop of images layered over the electrifying sounds of static energy (see fig. 3).

My experience of Nielsen's media installation immediately reminded me of Park's exhibition seen two years earlier. It evoked, in remarkably similar ways, powerful and contradictory feelings of sadness, elation, gratitude, and yearning. Of course, the crackling soundtrack and fuzzy images did not conjure vivid memories of my Korean ancestors. Rather, I felt "as if [I had] just entered into a metaphysical universe / a subconscious cognitive space" (Nielsen 2012). When I closed my eyes, I became acutely aware that I had entered a sacred space, one that enabled me to feel and recognize a powerful presence and energy far beyond—yet also within—myself.

In her artist statement, Nielsen explains how her interest in electromagnetic energy developed after learning that static is the by-product of radiation from the Big Bang that, according to many scientific theories, took place over fourteen billion years ago. She describes static to be a form of "ancient media" that inspires the work: "I intend to relay the relationship between human inner space, the natural world, and the mysterious life force that permeates creation. This practice of Cree metaphysics provides insight into the origin and nature of knowledge, with the result that there is a deeper understanding of the natural order; this spiritual understanding and connectedness is the foundational principle of the Cree ethos" (Nielsen 2012).

Electromagnetic energy is the main medium to articulate Nielsen's cultural understanding of Creation or Genesis, which is imagined to be part of a cycle or continuum (see figs. 4a–4d). As A Creation relays a Cree cosmological understanding to address current environmental crises, it also enables viewers to awaken to a higher spiritual consciousness and recognition of how the land connects our past, present, and future.

Nielsen's creative application of Cree metaphysics resonates strongly with Wanda Nanibush's (2015) description of contemporary Indigenous media arts. Drawing on Gerald Vizenor's concept of "survivance," a term that denotes "survival, resistance and presence," Nanibush (2015: para. 1) explains that Indigenous media artists "rewrite colonial histories from the perspective of Indigenous experience, visual culture, and oral history" and experiment "with medium in order to represent Indigenous worldviews, which often favour non-linear narrative; visual abstractions of historical events; interconnectedness of body and mind, nature and culture; the politics of space; as well as cyclical and geological philosophies of time."

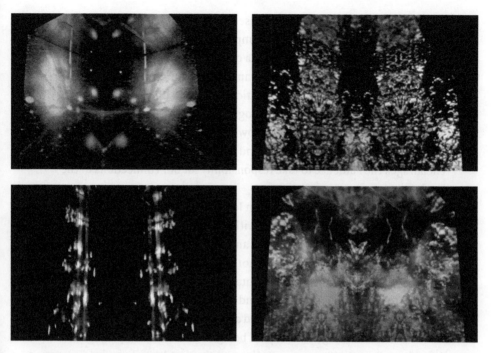

Figures 4a–4d. Video stills from *A Creation*. Images courtesy of Tannis Nielsen.

Correspondingly, in its completion, *A Creation* includes transcribed Elder teachings in the Cree and English languages. The combination of soundscapes plays alongside additional video art and performance recordings. Each of the six visual and audio streams incorporate the four elements of earth, water, air, fire, and "film from the tar sands project, Attawapiskat and various other Indigenous landscapes that have been greatly affected by industrial consumption. . . . The destruction of the land will be shown in relation to the destruction of society and portrayed in direct contrast to the teachings" (Nielsen 2012). The videos are projected and mounted onto reflective surfaces of aluminized mylar that mimic the effects of light on water. A large pool of water is placed on the floor where audience members can step into it, barefoot. Nielsen's intention is for the audience to be metaphorically "*baptized*" or "anointed into understanding the Cree ethos," which highlights a creation of relational alliances with nonhuman entities that are both natural and supernatural. Additionally, "These relationships extend to the participation level, where everything in the world takes part in the experience that the spirit of things is all one" (Nielsen 2012).

The Cree-*baptism* is, of course, Nielsen's subtle yet deliberate inversion of the Christian proselytizing that accompanies settler colonialism—but the actual presence of water also signals a cleansing, meditation, or healing ritual. By and large, *A Creation's* participatory actions and media effects serve to amplify the audience's sensation of being "submerged . . . into a deep subconscious inner world and cognitive space" (Nielsen 2012). In this way, *A Creation* gives recognition of how spiritual and ancestral knowledge can lead to deeper understandings and appreciation of the land—and it encourages the audience to take responsibility for our connections to the land.

Nielsen's activist background as an Idle No More organizer is certainly reflected in *A Creation's* engagement with the politics of decolonization and Indigenous sovereignty. It belongs to an Indigenous futurist movement, which, as Danika Medak-Saltzman (2017: 143, 144) explains, "serves to counter persistent settler colonial fantasies of Native disappearance" and "[relies] on Indigenous innovation and creativity to bring about change in ways that are always-already informed and supported by Indigenous political concerns and Indigenous ways of being in the world." In particular, *A Creation* reflects Indigenous narrative traditions and prophesying strategies for bringing forth better futures that are rooted in an ethic of responsibility.

In her commissioned catalog essay published in 2017, Nielsen relays how Indigenous women's expressions of sovereignty involve the protection of the Earth and matriarchal governance. For Nielsen, Indigenous women's governance precedes and remains incommensurable with Western feminist theories that are imbedded in settler colonial values of individualism and capitalist development that evacuate women's responsibilities to the land:

> As Indigenous women we know that we are a direct manifestation of Earth in human form. Our respect for Earth/Mother is the epistemological foundation of our matriarchal society. This respect/reverence is also offered to our women, who are viewed as sacred (as life-givers). It is this matriarchal "way of being" that later influenced settler ideas of feminist theory, and this is why I don't call myself a feminist, as much as I am part of the original matriarchy. With this relationship between women and Earth, we know too that when the land is exploited, so too are the women who live within the desecrated ecosystems. (Nielsen 2017: para. 5)

Nielsen's refusal to claim a feminist identity demonstrates her awareness that "the complexity of interpreting sovereign nationhood demands more than mainstream feminist theoretical approaches have to offer" (Mithlo 2009: 18). As Nancy Marie Mithlo contends, shifting constructions of time, space, and notions of community are crucial for an Indigenous feminist analysis to be relevant. In this regard, Nielsen's artistic themes and praxis reflect a wide engagement and relational understanding of interlocking struggles and complicities across languages, nations, geographies, and histories. In addition to her solo work, for example, Nielsen cocurated, with Vicky Moufawad-Paul, a group exhibition featuring James Luna, Emily Jacir, Erica Lord, and John Halaka in 2008 called *Enacting Emancipation*. This exhibition recognized the sixtieth memorial of the 1948 Palestinian Nakba (catastrophe) and formation of the Israeli state, featuring multimedia installations and performances by First Nations and Palestinian artists exploring the interconnectedness of Indigenous experience under colonialism as Fourth World peoples. *Enacting Emancipation* placed importance on contrasting diverse but localized modes of Indigenous resistance. Ultimately, it showcased how a universal, international system of colonial technique and strategy led to differences of defense that are "culturally based and inheritably Indigenous" (Nielsen and Moufawad-Paul 2008). Nielsen writes: "Although knowledge system(s) stemming from Turtle Island are not universal in nature, a common teaching—amongst an array of ideology—tells us that the Land we are fighting to protect—is Our Mother." Recognizing the shared struggles in relation to stolen and occupied land, the curators suggest that "what is at stake in claims to Indigenous identity in North America and in Palestine is the refusal to foreclose on the possibility of decolonization" (Nielsen and Moufawad-Paul 2008). Building on this sentiment, *A Creation* inspires audiences to imagine and bring into existence alternative realities and work collectively in what Leanne Betasamosake Simpson (2016) describes as practices of "Indigenous resurgence and co-resistance."

## Pedagogies of Land and Place: Indigenous Resurgence and Co-resistance

I bring together Park's *Forgotten Dreams* and Nielsen's *A Creation* in an effort to give language to a powerful healing force and awakening that I feel inside me, a kind of heightened intuition guided by loving desires of the heart and spirit. Taken together, these creative works offer a crucial opportunity to think through difficult questions about Indigeneity, diaspora, and the politics of relationality, which are the central preoccupations of this essay. In theoretical parlance, I bring Indigenous and women of color feminist theories into "productive" conversation by paying attention to how both frameworks draw on the significance of lived experience, embodied knowledge, and spirituality to advance a feminist politics.[13] But I regard as imperative Danika Medak-Saltzman's and Antonio Tiongson Jr.'s (2015: 2–3) caveat "that the influx of usage of Indigeneity has come to be associated with imbuing one's work with academic cachet but not with an associated sense of responsibility to Indigenous communities or to furthering Indigenous studies scholarship in a meaningful way." My heart urges me to dig deeper, to name truths that may be hard to ingest. Honesty requires humility.

Although they provide similar tools for critical inquiry, women of color and Indigenous feminisms do not share an equivalence that can simply be "added" together. Deborah A. Miranda (2003: 344) indicates, for instance, that Indigenous women and women of color are incongruously positioned in relation to land: "There is something intrinsically different about being an Indian woman in the Americas, which the work of other women of color in this country cannot express: we inherit and still live histories and oppressions designed to legally enforce Indian identities not just disempowered but genetically incapable of autonomy." Indigenous feminist projects are distinct because Indigenous women continue to "live out the generations of civil rights injustices such as the denial of documented treaty rights and the deadly form of literacy, wrought in Indian Boarding Schools, meant to further enslave rather than empower" (Miranda 2003: 345). Audra Simpson (2016) puts it bluntly: "The state is a Man."

Accordingly, transnational feminist projects relying on models of social justice that reinforce state-based frameworks of multicultural inclusion and recognition inevitably fail to meet the goals of Indigenous decolonization and sovereignty. An Indigenous feminist lens magnifies the gender-specific realities of settler colonialism, land theft, and Indigenous disappearance that are not fully addressed by women of color approaches. In this way, as Harsha Walia (2014: 45) explains, women of color must refuse "to replicate the Canadian state's assimilationist model of liberal pluralism, forcing Indigenous identities to fit within our existing groups and narratives. The inherent right to traditional lands and to self-determination is expressed collectively and should not be subsumed within the discourse of individual or human rights."

Strategies of institutional resistance that rely on state-based logics are not only limited by an intensified neoliberal climate but also through liberal humanist frameworks that invoke modern Western concepts of identity, subjectivity, agency, and freedom. As mentioned earlier, for example, Korean Canadian citizens largely benefit from our complicity in settler state colonialism and liberal multicultural policies that promote the cultural, economic, and political disempowerment of Indigenous peoples and their territorial claims through violated treaty agreements and rights of sovereignty (Lee 2017). Strategies of resistance are often incommensurable with respect to Indigenous perspectives on land, which exceed state-based frameworks (Tuck and Yang 2012). Thus, decolonial resistance is repeatedly fraught with conflict and contradiction among diasporic and Indigenous communities in relation to white, state-based contexts.

The layered, complex, and messy strategies of decolonial resistance among Black, Indigenous, and people of color warrant significant consideration. There is a heightened splintering within grassroots activist communities across Turtle Island to create necessary Black, Indigenous, and People of Color (BIPOC) distinctions, which signals both a coalitional ethic and a paradoxical reflection of the frenzied neoliberal pursuit of state recognition within and outside of the academy. Along these lines, the Black queer feminist scholar Tiffany Lethabo King (2019) questions the prospect of political coalition between Black and Indigenous communities by outlining their fraught asymmetrical histories in relation to land and sovereignty. King articulates how, in contrast to Indigenous groups, sovereignty is an option that is not historically available to Black peoples. As a result, Black people are frequently—and violently—induced into citizenship and settlement, furthering the genocidal project. Correspondingly, Indigenous folks often seek recognition from the nation-state through anti-Black practices, which include slavery in the case of the Cherokee nation, and repeatedly rely on nationhood discourses that are inaccessible to African Americans. King (2019: 160) further elaborates: "When interdependence and cooperation do occur, they often happen in zones and territories that are hard to travel to and are often forged under conditions of duress." In this vein, state-based modes of resistance fail to interrupt how white settler human subjectivity is established through the state ownership of the nonhuman Black Other. Asian, Latinx, South Asian, and other people of color are unevenly situated within deeply complicated conditions of colonial migration and overlapping histories of indenture that involve the necessary dehumanization of non-white bodies to justify the exploitative, extractive, and violent demands of global capitalism.

To challenge and disrupt these oppressive capitalist and settler colonial demands, Leanne Betasamosake Simpson (2016: 30–31) proposes models of justice founded on Indigenous principles of relationality, "land as pedagogy" and "constellations of co-resistance" that emphasize place-based resurgence, accountability, and radical coalition-building rather than an engagement with white settler anxieties:

> We can't achieve Indigenous nationhoods while replicating anti-Blackness. We can't have resurgence without centering gender and queerness, and creating alternative systems of accountability for sexual and gender violence. Therefore, we need to create constellations of connections with other radical thinkers and doers and makers. We need to build mass movements with radical labor, with Black communities, with radical communities of color. We need to stop providing space for the "What can white allies do" questions and set up spaces where we can connect with other social movements and create constellations of mutual support and co-resistance.

The politics of relationality holds us accountable for related but distinct modes of oppression and foregrounds how we are all invited to participate in interlocking systems of denial, extraction, and dispossession. Yet negotiating the politics of relationality is especially tricky in this historical moment when, for example, Black Lives Matter is entangled with official discourses of Truth and Reconciliation in Canada. If the analytic power of relationality enables us to perform "radical coalition work," we must recognize that political alliances between Indigenous and diasporic communities are more powerful when they are not based on shared victimization, but when they acknowledge how we can be complicit in each other's victimization (Cohen 1997: 457). The complex layering of racial inequities and colonial injustice among BIPOC communities calls for a highly perceptive approach to activist solidarity work. Indigenous genocide, slavery, and anti-Blackness generate acts of resistance under conquistador colonialism that diverge and converge unpredictably. Noting this complexity, Tamara K. Nopper (2015: para. 28) asserts, "As a recognition of settler colonialism gains more traction in the academy and activist spaces, we may also consider the ethics of how settler colonialism is inserted into conversations addressing non-Black people of color's / immigrants of color's structural relations with Black people." Nopper suggests that as radicalized non-Black people of color address their own settler complicity in relation to Indigenous peoples, they must also recognize their responsibilities to Black and other people of color communities on Turtle Island. Neoliberal multiculturalism heightens competitive binaries among Black and Asian communities when they seek state recognition through a politics of respectability.[14] Black feminist intellectuals such as Andrea J. Ritchie (2017) and Robyn Maynard (2017) powerfully illustrate how Black criminalization and anti-Blackness are denied and downplayed under the white savior rubric of protectionism, tolerance, and benevolence in the national imaginary. The awkward silences and hostile divisions between Asian and Black communities can be directly linked to the aftermath of slavery. The resurgence of anti-Asian racism must therefore account for the pervasive and haphazard replication of anti-Blackness in Asian communities that manifests in colonial violence at the expense of solidarity.[15]

Accordingly, I move away from humanist affect theories that rely on claims of sovereignty to heal from and disrupt systems of heteropatriarchy and white supremacy. Black lesbian and Indigenous feminisms reveal that spiritual relationalities offer a formidable paradigm for rethinking solidarities and decolonial resistance among BIPOC groups. Tiffany Lethabo King's (2019) persuasive insights in *The Black Shoals: Offshore Formations of Black and Native Studies* encourage me to theorize spiritually inspired decolonial resistance in Indigenous and diasporic feminist art and media. Although the erotic is frequently assessed as personal and irrelevant to political activism, King (2019: 146) echoes Indigenous scholars like Billy-Ray Belcourt to "imagine the space of the erotic as a space of decolonial possibility." King finds promise in erotic knowledge for how it confronts liberal concepts of sovereignty and selfhood to enact a project of futurity that affirms Black and Indigenous life rather than the persistent script of Black suffering or Indigenous genocide in popular culture. King (2019: 147) cites Audre Lorde's concept of the erotic: "Specifically, how its power functions as a kind of bridge that can lessen the threat of difference" that inspires us to "engage the threat and our fear of difference to come to a place that allows us to be with and for one another." Erotic knowledge goes far beyond privatized sexual relations and commodified romance among individuals and instead embraces the intricate interconnectedness of all life and land. Erotic knowledge indicates a spiritual relationality between human and nonhuman beings, environments, races, and communities of difference. It signals the crucial interplay between love, survival, decolonial resistance, and community formation. Alongside King (2019: 142), I wish to foreground "new endings to troubling histories" in a concerted effort to decolonize projects of transnational feminist solidarity through a nuanced recognition of multifarious ancestries and politics across communities of difference.

Sara Ahmed (2017) reminds us that our citations can be strategic and radically feminist acts. Whether it is through my research, teaching, or community work, I must be vigilant and pay tribute to Indigenous, Black, and other women of color thinkers and organizers without appropriating, flattening out, or conflating our experiences, what M. Jacqui Alexander (2005: 268) describes in terms of "be[ing] rooted in the particularities of our cultural homes without allegiance to the boundaries of the nation-state, yet remain[ing] simultaneously committed to a collectivized politic of identification and solidarity." In linking together Nielsen's and Park's artwork, I do not suggest that the effects of heteropatriarchy, racism, and settler state capitalism experienced by Indigenous and Korean diasporic women in Canada are equivalent. Rather, my reading of Park's *Forgotten Dreams* and Nielsen's *A Creation* enacts a politics of spiritual relationality that highlights how Indigenous and diasporic feminist media artists "refuse the constraints of colonial narratives on creative production, and [reorient] art-making to effect resurgent practices and Indigenous ways of being" (Martineau and Ritskes 2014: ix). *Forgotten Dreams* employs a decolonial aesthetic that gestures to spiritual ways of knowing and being through a contemporary invocation of Korean ancestral traditions. It strongly resonates with Nielsen's innovative media strategies of "survivance" that bring Indigenous creation stories to the present. By extension, I honor the intellectual and spiritual traditions of Black, Indigenous, and women of color feminists to disrupt the (neo)colonial logics of settler state capitalism.

What I find particularly exciting in Park's and Nielsen's creative works is that they avoid—and, in some ways, refuse—the essentializing conundrums of constructing identity or the "burden of representation." The modern liberal fantasy of progress and development relies on dualistic logics of primitive and civilized subjects. Crucial to this colonial logic is the idea that non-Western cultural traditions are traditional, backward, and barbaric, in which modern Indigenous women and people of color cannot exist or are paradoxically deemed inauthentic. Although each work is informed and shaped by specific histories, geographies, and place-based knowledges, both *A Creation* and *Forgotten Dreams* do not require or insist on audiences to recognize an authentic Other. Rather, we are invited to experience the powerful sacred knowledges of Indigenous and Korean women, epistemologies that have been systemically evacuated and devalued under the conditions of settler state colonialism and late global capitalism. Their dreams, memories, desires, creation stories, and celebratory rituals of life and death depart from colonialism's hyper-individualism. They remind and inspire us to (re)imagine alternative worlds based on our collective sacred matrilineal knowledges. I draw attention to these shared practices of creative resistance to build deeper relationships of solidarity among diasporic and Indigenous women—relationships that are based on our sacred responsibilities to all forms of life.

......................................................................................................

**Ruthann Lee** resides on unceded Syilx territory where she is associate professor of cultural studies at the University of British Columbia Okanagan. She teaches about media activism and has published essays about queer representations of race and masculinities in popular culture. She is interested in the politics of decolonization in feminist media art.

**Notes**

Special thanks to Tannis Nielsen and Rosa Sungjoo Park for inspiring me to engage with their work. I am grateful for the suggestions from my anonymous reviewers at *Meridians*, as well as the generous feedback and support provided by LiLynn Wan, Gulzar R. Charania, R. Cassandra Lord, Alifa Bandali, K.A. Hogan, Allison Hargreaves, and Anne-Marie Estrada.

1　See, for example, corresponding work on feminist spirituality by Gloria Anzaldúa (2015), Aimee Carrillo Rowe (2008), Omise'eke Natasha Tinsley (2018), bell hooks (2000), and Roxana Ng (2008, 2006).

2　For additional writings on settler colonial complicity and feminist accountability by women of color scholars, see Lawrence and Dua 2005; Day 2016; Palacios 2016; Walia 2014; Patel, Moussa, and Upadhyay 2015; Wong 2012, 2008; Jafri 2016; Phung 2019, 2015; Sehdev 2011; Kaur 2014; Charania 2022; and Lai 2015.

3　Malissa Phung (2015) cites Larissa Lai to claim that Asian Canadians are indebted to Indigenous peoples for these insights. Although this transactional language certainly resonates with a segment of Chinese Canadian histories, I depart from this terminology for it can depict respectability politics, notions of obedience and subservience that dangerously reconsolidate model minority stereotypes under the context of neoliberal multiculturalism.

4　Many pertinent scholarly collections similarly document BIPOC digital media activism, importantly noted by my anonymous reviewer. See, for example, the special issue of *Studies in American Indian Literatures* edited by Joanna Hearne (2017) and the Black Code special issue in *Black Scholar* edited by Jessica Marie Johnson and Mark Anthony Neal (2017).

5    Helen Lee's (1998: 292) landmark essay offers a selected filmography of works
     by and about Korean North American women (including Theresa Hak Kyung
     Cha's and her own films) and considers how shared experiences of *kyop'o* (over-
     seas Korean) women inform aesthetic practices "from the perspective of cul-
     tural displacement and feminist intervention."

6    *Mudang* literally translates into "people who believe in spirits." Although it is
     the more commonly used term, it also has derogatory connotations. The cul-
     tural anthropologist Laurel Kendall uses the less common term, *mansin*, mean-
     ing "ten thousand spirits," in a gesture of respect. See Kendall 1988 and 2009.

7    Korean women become shamans through spontaneous calls from ancestral
     spirits that will not go away until the woman accepts her destiny to be a *mudang*.
     *Mudang* interact with gods and ancestors by divining their presence and perform-
     ing specialized *kut* rituals to placate them and sustain their favour. *Kut* can involve
     feasting, chanting, drumming, and singing and are organized to "address afflic-
     tion, send ancestors to paradise, and secure blessings and prosperity. . . . More
     than merely incarnating the deities and the dead, *mansin* call upon the spirits'
     power to purify, exorcise, heal, and bring good fortune" (Kendall 2009: xx).

8    I thank my anonymous reviewer for this insight.

9    Korean cultural anthropologists and feminist historians concur that shaman-
     ism in modern Korea is best understood by locating it within Korean's colonial
     history. Korea was a battlefield for wars fought by other powers such as the
     Sino-Japanese War (1894–95) and the Russo-Japanese War (1904–5), which
     were followed by non-Western colonial occupation from Japan (1910–45) and U.
     S. imperialism during the Korean War (1950–53). During the 1890s, British and
     American travel writers and Christian missionaries described *mudang* as Korean
     female shamans who practiced superstition and worshipped the devil. *Mudang*
     were thus typically characterized by Westerners as undesirable and "unmod-
     ern" subjects. However, Korean court officials denigrated *mudang* as "uncivi-
     lized" subjects long before Western colonial discourses saturated the Korean
     public sphere in the late nineteenth century. When the Meiji government com-
     missioned ethnographic studies of Korean Indigenous subjects during the Jap-
     anese colonial occupation, *mudang* were further characterized by scholars and
     public intellectuals as threats to modernity: "During the colonial period . . .
     most people writing about *mudang* saw them as a menace to the nation. . . .
     *Mudang* were said to contaminate the nation by generating and spreading dis-
     eases, illnesses, depleting national resources, and generally wreaking social
     havoc" (Hwang 2007: 104).

10   In fact, under the Law for Conservation of Cultural Property established in 1962,
     *mudang* can officially register as authentic "Indigenous" Korean subjects where
     shamanic rituals are recognized as "folkloric theatrical performances" and "some
     shamans have been designated as living national treasures" (Lee 2009: 192).

11   In her self-reflexive reading of Vancouver-based artist David Khang's multime-
     dia works, Christine Kim (2013) describes her frustration and anxiety over
     simultaneously wanting and claiming to "know" the experience of Koreanness,
     particularly of *han*. For Kim, Khang's work opens up new possibilities for the

formation of publics based on a "geopolitics of feeling and the local and global structures that shape memory" (Kim 2013: 27). However, these "postcolonial intimacies" are paradoxically contingent upon the ability to access the vastly uneven histories of Asia or Korea that, in the Western academy, are produced and filtered through Orientalist frames.

12  A *Creation* has since been featured in a joint exhibition curated by Amy Malbeuf and Jessie Ray Short, *Lii Zoot Tare (Other Worlds)*, showcasing Métis artists in the Agnes Etherington Art Centre at Queen's University, situated on traditional Anishnaabe and Haudenosaunee Territory. See https://agnes.queensu.ca /exhibition/other-worlds/.

13  Rosa Sungjoo Park has not self-identified as a feminist, and I heed Tannis Nielsen's stated refusal to embrace the label "feminist." Here I acknowledge my desire to advance my own feminist agenda by claiming (even if I am "granted permission" to do so) their work under this umbrella.

14  See, for example, Kim 2000; Jun 2011; and Hong 2020. Scholar Strike Canada's online teach-in exemplifies the tense complications of Black-Asian alliances in North America and illustrates how the Defund the Police movement can mobilize multiple racialized communities in unprecedented yet promising ways. See Scholar Strike Canada 2021.

15  Elaine H. Kim (1998) describes how Asian Americans are insidiously positioned to denigrate Blackness through model minority discourse in an early assessment of Black-Asian race relations in the United States.

**Works Cited**

Ahmed, Sara. 2012. *On Being Included: Racism and Diversity in Institutional Life.* Durham, NC: Duke University Press.

Ahmed, Sara. 2017. *Living a Feminist Life.* Durham, NC: Duke University Press.

Alexander, M. Jacqui. 2005. *Pedagogies of Crossing: Meditations on Feminism, Sexual Politics, Memory, and the Sacred.* Durham, NC: Duke University Press.

Amadahy, Zainab. 2011. "Why Indigenous and Racialized Struggles Will Always Be Appendixed by the Left." *Rabble.ca*, July 10. http://rabble.ca/news/2011/07/why -indigenous-and-racialized-struggles-will-always-be-appendixed-left.

Anzaldúa, Gloria. 2015. *Light in the Dark / Luz en lo oscuro: Rewriting Identity, Spirituality, Reality.* Durham, NC: Duke University Press.

Canadian Association of University Teachers. 2017. *Guide to Acknowledging First Peoples & Traditional Territory.* Ottawa: CAUT.

Carrillo Rowe, Aimee. 2008. *Power Lines: On the Subject of Feminist Alliances.* Durham, NC: Duke University Press.

Cha, Theresa Hak Kyung. 1982. *Dictée.* New York: Tanham Press.

Charania, Gulzar R. 2022. "Lonely Methods and Other Tough Places: Recuperating Anti-racism from White Investments." *Feminist Theory* 23, no. 1: 61–75.

Cho, Grace M. 2007. *Haunting the Korean Diaspora: Shame, Secrecy, and the Forgotten War.* Minneapolis: University of Minnesota Press.

Chuh, Kandice. 2003. "Discomforting Knowledge; or, Korean 'Comfort Women' and Asian Americanist Critical Practice.'" *Journal of Asian American Studies* 6, no. 1: 5–23.

Cohen, Cathy J. 1997. "Punks, Bulldaggers, and Welfare Queens: The Radical Potential of Queer Politics?" *GLQ: A Journal of Lesbian and Gay Studies* 3, no. 4: 437–65.

Day, Iyko. 2016. *Alien Capital: Asian Racialization and the Logic of Settler Colonial Capitalism.* Durham, NC: Duke University Press.

Driskill, Qwo-Li, Chris Finley, Brian Joseph Gilley, and Scott Lauria Morgensen, eds. 2011. *Queer Indigenous Studies: Critical Interventions in Theory, Politics, and Literature.* Tucson: University of Arizona Press.

Garcia-Rojas, Claudia. 2016. "(Un)Disciplined Futures: Women of Color Feminism as a Disruptive to White Affect Studies." *Journal of Lesbian Studies* 21, no. 3: 254–71.

Gunew, Sneja. 2016. "Excess of Affect: In Translation." *Hecate* 42, no. 2: 7–22.

Haig-Brown, Celia. 2012. "Decolonizing Diaspora: Whose Traditional Land Are We On?" In *Decolonizing Philosophies of Education*, edited by Ali Al. Abdi, 73–90. Rotterdam: SensePublishers.

Hearne, Joanna. 2017. "Native to the Device: Thoughts on Digital Indigenous Studies." *Studies in American Indian Literatures* 29, no. 1: 3–26.

Hong, Cathy Park. 2020. *Minor Feelings: An Asian American Reckoning.* New York: One World.

hooks, bell. 2000. *All About Love: New Visions.* New York: William Morrow.

Hwang, Merose. 2007. "The Mudang: The Colonial Legacies of Korean Shamanism." In *Han Kut: Critical Art and Writing by Korean Canadian Women*, edited by the Korean Canadian Women's Anthology Collective, 103–19. Toronto: Inanna.

Jafri, Beenash. 2016. "Ongoing Colonial Violence in Settler States." *Lateral: Journal of the Cultural Studies Association* 6, no. 1. https://doi.org/10.25158/L6.1.7.

Johnson, Jessica Marie, and Mark Anthony Neal, eds. 2017. "Introduction: Wild Seed in the Machine." *Black Scholar* 47, no. 3: 1–2.

Jun, Helen Heran. 2011. *Race for Citizenship: Black Orientalism and Asian Uplift from Pre-Emancipation to Neoliberal America.* New York: New York University Press.

Kaur, Min. 2014. "Honoring Gaswentah: A Racialized Settler's Exploration of Responsibility and Mutual Respect as Coalition Building with First Peoples." In *Politics of Anti-racism Education: In Search of Strategies for Transformative Learning*, edited by George J. Sefa Dei and Mairi McDermott, 165–74. Dordrecht: Springer.

Keating, AnaLouise. 2008. " 'I'm a Citizen of the Universe': Gloria Anzaldúa's Spiritual Activism as Catalyst for Social Change." *Feminist Studies* 34, nos. 1–2: 53–69.

Keller, Nora Okja. 1998. *Comfort Woman.* New York: Penguin.

Kendall, Laurel. 1988. *The Life and Hard Times of a Korean Shaman: Of Tales and the Telling of Tales.* Honolulu: University of Hawai'i Press.

Kendall, Laurel. 2009. *Shamans, Nostalgias, and the IMF: South Korean Popular Religion in Motion.* Honolulu: University of Hawai'i Press.

Kim, Christine. 2013. "Intimating Asias, Postcolonial Possibilities, and the Art of David Khang." *Interventions* 15, no. 1: 24–36.

Kim, Clare Jean. 2000. *Bitter Fruit: The Politics of Black-Korean Conflict in New York City.* New Haven, CT: Yale University Press.

Kim, Elaine H. 1998. " 'At Least You're Not Black': Asian Americans in U.S. Race Relations." *Social Justice* 25, no. 3: 3–12.

King, Tiffany Lethabo. 2019. *The Black Shoals: Offshore Formations of Black and Native Studies*. Durham, NC: Duke University Press.

Kovach, M. 2013. "Treaties, Truths, and Transgressive Pedagogies: Re-imagining Indigenous Presence in the Classroom." *Social Studies* 9, no. 1: 109–27.

Lai, Larissa. 2015. "The Look of Like: Shooting Asian/Indigenous Relation." In *Migration, Regionalization, Citizenship: Comparing Canada and Europe*, edited by Katja Sarkowsky, Rainer-Olaf Schultze, and Sabine Schwarze, 181–94. Wiesbaden: Springer.

Lawrence, Bonita, and Enakshi Dua. 2005. "Decolonizing Antiracism." *Social Justice* 32, no. 4: 120–43.

Lee, Helen. 1998. "A Peculiar Sensation: A Personal Genealogy of Korean American Women's Film." In *Dangerous Women: Gender and Korean Nationalism*, edited by Elaine H. Kim and Chungmoo Choi, 291–322. New York: Routledge.

Lee, Jonghyun. 2009. "Shamanism and Its Emancipatory Power for Korean Women." *Affilia: Journal of Women and Social Work* 29, no. 2: 186–98.

Lee, Kun Jong. 2004. "Princess Pari in Nora Okja Keller's *Comfort Woman*." *positions: asia critique* 12, no. 2: 431–56.

Lee, Ruthann. 2017. "Using Indigenous Feminist Land Ethics to Queer the Korean Missionary Position in Canada." *TOPIA* 38: 103–13.

Lorde, Audre. (1978) 1984. "Uses of the Erotic: The Erotic as Power." In *Sister Outsider: Essays and Speeches*, 53–59. Trumansburg, NY: Crossing Press.

Lowe, Lisa. 1994. "Unfaithful to the Original: The Subject of *Dictée*." In *Writing Self, Writing Nation: Essays on Theresa Hak Kyung Cha's Dictée*, edited by Elaine H. Kim and Norma Alarcon, 35–69. Berkeley, CA: Third Woman Press.

Malbeuf, Amy, and Jessie Ray Short. 2022. "*Lii Zoot Tare (Other Worlds)*." https://agnes.queensu.ca/exhibition/other-worlds/ (accessed March 9, 2022).

Martineau, Jarrett, and Eric Ritskes. 2014. "Fugitive Indigeneity: Reclaiming the Terrain of Decolonial Struggle through Indigenous Art." *Decolonization: Indigeneity, Education, and Society* 3, no. 1: i–ix.

Maynard, Robyn. 2017. *Policing Black Lives: State Violence in Canada from Slavery to the Present*. Winnipeg: Fernwood.

Medak-Saltzman, Danika. 2017. "Coming to You from the Indigenous Future: Native Women, Speculative Film Shorts, and the Art of the Possible." *Studies in American Indian Literature* 29, no. 1: 139–71.

Medak-Saltzman, Danika, and Antonio Tiongson Jr. 2015. "Racial Comparativism Reconsidered." *Critical Ethnic Studies* 1, no. 2: 1–7.

Miranda, Deborah A. 2003. "What's Wrong with a Little Fantasy? Storytelling from the (Still) Ivory Tower." *American Indian Quarterly* 27, nos. 1–2: 333–48.

Mithlo, Nancy Marie. 2009. "'A Real Feminine Journey': Locating Indigenous Feminisms in the Arts." *Meridians* 9, no. 2: 1–30.

Nakamura, Lisa. 2014. "Indigenous Circuits: Navajo Women and the Racialization of Early Electronic Manufacture." *American Quarterly* 66, no. 4: 919–41.

Nanibush, Wanda. 2015. "The Earliest Adapters: Survivance in Indigenous Media Arts." *Voz a Voz*. http://www.vozavoz.ca/feature/wanda-nanibush.

Ng, Roxana. 2006. "Exploring Healing and the Body through Indigenous Chinese Medicine." In *Indigenous Peoples' Wisdom and Power: Affirming Our Knowledge through Narratives*, edited by Julian E. Kunnie and Nomalungelo L. Goduka, 95–114. London: Routledge.

Ng, Roxana. 2008. "Decolonizing Teaching and Learning through Embodied Learning: Toward an Integrated Approach." In *Sharing Breath: Embodied Learning and Decolonization*, edited by Sheila Batacharya and Yuk-Lin Renita Wong, 33–54. Athabasca, AB: Athabasca University Press.

Nielsen, Tannis. 2012. "A *Creation*: Artist Statement." Unpublished document.

Nielsen, Tannis. 2017. "We Can't Compete, We Won't Compete, We Can't Keep Up, We Won't Keep Down." *#silenceisviolence* exhibition catalog, edited by Heidi Cho, Deirdre Logue, Allyson Mitchell, and Morgan Sea, n.p. Scarborough: University of Toronto Scarborough.

Nielsen, Tannis, and Vicky Moufawad-Paul. 2008. "Enacting Emancipation." Exhibition catalog essay. Toronto: A Space Gallery.

Nopper, Tamara. 2015. "On Terror, Captivity, and Black-Korean Conflict." *Decolonization: Indigeneity, Education, and Society* (blog), September 24. https://decolonization.wordpress.com/2015/09/24/on-terror-captivity-and-black-korean-conflict/.

Palacios, Lena. 2016. "Challenging Convictions: Indigenous and Black Race-Radical Feminists Theorizing the Carceral State and Abolitionist Praxis in the United States and Canada." *Meridians* 15, no. 1: 137–65.

Park, Rosa Sungjoo. 2014. "Forgotten Dreams: Meditations on Narrative Space." MFA thesis, University of British Columbia.

Patel, Shaista, Ghaida Moussa, and Nishant Upadhyay. 2015. "Complicities, Connections, and Struggles: Critical Transnational Feminist Analysis of Settler Colonialism." *Feral Feminisms* 4: 5–19.

Phung, Malissa. 2012. "The Diasporic Inheritance of 'Postmemory' and Immigrant Shame in the Novels of Larissa Lai." *Postcolonial Text* 7, no. 3: 1–19.

Phung, Malissa. 2015. "Asian-Indigenous Relationalities: Literary Gestures of Respect and Gratitude." *Canadian Literature* 227: 56.

Phung, Malissa. 2019. "Indigenous and Asian Relation Making." *Verge: Studies in Global Asias* 5, no. 1: 18–30.

Ritchie, Andrea J. 2017. *Invisible No More: Police Violence against Black Women and Women of Color*. Boston: Beacon Press.

Schaeffer, Felicity Amaya. 2018. "Spirit Matters: Gloria Anzaldúa's Cosmic Becoming across Human/Nonhuman Borderlands." *Signs: Journal of Women in Culture and Society* 43, no. 4: 1005–29.

Scholar Strike Canada. 2021. "Anti-Asian Racism Undone." Online teach-in, May 29–30. https://www.scholarstrikecanada.ca/anti-asian-racism-undone.

Sehdev, Robinder Kaur. 2011. "People of Colour in Treaty." In *Cultivating Canada: Reconciliation through the Lens of Cultural Diversity*, edited by Ashok Mathur, Jonathan Dewar, and Mike DeGagne, 263–74. Ottawa: Aboriginal Healing Foundation.

Simpson, Audra. 2016. "The State is a Man: Theresa Spence, Loretta Saunders, and the Gender of Settler Sovereignty." *Theory and Event* 19, no. 4: N_A.

Simpson, Audra, and Andrea Smith. 2014. Introduction to *Theorizing Native Studies*, edited by Audra Simpson and Andrea Smith, 1–30. Durham, NC: Duke University Press.

Simpson, Leanne Betasamosake. 2016. "Indigenous Resurgence and Co-resistance." *Critical Ethnic Studies* 2, no. 2: 19–34.

Smith, Andrea. 2010. "Queer Theory and Native Studies: The Heteronormativity of Settler Colonialism." *GLQ: A Journal of Lesbian and Gay Studies* 16, nos. 1–2: 41–68.

Son, Elizabeth W. 2016. "Korean Trojan Women: Performing Wartime Sexual Violence." *Asian Theatre Journal* 33, no. 2: 369–94.

Son, Elizabeth W. 2018. *Embodied Reckonings: "Comfort Women," Performance, and Transpacific Redress*. Ann Arbor: University of Michigan Press.

Tinsley, Omise'eke Natasha. 2018. *Ezili's Mirrors: Imagining Black Queer Genders*. Durham, NC: Duke University Press.

Tuck, Eve, and K. Wayne Yang. 2012. "Decolonization Is Not a Metaphor." *Decolonization: Indigeneity, Education, and Society* 1, no. 1: 1–40.

Turner, Dale A. 2006. *This is Not a Peace Pipe: Towards a Critical Indigenous Philosophy*. Toronto: University of Toronto Press.

Vowel, Chelsea. 2016. "Beyond Territorial Acknowledgements." *âpihtawikosisân* (blog), September 26. http://apihtawikosisan.com/2016/09/beyond-territorial-acknowledgments/.

Walia, Harsha. 2014. "Decolonizing Together: Moving beyond a Politics of Solidarity toward a Practice of Decolonization." In *The Winter We Danced: Voices from the Past, the Future, and the Idle No More Movement*, edited by the Kino-nda-niimi Collective, 44–50. Winnipeg: ARP Books.

Wong, Rita. 2008. "Decolonizasian: Reading Asian and First Nations Relations in Literature." *Canadian Literature* 199: 158–80.

Wong, Rita. 2012. "Cultivating Respectful Relations: A Response to Leroy Little Bear." *Journal of Chinese Philosophy* 39, no. 4: 528–36.

Sônia Bone Guajajara and Célia Xakriabá
Introductory Note by Malcolm McNee
Translation by Elena Langdon

......................................................................

# Indigenous Women on the Frontlines of Climate Activism
## The Battle for Environmental Justice in the Amazon

Abstract: In this public address, transcribed and translated from the Portuguese, two leaders of Brazil's pan-ethnic Indigenous rights movement, Sônia Bone Guajajara and Célia Xakriabá, describe their respective formation, their involvement in environmental and human rights struggles, and the global stakes involved in the recognition and protection of the traditional territorial claims and land-use practices of Indigenous peoples in the Brazilian Amazon and beyond.

## Introduction

In February 2020, Smith College hosted Sônia Guajajara for a week of events and exchanges as the Lewis Global Studies Center's Global Leader-in-Residence. She was accompanied by another dynamic young leader of Brazil's Indigenous rights movement, Célia Xakriabá. Together, they presented this powerful public address, "Indigenous Women on the Frontlines of Climate Activism: The Battle for Environmental Justice in the Amazon," drawing clear connections between the global climate emergency and Indigenous women's leadership in territorial struggles in the Brazilian Amazon and beyond. In addition to their public talks, Sônia and Célia visited classes and met with students and faculty of Portuguese and Brazilian Studies, Latin American and Latino/a Studies, Environmental Studies, the

MERIDIANS · feminism, race, transnationalism   23:1 April 2024
DOI: 10.1215/15366936-10926992 © 2024 Smith College

Indigenous Smith Students Alliance, and community climate and environmental justice activists. Sônia's visit to a newly created Portuguese course, "Indigenous Brazil: Past, Present, Future," was particularly gratifying to me, and, as a form of public-facing, experiential learning, students in that class worked collaboratively to transcribe their talks. Their contribution facilitated the translation later done by Elena Langdon and published here at the invitation of the *Meridians* editor, Dr. Ginetta E. B. Candelario.

Sônia Bone Guajajara is among the most active, tireless, and fearless voices of opposition to the destructive and retrograde authoritarian reversals in Brazilian social and political life of recent years. Hers is also a key voice in the transnational movement to address our collective climate emergency, forcefully representing the Global South and, more precisely, the critical role of Indigenous peoples and other forest protectors on the battle lines. She was born and grew up in the Arariboia Indigenous Territory of the Guajajara/Tentehar people in the central west of Maranhão State, at the eastern edge of the Amazon Forest. Among the first generation in her community to gain access to the formal education system in Brazil, she worked as a domestic and childcare worker between the ages of ten and fourteen in a nearby town, Amarante, in order to attend middle school. At fifteen, with support from FUNAI, the Brazilian National Indian Foundation, she attended high school in a more distant city, Imperatriz. Overcoming fears of leaving her family and community, she resolved to pursue her dream of continued studies, completing high school and a teacher certification program in the state of Minas Gerais.

Fulfilling a promise to her family, she returned home and began work as a teacher's aide and health educator. Her drive to serve her community in these roles eventually led her to complete undergraduate and graduate degree programs in nursing, linguistics, and special education. Through her studies and professional activities, she increasingly became aware of the fundamental importance of community organizing and political activism to the well-being and even survival of her own and other Indigenous communities, locally and across Brazil. A particularly transformative moment was her participation in discussions following a pan-ethnic Indigenous people's march in 2001 in Brasília. This led to her protagonism in reviving the Confederation of Indigenous Peoples of Maranhão, which she was elected to help lead as executive secretary in 2003. She served in this role until 2009, when she was elected vice-coordinator of the Confederation of Indigenous Peoples of the Brazilian Amazon, a position based in

Manaus that she held until 2013. She was the first woman to take on such a prominent leadership role in the Indigenous movement in Brazil, and she has since worked as part of the executive coordination of APIB, the Articulation of Indigenous Peoples of Brazil, based in São Paulo and Brasília. APIB is presently the most effective nationwide organization advocating for the human rights and territorial claims of all of Brazil's Indigenous peoples, coordinating alliances and solidarity campaigns nationally and internationally.

She has attended all but one of the COP climate change meetings for the last decade, and she has brought her voice and representation of Brazil's Indigenous peoples to the U.N. Human Rights Council, the U.N. Permanent Forum on Indigenous Issues, and the E.U. Parliament. In 2018, she was nominated by the PSOL, the Party of Socialism and Freedom, to run for the vice presidency in Brazil, cochairing the ticket with the housing rights activist Guilherme Boulos. In 2022, she was elected to Brazil's Federal Chamber of Deputies and was subsequently appointed by the newly elected government of Luiz Inácio Lula da Silva to a cabinet position, as head of a new Ministry of Indigenous Peoples.

Guajajara was joined in her residency at Smith by Célia Xakriabá, who also serves on the executive coordination of APIB. She grew up in northern Minas Gerais, studied at an Indigenous school in her community, and then graduated as part of the first class admitted to a specialized, intercultural degree program for Indigenous students at the Federal University of Minas Gerais. She completed a master's degree in education at the University of Brasília and was the first Native Brazilian to work for the secretary of education of Minas Gerais, designing programs to support Indigenous teachers, schools, and curricula. She is now completing a PhD in anthropology. In addition to her advocacy for territorial and human rights for Indigenous peoples, she remains active in language and cultural revitalization projects, developing materials and pedagogies to support teaching of and in Indigenous languages. She too was elected federal deputy in 2022 and is affiliated with the PSOL.

In short, these are two extraordinary leaders, and the stakes of their activism, in Brazil and beyond, could not be higher. Their personal journeys, courage, and vision, as shared in the talks registered here, clearly signal why active solidarity with Indigenous peoples and this new generation of women leaders in Indigenous territorial struggles is so critical to transnational efforts to envision, recover, and sustain livable planetary futures. After her visit, Sônia Guajajara continued to face down the disastrously necropolitical and genocidal policies of the Jair Bolsonaro government in Brazil. In March 2021 she was put under federal police investigation for a web-based documentary series, *Maracá: Indigenous Emergency*, produced with APIB to denounce the failure of the Brazilian government to adequately protect Indigenous communities from the devastation of the COVID-19 pandemic. An international solidarity campaign in response helped lead to a suspension of that probe, but she, along with other Brazilian Indigenous leaders and communities, remains vulnerable to continued attacks. Between that vulnerability and the strength of their resistance, the future of the Amazon and our planetary future lie in the balance.

—Malcolm K. McNee, Smith College

**Part I: Célia Xakriabá's Speech**
I am Célia Xakriabá. I come from the Cerrado biome. We must recognize that the Amazon is not the only target for ecocide; the Cerrado—the second largest biome in Brazil—is also a target. Ninety percent of soy exports from Brazil come from the Cerrado region. To understand the criminal fires happening in the Amazon, one must know that such fires have historically burned the Cerrado biome. They are the same fires that burn the Guarani houses of worship. They are also the fires that have burned and raped Indigenous women's bodies. I come from the Cerrado region, and each time they ask us why we carry on this fight abroad, we ask in return, "What would you do if your mother were being taken from you? What would you do if they took your right to live, not only in your communal home, but especially in your internal home— in other words, your territory?"

Demarcation of Indigenous territories in Brazil has occurred only after Indigenous leaders were murdered. The Xakriabá territory is no different. We live in the Cerrado biome. Our land was demarcated after the 1987 murder of a Xakriabá leader. It was the first crime recognized in Brazil as Indigenous genocide. But only a third of the original Xakriabá land was demarcated. People always ask us women and especially young people, "Are you Xakriabá? Do you know how to swim? Do you live off the river? Do you fish for sustenance?" and most young people say "no." We compare this absence of the river to a child taken from a mother's breast. We manage to grow up, but we grow up with trauma. Our children and young people did not drown in the river, but instead drowned in the absence of that river.

Indigenous women help reduce climate change. Much worse than climate change is its speed. People say we don't have much time for our fight. People repeat that the fight against accelerated climate change is a fight against time. My grandfather says it is not a fight against time, but a fight to *take back* time, for this idea of being pressed for time also accelerates capitalism. Indigenous people currently represent a threat to the government—to the Bolsonaro government and capitalism—because we present a real possibility of life uncontrolled by time. In Brazil, congresspeople who represent agribusiness interests always ask us, "Why are Indigenous people against capitalism?" I tell them to reverse the question so we can reverse the answer. "Why are you and capitalism against Indigenous people?" We do not represent a threat to capitalism or climate change. It is the reverse: capitalism and climate change are an imminent threat to Indigenous people and to humanity.

When I think about capitalism, I also reflect on monoculture. Everyone knows that healthy food means a variety of food, with plenty of color. So why don't people think that a healthy society is one with variety and diversity? My region is threatened by eucalyptus monoculture, for example, and they say not even ants seem to survive where eucalyptus has been planted. So how can a society that lacks diversity survive, with its monoculture of bodies? I also think about universities that lack diversity of ideas. Won't such uniform thinking also make the land unproductive? I feel very strongly about this, because questioning capitalism is not the responsibility of world leaders alone. Society also needs to change its behavior. How many of us have asked—and how many of you have asked—how many Indigenous faculty members are at your university? How many of you have asked, or would be willing to ask yourselves, how many Indigenous women you helped elect?

The main explanation for climate change is that diversity has been killed. If the United States had the diversity of Indigenous people it used to have, we wouldn't be living this moment of accelerating climate change. Every society that kills the diversity of bodies is threatened by the monoculture of bodies and ideas. To reverse the acceleration of climate change we cannot repair the wrongs with the same illness. We cannot heal the Earth with the poison that killed it.

When we think about questioning political structures, and how we think about the environment, in Brazil and abroad—especially an export economy that tries to export Indigenous life— in order to fight the entire system, we must question the colonizing matrix. I misspoke! It is not a colonizing matrix, but a "patrix," for it comes from patriarchy. We need to think about the contributions of women's bodies. The twenty-first century is many things, but mainly it belongs to women and Indigenous women.

The empowerment of Indigenous women is key to this struggle. People are always asking what we have done to fight climate change. We defend territory with our very lives. Indigenous people are the world's thermometer. The day we stop breathing the very air of our territories, the rest of humanity will not be able to breathe either. Rather than responding to the repeated question about Indigenous people's contribution, I have often replied that Indigenous women simply wish to be truly recognized. We are the first scientists. We are pulmonologists; we care for the world's lungs. This idea is important. When Paulo Paulino Guajajara was killed, people did not reflect on this. They think the only ones who suffered a loss were Indigenous Brazilians, or only the Guajajara people. Last year 138 Indigenous leaders were "felled." For each leader they kill, millions of trees are felled, and this impacts the world's capacity to breathe. If people who are not victims of the territorial fights in which Indigenous people risk their lives do not realize this and do not join the fight with us, we will all die for the same reason: the poison that arrives at our table.

Eating should be synonymous with feeding one's body. But currently, eating is synonymous with being poisoned. People ask where the fight against capitalism begins, or even where capitalism and agribusiness begin. We are faced with agribusiness at the day's first meal; it starts with the food at our table. The situation requires us to think about systematic struggle, especially over common habits and behaviors.

Regarding capitalism in Brazil, last week the Brazilian government said, "Indigenous people want to be like us. They're becoming more human and evolved, like us."

We, Indigenous people, Indigenous women, are rising up even stronger now, since the Bolsonaro government attacked a woman first. People ask, "Who was this woman?" I say it was Earth. When Mother Earth is attacked, we need to rise up. Not only our lives are at stake, but especially our way of life. Because Indigenous people do not die only when leaders are murdered, but also when our identity is murdered. We die twice. It is important to say this because in the past, agribusiness and its supporters in Congress targeted only our bodies, like they did in 1500. Today the weapons are more sophisticated; they are also trying to kill our voices. We do not use the same weapons as our enemies, but we are armed. We fight with the power of spirituality, nourished by our territories.

We are suspicious of any plan to evolve that cannot produce its own food. During our campaign in Europe, "Not One More Drop of Indigenous Blood," Europeans told us they had few native fruits, that they were all imported from other countries because they cannot produce their own food. When they say Indigenous people do not help make Brazil a first world country, we say the most important thing is to recognize we were first in Brazil—we are its original people. Humanity is not yet extinct because our way of life continues. It is very important to consider not just the environment, but all of life, nature, and territory, as part of Indigenous life and its contributions.

In this sense, we wonder whether universities are also responsible for the epistemicide, for they also have tried to kill our way of knowing. Today we go to a university and people ask us, "How do you feel about being the first Indigenous woman to go to college? Sônia Guajajara, how do you feel about being the first Indigenous woman to run for vice president? Joenia Wapichana, how do you feel about being the first Indigenous woman elected to the Federal Congress? Indigenous women, how do you feel?" We tell them we don't feel more important for being first. It's actually double the responsibility. We need to ask: Why are we first, when it is already the twenty-first century? This is a very important point, because with our way of knowing, we, Indigenous people, represent a real epistemology of healing.

The planet and financial and political systems are in crisis, but so is science. We, Indigenous people, say that no government, no governing project, will kill science, because science is born inside us and on our Indigenous lands. So it will never be murdered. Not even the fires burning the Amazon, or fires burning the Cerrado region—or burning Indigenous bodies in Brasília, like we saw with the leader Galdino Pataxó[1]—can burn our memory and the powerful orality of Indigenous people.

We Indigenous women are Earth's womb. When the government eases gun laws, we Indigenous women are the main targets. The proliferation of guns pierces our wombs and the Earth's womb, threatening future generations. To speak of environmental justice and climate change, the best way out—the best strategy—is to better protect and demarcate more Indigenous lands. Demarcating these territories is good not only for Indigenous people; it is good for humanity.

I am going to end by saying that Indigenous people are rising up, and that we, Indigenous women, keep resisting because if we must die, it should be because we are speaking out and not because we are silent. Historically, silence has killed many Indigenous women, and has continued killing an entire continent. That is why we fight against the genocide of Indigenous people in Brazil. We fight the ecocide of humanity. We defend humanity through the science of territory, for we believe we will learn much more with living trees than with dead paper. I am sure that even when they burn all paper, our orality and our memory will endure.

**Part II: Sônia Guajajara's Speech**

Good evening, everyone. I want to thank you for your invitation to come here, to share our story, our fight, everything we have done for Brazil. A fight we are in today, but that has lasted 520 years. Our presence here, and in Brazil, symbolizes and shows our perseverance. If we were not such a resilient people, we would have been exterminated. We would not exist. When we speak of our history, we recall so much sadness and pain that all our ancestors endured, that many peoples endured. Pain endured by so many women raped by colonization, by the entire colonial period, by the dictatorship, so that today we can rise and say: we no longer accept any type of colonization or any type of rape, any type of control over our lives.

When we rise up and continue fighting, the good we do is not just for us. We are helping the entire world. Today we fight especially against this highly predatory economic model that destroys Mother Earth, kills biodiversity, and tries to kill our diversity, our way of life. Because of our fight and our battles, we are persecuted, murdered, cast as criminals, imprisoned every day. Our fight directly confronts economic and political power. These are very powerful forces that always work together to eliminate anyone who dares get in their way. Today we are seen as an impediment to progress, to development. It is true that we are against development, because for us development should include people. Development as it is practiced now excludes people. It continually increases inequality. It puts those without material goods at the margins. They try to do that with us every day.

In Brazil it has gotten worse with the Bolsonaro administration, which frames Indigenous people as its main enemies. It places poor and marginalized women, Black men and women, all in a vulnerable position. We continue to work together, for we know our fight cannot be isolated. We need to unite to empower those who have had their rights stolen, to rise up together. Land is the main object under dispute now, for political and economic power. And we are constantly battling. We fight not for land but for territory. For Mother Earth.

Earth is not a material asset for us, an asset to sell or negotiate. We treat Earth like our mother. We have always asked, Who would dare to bargain away their mother? Or sell their mother? Or destroy their mother? Would anyone do this? I don't think so. We treat Earth in the same way; we see her as our mother. She gives us life, food, sustenance—everything we need. Since we have this natural relationship, we won't allow Earth to be destroyed.

When we fight for territory, we are fighting for space, because the relationship is not just about contact, or a place to live, but also a connection to our heritage. It is how we relate to our ancestors, our history, and to our spirits, who live there and protect us, who keep us connected and give us strength to continue fighting. Territory for us is a sacred place, with water, trees, animals, and the air we need to breathe. That is why wherever Indigenous people live, territory, forests, and preserved biodiversity are present. Wherever Indigenous people live, there is clean water. Wherever Indigenous people live, there is healthy food, with no pesticides. That is why we continue our defense, because we believe we're doing the right thing. We are not afraid of confronting any government. We do not have to accept any unfair policies or laws that want to destroy our lives, our history, our way of life.

Since 1500, when Europeans arrived in Brazil, economic and national development plans were always based on exterminating Indigenous peoples. They were always based on exploiting natural resources. Destruction has always been the foundation on which policies are built. That is why our numbers are dwindling. The official number from the 1500s, which is probably low, is five million, and the latest Brazilian census says there are fewer than one million of us, that in Brazil there are 917,000 Indigenous people. There must be more, right? I wasn't counted. Were you, Célia? There must be more, right? So the latest census says 917,000. We have been able to maintain 274 spoken languages in Brazil. While many have gone extinct, we still speak 274 languages throughout the country. We are still 305 distinct Indigenous peoples, 305 ethnicities across the 26 states. And yet every day, wherever we go, we still hear that Brazilian Indigenous people are all in the Amazon, as if that were the only place where we live. Because people still think we're like savages, running around naked, hunting and fishing the whole time. How can we continue to hunt and fish when they are taking away our rights to do so?

We are forced to interact with another culture, to live a different life. We consider the interaction good, healthy, and permissible, because we take what we need, yet still keep our culture. The government is now trying to impose what it calls "integration." When it says "integration," it means we must give up our culture, our way of life, and integrate into another one.

When it says that, it is saying that one culture is better than another, that one outweighs the other, and that we must abandon our own, because it's no good and gets in the way. So they want us to adopt a different culture or way of life. We also fight this "integration" model of the Bolsonaro administration.

There are 305 peoples, each in contact to different degrees. Some peoples have been in contact with non-Natives for five hundred years, while others average about one hundred years, which is considered recent contact. Some communities are totally urban, living in cities. They are in the city, but still Indigenous. And some of our peoples have not had any contact with outsiders—not even with other Indigenous people living in the same territory. There are 114 confirmed peoples who live in voluntary isolation. The government insists on calling them "isolated peoples." We call them "autonomous peoples," because they are there by choice, of their own volition. If they wanted contact, they would have approached others, they would have asked for help already. We must respect their decision. We must fight for guaranteed territory so they can continue where they are and continue their way of life. That is another reason for our fight. It is for those who are not here to speak and demand protection for their territory.

All this motivates our fight against illegal logging on Indigenous land, against mining on Indigenous land, against agricultural expansion, agribusiness, and increased monoculture. Congress tries to enact new laws every day to permit deforestation for the sake of agricultural expansion. This fight is no small feat, not at all, because we deal with government and big companies. Government on one side and companies on the other, while we fight their economic power—power that focuses every day on getting more money, more profit, telling companies to exploit more, to increase their production, to grow the economy, that frames the GDP and the stock market as the most important things to focus on. People keep believing the country is doing well when the stock market is up, when GDP is up.

Few ask themselves how many people lose access to food because of this agricultural expansion, an expansion for big companies, for commodities. How many people are left without clean water because of mining? Minerals have contaminated the water that runs through communities and cities. How many people look at polluted rivers in cities or elsewhere, and are upset by this? How many people look at the river and imagine it could be clean and that everyone could have access to it? How many people get upset when they see government entities cutting down trees in their city to build a plaza, or to build a parking lot? How many people get upset or feel the need to fight this?

Many people, even those here today, think that cutting-edge technology is the answer, that the economic crisis and climate change will be resolved with it. But we always ask ourselves, What kind of new human do we want to create in order to resolve all this? What needs to be done for humans to feel responsible for slowing down climate change? What needs to be done to decarbonize politicians' minds? How do we restore people's hearts? How do we make more people take up this fight? Every day they simply give us more talk.

I come from the Araribóia Indigenous territory. I did not go to a city until I was fifteen. I had never seen a utility pole. I did not see paved roads until I was fifteen. I went to the big city because I had always wanted to go. I dreamed about leaving since I was a girl. I dreamed about traveling. I knew that if I stayed there in my place, in that way, I would be like everyone else. And as much as I liked my place and being close to my family, I was restless. I knew I could not help or change anyone by being there, because I too was always accepting the same things. I always wanted to leave, to see the world. I saw the world even before traveling, because I read a lot and knew the stories. When I came to the United States for the first time, I felt like I already knew it all because I knew a lot of the history, including the extermination of Native Americans, and how the government treated them here.

When I left, I discovered there were many things to do and to change, and that I couldn't do it alone. We needed to gather and bring along more people. I knew that many Indigenous people did not have demarcated land, so I started organizing cooperatives, to strengthen the Indigenous movement and fight for territory. We started with Indigenous movements at the state level, then regional and national, and now we talk about Indigenous presence and our way of life at an international level. We are currently 5 percent of the population. Globally, Indigenous people make up 5 percent of the population. Those 5 percent are able to protect 82 percent of the world's biodiversity. 82 percent. We can still protect most of the planet's freshwater, which is in the Amazon. Brazil has the world's two largest aquifers. One is in the Amazon and the other in the southeast. And there are Indigenous lands in those very places.

People ask us, especially in Brazil, "Why do Indians want so much land?" In Brazil we are less than 1 percent of the population. Less than 1 percent. We occupy 13 percent of the national territory. Is that a lot? Do you think it is a lot? It seems to be, right? Agribusiness lobbyists tell us every day that it is too much! Bolsonaro says we do not need this land. He says land demarcation in Brazil is abusive. But when you look at it from the other side, you see that 46 percent of rural property is owned by 1 percent of agribusiness landowners. Forty-Six percent—isn't that a big number? Isn't it too much for 1 percent? You can do the math. What is on our 13 percent of Indigenous land? Can anyone guess? We have forests, biodiversity, clean water, headwaters. . . . It is all in that 13 percent. But it is not much, right? It is too little. What do you see in the 46 percent? What do you see? Cattle, soy, eucalyptus, sugarcane—you see monocultures.

We can compare the two sides. What does each offer the planet? On one side you have eucalyptus, which sucks up water and dries up all the headwaters. It dries up rivers, streams, and creeks. And what does soy production offer? Poison. Pesticides that poison everyone around it. In Brazil, pesticides are sprayed by helicopter. They are dumped all over everything. People, water, whatever is there. And what do we have on Indigenous land? Standing forests, which regulate the rain, distributing it everywhere. Forests store carbon dioxide that would otherwise be emitted into the air. They reduce carbon emissions. They also help balance oxygen levels for the entire planet. This oxygen circulates globally, and everyone gets it. We need standing forests to ensure our air.

Célia said we are all the world's pulmonologists, that we are responsible for the lungs of the world. Everyone looks at the Amazon and sees the forest and the animals. But few know there are people, too. Few realize that it is us, with our way of life, who ensure that forests stay standing. We protect biodiversity. Few know that it is us, with our way of life, who sustain that. How do we sustain it? We sustain it through our daily fight on the steps of Congress. We take on rubber bullets, pepper spray, police brutality, jail time. But we keep going. We are paying with our own lives to maintain biodiversity. That is why we do not accept gestures of pity. We do not want anyone's pity. We do not want to be seen as helpless, or as savages or non-humans, as Bolsonaro calls us.

We want people to see our power to ensure life on this planet, to ensure that all have water, clean water, rain, and the air that everyone breathes. We are here telling you about what we do, what we protect, the fight we carry on. Of course other factors help ensure this balance, help regulate the rain. But we are part of this power. We always say we are not part of Brazil, that instead, Brazil is part of us. We were the first there, so Brazil is part of us.

And we want to carry on this fight for Brazil, for our place. We carry on this fight politically every day and we carry on the narrative fight on social media. Since we now have Internet and access to this mode of communication, we must use it to give visibility to the Indigenous reality. We need to show what we do and what others need to do to join us. If people do not know us, they will not approach us. The government sees us as a barrier, as enemies, and many still see us as savages, and they do not approach—they're afraid. They do not want to know or meet us, and so there is a detachment. Because of this detachment there are many unknowns about Indigenous life around the world. And schools that should be addressing these unknowns with students of all ages are failing to do so. People in their forties or fifties do not know anything about Indigenous reality. One of the ways for people to know us better would be for schools to teach topics on Indigenous people, about how many we are, how we live, where we are, what we do. And especially to speak of the conflicts we face.

They should no longer romanticize Indigenous people, treating them like beautiful objects in a novel. Schools must show us as we are now, and the battles we fight, the conflicts we are put in, and all the political struggles we undertake so we can continue to live. We are still at the frontlines of this fight. At the frontlines against a predatory economic system. At the frontlines against climate change. Wasn't that the theme? Fighting climate change.

Our very way of life fights climate change. In 2019 we held Brazil's first Indigenous women's march. Many people ask, Why didn't you come before? But we were here before. We have been fighting all of this for five hundred years. But at some point our local fight is no longer enough. We must rise up and call on more people to join hands with us. In August of 2019, we made it to Brasília for International Indigenous Peoples' Day. Over three thousand Indigenous women gathered. They left their lands and made their way there.

Many had to confront their partners to be able to go. Because in addition to inviting them, we also had to convince our people that forbidding female participation is not cultural. Subservience is not cultural. To stand on the margins is not cultural. It is a legacy of colonialism; it is part of the colonization we lived and complied with. We complied with machismo, domestic violence, and barring women's participation. We must break this barrier. The colonial, *machista* barrier that many Indigenous people still see as culture. We must confront that.

We brought three thousand women to Brasília. We carried out the first march and every woman who went returned knowing she had changed. They said, "I want to join in, I want to continue on, I want to participate. I know this fight depends on us." It was a very important march. The first in Brazil but also the first Indigenous women's march in the world. And as a continuation of that march, this year we are organizing an Indigenous women's caravan throughout Brazil. We are going to each state in Brazil, meeting women from different communities, from all the territories, and we are going to discuss the same theme as this talk today: the role of Indigenous women in confronting climate change. We will also discuss and support Indigenous women running for office. Because we belong in institutional politics as well.

We now have one woman elected to Congress, but one is not enough. Our fight is collective; we need more than one. We will support Indigenous women running for office at all levels of institutional politics—municipal, state, and national offices—and even the presidency, right? Let's keep it up. This women's caravan will travel throughout Brazil and on September 5, International Indigenous Women's Day, we'll have an international gathering in Brazil. It is a call from Brazil's Indigenous women to women around the world. We want other women to join us; this fight is not ours alone. We can no longer bear this responsibility alone. Other women must join us and take responsibility. Up until now we have been carrying out this struggle in our own space, but now we want to internationalize, to globalize our fight.

Globalization isn't just for the market. We must organize globally to make the market meet the needs of our localities. We can no longer allow an economic model based on agribusiness and on monoculture to keep reducing the diversity of grains. Today, this monoculture model reduces grain production by 25–30 percent. That is what we eat; it is our food. Also, it has been proven that 80 percent of the world's food is produced by family farms. In Brazil, 70 percent of the food comes from family farms. We must keep fighting to decentralize land use. With that, we can diversify food production. Will big business do this? No. We are the ones who will do this: farm workers, small producers, Indigenous people, *quilombolas*, and traditional communities.

We are the ones who live on and depend on this territory. The territory we have is for planting, for living. We cannot be like those who treat land like an asset for market transactions. We must keep fighting for our relationship with our territory. That is why we need more people to join us. They must understand and reconnect with Mother Nature. They must understand this connection will ensure our future. We do not have a Plan B nor a Planet B. Our path forward is to fight.

*Translated from the Portuguese by Elena Langdon and edited by Malcolm K. McNee*

## Transcription of Original Portuguese

*Parte I: Comunicação de Célia Xakriabá*

Eu sou Célia Xakriabá e venho da região do bioma do Cerrado. É importante reconhecer que não apenas a Amazônia está na mira do ecocídio, mas também o Cerrado, que é o segundo maior bioma do Brasil. Hoje, 90% da soja exportada pelo Brasil vem da região do Cerrado. Para compreender o fogo criminoso que acontece na Amazônia, é preciso compreender que esse fogo historicamente queima o bioma do Cerrado. É o mesmo fogo que queima as casas de reza indígena Guarani. Também é o fogo que historicamente queimou e estuprou os corpos das mulheres indígenas. Eu venho do bioma do Cerrado, e todas as vezes que nos perguntam por que fazemos essa luta no exterior, nós perguntamos: "O que vocês fariam se sua mãe estivesse sendo arrancada"? O que você faria se arrancassem o seu direito de viver, não apenas da sua morada coletiva, mas principalmente da sua morada interior, que é o território?" Todos os territórios indígenas no Brasil só foram demarcados depois da morte, da execução de lideranças indígenas. No território Xakriabá não é diferente. Vivemos na região do bioma do Cerrado, e o território só foi demarcado após o crime contra uma liderança Xakriabá, em 1987. Foi o primeiro crime reconhecido como genocídio indígena no Brasil. Mas só foi demarcado um terço do território originário Xakriabá. Sempre a população pergunta para as mulheres e principalmente para os jovens: "Vocês são Xakriabá? Vocês sabem nadar? Vocês vivem no rio? Vocês vivem da pesca"? E a maioria da juventude diz que não, porque essa ausência do rio nós comparamos a um filho retirado da amamentação no peito da mãe. Nós crescemos, mas crescemos com traumas. Os jovens e crianças não se afogaram no rio, mas a ausência do que não vivemos no rio nos afogou.

É importante dizer que as mulheres indígenas contribuem para a redução das mudanças climáticas. Muito pior do que a mudança climática é a velocidade com que ela acontece. As pessoas falam que temos pouco tempo para nossa luta. As pessoas reproduzem a fala de que a luta contra o aceleramento das mudanças climáticas é uma luta contra o tempo. Meu avô diz que não é uma luta contra o tempo; é uma luta pela retomada do tempo. Porque essa noção da velocidade do tempo também faz o capitalismo acelerar. Hoje os povos indígenas representam uma ameaça ao governo, tanto o governo brasileiro, de Bolsonaro, como para o capitalismo, porque apresentamos uma real possibilidade de vida que não é controlada pelo tempo. Constantemente no congresso nacional, no Brasil, somos questionados por deputados da bancada ruralista que dizem: "Por que os povos indígenas são contra o capitalismo"? E eu falo que a pergunta é ao contrário e a resposta também. Por que a bancada ruralista e o capitalismo são contra os povos indígenas? Porque nós não representamos uma ameaça ao capitalismo e às mudanças climáticas. Pelo contrário, o capitalismo e as mudanças climáticas representam uma eminente ameaça aos povos indígenas e à humanidade.

Pensando sobre o capitalismo, eu também reflito sobra a monocultura. É consenso para todos que comida saudável é aquela que tem diversidade na mesa, aquela que tem cor também. E por que as pessoas não pensam que uma sociedade saudável é aquela que tem diversidade? Minha região é ameaçada pela monocultura de eucalipto. Se no lugar onde se planta eucalipto possivelmente nem formigas sobrevivem, uma sociedade onde não há diversidade também vai sobreviver? Com monocultura de corpos? Fico pensando também numa universidade que não tem diversidade do pensamento. Esse pensamento também vai tornar a terra improdutiva?

Isso para mim é muito forte, porque a responsabilidade de questionar o capitalismo não está apenas nos governos em vários países, mas também na mudança de comportamento da sociedade. Quantos de nós já nos fizemos a pergunta, quantos de vocês já se perguntaram: Quantos professores indígenas vocês têm na universidade? Quantos de vocês se perguntaram, ou estariam dispostos a se perguntar, em quantas mulheres indígenas vocês já votaram?

A principal explicação para as mudanças climáticas é que a diversidade foi morta. Se nos Estados Unidos houvesse a diversidade de povos indígenas que havia antes, nós não estaríamos nesse momento de aceleramento das mudanças climáticas. Toda sociedade que mata a diversidade de corpos está ameaçada pela monocultura de corpos e de pensamento.

Tenho dito que para reverter o processo de aceleramento das mudanças climáticas não dá para curar o mal com a mesma enfermidade. Não se pode curar a terra com o veneno que a fez morrer. Quando pensamos em questionar a estrutura da política, dos processos de pensar a questão ambiental, tanto no Brasil como no exterior, principalmente a exportação em massa, que tenta exportar a vida dos indígenas, para fazer uma luta antissistêmica, temos que questionar a matriz colonizadora. Aliás, eu errei! Não é uma matriz colonizadora, mas uma "patriz" colonizadora. Porque vem do patriarcado.

Precisamos pensar quais são as contribuições dos corpos das mulheres. Porque o século XXI é de muitas coisas, mas é principalmente das mulheres e das mulheres indígenas. O fortalecimento das mulheres indígenas evoca a força da luta. Constantemente as pessoas perguntam o que temos feito contra as mudanças climáticas. Nós defendemos o território com nossa própria vida. Os povos indígenas são o termômetro do mundo. O dia em que nós, povos indígenas, pararmos de respirar em nossos territórios, toda a humanidade também não conseguirá respirar.

Em vez de responder a essa pergunta exaustiva sobre a contribuição dos povos indígenas, tenho dito que as mulheres indígenas querem ser verdadeiramente reconhecidas. Pois somos as primeiras cientistas. Somos como doutores em pneumologia, porque cuidamos do pulmão do mundo. É importante fazer essa reflexão, porque quando mataram Paulo Paulino Guajajara, como foi apresentado no vídeo, as pessoas não fizeram essa reflexão. Pensam que quem sofreu com a dor da perda foram apenas os indígenas do Brasil, foi apenas o povo Guajajara. No ano passado foram tombadas 138 lideranças indígenas. Cada vez que tombam uma liderança indígena, milhões de árvores passam a ser tombadas. Isso atinge a respiração do mundo. É preciso reconhecer que se as pessoas não se sensibilizarem em estar na luta junto com os povos indígenas, por não estarem sujeitas a morrer pelos conflitos territoriais aos quais os povos indígenas estão sujeitos a morrer, nós vamos morrer por algo em comum, que é pelo veneno que chega à nossa mesa.

A alimentação deveria ser sinônimo de alimentar o corpo. Mas hoje, alimentar também é sinônimo de envenenar. As pessoas perguntam onde começa a luta contra o capitalismo, ou onde o capitalismo começa, onde o agronegócio começa. Nós damos de cara com o agronegócio na primeira refeição do dia. Ele começa pelos pratos que chegam em nossa mesa. Então requer pensar uma luta de sistema, mas principalmente uma luta comportamental.

Pensando nessa questão do capitalismo no Brasil, semana passada, o governo brasileiro disse que "os povos indígenas querem ser iguais a nós.

Eles estão ficando mais humanos e mais evoluídos como nós." Nós povos indígenas, mulheres indígenas, nos levantamos com muito mais força agora, porque a primeira pessoa atacada pelo governo Bolsonaro foi uma mulher. As pessoas perguntam quem foi essa mulher. Eu digo que foi a Terra. Quando a mulher Terra é atingida, nós precisamos nos levantar. O que está em jogo não é apenas a nossa vida, mas principalmente o nosso modo de vida. Porque os povos indígenas não morrem apenas quando as lideranças são executadas, mas também quando executam nossa identidade. Nós já morremos duas vezes. É importante dizer isso, porque antes todo o agronegócio, a bancada ruralista, queriam apenas executar os corpos indígenas como aconteceu em 1500. Hoje é com armas sofisticadas. Mas agora também estão tentando matar as nossas vozes.

O fato de não lutarmos com a mesma arma do inimigo, que são as armas de fogo, não significa que nós estamos desarmados. Lutamos com a força da espiritualidade, alimentada pelo território. Desconfiamos de qualquer projeto de evolução que não consegue produzir nem seu próprio alimento. Na jornada "Sangue indígena, nenhuma gota a mais," que fizemos na Europa, os europeus falavam que havia poucas frutas nativas, que tudo era importado de outros países, porque eles não conseguem produzir o próprio alimento.

Quando falam que os povos indígenas não contribuem para que o Brasil seja um país de primeiro mundo, nós falamos que o mais importante é reconhecer que somos os primeiros do Brasil, somos originários. É por conta desse modo de vida que a humanidade ainda não foi exterminada. É muito importante pensar não exatamente no meio ambiente, mas na totalidade da vida, da natureza e do território como parte e a contribuição dos povos indígenas.

Nesse sentido, também questionamos a universidade por ser responsável pelo epistemicídio, porque também tentaram matar nosso modo de conhecimento. Hoje chegamos na universidade e as pessoas perguntam:

—Como você se sente sendo a primeira indígena a chegar na
   universidade?

—Sônia Guajajara, como se sente sendo a primeira indígena a lançar
   uma candidatura a vice-presidente?

—Joênia Wapichana, como se sente sendo a primeira mulher indígena a
   chegar no congresso nacional?

—Mulheres indígenas, como que vocês se sentem?

Falamos que não nos sentimos mais importantes por ser as primeiras. Na verdade, nos dá uma responsabilidade redobrada de questionar o porquê que só agora, no século XXI, nós somos as primeiras.

É muito importante fazer essa reflexão, porque nós povos indígenas, com nossa forma de conhecimento, representamos uma forma real de uma epistemologia de cura. Não é apenas o planeta, o recurso financeiro e a política que estão em crise. A ciência está em crise. Nós povos indígenas falamos que nenhum governo, nenhum projeto de estado vai conseguir acabar com a ciência. Porque a ciência nasce dentro de nós e em nossos territórios indígenas. Então nunca vai ser executada. Nem mesmo o fogo que queima a Amazônia, nem mesmo o fogo que queima o Cerrado e que queimou corpos indígenas em Brasília—como foi o caso do líder indígena Galdino Pataxó—não consegue queimar a nossa memória e a força da oralidade dos povos indígenas.

Nós mulheres indígenas somos o útero da terra. Quando existe autorização do governo para flexibilização do armamento, nós mulheres indígenas somos as principais miras. Certamente, a flexibilização do armamento atinge nossos úteros e o útero da terra, comprometendo as gerações futuras. Para falar de justiça ambiental, de mudanças climáticas, temos que entender que a melhor saída, a grande estratégia, está no fortalecimento e na demarcação dos territórios indígenas. Demarcar os territórios indígenas não é só um bem prestado aos indígenas, mas um bem prestado à humanidade.

Vou encerrar dizendo que nós povos indígenas fazemos esse levante de luta, e nós mulheres indígenas continuamos resistindo, porque decidimos que se for para morrer, que seja porque estamos falando, e não porque permanecemos em silêncio. Porque historicamente o silêncio matou muitas mulheres indígenas. E continuou matando um continente inteiro. Por isso que nós lutamos contra o genocídio dos povos indígenas no Brasil. Lutamos contra o ecocídio na humanidade. E fazemos essa defesa a partir da ciência do território, porque acreditamos que vamos continuar aprendendo muito mais com a árvore viva do que com o papel morto. Certamente, no dia em que conseguirem queimar todos os papéis, a nossa oralidade e a nossa memória serão capazes de resistir. Obrigada.

*Parte II: Comunicação de Sônia Guajajara*

Olá, gente. Boa noite a todas e todos. Quero agradecer o convite que nos fizeram para estarmos aqui compartilhando a nossa história, a nossa luta, tudo o que temos feito no Brasil. Uma luta que fazemos agora, mas que já dura 520 anos. A nossa presença aqui, a nossa presença no Brasil já simboliza, já mostra a nossa resistência. Se não fôssemos um povo tão resistente, teríamos sido exterminados. Já não existiríamos.

Falar da nossa história é rememorar toda uma tristeza, uma dor que foi sofrida por todos os nossos antepassados. Por muitos povos. Por muitas mulheres que foram estupradas pela colonização, por todo o período colonial, pela ditadura, para que hoje pudéssemos nos levantar e dizer que já não aceitamos nenhum tipo de colonização. Nenhum tipo de estupro, nenhum tipo de imposição nas nossas vidas.

Quando a gente se levanta e segue na luta, a gente não traz benefícios apenas para nós. A gente está trazendo benefícios para o mundo inteiro. Hoje a nossa luta é especialmente contra esse modelo econômico, que é altamente predatório, destrói toda a Mãe Terra, acaba com toda a biodiversidade e tenta acabar com a nossa diversidade. Acabar com nosso modo de vida. Por fazer essa luta, esse enfrentamento todo, a gente é perseguida, a gente é assassinada, a gente é criminalizada, a gente é presa todos os dias. Porque a luta que a gente faz confronta diretamente o poder econômico e o poder político. São forças muito poderosas que sempre se articularam para acabar com qualquer um que passasse na sua frente. Hoje somos vistos como esse empecilho. Esse empecilho ao progresso. Esse empecilho ao desenvolvimento.

A gente é mesmo contra o desenvolvimento. Porque para nós o desenvolvimento serviria se incluísse as pessoas. O desenvolvimento que é adotado é uma forma de excluir as pessoas. Aumenta cada vez mais a desigualdade. Coloca quem não tem recursos materiais à margem de todos os processos. Tentam fazer isso com a gente todos os dias. No Brasil, isso se intensificou com a eleição do presidente Bolsonaro, que coloca os povos indígenas como seus principais inimigos. Coloca mulheres pobres da periferia, negros e negras, todos nessa situação de vulnerabilidade. A gente segue se articulando, porque entendemos que a luta dos povos indígenas não pode ser uma luta isolada. Precisamos estar conectados para fortalecer quem tem seus direitos retirados, para que juntos façamos esse enfrentamento.

Hoje a terra se tornou o principal objeto de disputa pelo poder político e pelo poder econômico. E fazemos uma luta constante, não pela terra, mas pelo território. Pela Mãe Terra. Para nós, a Terra não é um bem físico, um bem que se vende e se negocia. Nós tratamos a Terra como nossa mãe.

Temos dito sempre para todo mundo: "Quem tem coragem de negociar a sua mãe? De vender sua mãe? De destruir a sua mãe? Alguém tem coragem?" Creio que não. Tratamos a Terra com essa mesma relação. A Terra para nós é mãe, é quem dá a vida, o alimento, o sustento, tudo o que precisamos. Por termos essa relação natural, não permitimos a destruição da Mãe Terra.

Quando lutamos por um território, estamos lutando por um espaço, porque temos uma relação não somente de contato, de um lugar para ficar, mas é uma relação com nossa ancestralidade, com nossos antepassados, com nossa história e com nossos encantados, que estão ali e nos protegem. Eles nos mantêm sempre nessa conexão que nos dá força para seguir lutando.

O território para nós é esse lugar que tem o sagrado, que tem a água, que tem as árvores, os animais e o ar que precisamos para respirar. E é por isso que onde tem a presença indígena tem território, tem floresta, tem biodiversidade preservada. Onde tem a presença indígena tem água limpa. Onde tem a presença indígena têm alimentos saudáveis, sem agrotóxicos. Por isso seguimos nessa defesa, porque acreditamos que estamos fazendo o certo. Não temos medo de enfrentar nenhum governo, porque não somos obrigadas a aceitar nenhuma política injusta, nenhuma lei injusta que queira acabar com nossa vida, acabar com a nossa história, acabar com nosso modo de vida.

Desde 1500, quando os europeus chegaram no Brasil, o plano de desenvolvimento econômico, ou de desenvolvimento nacional, sempre teve como base o extermínio dos povos indígenas. Sempre teve como base a exploração dos recursos naturais. Sempre teve como base toda essa política de destruição. É por isso que nosso povo foi totalmente reduzido. De 5 milhões estimados na escrita—embora a gente acredite que eram mais— hoje, no Brasil, somos menos de 1 milhão, segundo o último censo do IBGE. Hoje, no Brasil, somos 917 mil indígenas contabilizados. Deve ter mais, né? Eu não fui contada. Você foi contada? Deve ter mais, né?

Então somos 917 mil, segundo o último censo. Nós conseguimos manter 274 línguas faladas no Brasil. Embora tenham conseguido acabar com muitas, ainda falamos 274 línguas em todo o Brasil. Ainda somos 305 povos indígenas diferentes; 305 povos distribuídos nos 26 Estados. E ainda somos obrigadas a escutar todos os dias, por onde passamos, que os indígenas do Brasil estão na Amazônia. Que só tem indígena na Amazônia. Porque ainda se tem a ideia do indígena como um selvagem. Ou como aquele que tem que andar nu, andar o tempo todo caçando, pescando. Como que vamos continuar caçando e pescando, se estão tirando esse direito de caçar, pescar, nadar? Somos obrigados a interagir com outra cultura, a viver uma outra vida. Para nós, essa interação é boa, é permitida, é saudável, porque a gente tira o que precisa, mas mantemos nossa cultura.

O que o governo quer fazer hoje é a tal da "integração." Quando ele fala "integração," quer dizer que temos que largar nossa cultura, nosso modo de vida, e nos integrar a uma outra cultura. Quando ele fala isso, está dizendo que tem uma cultura que é melhor que a outra, que uma cultura se sobrepõe à outra, e que somos obrigados a largar a nossa, porque a nossa não presta, a nossa é ruim, atrapalha. Então temos que adotar outra cultura, outro modo de vida. Então também lutamos contra isso, contra essa "integração" que está sendo anunciada pelo governo Bolsonaro.

Além dos 305 povos contatados, cada um em diferentes níveis, temos povos com 500 anos de contato com a sociedade não indígena. Temos povos que têm em média cem anos de contato, o que chamamos de contato recente. Temos povos totalmente em contexto urbano, vivendo na cidade, que estão ali, mas são indígenas. E temos povos ainda sem nenhum contato com a sociedade, nem mesmo com indígenas que estão no mesmo território. Já foram confirmados 114 grupos de povos que vivem em isolamento voluntário. O Estado insiste em chamá-los de "povos isolados." Nós os chamamos de "povos autônomos," porque estão ali por decisão própria, por escolha. Se eles quisessem contato, já teriam se aproximado, já teriam vindo buscar ajuda. Temos que respeitar essa decisão deles. Temos que lutar pela garantia do território para que eles possam continuar ali, para que possam continuar com seu modo de vida. Por isso nós também fazemos essa luta. Por eles, que não estão aqui para falar e exigir a proteção do território.

Tudo isso nos faz lutar constantemente contra a exploração ilegal de madeira nos territórios indígenas. Contra a exploração de minério nos territórios indígenas. Contra a expansão agrícola do agronegócio por meio das monoculturas. Todos os dias vemos medidas no congresso nacional para tentar aprovar leis autorizando o desmatamento para a expansão agrícola. Nós fazemos essa luta que não é pouca, não é pequena. Porque a gente mexe com o governo e com os grandes empresários. De um lado o governo, do outro os empresários, e nós estamos lutando contra esse poder econômico, um poder que tenta todo dia mostrar que é preciso enriquecer, ter mais lucro, que as empresas têm que explorar mais para aumentar a produção para o crescimento econômico. Isso faz com que as pessoas entendam que o mais importante é o Produto Interno Bruto—o valor do PIB, o valor da Bolsa de Valores.

As pessoas seguem acreditando que o país está bem quando a Bolsa está bem, quando o PIB está bem. Poucos se perguntam sobre quantas pessoas estão deixando de ter acesso ao alimento por conta dessa expansão agrícola, uma expansão para atender grandes empresas, atender as *commodities*. Quantas pessoas estão deixando de ter água limpa por conta da exploração de minério? Minério que contaminou a água, que passa em seu território, em sua cidade. Quantas pessoas olham para os rios poluídos nas cidades, seja aonde for, e se comovem com isso? Quantas pessoas olham para o rio e imaginam que ele poderia ser limpo para que todos tivessem acesso? Quantas pessoas se comovem ao ver o poder público destruindo, cortando as árvores da sua cidade para fazer uma praça, para fazer um estacionamento? Quantas pessoas se comovem ou se sentem responsáveis para lutar contra isso?

Muitas pessoas, até mesmo a gente que está aqui, pensam que as respostas estão nas altas tecnologias. Para resolver a crise econômica, resolver as mudanças climáticas, muita gente sempre espera que as altas tecnologias vão resolver. Mas a gente sempre se pergunta: Qual o novo ser humano que queremos para resolver tudo isso? O que tem que se fazer para a gente ter humanos que se percebam responsáveis por frear essas mudanças climáticas? O que é preciso fazer para descarbonizar a mente dos governantes? Mas também restaurar o coração das pessoas. Como cada um se percebe dentro dessa luta?

A cada dia nos falam novas palavras. Eu venho do território indígena Araribóia. Até os 15 anos, eu nunca tinha ido numa cidade. Eu nunca tinha visto um poste de luz elétrica. Até os 15 anos, eu nunca tinha visto asfalto. E fui para a cidade grande porque sempre tive vontade de ir. Desde menina eu sonhava em sair, sonhava em viajar. Eu sabia que se continuasse ali, naquele meu lugar, daquele jeito, eu seria como todo mundo. E por mais que eu gostasse do meu lugar, de estar perto de minha família, eu me sentia muito inquieta. Porque eu sabia que ali eu não poderia ajudar e mudar ninguém, porque eu também estava sempre aceitando as mesmas coisas. Eu sempre quis sair, sempre quis conhecer o mundo.

Eu conheci o mundo mesmo antes de sair por ele, porque eu lia muito e já via as histórias. Quando vim aos Estados Unidos pela primeira vez, parecia que eu já conhecia tudo, pois eu já conhecia muito dessa história, inclusive do extermínio dos povos indígenas nesse país, como o governo tratava os povos indígenas aqui. Quando eu saí, descobri que havia muita coisa, muita coisa para ser feita, para mudar, e que não conseguiria fazer isso sozinha. A gente tinha que juntar mais gente, trazer mais pessoas.

Foi com esse sentimento, de que muitos povos indígenas ainda não tinham sua terra demarcada, que eu me propus a organizar coletivos, fortalecer o movimento indígena e emplacar essa luta em defesa dos territórios. E seguimos a partir do movimento indígena no estado, na região, a nível nacional, e hoje a gente chega no internacional, falando da presença indígena e do sentido do nosso modo de vida.

Hoje somos 5% da população mundial. Nós indígenas no mundo inteiro somamos 5% da população mundial. Esses 5% conseguem proteger 82% da biodiversidade que ainda existe no mundo. 82%. Nós ainda conseguimos proteger a maior parte da água doce do planeta, que está na Amazônia. O Brasil tem os dois maiores aquíferos: um na Amazônia e outro no Sul e Sudeste. E há territórios indígenas onde estão esses aquíferos. As pessoas nos perguntam, especialmente no Brasil, "para que esses índios querem tanta terra?" No Brasil, somos menos de 1% da população. Menos de 1%. Nós ocupamos 13% do território nacional. É muito? Vocês acham muito? Parece muito, né? Os ruralistas nos dizem todo dia que é muito! Eles falam que é demais. Bolsonaro diz que não precisamos dessa terra. Diz que a demarcação de terras no Brasil é abusiva. Quando você faz a conta ao inverso, você vê que 1% da população ruralista detém 46% da propriedade rural. 46%—esse número não é grande? Não é muito para esse 1%? Você pode comparar. O que tem nos 13% de terra indígena? Alguém pode me ajudar a imaginar e lembrar? Tem floresta, biodiversidade, nascentes de água limpa, está tudo aqui nesses 13%. Mas é pequeno, né? É pouco. Nos 46% o que você vê? Você vê o quê? Gado, soja, eucalipto, cana de açúcar. Você vê as monoculturas.

A gente pode comparar os dois lados. O que cada um oferece para o planeta? Desse lado você pega os eucaliptos que sugam a água, secando todas as nascentes. Seca rios, igarapés e riachos. E o que oferece a produção de soja? Veneno, agrotóxico que contamina todos que estão em volta. No Brasil, se aplica agrotóxico de helicóptero. Jogam e atinge todo mundo—as pessoas, a água, tudo que está ali. E o que tem na terra indígena? A floresta em pé, que garante a regulação da chuva, que manda chuva para todos os lugares. As florestas seguram o carbono; o gás carbônico que seria jogado na atmosfera está ali, guardado, evitando que esses gases sejam emitidos.

E ainda consegue equilibrar todo o oxigênio que vai para o mundo todo. Como é global, o oxigênio circula e chega para todos. Nós precisamos das florestas em pé para garantir o ar.

A Célia falou que somos os pneumologistas do mundo, que temos o maior pulmão do mundo. Todo mundo olha para a Amazônia. Todo mundo vê as florestas e os bichos. Mas poucos sabem que tem gente lá. Poucos imaginam que somos nós, com nosso modo de vida, que garantimos a floresta em pé. Garantimos a proteção da biodiversidade. Poucos sabem que somos nós, com nosso modo de vida, que sustentamos aquilo. E a gente sustenta como? Sustentamos com a luta que travamos todos os dias lá na porta do congresso nacional. Levando bala de borracha, spray de pimenta, apanhando da polícia, sendo preso. Mas a gente vai para lá. Estamos pagando com nossa própria vida para manter a biodiversidade. Por isso não aceitamos que nos olhem com pena. Não queremos que ninguém tenha pena de nós, e nos veja como coitadinhos, ou selvagens, como diz Bolsonaro, ou como não humanos, que ele também diz.

Queremos que as pessoas vejam a potência que somos para garantir a vida no planeta, para garantir a água que chega para todos. A água limpa, a chuva, o ar que que todos respiram. Estamos aqui contando o que a gente faz, o que a gente protege, a luta que a gente trava. É claro que existem outros fatores que ajudam a garantir esse equilíbrio, que ajudam a regular a chuva. Mas nós também somos parte dessa potência. Estamos sempre falando que nós não somos parte do Brasil; o Brasil é que é parte de nós. Somos os primeiros ali, então o Brasil é parte de nós.

E nós queremos fazer essa disputa pelo Brasil. Essa disputa pelo nosso lugar. Fazemos essa disputa lutando politicamente todos os dias, e também fazemos a disputa de narrativas nas redes sociais. Se hoje temos internet e acesso a esse meio de comunicação, temos que utilizá-los para dar visibilidade à realidade indígena, para mostrar o que fazemos e o que as pessoas precisam fazer para estar junto com a gente. Se as pessoas não conhecem, elas não se aproximam. O governo nos olha como um empecilho, como inimigos, e muitos ainda nos olham como selvagens. E então não se aproximam, têm medo. Não querem saber, não querem conhecer, por isso há esse distanciamento. Por causa do distanciamento há muito desconhecimento sobre a vida dos povos indígenas no mundo inteiro. E as escolas, que deveriam adotar materiais para trabalhar com os estudantes de todas as séries, também se isentam disso. Então as pessoas chegam aos quarenta, cinquenta anos e não sabem nada da realidade indígena. Uma das formas das pessoas nos conhecerem melhor seria se desde as primeiras séries as escolas adotassem disciplinas sobre os povos indígenas—não que disciplinem a gente—falando de quantos são, como vivem, onde estão, o que fazem. E principalmente falar dos conflitos existentes.

Não é mais falar dos povos indígenas com aquele romantismo do passado, os povos indígenas bonitos dos romances. Tem que mostrar como são os indígenas hoje, os confrontos que a gente trava, os conflitos que são colocados. E toda a luta política que a gente faz para continuar existindo. Hoje, nós seguimos na linha de frente dessa luta. Na linha de frente contra esse modelo econômico totalmente predatório. Na linha de frente contra as mudanças climáticas. Não era esse o tema? Contra as mudanças climáticas.

O nosso modo de vida já é por si só um enfrentamento às mudanças climáticas. Ano passado, realizamos no Brasil a primeira marcha das mulheres indígenas. Muita gente pergunta: "Por que vocês vieram só agora?" Não, não chegamos só agora. Há quinhentos anos a gente luta contra tudo o que está aí. Mas chega uma hora que nossa luta local não é mais suficiente. E nós temos que levantar e chamar mais pessoas para dar as mãos. Chegamos em Brasília em agosto do ano passado, no Dia Internacional dos Povos Indígenas. Reunimos mais de três mil mulheres, que saíram de seus territórios, todas deram um jeito de chegar.

Muitas enfrentaram seus companheiros para poderem ir. Além de fazermos esse chamado, nós ainda temos que mostrar ao nosso povo que a proibição da participação das mulheres não é cultural. Não é cultura ter essa subserviência. Não é cultura você ficar à margem. Isso é herança colonial. Isso faz parte de todo o processo de colonização que a gente viveu e que nossos povos também aderiram. Aderiram a um tipo de machismo, de violência doméstica e à proibição da participação das mulheres. Nós temos que romper essa barreira. Essa barreira colonial, machista, que por muitos povos ainda é vista como cultura. Nós temos que fazer esse enfrentamento.

Conseguimos trazer três mil mulheres para Brasília. Realizamos a primeira marcha, e cada uma que foi voltou sabendo que não era mais a mesma. Elas falaram "Eu quero estar junto," "eu quero continuar," "eu quero participar," "eu sei que essa luta depende de nós." Então essa marcha foi muito importante. A primeira marcha das mulheres no Brasil, mas é também a primeira marcha das mulheres indígenas do mundo. E como continuidade dessa marcha, vamos realizar esse ano a caravana de mulheres indígenas pelo Brasil. Vamos circular por todos os estados brasileiros, nos reunindo com mulheres de todos os povos, de todos os territórios e vamos discutir exatamente o tema dessa palestra: o papel das mulheres indígenas para conter as mudanças climáticas. Vamos também discutir e impulsionar as candidaturas das mulheres indígenas. Porque esse lugar na política institucional é nosso também.

Nós temos hoje uma mulher deputada federal, eleita na eleição passada. Mas uma é pouco. A nossa luta é coletiva. Onde tem uma, nós temos que levar mais. Vamos impulsionar candidaturas de mulheres indígenas para ocupar todos os níveis da política institucional. Desde o seu município, ao seu estado e ao nacional—e até a presidência, né? Vamos seguir. Vamos realizar essa caravana de mulheres pelo Brasil, e no dia 5 de setembro, Dia Internacional da Mulher Indígena, realizaremos esse encontro internacional no Brasil. É um chamado das mulheres indígenas do Brasil para as mulheres do mundo, para que outras mulheres possam se juntar a nós. Porque essa luta não é só nossa. Não estamos mais dando conta de carregar essa responsabilidade sozinhas. Outras mulheres têm que chegar junto e assumir a responsabilidade. E se nós estivemos até agora fazendo essa luta, no nosso lugar, nós queremos agora internacionalizar, globalizar a nossa luta.

Não é só o mercado que tem que ser globalizado. Nós temos que nos organizar globalmente para poder trazer o mercado para o local. Não podemos mais permitir que esse modelo econômico com base no agronegócio, nas monoculturas, seguir reduzindo a produção da diversidade de grãos. Da forma que está hoje, esse modelo da monocultura reduz entre 25% e 30% a produção de grãos, que é o que comemos de verdade, que é o nosso alimento. Além disso, está comprovado que 80% da alimentação no mundo é produzida pela agricultura familiar. No Brasil, 70% da alimentação que chega à mesa das pessoas vem da agricultura familiar. Nós temos que seguir lutando pela descentralização do uso da terra. E com isso diversificar a produção dos alimentos. Os grandes empresários farão isso? Não. Quem vai fazer isso somos nós. É o trabalhador rural, o pequeno produtor, nós indígenas, os quilombolas, comunidades tradicionais.

Somos nós que vivemos e dependemos desse território. Temos o nosso território como um lugar de plantar, de viver. Não como eles, que têm a terra como um mercado, como um bem para negociar. Temos que seguir lutando por essa relação. E para isso mais pessoas têm que chegar junto. Têm que entender, têm que se reconectar com a mãe natureza, têm que entender que é exatamente essa conexão que garantirá nosso futuro. Não temos um plano B. Não temos um planeta B. E o nosso caminho é a luta.

..........................................................................................

**Malcolm McNee** is associate professor and chair of the Department of Spanish and Portuguese at Smith College, where he teaches Portuguese and a range of interdisciplinary humanities topics in Afro-Luso-Brazilian studies. He is author of *The Environmental Imaginary in Brazilian Poetry and Art* (2014), which examines a range of artistic responses to environmental change and vulnerability in contemporary Brazil, from efforts to connect art with activism to conceptually oriented interrogations of ideas of nature, place-making, and ecology. He is currently working on an anthology of Brazilian environmental writing in translation and coediting a volume on ecology and contemporary Indigenous thought in Brazil.

**Elena Langdon** has been a professional translator and interpreter since 2001. She holds a master's degree in translation studies from the University of Massachusetts Amherst and is certified as a Portuguese-to-English translator by the American Translators Association. Elena grew up in southern Brazil and feels a deep connection to Native peoples everywhere, perhaps in part because as a child, her anthropologist parents told her cosmology tales of the Siona and Barasana people as bedtime stories.

## Note

Transcription collaboratively done by Smith College students enrolled in POR228, "Indigenous Brazil: Past, Present, Future": Melisa Aguila Rua, Maddie Haines, Emily Jaruszewski, Amanda Maia, Sarah Shuler-Barwick, Lexie Stephens, Emilia Tamayo, Isabel Teixeira, Em Tejada Jaquez, Michelle Tsai Gomez, Yesenia Villatoro Ramirez, and Sasha Zeidenberg, and revised by Elena Langdon and Malcolm K. McNee.

1    Galdino Pataxó was a leader of the Pataxó-Hã-Hã-Hã people of southern Bahia state. In 1997, while he was in Brasília negotiating land claims for his community, he was burned to death by a group of upper-class youth, in a brutal hate crime that shocked the conscience of Brazil and the world.

Eman Alasah

.......................................................................................

# The Palestinian Feminist Movement
# and the Settler Colonial Ordeal
An Intersectional and Interdependent Framework

Abstract: In light of recent developments in both the (anti)colonial and feminist discourses surrounding the settler colonial condition of Palestine, this article revisits and expands intersectionality as an analytical tool that captures manifold paradigms of subjugation. By considering the various ways in which colonial hegemony and patriarchal authority empower, substantiate, and contribute to one another, the article proposes interdependence as a more comprehensive analytical concept that, in addition to accentuating the multiplicity of oppressive structures, illuminates how they interact within a broader, complex matrix of power. The article positions the Palestinian feminist anticolonial struggle in relation to wider debates on Black, transnational, and Third World feminisms to contextualize the movement. The article eventually turns to contemporary examples of intersectional feminist mobilization that exemplifies the nuanced and ever developing nature of the movement.

The past few years have witnessed a remarkable shift in the global debates revolving around the question of Palestine. For the most part, this shift has been positive: the Israeli government has been condemned, in an unprecedented manner, for its racist and discriminatory colonial policies against the Indigenous people of the land it occupies. Denunciations of Israel for committing the crime of apartheid from organizations like Human Rights Watch, Amnesty International, and the International Criminal Court have indeed instigated an unparalleled alteration in the global discourse on the

MERIDIANS · feminism, race, transnationalism   23:1 April 2024
DOI: 10.1215/15366936-10926920 © 2024 Smith College

matter. Largely, this shift comes as a result of the increasingly chauvinistic discourse that dominates Israeli politics, which manifests itself in the striking turn toward the political Right in the government, as well as in the unmistakable upsurge in settler violence against Palestinians. But these changes are paralleled in another scope; that is, in Palestinian gender and feminist politics. The good tidings that arose with the progress made by various feminist and queer organizations like AlQaws, Aswat, the Palestinian Feminist Collective, and Tala'at, among others, mark an evolutionary turn in the Palestinian feminist movement. Nonetheless, this optimistic development was escorted by a regressive current that culminated in the withholding by the Palestinian Authority of its ratification of the Convention on the Elimination of All Forms of Discrimination against Women (CEDAW), largely due to the massive wave of vilification publicized by tribal and conservative circles. Put into perspective, the progressive and regressive shifts in both discourses, the national and the feminist, cannot go unnoticed, as they present an interdependent, thought-provoking matrix that requires revisiting the notion of intersectionality, as well as mapping the shift in Palestinian gender and queer politics.

By relating existing theoretical frameworks to the ongoing settler colonial context of Palestine, this article examines recent developments in Palestinian feminist thought by arguing that a better understanding of intersectionality requires the examination of the overarching matrix of domination that sustains oppression, as well as consideration of how overlapping oppressive structures contribute to one another. In other words, patriarchy and colonial violence do not simply intersect but rather empower and perpetuate the sustainability of one another. This creates a dynamic of interdependence and reciprocity, according to which several oppressive structures become inseparable from and contingent on each other; a proposition that the intersectional theoretical framework fails to expound. The importance of this approach is that it allows us to think of comprehensive, effective, and thorough emancipatory paradigms, as it does not assume that one mode of oppression is more vicious or more tolerable than another. Furthermore, it looks into the ways in which changes in one structure of power bear impact on the other. First of all, I will commence by referring to relevant strands of feminist thought that centralize the intersectional experiences of women of color, focusing mainly on Black, transnational, and Third World feminisms. I will then examine the ways in which gender and racial structures of oppression in the Palestinian context intersect with, connect to, and empower one another. Subsequently, I will examine the progress of Palestinian feminist resistance, by drawing attention to recent developments in discourse and strategy as modeled by two exemplary antipatriarchal, anticolonial organizations. While the main focus will be on Palestine as a site of contemporary settler colonialism, the arguments can apply to other contexts of ethnic and gender inequality where multiple oppressive paradigms hinge on one another. Therefore, the article aims to examine the Palestinian anticolonial feminist movement by expanding and revisiting the concept of intersectionality, which originated in Black feminist thought.

## Feminisms Reexamined: Black, Transnational, and Third World Feminism

In examining the various forms of oppression inflicted on Black women in the United States, Kimberlé Crenshaw (1991: 1265) uses intersectionality to "describe the location of women of colour both within overlapping systems of subordination and at the margins of feminism and antiracism," while highlighting the conundrum that racism is typically not problematized in feminist discourses, while sexism is overlooked in the antiracist struggle. Therefore, intersectionality appears as a highly significant analytical framework that addresses the "dynamics of difference and sameness" (Cho, Crenshaw, and McCall 2013: 787) as well as the manifold arrangements of power that marginalize Native women, women of color, and women in colonial contexts. Intersectionality resolves the problem of single-axis, subtractive, and reductionist analyses of power, stressing the significance of multidimensional and multilayered analytical frameworks. Angela Davis (2016: 4) proposes that the main problem faced by Black women in the United States was that they were pushed to choose one affiliation. Specifically, they were "frequently asked to choose whether the Black movement or the women's movement was most important," to which the response was that "this was the wrong question," as the accurate question should be "how to understand the intersections and interconnections between the two movements" (Davis 2016: 4). Hence, one might think of intersectionality as a "nodal point [rather] than as a closed system" (Cho, Crenshaw, and McCall 2013: 788), in which overlapping, conflicting, or complementary configurations of power such as race and gender transpire. Intersectionality, as Amanda Gouws (2017: 22) points out, tackles issues of "difference and sameness simultaneously in a form of liberatory praxis." Thus, an intersectional framework is crucial in radical and emancipatory politics. Due to its novelty and flexibility, critics have argued that the field of intersectionality studies requires further elaborations on its theoretical and practical application across and within other national contexts, given that the field of inquiry has hitherto centered on the experiences of Black women in the United States (Cho, Crenshaw, and McCall 2013: 807). In particular, more research needs to be conducted on intersectionality in settler colonial contexts, given the peculiar interplay between place/space and gender politics within settler colonial frameworks (Gouws 2017: 26).

Building on Crenshaw's work, Patricia Hill Collins maintains that, while intersectionality explains how different structures of power work together in marginalizing certain groups, particularly women of color, the analytical framework needs to be understood within the larger structure, which she refers to as the matrix of domination. The *matrix of domination* describes the "overall social organization within which intersecting oppressions originate, develop, and are contained" (Collins 2000: 228). Thus, it defines the overall organization of power in a given society. In other words, intersecting oppressive structures require social, political, and legal institutions—that is, a matrix of domination—that regulate and maintain the patterns of subjugation faced by marginalized groups. According to Collins, any matrix of domination has two main features. First of all, it has a specific arrangement of overlapping oppressive structures. The ways in which they overlap, and the forms of oppression faced, vary over time and place, and are thus context specific. Second, Collins refers to four interconnected domains through which systems of oppression within a matrix are organized: structural, disciplinary, hegemonic, and interpersonal. She explains that "the structural domain organizes oppression, whereas the disciplinary domain manages it. The hegemonic domain justifies oppression, and the interpersonal domain influences everyday lived experience and the individual consciousness that ensues" (Collins 2000: 276). Oppression, therefore, is operated through a complex structure that functions to safeguard its arrangement, durability, and legitimacy.

The significant contributions offered by Black feminist theorists and critics have been further criticized, restructured, and adjusted to accommodate the experiences of women in the Third World, the Global South, and the peripheries. Consequently, Third World feminism and transnational feminism emerged as movements that primarily challenged and rejected the inaccurate universalism assumed by white feminism, while building on and expanding Black feminist thought, given that the latter often failed to address the struggles of Indigenous women, or women who identified as neither Black nor white. Hence, transnational and Third World feminisms have primarily focused on women of the Third World rather than on women of color in the first world, as well as on the various forms of oppression and resistance in the formerly colonized world. However, it is important to note that transnational feminism and Third World feminism are distinct, as Ranjoo Herr (2014) points out. Their chief point of contention is their approach to the nation-state; while Third World feminists adopt a relatively positive attitude toward nationalism and the nation-state, transnational feminists consider nationalism as patriarchal and gendered in nature, which renders it detrimental to gender equality. Moreover, Herr argues that Third World feminism has mainly focused on the different forms of oppression inflicted on and resistance prompted by Third World women within their local and national contexts, whereas the focus of transnational feminism has been on networks and movements that transcend the national and local spheres of struggle and organize on transnational and international levels.

Both frameworks prove to be as problematic as they are beneficial when discussing feminism in Palestine. Transnational feminism, as Herr argues, lacks coherence and consistency, particularly in its approach to the nation-state. She accurately observes that the ambiguities of the movement in this regard "undermine the transnational feminist claim that it represents Third World women's interests, as nation-states and nationalism have crucial relevance for Third World women's activism" (Herr 2014: 3). For a stateless people fighting for the right of self-determination through the creation of an independent sovereign state, transnational feminism seems to be a reductive framework for Palestinian women, whose oppression is largely, though not completely, caused by the lack of a sovereign nation-state. In her critique of transnational feminism, Herr (2014: 3) further points out that the transnational "leaves the local/national, an extremely important arena of Third World women's activism and the proper domain of Third World feminism, under-theorized." Transnational feminism thus undervalues the daily, local struggle on the ground in a context of continuing settler colonialism. Third World feminism, on the other hand, is similarly problematic due to its focus on the local/national at the expense of the transnational, as Herr (2014: 25) contends. Nevertheless, Herr (2014:

25–26) argues that a transnational approach is necessary for a comprehensive understanding of gender oppression in the Third World, because Third World women "in their own local and national contexts have become increasingly implicated in the operations of neoliberal global capitalism under the conditions of a tightly integrated global economy." Particularly in a geopolitical context that can be considered as reflective of global political dynamics as Palestine, given the involvement of various international actors, it is necessary to consider the transnational dimension of the struggle. Moreover, transnational feminist solidarity has always proved to be substantial in shaping the discourse on Palestine, particularly given the countless similarities and overlaps of struggle with women from other colonial contexts. Therefore, as Herr concludes, Third World feminism and transnational feminism need to collaborate at several junctures of their analyses in order to reach a comprehensive understanding of the various matrixes of domination and intersectionalities of oppression. Overall, what distinguishes all these diverse strands of feminism from Western, white, and liberal feminist waves is their perceptive attention to race and ethnicity as other primary dimensions of oppression. Universalism is also dismissed in these movements, which is based on the premise that oppressions vary among different women in different cultural and national contexts. There is no universal, collective experience that applies to all women. Global sisterhood in its Eurocentric sense is thus overturned by these strands of feminism because, even though solidarity remains indispensable, experiences of oppression vary immensely and cannot be homogenized, reduced, or universalized.

While Black feminist and Third World feminist theoretical frameworks address the ways in which several power structures intersect with and converge in each other, they often fail to shed light on the ways in which these structures of oppression interact. Therefore, by shedding light on current developments in Palestine, I will attempt to scrutinize the ways in which patriarchal violence and settler colonialism redefine, strengthen, and contribute to one another by arguing that the two structures largely interdepend on and do not just intersect with one another, which complicates and reconfigures the matrix of domination. Hence, interdependency seems to be a critical framework that addresses social and political inequalities in ways that intersectionality does not. It allows for the conceptualization of a broader framework that inspects the ways in which several oppressive structures within the broader matrix of domination empower and contribute to the sustainability of one another.

The matrix of domination in the context of Palestine, as I will demonstrate, is complicated by the overlap, coexistence, and interdependence of two political arrangements that collude in oppressing Indigenous women: one is Native, while the other is colonial. The endurance of one necessarily insinuates the continuity of the other. The manifestations of oppression, however, vary from other contexts of colonialism, for each case of colonization has its own particularities. Settler colonialism is based on the logic of elimination, as Patrick Wolfe (2006) argues, which renders the dehumanizing colonial discourse into an annihilating and eradicating praxis. It is therefore a more violent structure that entails more radical modes of resistance than in contexts of exploitation colonialism, surrogate colonialism, trade colonialism, and other types identified by postcolonial critics (Healy and Dal Lago 2014). Therefore, it is important to note that Zionism as a settler colonial discourse from the onset has not always been attentive to internal gender dynamics in the conventional way. As will be demonstrated, it has occasionally used gender politics for legitimizing effects, but overall, it has largely maintained its eliminative dimension, or what Wolfe refers to as the "logic of elimination." While other colonial powers claimed that they aimed at civilizing and exerting power over the Natives, settler colonialism strategically sought their annihilation. Hence, Nada Elia (2021b) writes that Zionism has "always wanted them [Palestinian women] dead." She elaborates on the Zionist perception of Palestinian women as a "demographic threat," in reference to motherhood and childbearing, which outweighs the archetypal colonial discourse that aims at saving Indigenous women from their male counterparts.

## Israeli Settler Colonialism and the Reinforcement of Local Patriarchy

Much research has been conducted on the ways in which Israeli policies authorize, empower, and reconfigure the already existing patriarchal structure in Palestine. The manifestations of colonial violence are observable in two ways. First, colonial measures target all Natives unexceptionally, including women. Second, colonial violence functions by reshaping prevailing patriarchal practices. In a significant study, Nadera Shalhoub-Kevorkian (2014: 1) points out that the settler colonial regime has ever since 1948 actively "sought to manipulate patriarchal forces within the colonized society" in a way that is similar to other colonial regimes. In a study on gender-based violence during the time of the Second Intifada, Shalhoub-Kevorkian (2005) draws attention to the consequences of colonial violence on domestic gender dynamics by looking into the mounting violence against women domestically, which comes as a consequence to the humiliation, violence, and subjugation inflicted on men. Projection of violence becomes an unwarrantable yet explainable psychological defense mechanism through which men traumatized by colonial aggression manage and cope with their humiliation.

In other respects, colonialism has contributed to patriarchal hierarchy through preventing social change and hindering the natural course of progress. To Indigenous people, change is often problematic, as it represents the abandonment of the Native culture and identity, which they attempt to preserve from colonial influence as part of the anticolonial struggle. The maintenance of traditional gender roles has often been perceived as essential in preserving precolonial—that is, pre-1948—identity among Palestinian communities, as Rosemary Sayigh (2007) indicates in her research conducted in the refugee camps in Lebanon. While the research might be perceived as context specific, the results resonate with Nativist discourses that position gender hierarchy as central in precolonial Native cultures, which accordingly designate the preservation of patriarchal oppression as necessary in resisting colonialism. Furthermore, Nada Elia (2021b) argues that the regression that arises from the tendency to preserve the Native culture brings about a "time freeze" in the natural progress of societies. She further elaborates on how liberal democracy, feminism, and LGBTQ rights in Israel are contrasted in Palestine; the more Israel avows itself as progressive, the more conservative sectors in Palestine register those progressive values as colonial, and thus detrimental. By the same token, Shalhoub-Kevorkian (2014: 4) argues that continuing colonial policies of displacement, violence, and fragmentation "sowed intense fear and confusion" within Palestinian society, which "reacted by redoubling its efforts to protect itself . . . by safeguarding the family from displacement, poverty, [and] hardship." Protecting the family unit from disintegration predictably included the maintenance of patriarchal authority, gender hierarchy, and heteronormativity, which have always symbolized the ideal arrangement of the family.

Other researchers have examined the ways in which colonial occupation "impacts the internal dynamics of Palestinian society, serving to diminish the strength of women's presence and reinforce adherence to traditional gender roles" (Dana and Walker 2015: 488–89). This is not necessarily achieved by means of cultural influence, but because "restricted mobility

and exposure to different forms of harassment by Israeli soldiers and settlers compels Palestinian families to impel their daughters to stay at home
in order to protect them," which brings to light how gender hierarchy,
macho masculinities, and patriarchal embargoes are often indirectly
empowered by violent colonial measures (Dana and Walker 2015: 489).
Because the public sphere is unsafe for colonial subjects, including women,
patriarchal protectiveness becomes justified and normalized. To exemplify
how colonial measures interfere with internal gender politics, research has
been conducted on the experience of women crossing checkpoints in the
West Bank, and how it "brings the politics of gender and occupation to the
fore," highlighting the ways in which "colonial security mechanisms situate women within colonial patriarchies" (Griffiths and Repo 2021: 252).
Furthermore, it can be argued that colonialism blocks any attempts for
social change through the urgency and immediacy it epitomizes for colonized subjects. Priorities, in a context of ongoing colonialism, are reshaped
by colonized subjects in a way that makes other concerns secondary to the
national struggle for decolonization, often in disregard to the fact that
national liberation remains inadequate and unfulfilling if it excludes marginalized elements of the Native society. As Sophie Richter-Devroe (2008:
36) writes, Palestinian women are expected to "view themselves, first of all,
as Palestinians resisting the occupation, before their status as women in
patriarchal society can be discussed." Any activism that exclusively targets
gender inequality is perceived as a form of duplicity to the urgent, anticolonial cause. Hence, feminist activism has always had to accommodate the
culture by assuming an anticolonial approach beside its main social and
cultural reformative object.

## How Does Patriarchy Contribute to Legitimizing
## Colonial Discourse?

Research has been extensively conducted on the ways in which colonialism
empowers oppressive Native practices in the Palestinian context. However,
inquiries about how patriarchy authorizes and contributes to colonial discourse have only recently been instigated. In the field of postcolonial studies, it is a well-established premise that colonialism often assumed an
enlightening, redeeming, and civilizing role, according to which the white
man had a burden, a mission, and a duty to perform on colonial subjects. It
is the white man's burden to enlighten and educate the primitive Natives.
The attitude of the colonizer to gender and women's issues has varied

immensely throughout time and place, yet one thing is consistent: it has always maintained its paternalistic and patronizing role. At times, white men exoticized, eroticized, and sexualized women, and sometimes men, of the Orient, which is manifested in the Orientalist discourse as Edward Said has long argued. At other times, like the French in Algeria during the liberation war, they assumed the role of saviors by encouraging the unveiling of Algerian women, while waging a war against the revolutionaries fighting for national independence (Lazreg 1990). In other cases, colonial discourse was justified by the necessity of saving Native women from Native practices. As Gayatri Spivak (1993: 93) has put it in the context of British India, it was "white men saving brown women from brown men." More recently, the same pretext has been utilized by the Americans to rationalize the imperialistically motivated invasion of Afghanistan, which initiated debates about whether Muslim women need saving from Muslim men, as Lila Abu-Lughod (2002) points out.

When it comes to the Zionist colonial discourse, similar tendencies can be traced. In a study about femicide among Palestinian communities in Israel, Nadera Shalhoub-Kevorkian and Suhad Daher-Nashef (2013) contend that social phenomena based on gender hierarchy and violence in contexts of colonialism cannot be explained without referring to the overarching structure that entitles them. Israeli propaganda makes use of an Orientalist cultural discourse to substantiate that gender-based violence, particularly femicide, is endemic to the Arab culture, while failing to reference the colonial structure that circuitously empowers gender-based violence at times, and directly perpetrates necropolitical violence against Indigenous women at other times. In this regard, Frances Hasso (1998: 458) has argued that Palestinian feminists, following the lead of feminists in other regions of the Global South, have characteristically turned away from discussing internal gender dynamics and Indigenous patriarchal practices in international feminist forums, because they regarded the emphasis on internal gender dynamics not just as a diversion from the more immediate struggle against global capitalist imperialism, but also as an overall agenda that contributes to the legitimization of international political and economic inequalities. In other words, feminists from the Global South refrained from airing the dirty laundry of their Native cultures so as not to offer international, mainly white, audiences a trump card to dismiss their demands for political and economic justice. Patriarchy at home, therefore, has always created a barrier for women from the peripheries, because it embodies a counter discourse that legitimizes imperialist discourses, mainly instigated by liberal white feminist currents.

More recently, the colonial discourse has shifted toward the domain of queer politics. LGBTQ rights have become a commodity to legitimize colonial violence through producing a discourse that uses the heteronormative patriarchal Indigenous culture as a pretext to justify colonial measures. To situate this approach within the larger global context, the notion of homonationalism appears to be useful. In *Terrorist Assemblages: Homonationalism in Queer Time*, Jasbir Puar (2007) introduces the conceptual frame of homonationalism in an attempt to understand the intricacies of how acceptance of homosexual subjects and normalizing homosexuality in a heteronormative world have become an indicator that gauges and determines the right and capacity for the national sovereignty of the state. In other words, as an analytic to understand current global politics, the term *homonationalism* proposes a framework that explains the criteria according to which a state can enact its legitimacy. She then examines the phenomenon of pinkwashing in the context of Palestine and Israel, which can be described as a discourse that utilizes the already prevailing patriarchy, sexual violence, and regressive Native traditions to authorize colonial discourse, adding another layer to the existing matrix of domination. *Pinkwashing*, according to Sarah Schulman who employed the term in the context of Israeli settler colonialism, is "a deliberate strategy to conceal the continuing violations of Palestinians' human rights behind an image of modernity signified by Israeli gay life" (Schulman 2011). Pinkwashing is primarily operational within a broader discourse of homonationalism. Puar (2013: 338) writes that

> Within this nexus of history and economy, Israel appears as a pioneer of homonationalism, being perfectly situated to encourage the normalization of some homosexual bodies in relation to an increasingly violent occupation of Palestine. This homonationalist history of Israel, or the rise of LGBT rights in Israel, parallels the concomitant increasing segregation of Palestinian populations, especially post-Oslo.

Pinkwashing can be perceived as a correlative fallacy, a sort of whataboutism that shifts the primary focus of the anticolonial discourse, which is decolonization and self-determination. It goes without saying that the discourse against pinkwashing does not imply the nonexistence of homophobia within the Indigenous Palestinian community, but it simply indicates that one form of oppression cannot be justified by another, and that a progressive element within a certain political structure does not conceal its oppressive facets. By advocating for the rights of the LGBTQ community and pinpointing the lack thereof among the Palestinian community and the wider Middle East, Israel diverts the debate from its record of human rights violations. Initially, pinkwashing was part of a broader campaign that was initiated in 2007 by the Israeli foreign ministry, the aim of which has been to revitalize the image of the state (Papantonopoulou 2014: 278). But pinkwashing is importantly an indication of the interdependence of oppressive structures, whether colonial or patriarchal, on one another. Heteronormativity and non-acceptance of LGBTQ rights in the conservatively religious and patriarchal Palestinian community entitle the discourse of pinkwashing to sustain the legitimacy of Israel within a global structure of homonationalism. Patriarchal restrictions and sexual violence in this case contribute to the sustainability of the colonial discourse that vilifies and dehumanizes the Indigenous people. It provides a supposedly reasonable pretext for the continuation of colonial hegemony based on a legitimized discourse, according to which the Natives are primitive, uncivilized, and unworthy of self-determination.

### Models of Resistance: The Intersectionality, Multiplicity, and Development of Palestinian Feminist Action

In *Palestinian Women's Activism: Nationalism, Secularism, Islamism*, Islah Jad (2018) chronicles the history of Palestinian women's activism by dividing it into roughly three periods, or "waves" as one might call them. The first wave, referred to by Jad as the "revolutionary period," designates the advent and growth of nationalist feminism, spanning from the British Mandate of Palestine in the early twentieth century until the First Intifada in 1987. To a considerable extent, and particularly subsequent to the rise of the Palestine Liberation Organization (PLO), Palestinian women's activism in the period was factional, in the sense that it functioned principally within the factional frameworks of the PLO, which consisted of the nationalist secular Fatah and the progressive leftist factions. This was the period in which women activists mobilized militarily and factionally with the various political movements that participated in the anticolonial struggle. During periods of this stage, "nationalism and feminism were largely successful as a combined project," argues Hasso (1998: 442) in her critical analysis of the Palestinian Federation of Women's Action Committees, which was affiliated with the Democratic Front for the Liberation of Palestine, a Marxist faction of the PLO. The second wave that Jad designates is the state-building phase succeeding the Oslo Accords in 1993, following which feminist activism was centralized, institutionalized, NGO-ized, and transformed from its grassroots origins into an elitist and exclusivist discourse. Therese Saliba (2000: 1088–89) writes that within the ambiguous transitional phase from grassroots intifada activism to bureaucratic state building, women's role in policy making was rather marginal, which casts light on the general ambiguity—or perhaps inadequacy—of (post)colonial governments in matters of gender. Within the newly established pseudo government, gender politics were not prioritized, partly because state building was a more urgent priority, and partly because of its lack of tangible sovereignty. The failures of the newly formed Palestinian Authority and its accompanying secular feminist discourse at the turn of the century led to the emergence of Islamic feminism as an alternative, popularized by the newly established Hamas, whose focus centered on rural and refugee— that is, on socially and economically marginalized—women. This third wave of feminist activism epitomized a contradiction to the previously secular and progressive waves, but it also coincided with and corresponded to the broader regional wave of Islamization. In her analysis of the movement, Jad does not dismiss feminist activism associated with the Islamic movement as regressive or traditional, but rather highlights its constant flux, flexibility, and willingness for dialogue, in an attempt to avoid the common denigration of Islamic feminist movements in feminist studies.

   In the aftermath of the Second Intifada and the 2006 factional division of power between the Islamic yet active Hamas in Gaza and the secular, progressive, yet passive Fatah in the West Bank, the Palestinian feminist movement shifted toward grassroots, decentralized, and localized forms of resistance instead of the earlier formal mobilization, as Sophie Richter-Devroe (2018) indicates in her seminal work *Women's Political Activism in Palestine: Peacebuilding, Resistance, and Survival*. As a result of the general sense of disenfranchisement and disenchantment, women moved away from factional and formal politics toward a passive, adaptive form of resistance that centered on daily survival under continuing colonial occupation, which she labels as the "infrapolitics of *sumud*." Unlike the perception of *sumud* (steadfastness) as a form of passive resistance, Richter-Devroe (2008) underscores the vital importance of daily acts of steadfastness, which often have been associated with women.

Little research has been conducted on feminist and women's activism in Palestine after the early 2000s. As is clearly visible, waves of feminist politics echo, resonate with, and correspond to colonial and decolonial politics, which signifies that any developments in one respect necessarily impinge on the other. To complement the discourse commenced above on intersectionality and the matrix of domination, I will now look into two contemporary movements as examples of intersectional feminist activism that target the overlapping and complementary structures of oppression. But before that, it is necessary to elaborate on the beforehand mentioned changes in the international discourse on Palestine and Israel, which, as will be demonstrated, had a strong bearing on feminist mobilization. One can argue that, after decades of silence, the narrative is being reshaped, and human rights violations in the region have come to the forefront of debates in the international community. In the beginning of 2021, B'Tselem, the Israeli Information Center for Human Rights in the Occupied Territories, proclaimed upon investigation that the Israeli government is an apartheid regime (B'Tselem 2021). In February 2021, the International Criminal Court has declared that it will carry out an investigation in the Occupied Palestinian Territories related to allegations of crimes against humanity, apartheid, and persecution. In March, a formal investigation was officially announced. Subsequently, in April 2021, Human Rights Watch issued a report in which it declared that apartheid is being implemented in Israel-Palestine: "Two primary groups live today in Israel and the OPT [Occupied Palestinian Territories]: Jewish Israelis and Palestinians. One primary sovereign, the Israeli government, rules over them" (Human Rights Watch 2021). These changes can be viewed as a cornerstone for subsequent changes in feminist politics, given the inseparability of struggles.

## Al-Qaws

In an unprecedented turn in Palestinian feminist politics, Al-Qaws, or the (rain)bow, a civil-society, grassroots, nongovernmental organization was officially founded in Jerusalem in 2007 with the main goals of creating a platform for LGBTQ and queer subjects, advocating for the rights of sexual minorities, and promoting sexual and gender diversity in Palestinian society. Their work includes running community centers, establishing a network among cultural and social civil-society institutions, and initiating a public discourse based on acceptance, inclusion, and diversity. The inseparability of queer and colonial politics lies at the heart of the task instigated by Al-Qaws. In the mission statement of the organization, it is clearly stated that "at individual, community, and societal levels, al-Qaws disrupts sexual and gender-based oppression, and challenges regulation of our sexualities and bodies, whether patriarchal, capitalist, or colonial."[1]

The inseparability and connectedness of oppressive structures of power is a significant premise of any anticolonial, feminist movement, because the personal is always political. As stated by the movement, "All political work intersects with issues that are sometimes dismissed as too personal, apolitical, or irrelevant to anti-occupation and de-colonial organizing, such as homosexuality and queer identity, non-normative gender."[2] Fighting colonialism without fighting patriarchy and heteronormativity, therefore, is insufficient, because comprehensive self-determination stands for the freedom from all forms of oppression, whether internal or external, native or foreign. The vision of the organization is decisively built on "anticolonial and queer-feminist values."[3] Accordingly, Israeli settler colonialism and the prevalent patriarchal, heteronormative, cisgender culture of Palestinian society are defined as the chief oppressive structures of power that necessitate dissent and transformation. This challenges the critique that was prompted by Palestinian activists and critics like Sa'ed Atshan, whose work *Queer Palestine and the Empire of Critique* (2020) proposes that the Palestinian LGBTQ movement has since its commencement in the early 2000s gradually sidelined queer politics in favor of a purely anticolonial discourse; an operational mode that he describes as a "radical purism" and designates as problematic.

What makes Al-Qaws particularly significant is its "border-defying" mission, which echoes transnational feminist discourses that undermine national boundaries and embrace holistic and inclusive approaches to resistance and solidarity. While their views on the nation-state are ambiguous and unspecified, they are clear about their decolonial mission, which dictates the dismantling of settler colonialism and apartheid. Queer liberation is transnational in essence, since homophobia is global and transcends national borders. This requires any queer liberationist movement to approach the struggle as transnational in the first place. Yet, the context-specific element of the discourse, which characterizes Third World feminism, is prevalent in the discourse of Al-Qaws, for the movement is primarily working to raise awareness about the subjugation and resistance in the local context of Palestine and Israel.

In an online resource published following the demonstrations of May 2021, Al-Qaws (2021) stated that "in a settler colonial context, no clear line can be drawn where colonialism ends and patriarchal violence begins. The fight against patriarchy and sexual oppression is intertwined with the fight against settler-colonialism and capitalism." The intersectional approach in the statement cannot be mistaken, since the mission of the movement is based on multidimensional, multitargeted struggle. The fact that no line can be drawn between colonial violence and patriarchal violence hints tortuously to the inseparability, complicity, and interdependency of the two oppressive structures.

In addition, the fight against strategies of pinkwashing is among the primary undertakings of the organization. Pinkwashing, the statement declares, "is a form of colonial violence" that weaponizes queer experiences to justify the colonial agenda on the one hand, and to promote narratives that estrange queer Palestinians from their native community on the other (Al-Qaws 2021). The Israeli efforts to present the country as gay-friendly emerge as part of a larger campaign that aims to cover up the human rights violation record that has been accumulating, and that recently became hard to conceal. The inclusion of homosexual subjects in the occupation army, for example, is one example of these efforts, and it does imply progress and inclusion. However, "for Palestinians the sexuality of the soldier at a checkpoint makes little difference," since all of them "wield the same guns, wear the same boots, and maintain the same colonial regime" (Al-Qaws 2020).

The organization elaborates on the intricacies and repercussions of pinkwashing, which is viewed as more than a mere strategy of propaganda. The presentation and promotion of Israel as gay-friendly implies that Palestinians—and Arabs more broadly—are the contrary in the binary opposition (Al-Qaws 2020). This enforces the belief that Palestinian society is essentially regressive, primitive, and unworthy of international solidarity, particularly given that support of Palestine is in principle advocated by the same progressive segments that equally advocate feminism and queer liberation. This categorization draws on the colonial, Orientalist discourse that has always degraded and silenced the Palestinian narrative.

Furthermore, tactics of pinkwashing target Palestinian communities "internally and psychologically" by imposing the idea that sexual diversity is foreign, colonial, and unnatural to the native culture (Al-Qaws 2020). As established in postcolonial studies, colonial values are often naturally internalized by native populations. Accordingly, queer subjects are estranged as anomalous, and queer liberation is excluded as colonial and alien. It further implies that a Palestinian cannot be queer, and a queer subject cannot be Palestinian, which forces queer subjects to relinquish a part of their identity for the sake of maintaining another. Moreover, pink-washing is problematic because it promotes the idea that the only form of liberation available for queer Palestinians is personal liberation, for only by escaping the patriarchal community is it possible to survive. This inevitably promotes the false belief that certain cultures are essentially unalterable, and therefore efforts for collective queer liberation are made to seem use-less. Significantly, queer individuals are not protected from colonial vio-lence, since the "fantasy of Israeli humanitarianism falls apart as soon as the colonial situation is taken into account" (Al-Qaws 2020). The expres-sion "there is no 'pink door' in the apartheid wall" indicates the unavail-ability of salvage for queer Palestinians as long as ethnic apartheid is practiced.

Naturally, the fight against pinkwashing has been criticized by several observers. Karin Stögner (2019: 104) argues, for instance, that "only by accusing Israel of pinkwashing is it possible for a feminist to avoid focusing on how gender and sexual rights are systematically violated in the Palesti-nian territories, by the Palestinian National Authority, by Hamas and Islamic Jihad, and by Islamic communities and their terror of virtue." But addressing Native patriarchal and homophobic violations is not avoided by organizations like Al-Qaws; on the contrary, reforming the Native culture and demanding gender and sexual equality is at the heart of their work. The principal aim of current feminist trends is to tackle all systems of oppres-sion, whether colonial or Native.

### The Palestinian Feminist Collective

In 2021, the Palestinian Feminist Collective, a U.S.-based organization of Palestinian, Arab, and American feminists, was established to promote an agenda for Palestinian social and political liberation. The praxis of the col-lective, as stated on the official website, is directed by two analytical frame-works: "anti-colonialism and life-affirming decolonization."[4] The inspiration to initiate the movement comes from Palestinian, Arab, Black, Indigenous, and Third World women's movements that have fought and are still fighting racist, colonial, patriarchal structures of power, centering Palestinian feminism "as a liberatory philosophy" for a vision of a better world.

To mark Women's History Month in March 2021, the collective initiated its first public pledge. With the motto "Palestine is a feminist issue," the collective aimed to acknowledge, raise awareness of, and promote the Palestinian feminist narrative of struggle, while focusing on the urgency of the Palestinian anticolonial cause, particularly in relation to U.S.-American policies toward the region. The pledge expresses rejection of all "appropriations" of feminist and queer discourses, which have often been exploited to dehumanize Palestinians and invalidate the anticolonial struggle. The pledge is loaded with statements against Israeli settler colonialism, which aims to annihilate the existence of the Indigenous people. Accordingly, the pledge coincides with the recent shift of the Western political discourse, in which Israeli expansionist measures have come to be critically recognized as a form of settler colonialism.

The intersectional, transnational approach of the collective is clearly articulated in their commitment to fight against gender-based and sexual violence, settler colonialism, global capitalism, and political oppression in Palestine, on Turtle Island—highlighting the analogous struggle of Native Americans—and beyond. The pledge centers Palestine as the target of the collective, but it situates it within a broader antiracist, anticolonial, anticapitalist struggle, while it highlights the legacies of solidarity movements between marginalized communities, particularly Palestinians, Blacks, Indigenous populations, Third World feminist movements, the working class, and the LGBTQ community. The pledge expresses discontent with white, liberal feminism in the United States and the West more broadly, which has frequently weaponized feminist discourses against marginalized groups in the peripheries, while it failed to address the gendered violence of settler colonialism and global capitalism.

The pledge on the website announces six points that will ensure an intersectional and decolonial feminist vision: acknowledging that Palestinian liberation is a critical feminist issue; supporting Palestinian freedom of speech and political mobilization; rejecting the conflation of anti-Zionism and anti-Semitism; heeding the call for Boycott, Divestment, and Sanctions; divesting from militarism; and finally, demanding the end of American complicity in supporting apartheid in Palestine. According to Nada Elia (2021b), the pledge mainly affirms the "indivisibility of justice" based on the premise that "liberation cannot be complete unless all structural violence is ended," since oppressions inevitably overlap and interdepend on each other. A comprehensive liberatory approach, she affirms, is one that seeks to end oppression "from within, as well as without."

**Toward a New Palestinian Feminist Mobilization**

In contrast to the feminist strands studied by critics like Jad and Richter-Devroe, more recent feminist movements are different in focus and approach. Transnationalism is fundamental to the more recent models of feminist action, as they correspond to transnational feminist discourses that centralize cross-border solidarity and networks rather than localities. This is not achieved by discounting the local, but rather by connecting the local to the global, because systems of oppression are often connected with one another through the overarching system of global capitalism. Transnationalism can be detected by looking into the scope of the Palestinian Feminist Collective, as it encompasses the experiences of women from the Global North and South, with varying ethnic, national, cultural, and religious backgrounds. It positions the experiences of Palestinian women within the transnational scope of sexual and racial injustice. In doing so, it suggests that not only oppressions are intersectional and interdependent, but also that we can speak of the intersectionality and interdependence of movements of resistance. Similarly, Al-Qaws emerged at a time in which queer politics arose globally as an urgent case of justice. Therefore, the resistance waged by the organization against both pinkwashing as a colonial strategy in Israel and homophobia as an element of religious and cultural regression in Palestine is transnational in essence, as it is tangled with a broader global movement of emancipation, which Sarah Schulman (2012) refers to as the "Queer International." The organization's efforts to "situate pinkwashing within its broader settler-colonial context" and "to make connections to other forms of colonialism and gendered/sexual oppression" manifest the transnational stance it endorses (Al-Qaws 2020). Transnationalism is also to be indicated by the attitude toward the nation-state. Nationalism is never alluded to as a means of liberation. Although decolonization may and does include self-determination, it is not directly indicated that the nation-state in the conventional sense of the word is the form through which independence is to be carried out. While nationalism has historically dominated the anticolonial discourse in the Palestinian feminist movement, it recently ceased to be a central strategy or object. This may be chiefly due to the gendered nature of nationalism, but also, it may be a strategy of transnationalization. While, as argued earlier, transnational feminism is problematic to nations still fighting for self-determination, it is a more efficient approach toward injustices, because it situates local struggles on a larger, broader, global scale, and it empowers solidarity movements.

Another observable difference is the approach and mobilization of the movements. Former activism was grounded on and corresponded to the official political discourse, as it echoed the political demands of the ruling body, whether it was the Palestine Liberation Organization before 1993 or the Palestinian Authority afterward. Before 1993, the political program designated armed resistance as the strategy for liberation, which Palestinian women revolutionaries like Leila Khaled, Dalal Moghrabi, and countless other names endorsed through military affiliation to the various factions of the organization. After 1993, diplomacy was validated as the means toward liberation, which at this point shifted from the former ideal of liberating historic Palestine to the acceptance of a two-state solution. Feminist activism followed the lead, as the feminist movement was institutionalized as part of the newly formed government. Recent activism, however, has adopted a grassroots, independent, and nonaffiliated approach, as it noticeably eschews following the political trajectory stipulated by the authority, which has been hitherto adopting the diplomatic strategy, aiming for the moribund two-state solution. The current feminist movement is largely hostile to the official pseudo government, which is fundamentally complicit in facilitating gender-based violence through its unwillingness to reform the patriarchal and homophobic legal system. It is further viewed as reactionary in the anticolonial struggle, as it opposes any form of resistance, whether armed or popular, due to its ratification of diplomatic negotiations as the authorized political agenda, which is generally viewed as regressive among anticolonial progressives and radicals. Furthermore, the contemporary feminist movement has been more inclusive in that it endorses queer liberation as a fundamental element of struggle against colonialism, patriarchy, and heteronormativity. This echoes Puar's argument that acceptance of queer rights constitutes a premise for legitimacy within the current global system, but it also hints at the development of Palestinian feminism into a more inclusive and nondiscriminatory movement that is responsive to global and local transformations.

## Conclusion

This article has illustrated that intersectionality as a critical framework needs to be expanded to include the ways in which various forms of racism and sexism interact with one another within the broader matrix of domination. Interdependence as a framework appears to be a more comprehensive theoretical tool, as it explains how structures of power can function in a complementary, interdependent manner. As demonstrated, male dominance is empowered by the persistence of settler colonialism, as Native cultures tend to condemn progress and change while under the threat of colonial annihilation. In the same vein, colonial discourse is corroborated through taking advantage of patriarchal, homophobic, and regressive elements in the Native culture. The analysis shows that prioritizing one struggle over the other is problematic. Any attempts at targeting colonial violence without fighting internal gender inequality proves futile, for it makes little to no difference for the Native woman whether oppression is exerted by an abusive partner at home or a heavily armed soldier at a military checkpoint. Likewise, targeting patriarchy without taking into account the wider colonial context is ineffective in that such an approach depoliticizes the highly politicized setting, in which internal gender dynamics are unavoidably restructured by colonial hegemony. Further research is required to empirically assess the theoretical observations made in this article. Yet, the examples of feminist mobilization examined substantiate that not just struggle, but also resistance is intersectional, inseparable, complex, and transnational. As Collins (2000: 203) writes, "If power as domination is organized and operates via intersecting oppressions, then resistance must show comparable complexity." The evolution, nuances, and threads of the Palestinian anticolonial, feminist movement is but an exemplar of this complexity, the particulars of which have the potential to contribute immensely to the analytical framework of intersectionality.

...........................................................................................................

**Eman Alasah** is a PhD researcher in postcolonial and literary studies at Northumbria University Newcastle. Her work focuses on contemporary Palestinian autobiographical and life writings within the framework of settler colonialism.

**Notes**

1   Al-Qaws, "About Us," http://alqaws.org/about-us (accessed July 20, 2021).
2   Al-Qaws, "About Us," http://alqaws.org/about-us (accessed July 20, 2021).
3   Al-Qaws, "About Us," http://alqaws.org/about-us (accessed July 22, 2021).
4   Palestinian Feminist Collective, https://actionnetwork.org/groups/palestinian -feminist-collective (accessed July 23, 2021).

**Works Cited**

Abu-Lughod, Lila. 2002. "Do Muslim Women Really Need Saving? Anthropological Reflections on Cultural Relativism and Its Others." *American Anthropologist* 104, no. 3: 783–90.

Al-Qaws. 2020. "Beyond Propaganda: Pinkwashing as Colonial Violence." *Al-Qaws*, October 18.

Al-Qaws. 2021. "Queer Liberation and Palestine." *Al-Qaws*, May 26.

Atshan, Sa'ed. 2020. *Queer Palestine and the Empire of Critique.* Stanford, CA: Stanford University Press.

B'tselem. 2021. "Apartheid." *B'tselem*, January 12. https://www.btselem.org/apartheid.

Cho, Sumi, Kimberlé Williams Crenshaw, and Leslie McCall. 2013. "Toward a Field of Intersectionality Studies: Theory, Applications, and Praxis." *Signs* 38, no. 4: 785–810.

Collins, Patricia Hill. 2000. *Black Feminist Thought: Knowledge, Consciousness, and the Politics of Empowerment.* London: Routledge.

Crenshaw, Kimberlé. 1991. "Mapping the Margins: Intersectionality, Identity Politics, and Violence against Women of Color." *Stanford Law Review* 43, no. 6: 1241–99.

Dana, Karam, and Hannah Walker. 2015. "Invisible Disasters: The Effects of Israeli Occupation on Palestinian Gender Roles." *Contemporary Arab Affairs* 8, no. 4: 488–504.

Davis, Angela. 2016. *Freedom Is a Constant Struggle: Ferguson, Palestine, and the Foundations of a Movement.* Chicago: Haymarket.

Elia, Nada. 2021a. "How Palestine Is a Critical Feminist Issue." *Middle East Eye*, March 25.

Elia, Nada. 2021b. "Israel-Palestine: How Subcontracting the Occupation Fuels Gendered Violence." *Middle East Eye*, July 2.

Gouws, Amanda. 2017. "Feminist Intersectionality and the Matrix of Domination in South Africa." *Agenda* 31, no. 1: 19–27.

Griffiths, Mark, and Jemima Repo. 2021. "Women and Checkpoints in Palestine." *Security Dialogue* 52, no. 3: 249–65.

Hasso, Frances S. 1998. "The 'Women's Front': Nationalism, Feminism, and Modernity in Palestine." *Gender and Society* 12, no. 4: 441–65.

Healy, Róisín, and Enrico Dal Lago. 2014. *The Shadow of Colonialism on Europe's Modern Past.* New York: Palgrave Macmillan.

Herr, Ranjoo Seodu. 2014. "Reclaiming Third World Feminism; or, Why Transnational Feminism Needs Third World Feminism." *Meridians* 12, no. 1: 1–30.

Human Rights Watch. 2021. "A Threshold Crossed: Israeli Authorities and the Crimes of Apartheid and Persecution." *Human Rights Watch*, April 27.

Jad, Islah. 2018. *Palestinian Women's Activism: Nationalism, Secularism, Islamism.* Syracuse, NY: Syracuse University Press.

Lazreg, Marnia. 1990. "Gender and Politics in Algeria: Unraveling the Religious Paradigm." *Signs* 15, no. 4: 755–80.

Papantonopoulou, Saffo. 2014. "'Even a Freak Like You Would Be Safe in Tel Aviv': Transgender Subjects, Wounded Attachments, and the Zionist Economy of Gratitude." *Women's Studies Quarterly* 42, nos. 1–2: 278–93.

Puar, Jasbir. 2007. *Terrorist Assemblages: Homonationalism in Queer Times.* Durham, NC: Duke University Press.

Puar, Jasbir. 2013. "Rethinking Homonationalism." *International Journal of Middle East Studies* 45, no. 2: 336–39.

Richter-Devroe, Sophie. 2008. "Gender, Culture, and Conflict Resolution in Palestine." *Journal of Middle East Women's Studies* 4, no. 2: 30–59.

Richter-Devroe, Sophie. 2018. *Women's Political Activism in Palestine: Peacebuilding, Resistance, and Survival.* Champaign: University of Illinois Press.

Saliba, Therese. 2000. "Arab Feminism at the Millennium." *Signs* 25, no. 4: 1087–92.

Sayigh, Rosemary. 2007. "Product and Producer of Palestinian History: Stereotypes of 'Self' in Camp Women's Life Stories." *Journal of Middle East Women's Studies* 3, no. 1: 86–105.

Schulman, Sarah. 2011. "Israel and Pinkwashing." *New York Times*, November 22.

Schulman, Sarah. 2012. *Israel/Palestine and the Queer International.* Durham, NC: Duke University Press.

Shalhoub-Kevorkian, Nadera. 2005. "Voice Therapy for Women Aligned with Political Prisoners: A Case Study of Trauma among Palestinian Women in the Second Intifada." *Social Service Review* 79, no. 2: 322–43.

Shalhoub-Kevorkian, Nadera. 2014. "Palestinian Feminist Critique and the Physics of Power: Feminists between Thought and Practice." *Feminists@law* 4, no. 1: 1–18.

Shalhoub-Kevorkian, Nadera, and Suhad Daher-Nashef. 2013. "Femicide and Colonization: Between the Politics of Exclusion and the Culture of Control." *Violence against Women* 19, no. 3: 295–315.

Spivak, Gayatri. 1993. "Can the Subaltern Speak?" In *Colonial Discourse and Post-colonial Theory: A Reader*, edited by Patrick Williams and Laura Chrisman, 66–111. Hemel Hempstead, Hertfordshire: Harvester.

Stögner, Karin. 2019. "New Challenges in Feminism: Intersectionality, Critical Theory, and Anti-Zionism." In *Anti-Zionism and Antisemitism: The Dynamics of Delegitimization*, edited by Alvin H. Rosenfeld, 84–112. Bloomington, IN: Indiana University Press.

Wolfe, Patrick. 2006. "Settler Colonialism and the Elimination of the Native." *Journal of Genocide Research* 8, no. 4: 387–409.

Ina Knobblock

........................................................................

# "A Rape of the Earth"
## Sámi Feminists against Mines

Abstract: This article is a Sámi feminist analysis of large-scale resource extraction in Sábme, the transnational Sámi territory spanning northern Fenno-Scandinavia and the Murmansk peninsula. Specifically, it centers on the mining of Indigenous land within the borders of the Swedish nation-state to explore the knowledge evolving from Sámi feminists engaged in the anti-mining struggle. Here, I argue that Indigenous epistemes—that is, the fore-grounding of relationality and interdependency between land, humans, nonhuman beings, and the natural environment—are foundational to the research participants' struggles against mining in Sábme. From within a Sámi knowledge system, mining entails fracturing the relational web of connection. Consequently, mining represents a multigenerational threat against the survival of Sámi body lands and lifeworlds.

## Introduction

Without the inclusion of Indigenous women's and LGBTQ2s' knowledge, "the academy cannot have a full understanding of colonialism as a process nor can it fully understand Indigenous resurgence" (Simpson 2017: 31). As part of the decolonization of the feminist academia, the Sámi feminist scholar Rauna Kuokkanen argues for expanding Nordic feminist theoretical and conceptual frames to include the impact of structural violence on Sámi women's lives. A central area of concern is the dispossession of Sámi land through Nordic settler colonial state policies and transnational capital operating on Sámi land. A vital issue is the ongoing industrial exploitation of Sábme,[1] the transnational Sámi territory spanning northern

MERIDIANS · feminism, race, transnationalism   23:1 April 2024
DOI: 10.1215/15366936-10927016 © 2024 Smith College

Fenno-Scandinavia and the Murmansk peninsula (Knobblock and Kuok-kanen 2015: 277–79; see also Kuokkanen 2019: 188–91, 231).

Between 2014 and 2017, I met with fourteen other Sámi feminists for conversations focused on learning and sharing feminist analyses and experiences. Specifically, these conversations addressed feminism as articulated, enacted, and negotiated from Sámi locations. Indeed, the extraction of natural resources, especially minerals, on Sámi land was a central topic, particularly in Swedish Sábme. All the people I met had opinions about mining, and many were Sámi women and nonbinary people serving as spokespersons and organizers protesting the mines as well as artists and other protesters.

In this article, I refer to four conversations with women engaged in the anti-mining protests as activists or supporters of the protests. They all self-identify as Sámi, as feminists, and grew up in the Swedish nation-state. I have chosen these conversations as these dialogues are particularly illustrative of the points I wish to make. To acknowledge their role in the anti-mining struggle, I also include a short analysis of the Sámi artist and anti-mining activist Ti/Mimie[2] Märak's spoken-word poem "What Local People," which was performed at the Gállok protest camp in 2013. This article's main aim is to explore the knowledge evolving from the research participants' analyses and experiences and from Märak's poetry. Specifically, this article addresses two questions from the perspectives and locations of Sámi feminists: What does mining mean and entail? How can the resistance to mines be conceptualized and understood?

Recently, a large amount of research in Sweden has focused on mining in Sábme (e.g., Blåhed and San Sebastián 2021; Cocq 2014; Nachet, Beckett, and MacNeil 2021; Persson, Harnesk, and Islar 2017; Raitio, Allard, and Lawrence 2020; and Sehlin MacNeil 2017). However, these valuable contributions have not specifically centered the narratives of Sámi women and nonbinary people.[3] An exception is Moa Sandström's (2020) dissertation, "Dekoloniseringskonst: Artivism i 2010-talets Sápmi" ("Decolonizing Artivism in Contemporary Sápmi"). Sandström collaborates with Ti/Mimie Märak and analyzes intersecting Indigenous, feminist, and queer subjectivities as spaces of decolonial resistance and critique (Sandström 2020: 61–63, 99–104, 174–88).

Complementing Sandström, my work adds to the growing field of Sámi feminist scholarship (e.g., Dankertsen 2020; Finbog 2020; Öhman 2017; Kuokkanen 2021). This intervention is located within broader Indigenous and decolonial intellectual and political movements. Arguing for the existence of ontological and epistemic pluralities, these interventions promote Indigenous resurgence and decolonial (re)imaginations of the world(s) (Simpson 2017; Tlostanova, Thapar-Björkert, and Knobblock 2019).[4]

## Mining in Sábme: An Overview

Mining on Sámi land has deep historical roots in Sweden. In the early modern period, starting in the seventeenth century, several metal works and mines were established. Carl-Gösta Ojala and Jonas M. Nordin (2015: 11) argue that "the early modern metal industries in Sápmi were part of a colonial discourse where the Sámi and their land, Sápmi, were regarded as assets for the Swedish Crown and industrialists supported by it." A notable example is the mine in Násavárre/Nasafjäll, where local Sámi were used as forced labor, coerced into transporting ore and other materials needed for mining (Ojala and Nordin 2015: 11–12).[5] Around the turn of the twentieth century, technological and logistical inventions enabled the extraction of the vast ore deposits in Giron/Kiruna and Málmmavárre/Malmberget. Thus, the colonial extractive process intensified with the development of large-scale mining complexes. Today, the state-owned mining company LKAB is Europe's largest iron ore producer. The mining industry is regarded as vital for economic growth and job creation, especially in the Northern regions (Ojala and Nordin 2015: 10–12; Sehlin MacNeil 2017: 8–10).

In the late twentieth century, fundamental changes were made to Swedish mining legislations to create a more coherent framework that would increase prospecting (Government of Sweden 1989, 1992). The reforms included the abandonment of the state's half-share of mining concessions, royalty fees at only 2 percent, and, in alignment with the Treaty of Rome, the removal of the requirement of Swedish citizenship for prospecting. In addition, the general corporate tax was lowered to 30 percent (Government of Sweden 1989). Together with a global rise in mineral prices, these reforms resulted in a "Swedish mining boom" (Anshelm and Haikola 2018: 9–11; Persson, Harnesk, and Islar 2017: 23).

In 2013, Sámi and environmental activists formed a coalition to protect the area of Gállok/Kallak, which is outside the municipality of Jåhkåmåhkke/Jokkmokk, just north of the Arctic Circle. Land protectors argue that the prospecting undertaken by the British company Beowulf Mining ignores the presence of Indigenous people in the area, especially the needs of the reindeer herding community Jåhkågasska tjiellde. Activists have blocked roads to stop exploration work in Gállok, demonstrated in Stockholm and other parts of Sweden, and initiated a petition demanding that the government prohibit mining in Gállok (Gruvfritt Jokkmokk 2021). Despite considerable protests, the Swedish government decided to grant the company Jokkmokk Iron Mines AB an exploitation concession for Gállok/Kallak in March 2022 (Government of Sweden 2022).

In addition to criticizing mining companies' discourses and actions, anti-mining activists criticize the Swedish state's position, especially the Swedish Minerals Act and its corresponding laws and regulations. They claim that the state's deregulation of the mining industry has significantly increased the pressure on Sábme and therefore increased the detrimental effects of extractive activities (Cocq 2014; Nachet, Beckett, and MacNeil 2021; Persson, Harnesk, and Islar 2017). For example, the Sámi anti-mining activist Marie Persson Njajta (2014), founder of the network Stop the Mine in Rönnbäck, makes the following observation:

> The current mineral legislation and mineral politics actuate increased exploitation—without reflection or concern for the coming generations. It is exploitation without protection for our children's and grandchildren's natural environment, health, land, water, and local primary produce, exploitation that doesn't contribute to viable local communities, funds for sanitation, or any substantial contribution to the state treasury. The mineral legislation also effectuates the colonization of the Sámi people. (my translation)

Mining, hydropower, forestry, and wind power produce "cumulative effects" (Larsen, Stinnerbom, and Wik-Karlsson 2017), whose combined negative impacts severely affect Sábme. Centrally, extractive industries have and continue to be significant contributors to the dispossession of Indigenous lands in Sweden (Lawrence 2014; Nachet, Beckett, and MacNeil 2021; Össbo 2021). Mining entails contamination of land and waterways, disrupting the Sámi traditional occupation of reindeer herding, and, concurrently, fragmenting Sámi lifeworlds, including land-based knowledge, histories, and identities (Cocq 2014; Sehlin MacNeil 2017: 8–10). The stress Sámi people experience, especially in reindeer herding communities, gives rise to adverse health effects (Blåhed and San Sebastián 2021). Furthermore, the bureaucratic and legal systems limit the possibilities for Sámi participation and influence in the mining permitting processes (Raitio, Allard, and Lawrence 2020).

## Relationality, Body Land, and Settler Colonial Erasure

Indigenous feminisms theorize colonial structures of domination and envision decolonial alternatives and futures, which ultimately critically reimagine the world. A core value is relationality, a foundational premise within Indigenous epistemes (Green 2007; Nickel and Fehr 2020; Suzack et al. 2010). Kuokkanen (2007b: 57; see also Kuokkanen 2017: 314) conceptualizes *episteme* as a "system of knowledge, way of thinking, worldview or traditional philosophy."

> The world as a whole comprises an infinite web of relationships, which extend and are incorporated into the entire social condition of the individual. Social ties apply to everyone and everything, including the land, which is considered a living, conscious entity. People are related to their physical and natural surroundings through their genealogies, their oral traditions, and their personal and collective experiences with certain locations. (Kuokkanen 2007b: 32)

As the quotation shows, Indigenous epistemes advance an interconnectedness between land, nature, and people, which assumes specific social, cultural, and ecological responsibilities (Kuokkanen 2007b: 32–33; see also Simpson 2017: 22–25; Finbog 2020: 14; Moreton-Robinson 2013: 338; Nilsson 2021: 15–18, 210–12). Everything is constituted in a relational sense, including the land, which is "a physical and spiritual entity of which humans are one part" (Kuokkanen 2007b: 33), and therefore relationality "requires attentiveness and a conscious commitment to uphold the act of being in relation with the non-human world and each other" (Altamirano-Jiménez 2020: 323).

In Abya Yala,[6] Indigenous feminists developed the notion of *body land* (*Cuerpo-Territorio*) to center relationality. Body land describes an "ontological relation, a continuum that does not separate human beings from territory and other beings" (Altamirano-Jiménez 2021: 218). However, body land is also a political statement encompassing manifold meanings in the struggle against the subjugation of Indigenous territories and bodies as it connects the violence done to the land and nonhuman entities and beings with the violence done to Indigenous communal and individual bodies. Together, these violent acts pose a multigenerational threat against Indigenous life (Altamirano-Jiménez 2021, 2020; Erpel 2018).

The notions of relationality and body land fundamentally differ from settler colonial and capitalist frameworks where land is primarily seen as a resource to possess and exploit for human benefit. Concurrently, Indigenous people are racialized as primitive Others on the brink of extinction, a classification that legitimizes and enables settler colonial ascendancy on Indigenous land (Simpson 2017: 75; Finbog 2020: 62). Using the logic of elimination, Patrick Wolfe (2006) captures the need for settler nations to disappear Indigenous peoples from the territory and therefore erase their historical and collective claim on the land. Settler states can enact such disappearance in different ways, such as through direct violence or the gradual undermining of Indigenous people's identities and rights.

A poignant example of Swedish eliminatory policy is the forced relocations of Sámi reindeer herders in the early twentieth century. After the adoption of the Reindeer Grazing Convention of 1919 between Sweden and Norway, Sámi reindeer herders from the northern Norrbotten county were closed off from their traditional pasturelands in northern Norway and the Swedish authorities forced them to relocate south. From the perspective of the Swedish and Norwegian states, the measure intended to decrease the impact of reindeer herding on the land, favoring the needs of farming and the settler agricultural communities (Lantto and Mörkenstam 2008: 31). However, for the relocated Sámi herders, the policy disconnected them from their traditional lands and practices, creating identity loss and intergenerational trauma (Labba 2020).

The Sámi archaeologist and museologist Liisa-Rávná Finbog argues that land dispossession is inextricably linked to Indigenous epistemicide, "the destruction of the knowledge and cultures of these populations, of their memories and ancestral links and their manner of relating to others and to nature" (Sousa Santos quoted in Finbog 2020: 21). Similarly, Kuokkanen (2007b: 1, 124) argues that the intertwined systems of colonialism, modernity, capitalism, and patriarchy have had a profound effect on Indigenous epistemes and their conceptualization of the life and land as a relationship in the form of erasure, silencing, or making its interrelated cultural and social practices appear backward or impossible. Relatedly, as pointed out by the Binizaá (Zapotec) scholar Isabel Altamirano-Jiménez (2020, 2021), today settler colonial states increasingly transfer their power to transnational corporations, which enable corporate interventions on Indigenous land. Arguably, as further discussed in my article's analytical section, this situation applies to the area of Gállok, where the British company Beowulf Mining operates with the support of the Swedish state's mining policies.

## Learning in Conversation

Within Indigenous methodologies, knowledge is conceptualized as a relational, collaborative, and situated process characterized by learning, responsiveness, and answerability (Simpson 2017: 16–17, 27–31; Kovach 2009: 14; Kuokkanen 2017; Smith 2012). Kim TallBear (2017: 82) argues for a "co-constitution" of knowledge with communities and their intellectual and political projects, which people may or may not be part of and invested in. However, equally important is "speaking in faith." Speaking in faith implies recognizing that perfect representation is always impossible, as there is an inherent incompleteness in all positions. To me, TallBear's methodology deeply recognizes relatedness and diversity within and between variously situated Indigenous peoples (cf. Driskill et al. 2011: 8).

I write as a Sámi-identified woman whose family originates from Málmmavárre/Malmberget, a dying mining town located on caved-in ground. Affected by the Swedish colonial state's assimilatory policies (cf. Öhman 2021), my family members have vacillated between recognition and denial of Sámi belonging. My specific situatedness from which I research enables me to see, reach, and analyze some social aspects relevant to the people participating in my research. However, other elements and interpretations might escape my notice. This inevitable situation does not render my analysis invalid, but it does make it inevitably partial.

Inspired by the working methods of Indigenous and Sámi feminists (Beads and Kuokkanen 2007; Helander-Renvall and Kailo 1998), my primary way to co-constitute knowledge (TallBear 2017: 83) is through conversations focused on learning and sharing Sámi feminist analyses and experiences. Central to my approach is treating all participants as knowledgeable subjects by softening or challenging the binary between researcher and researched, or in TallBear's (2017: 80) words, "the binary . . . between knowing inquirer and those who are considered to be the resources or grounds for knowledge production." I see participants in my projects as colleagues, peers, or mentors and, accordingly, all conversations emphasize participants' views, standpoints, and engagements.

The four conversations I cite have been translated from Swedish to English and slightly edited for clarity. After deliberation with the participants (cf. Svalastog and Eriksson 2010: 5), I assigned the participants pseudonyms to protect their privacy. They have also had the opportunity to read and comment on the transcripts and a nearly completed version of the article. Of course, my choice of illustrations and analyses does not cover the full complexity of the arguments made by each participant, and the dialogues do not represent all Sámi feminists' positions or speak for an authentic "we." My aim is not to reproduce racialized differences but to illuminate and explore excluded knowledge systems within feminist theory, particularly in the Nordic context.

### Anti-mining Struggle: Gender, Interconnectedness, and the Survival of Sámi Land and Life

The following excerpts are from my conversations with Sámi feminists engaged in the anti-mining struggle. The participants are quoted at length as I want to give ample space for their voices. Their thinking is interwoven with my analytical reflections in dialogue with select writings from Indigenous feminist theory centered around relationality, body land, and settler colonial erasure.

#### "Whatever You Do, It Will Affect Nature"

All participants referred to their relationship with the land when I asked them about their reasons to resist the mines in Sábme. Sagka, for example, explains its importance for her identity as Sámi:

> It would have been incredibly difficult to develop my Sámi identity without the land. There are so many connections to it, all the stories the land in my area carries and the knowledge and things I've learned that have made me who I am. . . . And the feeling of possibility to pass on what you have and have received over the generations. (conversation with author, 2014)

For Sagka, the land is central to her identity as Sámi. She is connected to the land through the stories and knowledge of the land passed down to her from previous generations. Accordingly, the land is equally central to conveying this identity to future generations. Hence, her comment is illustrative of a Sámi relational episteme (cf. Kuokkanen 2007b, 2017) where land and identity are woven intergenerationally.

Sagka further emphasizes the centrality of continuity concerning Sámi women's and mothers' engagement in the mining issue. Below she explores reasons for their engagement with regard to motherhood:

> I believe it becomes incredibly apparent [when you have become a mother]. Now you are in the position of having this person and this responsibility to do many things that are so hard to do under the present

circumstances. I know that it will be a struggle to give this small person the opportunity to learn its mother tongue, . . . in the same way as it is with the land. And everything from the fact that the child should not eat food contaminated by leaking mines and that we are one of the last remaining places where you can drink surface water and that we have edible wild animals that are good for your health, to the fact that you should be able to transmit that knowledge and those abilities to future generations. Naturally, it is a wake-up call. . . . So many women and mothers of small children have taken to the barricades and worked very hard, for example, in the mining issue. (conversation with author, 2014)

Becoming a mother, Sagka believes, motivates many women to defend their land and society for the sake of their children and the future of their culture. She connects the activism of mothers with these women's feelings of responsibility for their children and the protection and reproduction of their environments. Sagka's analysis suggests that motherhood—a deeply embodied experience for many people—spurs women to defend the Sámi body land against exploitation (cf. Altamirano-Jimenéz 2020, 2021). In protecting the land against intrusion, exploitation, and pollution, they care for their children, their children's bodies and, ultimately, for the futures of interlinked and sovereign Sámi body lands.

In response to my question regarding the relationship between feminism and anti-mining activism, Sagka continued by reflecting on feminism as an environmental issue:

> **Ina:** I have reflected that so many people I have talked to concerning feminist issues also have a strong engagement in mining issues.
> **Sagka:** Yes. I assume that if you are attentive to injustices, there are two issues that you cannot ignore. . . . In both cases, it is apparent. . . . Partly, it is this old, hackneyed thing that all issues are environmental issues. So it is probably very easy to think of the environmental issue as something very intimate.
> **Ina:** Please tell me more about how you think about this.
> **Sagka:** To me, it is so apparent if you take it a step further since the environment is such a precondition for all that we do. It is such a fundamental precondition for being a Sámi, to me at least. . . . So to stand firm on something, it must be there as a basis, and everything you do comes back to that. The essential thing in life that we know is that everything circulates. So whatever you do, it will affect nature. You may as well consider it since that

is how it will be. And that kind of awareness of things, I think, makes you prioritize differently sometimes. In that sense, feminism also becomes an environmental issue. And it is not such a big step to take in many ways, at least not when you consider it in terms of percentages of how the world is divided and how people act out of power or gender or whatever it may be. It is connected. (conversation with author, 2014)

As I understand her, Sagka sees the environment as fundamental to all aspects of life, including feminism, and sees nature and gender as interconnected nodes where injustice and inequality are enacted and made visible. The natural and social worlds are, within a relational worldview, not separate spheres but always interconnected. Accordingly, because social ties exist with everything, including the land (cf. Kuokkanen 2007b: 32), anti-mining activism and feminism are connected. Likewise, relations of domination are interwoven as inequalities in one area connected to disparities in other areas.

Sagka continues by observing how different bodies are positioned differently within intersecting power relations. Describing the stark difference between the mining advocates and their adversaries, she says, "It is so fascinating with the mining issue that so many older white men from a certain class are coming and on the other side of the barricade stands a group of Sámi mothers of small children" (conversation with author, 2014). She describes the subjects in the conflict in terms of gender, race, class, and location. The mining proponents represent masculinity, whiteness, and privilege. They are met by resistance from activists positioned as Indigenous, as women, and often as mothers.

For Sire, another participant in my research project, women's presence in anti-mining activism relates to the history of Sámi women's political participation. In our conversation in 2014, Sire told me that Sámi women asked themselves how they could take on a vital role in the Gállok resistance as they did in the Alta struggle. Indeed, Sámi feminist activism in tandem with environmental struggles has a long history. In the 1970s and 1980s, activists mobilized against the Norwegian government's plan to construct a large hydroelectric dam in the Alta River. Women had a central role as intellectuals, artists, and participants in acts of civil disobedience. For example, in February 1981, fourteen Sámi women occupied the office of Norwegian Prime Minister Gro Harlem Brundtland as part of the struggle to keep the Alta River free flowing (Halsaa 2020: 129–31). Starting from their intersectional realities, female activists eventually came to mobilize expressly as Sámi women. Eventually, the Sáráhkká[7] (Sámi Women's Organization) and the Sámi Nisson Forum[8] were established in Girón (Kiruna) in 1988 and Kárášjohka (Karasjok) in 1993, respectively. The Sáráhkká aims to promote Sámi women's interests, and the Sámi Nisson Forum aims to promote gender equality in Sábme (Knobblock 2022: 537).

According to Sire, the organization of reindeer husbandry necessitates that women take a central role in the struggle against mines:

> **Sire:** I believe the men have their hands full, taking care of the animals. They are wholly occupied with trying to find pasture for the reindeer.
> **Ina:** So then women take on this role?
> **Sire:** I believe that there is no time when you are out the whole day. But when you're not out the entire day, there is time. Focus.
> **Ina:** So you share the responsibility but in different ways?
> **Sire:** Yes, and I believe it is imperative that we who are not with the reindeer have to take on responsibility. We must because we can't think that the reindeer herders can take on this fight. They have to take care of the animals. The animals are the priority. (conversation with author, 2014)

Sire describes how the men take primary responsibility for the labor attached to reindeer husbandry, and the women take primary responsibility for the work involved in social and political activities. I would not interpret this as the typical gendered division of labor but rather as a system of gendered complementarity where men and women assume different but complementary roles in the work for the continuation of reindeer husbandry and the survival of the Sámi as an Indigenous people (cf. Kuokkanen 2007a: 74).

The historian Anna-Lill Ledman forwards a similar line of reasoning. She analyzes Sámi women's paid labor and economic contributions as a strategy to ensure the continuation of reindeer herding in their families (Ledman 2012: 117). Importantly, in another part of our conversation, Sire discusses the activities of full-time women reindeer herders. They occupy the same roles as men and therefore have the same responsibilities for the care of the animals.

Consequently, irrespective of working as full-time reindeer herders or shouldering the multiple responsibilities of care work, part-time work within reindeer husbandry, paid labor, and activism, Sámi women's involvement is substantial. However, the Swedish Reindeer Grazing Act of

1971 centers on the frequently male, active reindeer herder member in the
Sámi village (Amft 1998: 2000). Accordingly, men are positioned as reindeer husbandry's central subjects, whereas the criticality of women's contributions to reindeer husbandry and Sámi lifeworlds is downplayed.

Whether mothers or members of families involved in reindeer husbandry,
women's relationships to the land, their families, and their people function
as mobilizing factors for active participation within the collective struggle for
Sámi survival. In other words, as both Sagka and Sire reiterated, women's
anti-mining activism is predicated on a wish to reproduce Sámi relationships with the land through the transfer of knowledge over generations
and the protection of the lands necessary for reindeer husbandry.

*"A Rape of the Earth"*
Biret views the world as an interdependent whole, which is threatened by
mining and its unforeseeable long-term consequences. She traces the
impacts of mining through the interconnected levels of people, place, and
the earth: "It [the establishment of mines] is total consumption. It is a rape
of the earth. Of us. Because we are all one with everything, and we don't
know what will happen. What happens if we dig deep holes? Put in a larger
perspective, what happens with the land, the places, and the balance for
the earth and everything else?" (conversation with author, 2014). Biret's
descriptions of the mining as "total consumption" and "a rape of the
earth" allude to a consumer attitude toward nature and severe gendered
violence. This connection, I argue, is akin to the notion of the body land,
which captures the connection between violence against nature and violence against Indigenous people (cf. Altamirano-Jiménez 2020, 2021).
In other words, the consequences of the violence done to the land are felt by
the land and nonhuman beings as well as by Indigenous bodies, who are
interconnected with the land.

A vital context to Biret's quote is Indigenous peoples' experiences of
gendered and sexualized violence in settler colonial contexts. While men can
be raped, sexual assault and rape are particularly gendered acts of violence
disproportionately experienced by women and nonbinary people in
Indigenous communities. The reasons behind and consequences of gendered and sexual violence are complex, especially as they intersect with
colonial frameworks and their production of social and economic vulnerabilities. A significant need for further research has been identified,
especially in the Sámi context (Kuokkanen 2019: 179–216). However, in

Norway, the statistical survey Saminor II showed that both Sámi women and men report higher exposure to interpersonal violence than non-Sámi individuals. The prevalence of violence was highest among Sámi women (Eriksen et al. 2015, 2021).

Possibly, women and nonbinary people's experiences of living in bodies exposed to gendered and sexual violence adds another dimension of understanding for the land as a living entity penetrated and violated by extractivist interventions. Put differently, Biret's comparison between mining and rape resonates with Indigenous gendered experiences of embodying body lands whose boundaries are continually overstepped and violated.

Sire also discusses the grave consequences of disrupting the relationship with the land and the natural environment. However, she equates this disruption with death:

> **Sire:** If there were to be a mine in Gállok, . . . if we can't stop the exploitation happening and that were to happen [*silence*], then we would die. And I do not believe anything else.
>
> **Ina:** So would you describe the establishment of mines as a threat against Sámi existence?
>
> **Sire:** Yes! That is why it is so essential for me to be engaged. . . .
>
> **Ina:** Is this also connected to your feeling for the land?
>
> **Sire:** Yes! And for me, it is connected to . . . our well-being is dependent [*silence*]. We die with the land. And that is what is happening. . . . I see no way for us to separate ourselves from the land. . . . And when the land is not well, and we are not separated from it, then they are digging in us. . . . And we die. (conversation with author, 2014)

As her comments show, mining is a source of great sadness for Sire. It is not that mining only breaks the Sámi's connection to the land, because according to Sire, the land and its people are inseparable. The consequence of industrial exploitation of the land is the inevitable destruction of the people, who will "die with the land." Sire's analysis cannot solely be understood on a metaphoric level. As critical settler colonial scholarship shows, settler colonial ascendancy depends on forms of Indigenous erasure, either physically or as an epistemicide that undermines Indigenous claims to the land (Wolfe 2006; Finbog 2020: 21).

Indeed, fundamentally, Indigenous relational epistemes speak to the interconnection of Indigenous bodies and lands; physically, culturally, and epistemically. Hence, relationality captures deeply embodied lived experience that makes us, as Indigenous individuals and peoples embedded in the land, susceptible to violence in multiplex ways. The Western category splits between human bodies and bodies of lands are nonexistent from within Sámi lifeworlds. Consequently, the violence against our lands is violence against our bodies and vice versa, or perhaps more accurately put, against our body lands (cf. Altamirano-Jiménez 2020, 2021). Quoting Biret, it is a "rape of the earth" or, paraphrasing her statement, a rape of our body lands. Alternatively, following Sire's reflection, "we die with the land" because mining entails an existential threat against Sámi body lands.

Márjá, a mother in a reindeer herder family, talks about the multiple threats to Sábme and the earth as a whole. She links them to her concerns for Sámi youth, including her children, their mental health, and their futures:

> **Márjá:** I've never lost hope, but this spring, I have felt that there are no boundaries regarding humankind's consumption and destruction of Mother Earth. . . . And then there are all the threats posed by the mines and the prospecting taking place everywhere, all over Sápmi. And no one is thinking—I mean, humankind is solely governed by money and isn't considering the environment and the treatment of nature. What it looks like and what remains. And it's even more challenging for a young person. . . . There are so many young Sámi who suffer and who have taken their own lives.
> **Ina:** Yes.
> **Márjá:** And it's terrifying when you, yourself, are the parent of . . . young people. Because everyone feels this pressure, everyone suffers, literally everyone. It's there all the time. And to know that so many young people are deeply depressed due to the situation. It makes you want to cry.
> **Ina:** Yes, as the parental generation.
> **Márjá:** Yes, indeed. Because you feel our heritage is forced upon us by the state, that is, involuntarily, our heritage is all the exploitation and threats and worry. (conversation with author, 2017)

Like Sire, Márjá discusses the land's well-being as the people's well-being. Her analysis points to connections between interlinked pressures on the land and mental illness among Sámi people, especially the prevalence of suicide among young reindeer herders and its consequences for the individual and the community (cf. Jacobsson, Stoor, and Eriksson 2020).

She explains that an involuntary heritage is "forced upon us by the state." This intergenerational burden is in the form of exploitation and threats of exploitation of Sámi land and causes worry and pain. It is also experienced by Sámi youth and manifests as depression and anxiety. This situation, she conveys, is a cause of great concern for the older generations. Her analysis points to how dispossession and exploitation of Sámi land connect to the destruction of Sámi culture. As a result, multiple generations experience anxiety for the future and struggle to ensure the survival of the Sámi people, land, and lifeworlds.

### "You Must See a Different Life, Different Values"

Historically, discourses and practices of the Swedish state positioned the Sámi as "children," an "uncivilized" and "underdeveloped" people in need of guidance and education from the majority society (Finbog 2020: 41–42; Lantto and Mörkenstam 2008: 29–34). The construction of Sámi inferiority was an inextricable part of colonial relations of domination: "Colonialism signifies not only the occupation of territories but also a certain type of relationship between the colonizer and the colonized in which the latter is considered inherently inferior ('uncivilised,' 'savage,' 'primitive')" (Kuokkanen 2017: 314). Today, colonial legacies often manifest through "epistemic ignorance"—"practices and discourses that actively foreclose other than dominant epistemes and that refuse to seriously contemplate their existence" (Kuokkanen 2017: 317). Epistemic ignorance, according to Kuokkanen (2017: 317), is a "form of subtle violence" where active nonrecognition brings about the disappearance of marginalized worldviews.

Biret sees a difference in the "approach to land and life" between Swedish society and the Sámi as an Indigenous people. Because of this difference, it is difficult for Swedish society to understand the situation from the viewpoint of the Sámi: "We are Indigenous people. We have a completely different approach to the land, to life. And I think it is hard for Swedish society to understand this. . . . You must think differently then. You must move outside your comfort zone. You must see a different life, different values" (conversation with author, 2014). Here, Biret is asking Swedish society to recognize the existence of Sámi worldviews and acknowledge its different conceptualization of land. In other words, the majority society needs to consciously shift their thinking from reproducing Swedish epistemic ignorance to engaging with Sámi people's perspectives on the mining issue.

Sagka sees a similar inability of Swedish society, especially government representatives, to recognize the situation from the viewpoint of the Sámi:

The actions of the state and the government are so incredibly unpleasant. . . . The Swedish representative claimed, I believe she is state secretary to Annie Lööf [the Swedish minister for enterprise and leader of the Centre Party at the time of the conversation], that reindeer herding and mining can coexist as if it is an indisputable fact that she for some reason knows better than the reindeer herders. And that you shouldn't believe what the media says and that you need to devote more energy to explaining the mining industry to the Sámi. Because they don't seem to understand it! . . . We have a history of being called a subhuman race—eternal children who don't know what is best for us. (conversation with author, 2014)

The inability or refusal to see the difference in values, according to Sagka, enables arguments that support the feasibility of the coexistence of mining, reindeer husbandry, and Sámi culture. Sagka interprets the state's arguments as a paternalistic discourse vis-à-vis the Sámi with clear links to the past. Mining, according to Sagka, is a continuation of unequal power relations between the Swedish majority and the Indigenous minority. In this discourse, Swedish culture continues to be constructed as the hegemonic norm. Therefore, for Sagka, equal dialogue between the state and the Sámi is impossible.

*"What Local People": A Poetic Refusal of Sámi Erasure*
"What Local People" is the title of a spoken-word poem performed by Ti/Mimie Märak on August 2, 2013, during a concert at the Gállok protest camp. In line with Sandström (2021: 5), I read the poem as an expression of *artivism*—artistic practice that aims for societal change—and interpret the poem as a story "with a purpose" (Sandström 2021: 75). The poem's title refers to a statement made by the then director of Beowulf Mining, Clive Sinclair-Poulton, at a presentation for shareholders in Stockholm in 2012. When asked about local opinions about a potential mine in Gállok, he responded by showing a forest landscape devoid of buildings and people while rhetorically asking his audience, "What local people?" His denial of Indigenous and local presences, cultures, and histories was met with substantial protests, among them Märak's poetic performance.

Sinclair-Poulton's assertion is a clear example of the colonial logic of terra nullius—marking Indigenous territories as wasteland and extractive zones (Cocq 2014: 6; Sandström 2020: 99). Altamirano-Jimenéz (2020: 325) makes a similar observation: "By making Indigenous peoples, their legal orders, histories and existing land tenures 'strategically invisible' (Cooper 2020), the violence of emptying the land is obscured." In response to this logic, Märak's (2013) poem adamantly refuses Sámi erasure:

> for every dam constructed / every tree you want to take down / every place you wish to blast /a thousand voices will burst forth / from us / who is / what local people / we who love and wish / that our greenery is preserved where it is / without you cutting it down / draining it / for the fact is that you choke a minority / know that we stand with one foot in the grave / but the roots go too deep to tear up / it will never work on us / we are not possible to bribe / so stop / you can't crack us / you will never break / us local people. (my translation)

In this excerpt, the text outlines the threats against the Indigenous minority—damming, deforestation, and the blasting of the ground from mining-related activities, resulting in a situation where "we stand with one foot in the grave." However, Sámi people will overcome such threats against Indigenous land-worlds and lifeworlds, because "the roots go too deep to tear up." As such, the performance is a speech act of defiance and refusal. The land is not terra nullius but an Indigenous space where people are rooted in the land and ready to protect it against exploitation (cf. Sandström 2020: 99–104).

As argued by Sandström, settler colonial and heteropatriarchal logics operate in a binary and hierarchical fashion. Consequently, the land is separated from humankind and subordinate to human interests similar to how gender and race are constructed according to logics of difference and stratification (Sandström 2020: 178–81). Thus, Indigenous nonbinary and women land protectors both embody and forward a different worldview when they protect the land against proponents of settler colonial and capitalist intervention. By resisting a dominant episteme founded on category splits such as human/nature and woman/man, they are forwarding relationality; or, in the words of Altamirano-Jiménez (2021: 218), body land as an "ontological relation, a continuum that does not separate human beings from territory and other beings."

I interpret Märak's poetic refusal of colonial logic through the regenerative aspect of body land: "the potential that emerges when these [Indigenous] bodies come together to refuse colonial power" (Altamirano-Jimenéz 2020: 101). While the notion of body land directs attention to the intertwined violence done to Indigenous land and bodies, it also captures the hope and possibilities that arise when bodies come together to resist settler colonial capitalist powers of "hierarchization of life" (Altamirano-Jiménez 2021: 215) as such refusal "is not mere self-preservation but the exercise of practices of relationality and freedom that center Indigenous life" (Altamirano-Jimenéz 2021: 218).

## Concluding Remarks

Mining entails fracturing the relational web connecting land, humans, and nonhuman beings. It represents a multigenerational threat against the survival of Sámi land, life, and knowledge systems. However, the participants express how a relational Sami episteme is unrecognized by state authorities and the Swedish majority, which invalidates and renders their resistance unintelligible. Thus, acknowledging their critique and positions requires challenging the power structures in multiple ways, including on epistemic levels.

In conclusion, I suggest that my conversational partners and Ti/Mimie Märak, through their spoken-word poem "What Local People," argue for an episteme that challenges the settler colonial and capitalist frameworks of the Swedish state and the mining industry. That is, their worldviews emphasize the interconnectedness of land, nature, and people and the necessity of protecting our interlinked lifeworlds today and for the future. Such an episteme, which foregrounds relationality and interdependency, is foundational to the research participants' struggles against mining in Sábme.

In the context of feminist scholarship, recognizing the impact of structural violence on Sámi women and nonbinary people would necessitate further critical analysis of the nexus of settler colonial and capitalist dispossession and fragmentation. Moreover, it would entail a recognition and inclusion of relationality. By incorporating the land in analyses of embodiment and emphasizing interconnectedness, the concept of body land contributes to feminist theory from within Indigenous epistemes. Arguably, interconnectedness entails a susceptibility to multiform acts of violence against the Sámi body land. However, as demonstrated through Märak's spoken-word poetry, our interconnectedness with the land is, at the same time, our strongest argument and foundation against colonial and industrial "rapes of the land." In their words, "We stand with one foot in the grave / but the roots go too deep to tear up."

**Ina Knobblock** is a Sámi and Tornedalian feminist scholar. Her doctoral dissertation, "Writing-Weaving Sámi Feminisms: Stories and Conversations" (2022) explores, illuminates, and analyzes Sámi feminist knowledges. She is a lecturer in gender studies at Gaskeuniversiteete/Mid-Sweden University, Sweden.

## Notes

I express my warmest gratitude to the research participants for sharing their knowledge and experiences. I also thank Diana Mulinari, Anna-Lill Drugge, and the two anonymous reviewers for their insightful and constructive comments on my work.

1 With the exception of quotations and the place names Násavárre and Giron, I use Lule Sámi orthography.

2 Timimie Märak has changed name and pronoun since the performance in 2013—from Mimie/she to Timimie/they. Following Sandström (2020: 61), in the context of the specific poem, I write the name Ti/Mimie to reflect that they created and first performed the poem using name Mimie.

3 Although my focus in this article lies on the narratives of women and nonbinary people, my intention is not to diminish or critique men's contributions to the anti-mining struggle. Therefore, while I do not include men's voices here, I agree with Kuokkanen's (2021: 311) statement that "Indigenous feminist analyses are not limited on discussing women's participation, roles, or views."

4 At the core of the terms *decolonization* and *resurgence* is a critical examination, (re)imagination, and (re)creation of the world grounded in Indigenous experiences and world-making practices (Simpson 2017: 191–98; Smith 2012: 204).

5 Place name in Sámi and Swedish, respectively.

6 Abya-Yala, which signifies "land in full maturity," is the name coined by the kunas of Panama and widely adopted by Indigenous peoples in 1992 to refer to the "territory and the indigenous nations of the Americas" (Walsh 2011: 5).

7 Sáráhkká is the name of a Sámi female deity.

8 *Sámi Nisson Forum* translates to Sámi Women's Forum.

## Works Cited

Altamirano-Jiménez, Isabel. 2020. "Possessing Land, Wind, and Water in the Isthmus of Tehuantepec, Oaxaca." *Australian Feminist Studies* 35, no. 106: 321–35.

Altamirano-Jiménez, Isabel. 2021. "Indigenous Women Refusing the Violence of Resource Extraction in Oaxaca." *AlterNative: An International Journal of Indigenous People* 17, no. 2: 215–23.

Amft, Andrea. 1998. "Silent in the Church: Sámi Women in Reindeer-Herding Society, 1886–1996." In *The Social Construction of Gender in Different Cultural Contexts*, edited by G.-M. Frånberg, 17–53. Stockholm: Fritzes.

Amft, Andrea. 2000. "Sápmi i förändringens tid: En studie av svenska samers levnadsvillkor under 1900-talet ur ett genus- och etnicitetsperspektiv" ("Sápmi in a

Time of Change: A Study of Swedish Sámi Living Conditions during the Twentieth Century from a Gender and Ethnic Perspective"). PhD diss., Umeå University.

Anshelm, Jonas, and Simon Haikola. 2018. Introduction to *Svensk gruvpolitik i omvandling: Aktörer, kontroverser och möjliga världar*, edited by Jonas Anshelm and Simon Haikola, 9–15. Halmstad: Gidlunds förlag.

Beads, Tina, and Rauna Kuokkanen. 2007. "Aboriginal Feminist Action on Violence against Women." In Green 2007: 221–32.

Blåhed, Hanna, and Miguel San Sebastián. 2021. "'If the Reindeer Die, Everything Dies': The Mental Health of a Sámi Community Exposed to a Mining Project in Swedish Sápmi." *International Journal of Circumpolar Health* 80, no. 1: 1935132.

Cocq, Coppélie. 2014. "Kampen om Gállok: platsskapande och synliggörande" ("The Struggle for Gállok: Place Making and Visibility"). *Kulturella perspektiv* 23, no. 1: 5–12.

Dankertsen, Astri. 2020. "Sámi Feminist Moments." In *Good Relation: History, Gender, and Kinship in Indigenous Feminisms*, edited by Sara Nickel and Amanda Fehr, 48–65. Winnipeg: University of Manitoba Press.

Driskill, Qwo-Li, Chris Finley, Brian Joseph Gilley, and Lauria Scott Morgensen. 2011. Introduction to *Queer Indigenous Studies: Critical Interventions in Theory, Politics, and Literature*, edited by Qwo-Li Driskill, Chris Finley, Brian Joseph Gilley, and Lauria Scott Morgensen, 1–28. Tucson: University of Arizona Press.

Eriksen, Astrid M. A., Ketil Lenert Hansen, Cecilie Javo, and Berit Schei. 2015. "Emotional, Physical, and Sexual Violence among Sámi and non-Sámi Populations in Norway: The SAMINOR 2 Questionnaire Study." *Scandinavian Journal of Public Health* 43: 588–96. https://doi.org/10.1177/1403494815585936.

Eriksen, Astrid M. A., Marita Melhus, Bjarne Koster Jacobsen, Berit Schei, and Ann-Ragnhild Broderstad. 2021. "Intimate Partner Violence and Its Association with Mental Health Problems: The Importance of Childhood Violence—The SAMINOR 2 Questionnaire Survey." *Scandinavian Journal of Public Health* 50, no. 8: 1–13. https//doi.org/10.1177/14034948211024481.

Erpel, Angela, ed. 2018. *Mujeres en defensa de territorios: Reflexiones feministas frente al extractivismo (Women Protecting the Land: Feminist Reflections on Extractivism)*. Santiago: Fundación Heinrich Böll.

Finbog, Liisa-Rávná. 2020. "It Speaks to You: Making Kin of People, Duodji, and Stories in Sámi Museums." PhD diss., Oslo University.

Government of Sweden. 1989. Directive 1988/89: 92. https://www.riksdagen.se/sv/dokument-lagar/dokument/proposition/om-ny-minerallagstiftning-mm_GC0392.

Government of Sweden. 1990. Directive 1989/90: 110. https://www.riksdagen.se/sv/dokument-lagar/dokument/proposition/om—reformerad-inkomst—och-foretagsbeskattning_GD03110.

Government of Sweden. 1992. Directive 1992/93: 238. https://www.riksdagen.se/sv/dokument-lagar/dokument/proposition/om-andringar-i-de-immaterialrattsliga-lagarna-med_GG0348.

Government of Sweden. 2022. Press release, March. https://www.government.se/press-releases/2022/03/government-grants-exploitation-concession-for-kallak-k-no-1/.

Green, Joyce, ed. 2007. *Making Space for Indigenous Feminism*. Black Point, NS: Fernwood.

Gruvfritt Jokkmokk. 2021. "Till näringsdepartementet, Sveriges regering: För levande kultur och ren natur i ett gruvfritt Jokkmokk" ("To the Ministry of Business, Industry, and Intervention, the Swedish Government: For a Living Culture and Clean Nature in a Jokkmokk Free From Mines"). Mittskifte.org. https://www.mittskifte .org/petitions/for-levande-kultur-och-ren-natur-i-ett-gruvfritt-jokkmokk.

Halsaa, Beatrice. 2020. "The (Trans)National Mobilisation of Sámi Women in Norway." *Moving the Social: Journal of Social History and the History of Social Movements* 63: 119–45.

Helander-Renvall, Elina, and Kaarina Kailo. 1998. "No Beginning, No End." In *No Beginning, No End: The Sami Sak Up*, edited by Elina Helander-Renvall, and Kaarina Kailo, 1–15. Edmonton: Canadian Circumpolar Institute.

Jacobsson, Lars, Jon Petter Stoor, and Anders Eriksson. 2020. "Suicide among Reindeer Herding Sámi in Sweden, 1961–2017." *International Journal of Circumpolar Health* 79, no. 1: 1754085.

Knobblock, Ina. 2022. "Sámi Feminist Conversations." In *The Sámi World*, edited by Sanna Valkonen, Áile Aiko, Saara Alakorva, and Sigga-Marja Magga, 535–50. London: Routledge.

Knobblock, Ina, and Rauna Kuokkanen. 2015. "Decolonizing Feminism in the North: A Conversation with Rauna Kuokkanen." *NORA: Nordic Journal of Feminist and Gender Research* 23, no. 4: 275–81.

Kovach, Margaret. 2009. *Indigenous Methodologies: Characteristics, Conversations, and Contexts*. Toronto: Toronto University Press.

Kuokkanen, Rauna. 2007a. "Myths and Realities of Sámi Women: A Post-colonial Feminist Analysis for the Decolonization and Transformation of Sámi Society." In Green 2007: 72–92.

Kuokkanen, Rauna. 2007b. *Reshaping the University: Responsibility, Indigenous Epistemes, and the Logic of the Gift*. Vancouver: University of British Columbia Press.

Kuokkanen, Rauna. 2017. "Indigenous Epistemes." In *A Companion to Critical and Cultural Theory*, edited by Imre Szeman, Sarah Blacker, and Justin Sully, 313–26. Hoboken, NJ: Wiley-Blackwell.

Kuokkanen, Rauna. 2019. *Restructuring Relations: Indigenous Self-Determination, Governance, and Gender*. New York: Oxford University Press.

Kuokkanen, Rauna. 2021. "Ellos Deatnu and Post-state Indigenous Feminist Sovereignty." In *The Routledge Handbook of Critical Indigenous Studies*, edited by Brendan Hokowhitu, Aileen Moreton-Robinson, Linda Tuhiwai Smith, Chris Andersen, and Steve Larkin, 310–23. Abingdon, U.K.: Routledge.

Labba, ElinAnna. 2020. *Herrarna satte oss hit: Om tvångsförflyttningarna i Sverige* (Sirdolaččat: The Deportation of the Northern Sámi). Stockholm: Norstedts.

Lantto, Patrik, and Ulf Mörkenstam. 2008. "Sámi Rights and Sámi Challenges: The Modernization Process and the Swedish Sámi Movement." *Scandinavian Journal of History* 33, no. 1: 26–51.

Larsen, Rasmus Kløcker, Kaisa Raitio, Marita Stinnerbom, and Jenny Wik-Karlsson. 2017. "Sámi-State Collaboration in the Governance of Cumulative Effects Assessment: A Critical Action Research Approach." *Environmental Impact Assessment Review* 64: 67–76.

Lawrence, Rebecca. 2014. "Internal Colonisation and Indigenous Resource Sovereignty: Wind Power Developments on Traditional Saami Lands." *Environment and
Planning D: Society and Space* 32: 1036–53.

Ledman, Anna-Lill. 2012. "Att representera och representeras: Samiska kvinnor i
svensk och samisk press, 1966–2006" ("To Be Represented and to Represent: Sámi
Women in Swedish and Sámi Press, 1966–2006"). PhD diss., Umeå University.

Märak, Ti/Mimie. 2013. "What Local People?" https://www.youtube.com/watch
?v=JiFcEvjIG8w.

Moreton-Robinson, Aileen. 2013. "Towards an Australian Indigenous Women's Standpoint Theory: A Methodological Tool." *Australian Feminist Studies* 28, no. 78: 331–47.

Nachet, Louise, Caitlynn Beckett, and Kristina Sehlin MacNeil. 2021. "Framing
Extractive Violence as Environmental (In)justice: A Cross-perspective from Indigenous Lands in Canada and Sweden." *Extractive Industries and Society*. https://doi
.org/10.1016/j.exis.2021.100949.

Nickel, Sarah, and Amanda Fehr, eds. 2020. *In Good Relation: History, Gender, and Kinship
in Indigenous Feminisms*. Winnipeg: University of Manitoba Press.

Nilsson, Ragnhild. 2021. "Att bearkadidh: Om samiskt självbestämmande och
samisk självkonstituering" ("To Bearkadidh: Sámi Self-Determination and Self-
Constitution"). PhD diss., Stockholm University.

Öhman, May-Britt. 2017. "Places and Peoples: Sámi Feminist Technoscience and
Supradisciplinary Research." In *Sources and Methods in Indigenous Studies*, edited by
Chris Andersen and Jean M. O'Brien, 152–59. Abingdon, Oxon: Routledge.

Öhman, May-Britt. 2021. "Morfars farmors syster Brita Stina Larsdotter Rim: Återta-
gande av lulesamisk och skogssamisk historia och identitet i ett bosättarkolonialt
Sverige" ("My Grandfather's Grandmother's Sister Brita Stina Larsdotter Rim:
Taking Back Lule Sámi and Forest Sámi History and Identity in Settler Colonial
Sweden"). *Tidskrift for Kjønnsforskning* 45, no. 4: 197–214.

Ojala, Carl-Gösta, and Jonas Monié Nordin. 2015. "Mining Sápmi: Colonial Histories, Sámi Archaeology, and the Exploitation of Natural Resources in Northern
Sweden." *Arctic Anthropology* 52, no. 2: 6–21.

Össbo, Åsa. 2021. "A Constant Reminder of What We Had to Forfeit." *International
Journal of Critical Indigenous Studies* 14, no. 1: 17–32.

Persson Njajta, Marie. 2014. "Dags att ändra minerallagstiftningen!" [Time to
change the mineral legislation!]. *Nätverket Stoppa gruvan i Rönnbäck* (blog),
March 24. https://stoppagruvan.wordpress.com/2014/03/24/dags-att-andra
minerallagstiftningen/.

Persson, Sofia, David Harnesk, and Mine Islar. 2017. "What Local People? Examining
the Gállok Mining Conflict and the Rights of the Sámi Population in Terms of
Justice and Power." *Geoforum* 86: 20–29.

Raitio, Kaisa, Christina Allard, and Rebecca Lawrence. 2020. "Mineral Extraction in
Swedish Sápmi: The Regulatory Gap between Sami Rights and Sweden's Mining
Permitting Practices." *Land Use Policy* 99: 105001.

Sandström, Moa. 2020. "Dekoloniseringskonst: Artivism i 2010-talets Sápmi"
[Decolonizing artivism in contemporary Sápmi]. PhD diss., Umeå University.

Sehlin MacNeil, Kristina. 2017. "Extractive Violence on Indigenous Country: Sámi and Aboriginal Views on Conflicts and Power Relations with Extractive Industries." PhD diss., Umeå University.

Simpson, Leanne Betasamosake. 2017. *As We Have Always Done: Indigenous Freedom through Radical Resistance*. Minneapolis: University of Minnesota Press.

Smith, Linda Tuhiwai. 2012. *Decolonizing Methodologies: Research and Indigenous Peoples*. 2nd ed. London: Zed.

Suzack, Cheryl, Shari. M. Huhndorf, Jeanne Perreault, and Jean Barman, eds. 2010. *Indigenous Women and Feminism: Politics, Activism, Culture*. Vancouver: University of British Columbia Press.

Svalastog, Anna-Lydia, and Stefan Eriksson. 2010. "You Can Use My Name; You Don't Have to Steal My Story—A Critique of Anonymity in Indigenous Studies." *Developing World Bioethics* 10, no. 2: 104–10.

TallBear, Kim. 2017. "Standing with and Speaking as Faith: A Feminist-Indigenous Approach to Inquiry." In *Sources and Methods in Indigenous Studies*, edited by C. Andersen and J. M. O'Brien, 78–85. Abingdon, U.K.: Routledge.

Tlostanova, Madina, Suruchi Thapar-Björkert, and Ina Knobblock. 2019. "Do We Need Decolonial Feminism in Sweden?" *NORA: Nordic Journal of Feminist and Gender Research* 27, no. 4: 290–95.

Walsh, Catherine. 2011. "Afro and Indigenous Life: Visions in/and Politics; (De)colonial Perspectives in Bolivia and Ecuador." *Bolivian Studies Journal/Revista de estudios bolivianos* 18: 50–69.

Wolfe, Patrick. 2006. "Settler Colonialism and the Elimination of the Native." *Journal of Genocide Research* 8, no. 4: 387–409.

Denise Schallenkammer

........................................................................

# The "Grandmother" of Indigenous Filmmaking in New Zealand
## Merata Mita—Film Is Her Patu

Abstract: With reference to Heperi Mita's documentary *Merata: How Mum Decolonised the Screen* (2018) about his mother, Merata Mita, this article illustrates the importance of Indigenous filmmaking by providing insights into the work and life of New Zealand's first female Māori filmmaker who made a feature-length narrative. Film is an important part of identity formation and shapes the perception of (Indigenous) cultures and peoples. From the late 1970s onward, there is a growing movement in Māori filmmaking which led to changes in the representation of Māori culture in film and influenced Indigenous filmmaking on a global scale. Merata Mita plays a major role in bringing Māori behind and in front of the camera and paved the way for Indigenous female filmmakers.

## Introduction

*Merata: How Mum Decolonised the Screen*, released in 2018, is an intimate portrayal of Merata Mita, one of New Zealand's first Indigenous female filmmakers (Goh 2019). After Mita's sudden death in 2010, her youngest son, Heperi Mita (see fig. 1), pieced together archival footage of Mita's cinematic works, interviews (with her), as well as private recordings (Mayer 2019). His documentary allows an insight into Merata Mita's life and work as a Māori,[1] activist, filmmaker, woman, and mother—through the eyes of her children, her own perspective, her filmic work, and through statements of other (Indigenous) filmmakers (NZFilm n.d.). Additionally, Heperi Mita gives an impression of New Zealand's sociopolitical climate, especially

MERIDIANS · feminism, race, transnationalism    23:1 April 2024
DOI: 10.1215/15366936-10926968 © 2024 Smith College

Figure 1. Merata Mita's son, director Heperi Mita, sifts through film reels for his documentary.

during the 1970s and 1980s, and outlines the beginnings and developments of "Indigenous Cinema."² The documentary shows how Merata Mita
changed the landscape of Indigenous participation in film by advocating
for accurate filmic representation of Indigenous narratives but also provides an insight into personal accounts of Mita and how her relentless and
fearless commitment to exposing social injustices affected her (family) life
(Mayer 2019).

Director Heperi Mita described his mother as a complex person who was
a lot of things to a lot of people: "To some people she was an icon of Indigenous filmmaking and to others she was radical" (Goh 2019). Mita's documentary shows Merata taking the audience through her life from being a
mother of six, to a political activist standing up for Māori and women's
rights, to one of Aotearoa's³ most known and impactful filmmakers.
According to her son, her impetus for becoming a filmmaker was the
effects of colonialism, oppression, misogyny, and sexism she experienced
on a personal level. In order to represent and change the situation for
women and Māori within New Zealand's society, she started filming (Goh
2019). Due to her cinematic works, Mita's public image oscillated between
"international heroine" and "domestic nuisance": "Merata's political
films highlighted the injustices for Māori people during the 1980s and

often divided the country" (NZFilm n.d.). Even though Mita became a forerunner in Māori filmmaking and an "international champion of women in indigenous film" (NZiff n.d.), her political films were not well received by many people within New Zealand at the time of their release, because she was (metaphorically speaking) holding up a mirror—and society did not like what it was seeing. Notwithstanding the negative feedback and the professional as well as personal difficulties she had to face as a result, Merata Mita stuck to her convictions and intentions and sent her films overseas to spread her messages (Goh 2019). For her, "The revolution isn't just running out with a gun. If a film I make cause[s] indigenous people to feel stronger about themselves, then I'm achieving something worthwhile for the revolution" (NZiff n.d.). In *Merata: How Mum Decolonised the Screen* (2018) she said: "Foot soldiers don't have a very high status, but they have to be very brave and very determined to keep fighting a war" (Dailymotion 2023, 00:02:08), which encapsulates her filmmaking philosophy. Jesse Wente, the first director of Canada's Indigenous Screen Office, reported in Heperi Mita's documentary that Mita acted as "the spark that actually set the fire" for "Indigenous Cinema" (Mayer 2019). She paved the way for Indigenous (female) filmmakers both overseas and in New Zealand and left an incredible legacy.

Heperi Mita's documentary (see fig. 2) and its relation to and relevance for current issues gave rise to a closer look at Merata Mita and her stated mission "to decolonise the screen, and to indigenise a lot of what we see up there" (Dailymotion 2023, 00:02:33). His compelling portrayal of his mother depicts and emphasizes her abiding international significance (NZiff n.d.) as an Indigenous filmmaker, activist, woman, and (single) mother who "speaks to wider experiences and universal struggles that are still being faced by indigenous filmmakers everywhere in the world" (Berlinale 2019). The discussion below provides a deeper insight into Merata Mita's life and work to demonstrate the importance and scope of her tireless commitment, both in the professional and personal sphere. For a better understanding, it is necessary to take into account the historical, political, social, and cultural contexts at that time. Therefore, a brief abstract on New Zealand (film) history follows. It becomes clear that Mita's groundbreaking activist filmmaking and cinematic lineage cross (ed) international boundaries and show Māori connections with Indigenous people worldwide (Asenap 2019): "Everything has an impact internationally. Everything we make has an impact on other societies, other

Figure 2. A film still from *Merata: How Mum Decolonised the Screen* (2018) showing Mita editing one of her films.

cultures, but particularly indigenous ones" (Mita 2002/2003: 34). This article is conceived as a kind of portrait in which Merata Mita speaks "directly" to the reader through numerous quotations to give more depth to her experiences and impressions through an autobiographical character. *Merata: How Mum Decolonised the Screen* (2018) can be regarded as a tribute and as a reminder of Mita's massive impact on Indigenous (female) filmmaking and its power to raise public awareness about social and political injustice as well as to revitalize and preserve cultural traditions, values, and identity.

## "Māori Renaissance" in New Zealand (Film) History

The history of narratives about Māori is marked by a lack of power. New Zealand's Indigenous population were regarded as popular objects of illustration among Europeans. Besides representing Māori through an ethnographic lens and treating them as research objects, Aotearoa's Indigenous people were also used as advertising media to attract visitors, which created a glorified image of Māori (Murray 2008: 17–18, 37).

Until the 1970s, the prevailing image of Māori was a stereotyped one constructed by Pākehā.[4] It "rested upon the assumption that non-European peoples were backward, primitive, quaint, sometimes even 'noble' but always different from the products of western civilisation" (Loomba 1998: 48). Up to this time, New Zealand's film industry was dominated by white males (Conrich and Davy 1997: 6). Thus, Indigenous people were not adequately represented in front of the camera, nor were they given the opportunity to be present behind it.

In the second half of the twentieth century, Māori and Pākehā came into closer contact due to demographic change. Many Māori left the countryside to find work in surrounding cities. As most of New Zealand's institutions within larger cities were European in character, there was a lack of alternative lifestyles. Further, Pākehā were not just expecting Māori to integrate into society but rather to assimilate and adapt to Western lifestyles. As a result of urbanization and its accompanying intercultural challenges, Aotearoa's Indigenous people were marginalized and forced to give up much of their culture and identity (King 2003: 440–42).

These developments led to a counterreaction: Protest groups were formed which called for actions to draw attention to the political insensitivity and social injustices toward Māori. The 1970s and 1980s were marked by social protests and events that gave rise to debates within media and political contexts about interethnic relationships. Within the 1970s, several (peaceful) protests took place (Bastion Point, Raglan Golf Course, South African Springbok Rugby Tour, etc.).[5] This period of time was characterized by radical social change that increasingly initiated discussions about biculturalism (Clelland-Stokes 2007: 172–73). By then, Māori cultural activism experienced a revival as part of the so-called Māori Renaissance (Martens 2012: 5). It can be considered a reactionary movement to years of discrimination which was triggered by certain developments within culture and society. Besides, it can be viewed as a kind of "ethnic mobilization" to reestablish Māori culture, language, and identity (Byrnes 1999: 72). This "renaissance" happened across various fields such as art, literature, and film. The arts have become an important "vehicle" for expressing resistance: "The struggle of survival of Māori identity and culture, was paradoxically fostered by . . . using the [tools] of the colonisers to subvert their dominant discourse" (Della Valle 2010: 9). Film in particular played and still plays a special role in this act of self-empowerment by Māori.

To illustrate the significance of this medium, a brief introduction to Indigenous filmmaking seems useful. Barry Barclay's Ngati (1987) is credited as being the first fiction feature film made by an Indigenous film-maker (Murray 2008: 1). Ngati has become a showpiece and prime example of Indigenous film (Martin and Edwards 1997: 128). The Māori filmmaker argued that films made by members of Indigenous communities do not fit into the already existing framework of "First," "Second," and "Third Cin-ema." Hence, Barclay introduced the category of "Fourth Cinema" to group films made by Indigenous people: "There is a category which can legiti-mately be called 'Fourth Cinema' by which I mean Indigenous Cinema—that's Indigenous with a capital 'I'" (Barclay 2003: 8).

His category refers to the "Fourth World" model, which comprises Indigenous populations in parts of the world where they are excluded from power and describes a process of decolonization based on the revitaliza-tion of Indigenous practices that colonization sought to destroy (Coulthard 2019: xii). Barry Barclay's concept of "Fourth World" aesthetic is based on the idea that being Indigenous is a shared experience; that Indigenous cultures are located outside any modern orthodoxy, which can unite cul-tures through a shared sense of exclusion (Murray 2008: 16–17). Thus, for the Māori filmmaker "Fourth Cinema" does not just comprise films made by Indigenous filmmakers, "but refers to a distinct politically engaged mode of filmmaking that has emerged from the shared Indigenous experi-ence of exclusion in postcolonial settler states and allows for film practices and images that are controlled by—and do justice to—Indigenous peoples and their concerns and customs" (Martens 2012: 3).

Films that fall under this new category are narratively and aesthetically structured to offer alternatives to the three former models. In order to explain elements of this framework, Barclay refers to the conceptual theory of "interiority" and "exteriority" (Waititi 2008: 1); for him, "interiority" is especially inherent in "Fourth Cinema" and distinguishes "Indigenous Cinema" from other categories (Milligan 2015: 354). The Māori filmmaker describes "exteriority" as "surface features" (e.g., rituals, posturing, lan-guage, use of elders, decor, attitudes to land, and the presence of children), while "interiority" refers to "the philosophical elements, the essence of Indigenous film and is a complex ingredient to convey" (Barclay 2003: 7). Both concepts are needed to articulate the film, as "exteriority" is the basis from which "interiority" is developed; they are intertwined and often a reflection of the other and consequently need to be in balance. However, "interiority" is achieved when what is seen on screen sounds true to those who are depicted in the story (Waititi 2008: 7–9).

Houston Wood agrees that it is useful to group Indigenous-made films under a single label, even though each Indigenous film is different from another. He argues that every film made by Native peoples reflects (more or less) the specific storytelling traditions of the Indigenous people being represented. Although these traditions are different from one another and each film differs, of course, in content, they share "a similar relationship to the dominant cinematic traditions that they, to various degrees, oppose" (Wood 2008: 1–2). From the 1970s onward, Indigenous filmmakers started to make films that offer decolonizing alternatives to films based on non-Indigenous traditions "that had excluded, confined and exoticised them [Māori] ever since the medium was introduced" (Martens 2012: 3). Therewith, they have contributed to the "Indigenization" of the silver screen (Martens 2012: 3). Although Indigenous films cannot per se save Native peoples' cultures from extinction, they are useful vehicles to strengthen them by revising stereotypical images of Indigenous peoples and increasing public awareness about Indigenous issues (Wood 2008: 2).

### Film as a Vehicle for Self-Determination and Resistance

Merata Mita of Ngāti Pikiao and Ngāi Te Rangi was born in 1942 as one of nine siblings. She grew up in Maketu, a town in the Bay of Plenty of Aotearoa's North Island, and had a rural upbringing on her whānau's[6] land (NZ on Screen n.d.). Becoming a filmmaker "was an accident" (Stutesman 1984: 3), Mita explained in an interview shortly after her documentary Patu! (1983)[7] was successfully screened at the Phoenix Film Festival in London in 1984. Her interest in filmmaking was sparked by experiences she had when she worked as a schoolteacher (Stutesman 1984: 2–3). Mita began integrating film and video into her teaching methods to reach students who were "mostly Māori, mostly condemned to failure" (NZ on Screen n.d.). In doing so, she realized how powerful images are, both in reaching people who do not have other communicative skills and in offering a way to express oneself. In 1977, Mita started collaborating on documentaries for New Zealand television about Māori culture. She helped a Pākehā filmmaker organize interviews with Māori (NZ on Screen n.d.); she recognized that the majority of the film crew did not feel the need to familiarize themselves with Māori cultural life so as not to run the risk of violating Indigenous values and norms. Merata Mita was shocked by how she was used to facilitate access to the locations and to Māori being filmed. As a result of these experiences, she decided to start making her own films: "I was fed up with film makers putting Māori under the microscope and misrepresenting them. . . . They rush to the Māori area when they want politics, rush to the Māori area without any inkling of understanding about the dynamics of that society, its history and culture" (Mita 2002/2003: 32).

In 1980, Mita worked for Television NZ, a channel that broadcast New Zealand's first weekly Māori news show. However, this program was aimed at the majority (Pākehā) audience. As a result, only 2 percent of the content was in Te Reo Māori:[8] "We were nice enough to believe that these were programmes by Māori, about Māori, for Māori, since we would occupy less than one percent of the total hours programmed by the two channels" (Mita 1996: 45). In Mita's opinion, the negative aspect of film is its commodity nature in the hands of capitalist countries in order to spread Western culture and ideology throughout the world, which has the effect of corrupting other peoples' Indigenous and ethnic values. She described this one-sided mode of filmic representations of Māori by Pākehā as a reflection of racially discriminatory politics in New Zealand (Mita 1996: 45). Though, one of its positive aspects is that "film has the power to destroy myths and demystify those areas of knowledge that are mystified" (Stutesman 1984: 4). As a consequence, this knowledge expands and becomes common property: "It became clear that Māori needed to be telling their own stories" (Mita 2002/2003: 32). Her concern was to bring Māori to the screen and provide viewers with realistic portrayals of Aotearoa's Indigenous culture in order to resolve long-established stereotypical images of Māori (Mita 1996: 49): "I want to fill [the screen] with Māori faces, Māori history, Māori culture and Māori ways of looking at life" (Mita 1986: 2).

Furthermore, as Māori people do not come from a literary heritage, it is an advantage to Mita transferring pictures of the mind to pictures on celluloid. Māori culture is based on whakapapa,[9] which is a form of genealogy; it is a whole history that is told in pictures. "So I've got these cultural, historical and ancestral links to storytelling through picture, which naturally gravitate towards film" (Stutesman 1984: 3). It became possible to transform these memory pictures and create a story "that you can see with your eye rather than with the mind's eye" (Stutesman 1984: 3). Merata Mita explained that she, as a filmmaker, is actually in the position of those who carried the oral tradition in olden days: the combination of a film's technical complexity with traditional Māori philosophy allows an unfragmented view of society that focuses on people rather than institutions. For Mita, filmmaking is "a continuation of the oral tradition"—a way to keep history and culture alive (Stutesman 1984: 3).

Through Indigenous filmmaking Merata Mita wants to open the people's eyes to what they have been closed to for a long time since the colonization of New Zealand by Europeans. She considers the medium of film as an instrument for demystifying the Māori way of life and its image (Stutesman 1984: 4): "I want my films to provide a vehicle especially for Māori people who have been so often misportrayed or portrayed through the eyes of a dominant culture whether domestic or foreign" (Mita 1986: 3). In doing so, she specifically directed her focus on social injustices and called for a complete shift and critique of dispossession and representation within New Zealand's society and film industry. Her interest in social issues stems from personal experiences as part of a marginalized cultural group: "[It] is a consequence of the fact that ever since I can remember as a kid, I've actually been on a collision course with politics and social reality in this country. That has heightened my awareness" (Mita 2002/2003: 31).

Her cinematic works *Bastion Point: Day 507* (1980) and *Patu!* (1983) went down in the history books of New Zealand because of their heavy documentary content (Peters 2007: 1). These two documentaries reflect the spirit of optimism within the "Māori Renaissance" at the time when several protest actions by Māori changed the public awareness about Aotearoa's Indigenous population and its culture.[10] In addition, she is the first (and only) female Māori filmmaker who has written, directed, and produced a feature-length film (Zimmer 2022). Her feature narrative *Mauri* (1988) (NZ on Screen n.d.) is about Māori identity and birthright and deals with the rhythms of birth, death, destiny, and the relationship with nature. She described *Mauri* (a love story that explores cultural differences and tensions within New Zealand) as "a probing enquiry into Māori cultural concepts and a parable about the schizophrenic existence of so many Māori in Pākehā society" (Mita 1996: 49). It seems no coincidence that Mita chose Eva Rickard as the female protagonist in her feature film. Rickard was an activist for Māori land rights and led the occupation of the Raglan Golf Course in 1978. It was land that had been gifted to the Crown by Māori in World War II but had not been returned and was used as a golf course instead.

*Bastion Point: Day 507* (1980) (see fig. 3) provides a glimpse into the second-largest Māori land/protest march as a backlash against the loss of their Indigenous culture and identity due to the adaptation to European values and norms demanded by Pākehā (partly under duress). Bastion Point (Auckland) was the site of the main Indigenous marae.[11] The government decided to sell it in 1977, whereupon hundreds of Māori occupied the

Figure 3. Bastion Point: Day 507 (1980).

marae for months. The peaceful Māori occupation was ended by a violent eviction in 1978. Merata Mita was on-site with a camera crew and documented the events (Belich 2001: 478).

The South African Springbok Tour in 1981 was considered to support South Africa's system of apartheid by some New Zealanders. When the government ignored the calls to cancel the tour, the New Zealand anti-apartheid movement organized peaceful protests to change its decision. With the beginning of the tour, the clashes between the police and the protestors got out of hand. Merata Mita recorded this massive civil disobedience. Her feature-length documentary Patu! (1983) (see fig. 4) depicts these stirring and brutal events that took place throughout Aotearoa in 1981 and can be seen as an act of resistance against racism and an expression of the courage and faith of the protestors and filmmakers (Murray 2013). It is mainly composed of footage of confrontations between opponents of the Springbok Rugby Tour and the police in various cities in New Zealand. The blurred and jerky images are due to handheld camera work, indicating that Mita was involved in the action. "Filming was dangerous and difficult. At times crews were beaten along with marchers. Police pushed cameras and camera crews aside" (Martin and Edwards 1997: 91).

During the production of Patu! Mita encountered a number of obstacles that were not only financial and legal but also private. Due to delays caused

Figure 4. *Patu!* (1983).

by police surveillance and the withdrawal of government funding, it took about three years for Mita's documentary to be completed (Mayer 2019). The Māori filmmaker faced difficulties raising funds; Mita described the process of funding independent films in New Zealand at the time as: "You beg, borrow and steal. . . . I mean, you can get small sums of money . . . from the Arts Council and the Film Commission, but the rest of it's just a real shit fight, every cent you can get" (Stutesman 1984: 10). Moreover, the footage had to be withheld until the conclusion of the court case to prevent it from being used as evidence: "The police got a court order . . . to use it [the television footage] in the trials against the people who'd been arrested. So I thought, right, the negative stays out of the country and we shifted the film around a lot" (Stutesman 1984: 4). In addition, Mita and her family faced physical and psychological violence as the police raided their family house, beat them, and strip-searched her (Zimmer 2022). She was criticized several times during filming for her radical approach and was accused of allegedly biased reporting: "I was asked repeatedly if I thought I was the right person to make the film, or why I was making it. The reason I was asked the questions was that some of those people told me they feared that the film would not be accurate because it would have a Māori perspective! The Pākehā bias in all things recorded in Aotearoa was never questioned" (Mita 1996: 47).

*Patu!* (1983) acted as a kind of mirror to highlight racism that still existed in New Zealand; it served as a catalyst for subsequent antiracist demonstrations in the country. "In exploring this cross-cultural divide, Mita's film also features a range of Māori talking heads who draw [a] direct parallel between the racist system of apartheid in South Africa, and institutional-ised racism within New Zealand culture" (Keown 2008: 201). For the coun-try's Indigenous population, Mita's documentaries about racism and the Pākehā's lack of understanding Māoritanga[12] are a tremendous achieve-ment. Even overseas, for example at the Phoenix Film Festival in London, *Patu!* received great attention (Stutesman 1984: 2); the filmmaker Ken Wlaschin called it the "major documentary of our time" (Mita 1986: 1).

Mita believes that every aspect of life is political because "as soon as you open your mouth you are in the arena of politics" (Stutesman 1984: 4). Above all, being born Indigenous is itself a political statement, as Heperi Mita recalls of his mother in his documentary (Zimmer 2022). "So I've been brought up knowing that being Māori is political, being a woman is politi-cal. I don't want to wear an elitist label that removes me from . . . things that I'm actively involved with, I'm not the detached observer. . . . I film the struggles that I've had experience in first-hand, like the Māori land occu-pations, anti-apartheid and anti-racist struggles" (Stutesman 1984: 4). Merata Mita earned great respect not only for her rigorous and relentless commitment to a realistic portrayal of Māori culture and identity in order to correct cinematic representations of Indigenous people that were marked by prejudice and stereotyping, but also because of her pathbreaking role as a female Māori filmmaker venturing into a medium dominated by (white) men: "As far as being radical, I only appear to be so because of the country's attitudes towards women and Māori, and to anyone who holds a particular point of view" (Mita 2002/2003: 31).

On the one hand, Mita was concerned with making the Indigenous people of New Zealand and their way of life visible (through film) and cor-recting distorted portrayals of Māori. On the other hand, she advocated for self-determination and equal rights for women, especially of Indigenous origin: "They [women] aren't going to be given the power, they have to fight for it like anyone else and they have to fight for it within their own ranks against the men who purport to support feminism. . . . The Māori women are the most oppressed, they are still on the level of fighting for basic sur-vival; there's not the luxury of that kind of western feminist movement" (Stutesman 1984: 8–9). It was not until *Patu!* that the presence of women within the New Zealand film industry became noticeable and visible (Martin and Edwards 1997: 91). After interviewing Merata Mita in 1983, the filmmaker of French–South African origin, Pascale Lamche, wrote the following: "Made on a tiny budget and under adverse conditions, it's [Patu!] a good example of how women's filmmaking continues to break through institutional and political barriers" (Stutesman 1984: 2).

## Conclusion and Outlook

"At the start, people used to look at me, you know, in utter disbelief when I've talked about filming and I think it was because there are not only no Māori filmmakers in the country but the fact that I was also a woman" (Dailymotion 2023, 00:2:45). Heperi Mita's *Merata: How Mum Decolonised the Screen* (2018) points out that Mita can be seen as a true foot soldier in the battle of portraying Indigenous narratives through film (see fig. 5). She did not make films for fame and she refused to wait for someone else to do it. Mita did not focus on innovative techniques; instead she fought for proper representation and documentation of those who fight for the same goals (Asenap 2019). Especially "when you have kids, you have an investment in the future, and you come out fighting again" (Mayer 2019).

Merata Mita's life and work as a female Indigenous filmmaker, activist, and mother have been shaped and driven by the pursuit of social and gender equality as well as the struggle against cultural oppression and racism, and for the preservation of Indigenous ways of life, traditions, and identity. For a long time, "stereotyped images of Māori have distorted the cultural basis of Māori identities" (Fleras and Spoonley 1999: 65), but in turn, the medium of film has been one of the most effective instruments in representing the struggle for survival and revitalization of Aotearoa's Indigenous people, their identity, and their culture (Martens 2012: 5, 18). In the course of her career as a filmmaker, Mita "emerged at the forefront of Indigenous cinema, both in her native country and internationally" (Zimmer 2022). She believed in producing films with Indigenous relevance to reinforce Indigenous values and an individual culture. When a Māori film is made, it refers to the Indigenous people of New Zealand only on the surface; in depth, it has the capacity of Indigenizing the screen in any part of the world it is shown and thus is a mouthpiece for all marginalities worldwide (Mita 1996: 54).

The education and promotion of young Māori were very important to Mita, so that they could gain a foothold in the film business (Mita 2002/ 2003: 34). She worked on many projects and coproductions and advised young (Indigenous) filmmakers and students (Mayer 2019). Adam Piron, the present-day director of the Sundance Institute's Indigenous Program,

Figure 5. A still from Heperi Mita's documentary showing his mother at work on a film set.

explained that Mita's filmic style can be described as following an "'Indigenous mind-set' . . . a collective view implying a responsibility to the community" (Zimmer 2022). Piron added that he sees her as a mentor whose legacy extends beyond those people who knew her. Merata Mita observed a lack of Native peoples being trained in film and television, which is one of the reasons for the underrepresentation of Indigenous and community stories. Throughout her career she became an advocate for Indigenous voices around the world. In order to continue and honor Mita's efforts, the Sundance Institute initiated the Merata Mita Fellowship for Indigenous Artists (Zimmer 2022).

Over the last decades, a growing body of Indigenous films has been developed. Therewith, "filmmaking has proven to be an increasingly significant vehicle for Indigenous people's self-representation" (Christensen 2017: 92). By now, those films cover a range of formats and differ in narrative and aesthetic film practices in order to express and negotiate Indigenous realities lived by Native peoples all over the world (Christensen 2017: 92). Whereas Heperi Mita's mother explains in his documentary that she cannot make "nice" films because her people experience ugly things, Merata Mita's view on contemporary Indigenous filmmaking changed in the course of its development (Zimmer 2022). Ever since Chelsea Cohen[13] watched *Bastion Point: Day 507*, she wanted to become a filmmaker herself. Her great role model was and is Merata Mita, with whom she worked on the documentary *Saving Grace: Te Whakarauora Tangata* (2011) shortly before Mita's death (Husband 2018). Aoetearoa's filmmaker Cohen, who is one of the directors of *Waru* (2017),[14] described Mita's perspective on contemporary "Indigenous Cinema" and her influence on her—as a female filmmaker—as follows:

> Merata talks about storytelling in phases. . . . When she was starting out, it was a matter of talking to ourselves and trying to come to terms with what was happening to Māori as a whole. . . . Kind of like unravelling decolonisation, and figuring out how you fit in that whole space. But now we're at a point where Māori films, and other indigenous films, have so much heart, and there are so many different layers to what people want to talk about. They don't have to be all dark and . . . sad stories. (Smith 2021: 497)

It could be argued that they are universal by character, but Indigenous by heart. Besides Chelsea Cohen, Briar Grace-Smith and Ainsley Gardiner collaborated on the anthology film *Waru*. The two female filmmakers made the film *Cousins* (2021), an adaptation of the novel of the same name by Patricia Grace, published in 1992. Merata Mita began working on this feature-length drama when she unexpectedly passed away in 2010. Through her work at the New Zealand Film Commission, Grace-Smith was aware of Mita's unsuccessful attempts to shoot *Cousins*. She knew about the difficulties Merata faced making the film, but still managed, along with Ainsley Gardiner as a producer, to complete Mita's unfinished film project. This film was very important to the Māori filmmakers because it not only allows insight and understanding into the Māori culture and the injustices many Indigenous peoples have to face, but also because it is a story about Māori women (Debelle 2021; Grater 2021). Most recently, the Māori filmmaker Paula Whetu Jones[15] follows in Merata Mita's footsteps by portraying the life of Dame Whina Cooper as a Māori leader, wife, and mother in the biographical film *Whina* (2022). The biopic chronicles the story of a Māori matriarch who stood up for the rights of her people and particularly for those of women. For Whetu Jones, "It's not just a 'Māori' story, it's a story about an extraordinary Māori woman, that has the potential to relate to everyone" (WIFT NZ 2022).

Merata Mita paved the way for Indigenous filmmaking. She acted as an inspiration, mentor, and companion for many (female) filmmakers of Native origin in New Zealand and around the world. In doing so, she stressed the power of Indigenous film to bring about and influence social change in any part of the world (Smith 2021: 497). In the end, Heperi Mita's intention of making a documentary about his mother was "to offer her story as an example that despite how hopeless some of these situations may feel, her triumphs are proof that those sacrifices are worth it" (Asenap 2019).

**Denise Schallenkammer** holds a master of arts in communication and media studies as well as in British and American transcultural studies. She is a PhD student at the Institute for Media Research at the University of Rostock and a research associate at the Sorbian Institute in Bautzen (Germany). Her dissertation project deals with the comparison of filmic depictions of the ethnic minorities of the Sorbs, Sámi, and Māori. Special attention is paid to the cinematic representation(s) of Indigenous identity. Her fields of work include cultural, (post) colonial, and Indigenous studies, as well as film and media studies.

**Notes**

1  Māori are New Zealand's Indigenous people (Ka'ai 2005: 13).
2  A more detailed description of what is meant by "Indigenous Cinema" is provided in the section on historical and contextual background information about New Zealand (film) history.
3  *Aotearoa* is the Māori name for New Zealand (Keown 2008: 205).
4  *Pākehā* is a Māori term for (white) inhabitants of New Zealand who are not of Māori ancestry.
5  More background information can be found in the descriptions of Mita's filmic works.
6  *Whānau* means "family" (Ka'ai 2005: 14).
7  *Patu* is a close quarter weapon; it is a flat double-sided striking weapon and is usually made from rough stone or bone (Basil 2012).
8  *Te Reo Māori*: Māori-language (Ka'ai 2005: 14).
9  *Whakapapa* means "genealogy," which is a key concept in Māori culture; it represents the core of Māori knowledge and is at the center of (cultural) identity discourse (Moura-Koçoğlu 2011: 15).
10  Detailed information is provided further below in the text.
11  The *marae* is a sacred open meeting area, a communal meeting house, and a traditional Māori-complex where particular rituals occur (Ka'ai 2005: 13).
12  *Māoritanga* means "Māori culture" (Hokowhitu 2008: 121).
13  Cohen is sometimes credited by her maiden name, Chelsea Winstanley.
14  *Waru* (2017) is a drama consisting of eight short films made by a collective of eight Māori women, who address and respond to pressing social problems in a

multilayered way based on an interior life (see previous remarks on Barry Barclay's concept of "Fourth Cinema") that is related to principles coming from Te Ao Māori (i.e., Māori worldview). See Ka'ai 2005: 13 and Smith 2021: 497.

15  Paula Whetu Jones directed *Whina* (2022) in collaboration with James Napier Robertson.

## Works Cited

Asenap, Jason. 2019. "A Maori Filmmaker and the Fight for Proper Indigenous Narratives. Hepi Mita Offers a Fascinating Look at His Mother's Life in *Merata: How Mum Decolonised the Screen*." *High Country News*, August 23. https://www.hcn .org/issues/51.16/tribal-affairs-maori- filmmaker-and-the-fight-for-proper -indigenous-narratives.

Barclay, Barry. 2003. "Celebrating Fourth Cinema." *Illusions*, no. 35: 7–11.

Basil, Keane. 2012. "Riri—Traditional Māori Warfare—Rākau Māori—Māori Weapons and Their Uses." *Te Ara—The Encyclopedia of New Zealand*. https://teara.govt.nz /en/riri-traditional-maori-warfare-page-3.

Belich, James. 2001. *Paradise Reforged: A History of the New Zealanders from the 1880s to the Year 2000*. Auckland: Penguin.

Berlinale. n.d. "*Merata: How Mum Decolonised the Screen*." https://www.berlinale.de/en /2019/programme/201912920.html (accessed March 16, 2022).

Byrnes, Giselle M. 1999. "Patrons of Maori Culture: Power, Theory, and Ideology in the Maori Renaissance." *Kōtare: New Zealand Notes and Queries* 2, no. 2: 71–73.

Christensen, Cato. 2017. "Indigenous Feature Film: A Pathway for Indigenous Religion?" In *Handbook of Indigenous Religion(s)*, edited by Greg Johnson and Siv Ellen Kraft, 92–107. Leiden: Brill.

Clelland-Stokes, Sacha. 2007. *Representing Aboriginality: A Post-colonial Analysis of the Key Trends of Representing Aboriginality in South Africa, Australian, and Aotearoa/New Zealand Film*. Højbjerg: Intervention Press.

Conrich, Ian, and Sarah Davy. 1997. *Views from the Edge of the World: New Zealand Film*. London: Kakapo.

Coulthard, Glen S. 2019. "Introduction: A Fourth World Resurgent." In *The Fourth World: An Indian Reality*, edited by George Manuel and Michael Posluns, iv–xxxvi. Minneapolis: University of Minnesota Press.

Dailymotion. 2023. "*Merata: How Mum Decolonised the Screen* (2019) Watch HD." Video, 01:28:08. https://www.dailymotion.com/video/x8j2240.

Debelle, Penelope. 2021. "Maori Women Find Their Voice in Powerful New Film." *Inreview*, May 26. https://inreview.com.au/inreview/books-and-poetry/2021 /05/26/poem-a-kind-of-love/.

Della Valle, Paola. 2010. *From Silence to Voice: The Rise of Maori Literature*. Auckland: Oralia Media.

Fleras, Augie, and Paul Spoonley. 1999. *Recalling Aotearoa: Indigenous Politics and Ethnic Relations in New Zealand*. Auckland: Oxford University Press.

Goh, Katie. 2019. "Merata Mita, the Filmmaker Who Decolonised the Screen." *Huck*, February 14. https://www.huckmag.com/article/merata-mita-filmmaker-new -zealand-declonised-the-screen.

Grater, Tom. 2021. "Array Releasing Bords New Zealand Indigenous Drama *Cousins*." *Deadline*, June 29. https://deadline.com/2021/06/array-releasing-new-zealand -indigenous-drama-cousins-1234782615/.

Hokowhitu, Brendan. 2008. "The Death of Koro Paka: 'Traditional' Māori Patriarchy." *Contemporary Pacific* 20, no. 1: 115–41.

Husband, Dale. 2018. "Chelsea Winstanley: My Idol Was Merata Mita." *E-Tangata*, August 19. https://e-tangata.co.nz/korero/chelsea-winstanley-my-idol-was -merata-mita/.

Ka'ai, Tānia M. 2005. "Te Kauae Mārō Muriranga-Whenua (The Jawbone of Muriranga-Whenua): Globalising Local Indigenous Culture—Māori Leadership, Gender, and Cultural Knowledge Transmission as Represented in the Film *Whale Rider*." *Portal Journal of Multidisciplinary International Studies* 2, no. 2: 1–15.

Keown, Michelle. 2008. "'He Iwi Kotahi Tatou'? Nationalism and Cultural Identity in Maori Film." In *Contemporary New Zealand Cinema: From New Wave to Blockbuster*, edited by Ian Conrich and Stuart Murray, 197–210. London: I. B. Tauris.

King, Michael. 2003. *The Penguin History of New Zealand*. Auckland: Penguin.

Loomba, Ania. *Colonialism/Postcolonialism*. London: Routledge, 1998.

Martens, Emiel. 2012. "Maori on the Silver Screen: The Evolution of Indigenous Feature Filmmaking in Aotearoa/New Zealand." *International Journal of Critical Indigenous Studies* 5, no. 1: 2–30.

Martin, Helen, and Sam Edwards. 1997. *New Zealand Film from 1912–1996*. Auckland: Oxford University Press.

Mayer, So. 2019. "Merata: The Maori Film Legend and Her Legacy." *British Film Institute*, October 7. https://www2.bfi.org.uk/news-opinion/sight-sound -magazine-features/merata-mita-maori-indigenous-pioneer-filmmaker-mum -decolonised-screen-documentary.

Milligan, Christina. 2015. "Sites of Exuberance: Barry Barclay and Fourth Cinema, Ten Years On." *International Journal of Media and Cultural Politics* 11, no. 3: 347–59.

Mita, Heperi, dir. 2018. *Merata: How Mum Decolonised the Screen*. New Zealand: Ārama Pictures.

Mita, Merata. 1986. *Listen to Women for a Change*. New York: Jane Addams Peace Association.

Mita, Merata. 1996. "The Soul and the Image." In *Film in Aotearoa*, edited by Jonathan Dennis and Jan Bieringa, 36–54. Wellington: Victoria University Press.

Mita, Merata. 2002/2003. "Stories Worth Telling." *Mana* 49: 30–35.

Moura-Koçoğlu, Michaela. 2011. *Narrating Indigenous Modernities: Transcultural Dimensions in Contemporary Maori Literature*. Amsterdam: Rodopi.

Murray, Mihi. 2013. "Patu! A Perspective." NZ on Screen. https://www.nzonscreen.com /title/patu-1983/background.

Murray, Stuart. 2008. *Images of Dignity: Barry Barclay and Fourth Cinema*. Wellington: Huia.

NZFilm. n.d. "Merata: How Mum Decolonised the Screen." https://www.nzfilm.co.nz/films /merata-how-mum-decolonised-screen (accessed March 16, 2022).

NZiff. n.d. "Merata: How Mum Decolonised the Screen." https://www.nziff.co.nz/2018/film /merata-how-mum-decolonised-the-screen/ (accessed March 16, 2022).

NZ on Screen. n.d. "Merata Mita." https://www.nzonscreen.com/profile/merata-mita
/biography (accessed March 16, 2022).

Peters, Geraldene. 2007. "Lives of Their Own: Films by Merata Mita." In *New Zealand
Filmmakers*, edited by Ian Conrich and Stuart Murray, 103–20. Detroit: Wayne
State University Press.

Smith, Jo. 2021. "Indigenous Insistence on Film." In *Routledge Handbook of Critical
Indigenous Studies*, edited by Brendan Hokowhitu, Aileen Moreton-Robinson,
Linda Tuhiwai-Smith, Chris Andersen, and Steve Larkin, 488–500. London:
Routledge.

Stutesman, Drake. 1984. "Interview with Merata Mita by Pascale Lamche." *Journal of
Cinema and Media* 25: 2–11.

Waititi, Kahurangi. 2008. "Māori Documentary Film: Interiority and Exteriority."
*MAI Review* 1: 1–10.

WIFT NZ. 2022. "Paula Whetu Jones on Her Feature Film *Whina*." https://www.wiftnz
.org.nz/news/news-archive/2022/jun/paula-whetu-jones-on-her-feature-film
-whina/.

Wood, Houston. 2008. *Native Features: Indigenous Films around the World*. New York:
Bloomsbury.

Zimmer, Vanessa. 2022. "Who Was . . . Merata Mita?" *Sundance Institute*, April 28.
https://www.sundance.org/blogs/who-was-merata-mita/.

Gina Athena Ulysse

## Tools of the Trade; or, Women's Works

> But long ago when the people were given these ceremonies, the changing
> began, if only in the aging of the yellow gourd rattle or the shrinking of the
> skin around the eagle's claw, if only in the different voices from generation
> to generation, singing the chants. You see, in many ways, the ceremonies
> have always been changing.
> —Leslie Marmon Silko, *Ceremony*

The Kwi—made from the kalbas or calabash tree (*Crescentia
Cujete*)—
are the simple, sacred, and profane holder of rasanblaj,
a gathering of ideas, things, people, and spirits,
(Though not necessarily in that order!).

In 2019, variations of these gourds known as calabash in the African diaspora, which exist all over the world, made themselves known to me as the
primary materials of a new commissioned installation work.

Too aware of stories concerning women as calabashes or women and
calabashes, this series of photographs featuring my work with the Kwi
present evidence of serendipitous encounters
between artist and medium,
energy and material
as well as the seen and unseen.

MERIDIANS · feminism, race, transnationalism   23:1 April 2024
DOI: 10.1215/15366936-10926976 © 2024 Smith College

Figure 1. Ochre.

Figure 2. Indigo.

Figure 3. Myrrh.

Figure 4. Kindling.

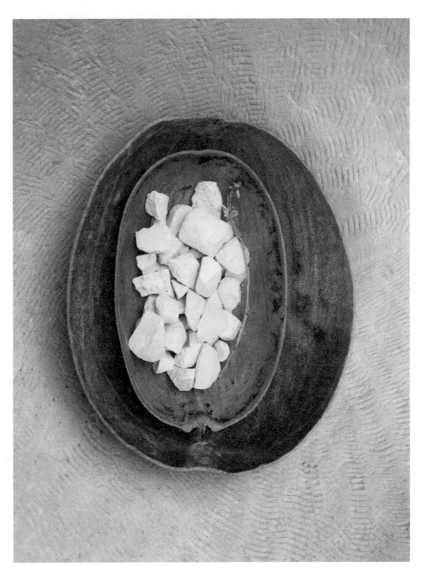

Figure 5. Sulfur.

Indeed, I did not set out to explore the relationship between gendered labor, the quotidian, and the spiritual. Yet here they were. Entanglements exposed:

The Sacred        Medicine       TheGreatWomb      Laundry

                  Conduit                        Bowls

                  Bluing      Cosmetics        Twinning

Source of Wisdom

                                        Water Bearer

            Measuring Device

Libations                    Belly                      Portals

       Rattle                         Spoons

            Divination

Cooking                      Foraging               Triplets

The wonder in these Kwi formations is enhanced by the organic patina and pigments from natural items that have utilitarian uses in what is associated with women's work. Such things imbued with colonial histories of extraction are also charged with properties that render them effective ingredients in all kinds of rituals and healing work.

Photo credit: All artwork and photographs are by © Gina Athena Ulysse (2019)

..................................................................................

**Gina Athena Ulysse** is a Haitian American feminist artist-scholar and professor of feminist studies at the University of California Santa Cruz. In the last two decades, she has been concerned with the expression and representation of the dailyness of Black diasporic conditions; her rasanblaj approach to her art and writing practice entails ongoing crossings and dialogues in the arts, humanities, and social sciences. She has been published in art catalogs as well as journals such as *Feminist Studies*, *Gastronomica*, *Frontiers*, *Journal of Haitian Studies*, *Interim Poetics*, *Kerb: Journal of Landscape Architecture*, *Third Text*, and others. Over the years, she has performed at a range of venues including the Bowery, the British Museum, Gorki Theatre, LaMaMa, Marcus Garvey Liberty Hall, MoMA Salon, and the MCA in Australia.

Mariam Georgis

········································································································

# Traversing Disciplinary Boundaries, Globalizing Indigeneities

## Visibilizing Assyrians in the Present

Abstract: The author's work spans the disciplinary boundaries of political science, Middle East studies, Indigenous studies, and their subfields. Broadly situated within critical theoretical bodies of knowledge, she focuses on an Indigenous nation in what is today known as Iraq. Her work is grounded within particular and fragmented locations that blur various lines and multiple layers of coloniality. This article offers a critical reflection of the invisibility in working on Indigeneity in southwest Asia within the structural imperatives of the academy. It takes up each of these themes by examining the fields of international relations and Iraqi studies to show how the story of Assyrians is invisible or unintelligible across these fields of political science and Middle East studies. Moreover, what the Assyrian story tells us about these disciplines and the multiplicity of coloniality (Patel 2019) is also rendered invisible. Despite the absence of Assyrians from Indigenous studies, the author sees this field as a site from which to potentially globalize Indigeneities. Specifically, she uses Indigenous feminism to construct a more nuanced framework into Assyrian histories, a framework that uses the lens of colonialism, land theft, erasure, and genocide to reframe the Assyrian experience as a remnant of the colonial global order.

## Introduction

While Middle Eastern studies (MES) has yet to contend with Indigeneity on a broad basis,[1] now, more than ever, political science and its subfields are inviting scholars to critically reflect on the ways in which our methods, canons, and assumptions contribute to the invisibilization, distortion, and

MERIDIANS · feminism, race, transnationalism    23:1  April 2024
DOI: 10.1215/15366936-10926936  © 2024 Smith College

narrow analysis of Indigenous politics and peoples. This concern for inserting or including Indigeneity, Indigenous analysis, and Indigenous peoples, however, materializes within the parameters, and in turn, constraints, of the discipline, which establish the conditions under which this insertion and inclusion takes place. More problematically, any analysis which does not fit neatly into an already existing or preestablished understanding of Indigeneity or peoples in the discipline becomes unintelligible, illegible, and invisible. This article brings Assyrians into conversation with Indigenous studies, Iraqi studies, international relations (IR) and other critical scholarship of global colonialism, decolonization, and race. In doing so, I am writing to challenge the ways in which Assyrians are made invisible in academic scholarship on Indigeneities, colonialism, decolonization, and solidarity across decolonial struggles. Even worse, when they are taken up, they are often framed in problematic, ahistorical, and distorted ways. I offer a critical reflection of international relations and Iraqi studies to show how the story of Assyrians is invisible or unknowable across these subfields of political science and Middle East studies. Moreover, what the Assyrian story tells us about these disciplines and the multiplicity of coloniality (Patel 2019) is also rendered invisible. This invisibility is the underlying foundation for myths perpetuated by states and scholars of the region on the extinction of the Assyrian people, leaving their territory ripe for the creation of states such as Iraq, Syria, Turkey, Iran, and more recently, the Kurdistan Region of Iraq.

Despite their absence from Indigenous studies, I see this field as a site from which to potentially globalize Indigeneities. I use Indigenous feminism to construct a more nuanced framework into Assyrian histories, a framework that uses the lens of colonialism, land theft, erasure, and genocide to reframe the Assyrian experience as a remnant of the colonial global order. In so doing, I argue the Assyrian story is a global Indigenous issue rather than a matter of domestic contentious politics. First, I situate myself as Assyrian, as part of the diaspora, and as a scholar of IR who has found this discipline lacking and distorting for my work, which brings an Indigenous feminist lens to the study of the "international" and southwest Asia (Middle East).[2] Second, I discuss the failures of the discipline of IR, which itself is implicated as a legitimator of the Westphalian state, the existing international order, and the colonial legacies that also produce Assyrian erasures, genocides, and displacements. Third, animated by the feminist principle of "the personal is political," I critique Iraqi studies and show the commonalities Assyrians share with other Indigenous peoples: invasion, dispossession, displacement, domination, marginalization, ongoing resistance, and the context of the invaders' mythmaking, which passes as political and cultural truth of the states founded on Assyrian territory. Finally, this article uses an Indigenous feminist lens to recount Assyrian histories as told by Assyrians to critique the disciplines of IR and Middle East studies.

**Traversing Disciplinary Boundaries: Being Assyrian in the Academy**

Spanning the disciplinary boundaries of political science, Middle East studies, Indigenous studies, and their subfields, I focus on a transnational Indigenous nation within the present-day political borders of Iraq, Syria, Turkey, and Iran. My work is grounded within particular and fragmented locations that blur various lines and multiple layers of coloniality. As my lived experiences are situated along multiple locations, histories, and languages, I reflect on the ways in which my work has been and continues to be shaped by my location in both marginal and hegemonic structures and spaces. I am an Indigenous woman from southwest Asia colonized by multiple waves of Arab and Muslim conquests long before British, Western Catholic, and Protestant missionaries, and later, American colonial violence displaced me from my homeland—rendering me a refugee, and then eventually, a settler on the stolen lands of Indigenous peoples *here*, where I become inadvertently complicit in settler colonialism in Canada. Within settler colonial Canada and its discourses of multiculturalism, I am also interpreted as a woman of color for the first time in my life—as Brown, which has become synonymous with terrorist and/or Muslim during the post-9/11 era and the height of anti-Muslim racism when an Iraqi or a Brown body can be nothing else.

Writing about the ongoing colonization and occupation of the Assyrian homeland in the making of modern states, including the ongoing project for Kurdish self-determination and statehood, I start by acknowledging my location on ancestral and unceded traditional Coast Salish Lands, including the Tsleil-Waututh (səÌ̓ilw̓ətaʔɬ), Kwikwetlem (kʷikʷəƛ̓əm), Squamish (Sḵwx̱wú7mesh), and Musqueam (xʷməθkʷəy̓əm) Nations. It is important for me to also draw attention to the history of my forced displacement from my traditional homeland through imperial and colonial wars and ongoing occupation of my village in what is today known as the Kurdistan Region of

Iraq, as the reason my family and I are presently on these lands.[3] In their thoughtful and careful answer to the question, "What can 'settler of colour' teach us?" Shaista Patel and Nisha Nath powerfully assert that "thinking about the place of settlers of colour in white settler colonialisms also necessitates firmly holding onto multiple colonialisms that bring racial-ized people to other occupied territories" (Patel and Nath 2022: 146). They remind us that "decolonization *here* will not and cannot happen without shaking the roots of imperialism, war, and ongoing invasions by white settler states that also function as aggressors of empire" (Patel and Nath 2022: 146; emphasis added). Drawing on this important contribution to the lineage of Black scholars and scholars of color who have carefully sought to trace their histories and contexts to understand their positionalities in white settler colonial states and contexts, I am thinking about my own ori-gins, interconnections of racial capitalism and invasion, and multiple forms of dispossession and dis/relocations to white settler colonial Canada. It is my intention in writing about the invisibility of Assyrians in academic scholarship to bring the Assyrian struggle in conversation and in solidarity with decolonial struggles and other intertwined liberation struggles across the globe. I am interested in using Indigenous feminist theoretical and methodological orientations to explore the interconnec-tedness of coloniality across time, place, and space. Despite important differences in history, context, even worldviews, Assyrians have something to contribute to our understanding of colonialisms and Indigeneities. Assyrian Indigeneity reveals a parallel connection to land and land-based politics, challenging the fundamental legitimacy of the global nation-state structure. They also share a connected lived experience of colonization in its different forms by different powers, which has resulted in their struggle against dispossession and erasure.

My earliest memory of my country of origin involves the sounds of war. But my earliest collective memory is that of a land lost, a people scattered, a nation divided by artificial borders and the politics therein but also of survival, resistance, and a refusal to be erased. As a scholar of IR, I cannot find myself in the story of the "global." Moreover, when IR does turn its attention to events or issues that relate to me, I find that it is not *me* doing the talking. Critical theories and specifically, scholarship within critical postcolonial, decolonial feminist approaches and writers from the Global South make the story of IR more relevant, yet I am still absent. Crossing disciplinary boundaries into Indigenous studies shows me that interconnected experiences exist, but even this field does not mention Assyrians or the experiences of expulsion in the making of the modern colonial states of Iraq, Syria, Turkey, and Iran and the ongoing self-labeled postcolonial project of Kurdish statehood. The Assyrian experience is seldom recognized as contemporary or Indigenous, and Indigenous studies, which is becoming more comparative, has yet to take up the Assyrian experience. This might be because Indigenous studies is place-based and scholars within this field are writing from their specific experiences of colonization and Indigeneity. As such, it is important to contribute to Indigenous studies by bringing in the Assyrian story and experiences of colonization and displacement in the context of southwest Asia to build these interconnections and globalize colonialisms and Indigeneities.

The field that seemingly has a greater likelihood of taking up the Assyrian experience is the one that has arguably the most vested interest in Assyrians' erasure. Scholars in this field continue to produce an archive of knowledge that is underpinned by our very absence. The "Near East," "Middle East," "Ancient Near East," "Oriental studies," and other such departments are in almost every university across the world, especially in the Global North in institutions that have studied the Other since contact. Colonial and Orientalist by their very nature, what is remarkable about these departments is the complete absence of Assyrians as a contemporary nation Indigenous to this region in the modern context. Specifically, the Middle East is the study of the "Arab World," the "Muslim World," and sometimes, "minorities," even by critical scholars of the region. Assyrian historian Sargon Donabed writes, "In Middle East Studies, scholars simply reproduce the metanarrative in a different light, which marginalizes Indigenous and minority groups to a citation in history" (Donabed 2015: 11). When Assyrians are mentioned, they are misrepresented because they are inserted as an ethnic and/or religious minority or as "Christian Arabs." Consider, for example, the Middle East Studies Association Conference in the United States with its notable erasure of Indigeneity in Iraq, Syria, Turkey, and Iran; absence of any mention of Assyrians in panels on any of these states; and number of panels on "ancient" Assyria where Assyrians are relics of the ancient past instead of contemporary political actors. This reality is formative to my understanding that writing Assyrians into the Western academy needs to be done within MES and Iraqi studies as well, within fields populated by scholars who come from the same place I do, and still discount Assyrians.

The states in the region known colonially as the Middle East are carved out of "ancient empires" by colonial powers. The Ottoman Empire's entry into the First World War ended its rule over the region, a territory long coveted by colonial powers and presently known as the Middle East in reference to its distance from Europe. The Franco-British division of this region due to the Allied victory was formalized by two Foreign Office and Quai d'Orsay officials: Sir Mark Sykes and Francois Georges-Picot in the now famous Sykes-Picot Agreement (Ouahes 2018: 13). Iraq and Syria were both created in this fashion under British and French Mandates while the Republic of Turkey was established by the Treaty of Lausanne as the successor to the Ottoman Empire in 1923. Having unified as an independent state in 1501 under the Safavid Dynasty, Iran was ruled without interruption until the Iranian Revolution when Iran became the Islamic Republic on April 1, 1979. This history is important and marks the "beginning" of the modern Middle East, which usually focuses on Arab nationalism; inter- and intracommunal conflict; authoritarianism; development; politics of the Islamic world, including sectarianism and militant Islam; and the question of Palestine/Israel. The fact that these concepts and ideas about the Middle East are themselves problematic, colonial, and Oriental has been taken up by many important scholars (Said 2014; Mahdavi and Knight 2012; Achcar 2013) and will not be rehearsed here as I am specifically concerned with the absence of Assyrians. Recently, there has been an increasing interest in studying "minority" groups, although the study of minorities has always been part of MES (White 2012; Zabad 2017; Rowe 2018). But the story of Assyrians in *Beth-Nahrain* begins much earlier. This is one of the reasons why Assyrians are usually seen—if they are seen at all—as relics of the ancient past. For political reasons, Assyrians are sometimes seen as disconnected from ancient Assyrians; today, inside Iraq (and elsewhere in southwest Asia) and in Western media and scholarship, Assyrians are referred to as a "Christian minority." The Assyrian identity is so politicized when it is used that I am frequently asked to explain who I am talking about or asked to *prove* Assyrians are descendants of ancient Assyrians in my work, which is both anti-Indigenous and political. The four modern states in question have been built through Arab, Turkish, Iranian, and Kurdish nationalisms on Assyrian land. These nationalisms and states are not the same, even though they are interrelated as they have been formed within one region. The specific historical formations and processes in each of these modern states have resulted in differing yet interconnected

Assyrian experiences inside each state. However, these states share two commonalities: first, their attempted erasure of Assyrian Indigeneity and second, assimilatory state mechanisms and policies to subsume the Assyrian nation within the larger state as minorities, even if these policies have taken different forms in each state. More importantly, acknowledging or recognizing the existence of Assyrians as a priori to these modern political entities with rightful claims to this land and its resources unravels the ongoing project of the making of these states, especially of the more recent project of a larger Kurdistan in/on these states.

While I find it problematic to respond to questions about the legitimacy of the Assyrian identity, for the sake of increasing awareness of the Assyrian nation through my work, I am using *Assyrian* here to refer to those who self-identify as Assyrian today[4] and who have always and continue to inhabit *Beth-Nahrain* ("the land between two rivers," often referred to as Mesopotamia by Western scholars).[5] *Mesopotamia* refers to southern and southeastern present-day Turkey; northwestern present-day Iran; northern present-day Iraq, which is presently established as the Kurdistan Region of Iraq (KRI); and northeastern present-day Syria, which is presently considered the Autonomous Administration of North and East Syria (known as *Rojova* in Kurdish). Assyrians speak Assyrian, sometimes referred to as a modern form of Neo-Mesopotamian Aramaic (commonly known as Neo-Aramaic and Neo-Syriac in scholarly work) with a heavy Akkadian influence, and also use classical Syriac as an ecclesiastical tongue (Donabed 2015: 3). Assyrian historian Alda Benjamen (2019) tells us the Akkadian and Sumerian influences in their language are indicative of their long presence in Mesopotamia or modern-day Iraq and neighboring countries. Those Assyrians who speak a derivative of this language today self-identify as "*Sūrōyō/Sūrāyā* derived directly from the Neo-Assyrian word Assūrāyu" (Donabed 2018: 118). The English word *Assyrian* is used to refer to this nation today in and to the English-speaking world.

Indigeneity is most often studied within settler colonial contexts where the settler is white and geographically bound to the Americas, Oceania, Scandinavia, the Arctic, and Russia. When studies of settler colonialism travel across continents, it is often (and more recently) associated with Palestine and Kashmir. Perhaps part of the reason for the absence of Assyrians might be that Assyrians whose scholarship focuses on Assyrians have only recently entered Western academia and/or are largely unknown to the English-speaking world. Benjamen (2022: 16) tells us the "absence of

Assyrians from scholarly discussion reflects not only their omission from national archives and libraries, but also a lack of language training among scholars." She also importantly reminds us that much of the Assyrian archives and cultural heritage have been destroyed, relocated, looted, or closed in certain nation-states (Benjamen 2022: 16). I add that the four states which make up the Assyrian homeland have been able to portray themselves as Arab, Turkish, and Iranian to the rest of the world. This is a credit to their nation-building projects both politically and academically, at home and abroad, in building these "nations" through the attempted erasure of the Indigenous peoples on whose lands those states are built. Using an Indigenous feminist lens, the following sections analyze the absence of Assyrians in the fields of IR and Iraqi studies.

**International Relations: The "Domestic" Is Global**
International relations as a discipline is concerned with solutions to the problem of war and violence in the international system. International politics in IR are predicated on the taken-for-granted colonial, Westphalian arrangement. This means that the state is the central actor and the main unit of analysis of conventional IR. Almost every undergraduate syllabus in the discipline is introduced to the "theories of IR" in a chronological order beginning with realism, liberalism, the "neo" schools of realism and liberalism, and then the critical theories of constructivism, Marxism, feminism (usually every type of feminism is covered in this week if feminism is allotted a week), and postcolonialism. Depending on the institution and on the professor, often the "critical" theories are lumped together in one week at the undergraduate level and only separated at the graduate levels. The politics inherent in the decisions around curriculum are interrelated to the reasons this process is wholly insufficient as it predisposes scholars to a colonial way of understanding, analyzing, and being in the world. These theories are then applied to concepts and conflicts such as terrorism, international institutions, war on terror, humanitarian intervention—concepts that are themselves mired in the politics inherent in the decisions related to curriculum and what becomes worthy of study in IR. Conventional IR is underpinned by many silences, absences, erasures, and distortions.

Postcolonial IR does the critical work of analyzing colonialism; empire; theoretical and methodological Eurocentrism; global inequality, exclusion and violence; and colonial legacies underpinning global structures and politics. One notable and seeming absence is Indigeneity. What I mean is that the discipline of Indigenous studies and insights made by Indigenous scholars on the condition of ongoing coloniality in a "postcolonial" world, the lived experiences of settler colonialism, and enduring Indigeneity are not present in the core of the IR discipline and sometimes not in the critical approaches such as postcolonialism. This might be because postcolonial scholars are writing and thinking about international politics from their locations as formerly colonized, even if colonial legacies that shape their lived experiences and their politics continue in the present day. It might also be because many Indigenous scholars are not in the field of IR; but this too is telling of the discipline's narrow and problematic focus on the "international" system and the taken-for-granted idea of the state. Jodi Byrd (Chickasaw) remarks how notable it is that postcolonial theory and American Indian studies rarely have been in conversation given that they formed within the academy almost simultaneously and share a concern with the ramifications of colonial legacies (Byrd 2011: xxxii). What this means for the study of global politics, then, is the erasure of so much ongoing violence, especially in the form of land dispossession and displacement in the making of modern territorial states. It also means that everyday people and communities are always the ones who bear the brunt of state-centric, colonial, and violent policies across the globe.

It is usually easy to forget because of how measurably colonial and Anglo/Eurocentric IR scholarship is, but there exists a tradition of the critical study of race and racisms in IR that dates to the field's inception in the late nineteenth century (Shilliam 2020: 2). Robbie Shilliam (2020: 2) reminds us that there are also many scholars who made significant contributions to the study of imperialism and the postcolonial condition in IR during the 1990s and 2000s.[6] While Iraq, Syria, Turkey, and Iran are not the specific focus of analysis in this literature, their position in the global racial hierarchy can be theorized using this lens. My work on Iraq is greatly indebted to this lineage of scholarship on race in IR, especially in relation to examining imperial powers' infliction of violence on the state of Iraq and more importantly, Iraqis. It is this profound respect and gratitude that compels me to challenge the categorization of Iraq in critical literature as a *postcolonial* state, referring to its independence from the British Mandate in 1932. The same can be said of Syria, which gained its independence in 1943. However, these states were constructed on Assyrian land, a fact that is strikingly absent from analyses of both states, even by critical scholars.

Iran is not studied as a postcolonial state because it was not formally colonized and is itself the remnant of the ancient Persian Empire whose own borders have been shaped and reshaped by various wars across the centuries. Nevertheless, its racialization as a Muslim state in southwest Asia within the global racial hierarchy is the major lens through which it is studied by critical IR today. Similarly, Turkey was not formally colonized and is also the relic of the Ottoman Empire but developed institutions like other postcolonial states in the region. However, Turkey straddles the line geographically (and culturally in certain respects) between southwest Asia and Europe, which has been a focal point in the way it is analyzed, especially in terms of its position in the global racial hierarchy. What I mean to say here is that while these states are racialized and are studied as such by critical IR, the taken-for-granted assumption of these states as legitimate and the absence of Indigeneity are what I am calling in question. When the legitimacy of these states is called into question or challenged by critical IR, it is usually with relation to the Kurdish struggle for statehood. The Kurdish struggle is also seen as postcolonial, liberatory, and even democratic and is often couched in these frameworks, with more recent analyses drawing from scholarship on Indigeneity.

Important critical scholars have done the work of revealing IR's colonial roots and the way in which Indigeneity has shaped and underpinned much of the discipline, despite Indigenous peoples' seeming absence from the story (Shaw 2002; Beier 2005; Nayak and Selbin 2013). Yet, Indigeneity and Indigenous politics remain on the margins of the discipline, gaining relevance only more recently. It is at this juncture in IR where I identify an opening for my research on Assyrians. But I find myself having to undo some of the work that has been done on Iraq, which has been the focus of my research so far; specifically, in terms of its postcoloniality, its "Arab" character, and its geographic location on Assyrian land. Similarly, I must complicate this narrative of Kurdish struggle for self-determination that critical IR seems to not only leave unquestioned, but support. Given the centrality of the state and, consequently, sovereignty to IR, nations within multination states in conflict often vie for independence because they view statehood as the answer to their political, economic, and social marginalization. In this context, the Kurdish desire for a state is understandable, even valid. But redressing the oppression Kurds have suffered and continue to suffer in the region must not be at the expense of building a state on occupied Assyrian land, resulting in Assyrians' continued expulsion and subjugation.

Despite IR's insistence that "territorial disputes" within states are not within the purview of the field, I am also situating Assyrians and their assertions of Indigeneity and nationhood in Iraq as an IR problem, and specifically as a problem of global colonial modernity and international state-building. Drawing on an understanding of history as a "selective, collective construction of significant events that form a unifying mythology" (Green 1995: 86) and its role in constructing the nation, I am making a link between the nation-building process and the removal of Indigenous inhabitants. This is not a case of intercommunal conflict where Assyrians and Kurds are competing within a state as is often depicted. But once a narrative is adopted, it is very difficult to unlearn and undo. The prevalence of this narrative is the reason I am often confronted with questions centering Kurdish futurity in the region when presenting my work on Assyrians such as, How, then, should Kurdish oppression be redressed? I am often accused of suggesting Kurds "do not deserve independence" and have to justify my work and make clear that Kurdish oppression and struggle for a state are valid but that they have manifested in colonial and violent ways. Centering Assyrian Indigeneity and nationhood is problematically understood as necessitating and/or denying the suffering of another people within what I argue is a colonial zero-sum understanding of self-determination as statehood. When confronted with these questions, I must make clear that while I agree Kurds have a right to self-determination, Kurdish self-determination must not come at the expense of Assyrian nationhood and sovereignty and result in the further dispossession of Assyrians from their native land to build a *Kurdistan*. Finally, I am always confronted with the need to distinguish between the governing elites of the Kurdistan Regional Government and Kurdish *people* to ensure my critique of the KRI is nuanced and not anti-Kurdish. But this too obscures the complicity of many Kurdish settlers in the KRI who explicitly or implicitly perpetuate and uphold Kurdish ethnonationalist supremacy, which is the foundational logic of the KRI and the ongoing illegal settlement of Assyrian land.

**Iraq as a Site of Indigeneity: Invisibilizing Assyrians**
Every department that studies southwest Asia includes the study of Iraq. One of the largest Iraqi studies archives is housed at the British Museum and mainly includes colonial documents, which have been significant in shaping scholarship on Iraq. Non-Iraqis have been studying Iraq, an oil-

rich, geostrategically important state, since its inception—even before that, if you count the European missionaries and their logs and descriptions of this region. Iraqis who study Iraq predominantly publish in Arabic if they are in Iraq and write mostly from an "Arab" perspective; or, if they publish in English, they are usually Iraqis who live in the diaspora. In this way, much of Middle East studies and Iraqi studies problematically focus on major power blocs and Iraq's colonial history with Western powers with little to no attention to Indigeneity. The Anglo-American invasion in 2003, the ensuing occupation, and decades of "democratic nation-building" catapulted Iraq to international and scholarly attention (again), including a debate on its possible dissolution between the three "major" power blocs: Shi'a and Sunni Arabs and Kurds. This debate and focus on the three major power blocs is not an accident: it reflects MES and Iraqi studies and how they have understood and continue to understand Iraq. The absence of Indigenous groups such as Assyrians in these problematic, yet taken-for-granted, analyses perpetuates and reinforces the ahistorical and colonial narrative of Iraq as an *Arab* state with a *Kurdish* "problem."

Despite notable work on "minorities" (Petrosian 2006; Taneja 2007; Youash 2008; Isakhan 2012), an analysis of Indigeneity, specifically, remains invisible in the Iraqi context. The continuation of the Assyrian identity from ancient to contemporary times, and the way in which coloniality has functioned across multiple frontiers, spaces, temporalities, and geographies, are markedly absent. The discounting of Iraq as a site of Indigeneity means that when Assyrians are included in the literature, they are constructed as a marginalized religious minority rather than as an Indigenous nation resisting ongoing dispossession from their homeland in the makings of various empires and states.[7] I argue that it is important to unpack the term *religious minority*, even if briefly, because these are strategic and politically motivated distortions of the Assyrian identity. I begin with the first portion of the label: reducing Assyrians to their religion is a colonial mechanism with which to deny Assyrians' ancient and ongoing attachment to their specific land in the making of Iraq and, more recently, the KRI. Sargon Donabed (2015) cites the role of Western Christian missionaries in triggering and instigating the fragmentation of the Assyrian identity and its connectedness to place. This is mainly because "almost all nineteenth-century information on the Assyrians that is studied or reproduced is based on sources by Western travelogues" (Donabed 2015: 42). It also allows for the further distortion of the Assyrian identity through a colonial divide-and-conquer strategy, which results in their fragmentation across sects, diluting their resistance and opposition to the state.

There are "Christians" in each state that sits on the Assyrian homeland; I argue that this label facilitates their absorption into the larger society as Arab or Kurd or Turk or Iranian. At the same time, in the context of Iraq, this label also facilitates the myth that all Iraqis, regardless of religion, are inheritors of the ancient Assyrian empire, despite the historical record telling us Arabs invaded this land in 633 CE (Travis 2010). In this way, as the state assimilates Assyrians into the larger society, it appropriates their history and culture to make the foundational myth that Iraq is "ancient."[8] It is a form of violent erasure when Assyrians are stripped of their ethnic identity and reduced to a religious group. Here I am drawing on Linda Tuhiwai Smith (Maori) and her argument that knowledge is central to the colonial project (Smith 2016). Smith's work on the complex ways that colonialism has been enacted through knowledge production underpins my argument that the erasure of the Assyrian identity from Iraqi studies is a form of epistemic violence with real material ramifications on the everyday lives of Assyrians in Iraq. In short, discursively erasing Assyrians allows for their "political unimagining" (Donabed 2015). Policy and practice are intertwined with theory and scholarship; knowledge enacts colonial policy wherein Assyrians are not considered because Iraq is built on their erasure and exclusion. In other words, imagining Iraq as an Arab state with a Kurdish problem gives rise to "solutions" to this perceived problem that undoubtedly exclude Assyrians because they do not exist. What *do* exist are "Christian" Arabs and Kurds (and Turks and Iranians), who can fit neatly into these states without compromising their Arab or Kurdish (or Turkish or Iranian) character, even as their insertion manifests in unequal citizenship. This logic underpins much of Arabization (Benjamen 2022; Donabed 2021; Georgis 2017), Kurdification (Hanna and Barber 2017; Donabed 2015; Petrosian 2006), and Turkification (Atto 2011), which are assimilatory (state or otherwise) practices and policies that Assyrians experience in these respective states presently, not only historically in the making of these states. The assimilation of Assyrians into larger societies and the expansion of these states on Assyrian territory are part of a continual process of reaffirming and reproducing these states. Indigenous scholars have discussed at length the dispossession of Indigenous communities and the perpetual need for land in the making of settler colonial states (Moreton-Robinson 2015; Green 2019). The connection with land, the dispossession of land, and the cultural and political project of recovering land as a means of recovering both identity and self-determination are shared among Indigenous peoples (Kuokkanen 2019; Tuck and Yang 2012), including Assyrians.

The second part of the label is the designation of Assyrians as a "minority," which is problematic for interconnected reasons that together serve to facilitate the political and cultural erasure of Assyrians as Indigenous. *Minority* as a mechanism of the state is designed to steer and define how Assyrians navigate their political existence and, subsequently, the strategies they adopt in their interactions with the state. For example, labeling them as a minority results in their demands for religious freedom and rights from the state because those are the parameters set up by the Iraqi state and the KRI to define them and their strategies of survival. This also impacts the strategies adopted by diaspora Assyrians in their activism, meaning in their attempts to be legible, their demands for Assyrian rights are couched in minority rights discourse because that is what the United States, Canada, Australia, and European states call Assyrians. It is worth noting here that Indigenous peoples in Canada have resisted the state's attempts to include them as minorities and as part of the multicultural project. The politics of recognition and rights as colonial, and their role in perpetuating colonialism, have been well theorized by Indigenous scholars (Coulthard 2014). *Minority* also obfuscates the processes involved in rendering Assyrians a minority in their homeland. Alda Benjamen (2018) uses the concept of *minoritization* in her study of Assyrians in Iraq to describe a process leading to the creation of minority groups. Rather than labeling Assyrians as minorities within Iraq, which erases the violent processes by which this nation came to be a minority, minoritization for Benjamen "signifies historical and contemporary practices of discrimination that marginalize communities and relegate them to an inferior status within the modern hierarchy of citizenship" (Benjamen 2018: 10–11). The framework of minoritization is essential as it describes the *processes* through which Assyrians became a minority in their homeland. It is not and should not be used as a sociopolitical label, category, or identity for Assyrians. That is, Assyrians are not a minority or a minoritized community; they are a nation that has undergone a process of minoritization specifically because they are Indigenous and modern nationalist state-building has historically and continuously necessitated their removal and erasure as Assyrians. Here I point first to the historical and ongoing forcible removal of Assyrians from their traditional homeland, and second to the political and cultural erasure of Assyrians as Indigenous or descendants of ancient Assyrians through assimilation policies and appropriation of Assyrian history to make modern nation-states within the global colonial order.

Perhaps the most problematic aspect of the minority label for Assyrians is the fact that Assyrian Indigeneity transcends their numerical status in each state. It is significant to note that most Indigenous populations are numerical minorities in the states built on their lands specifically as a result of the processes of colonization. Moreover, regardless of their number today, Assyrian sovereignty on their Native homeland and self-determination are Indigenous rights, internationally enshrined, transcending the borders of nation-states. Specifically, self-determination and sovereignty are Indigenous rights protected by the United Nations Declaration on the Rights of Indigenous Peoples (UNDRIP). Recognizing the right of Indigenous peoples to self-determination, UNDRIP "speaks powerfully to the importance of land and control of land" (Green 2017: 183). Putting aside the inherent coloniality of the human rights regime, at their core, self-determination and sovereignty rights challenge the supremacy of occupying states and their assertion of sovereignty over Indigenous territories. This becomes an important assertion especially when disrupting the state's and, in turn, the encompassing nation's moral authority to exercise sovereign rule over this land, which is stolen. Rather than appealing to the problematic notion of human rights, an Indigenous feminist lens problematizes the very idea of nation-states constructed on the theft of land, dispossession, and attempted erasure of Indigenous peoples.

### Indigenous Studies: Expanding Geographical and Temporal Boundaries

Let me say at the outset that my intention here is not to problematize Indigenous studies but to bring Assyrian Indigeneity in conversation with this body of knowledge. Like the scholarship on Indigeneity in Palestine, Kashmir, and elsewhere in Asia, Assyrian Indigeneity expands the geographical boundaries of Indigenous studies to look at the processes through which Indigenous peoples in the Global South have experienced interrelated forms of colonialism, including dispossession, conquest, and the settlement of their land, contributing to furthering our understanding of the globality and "multiplicity of coloniality" (Patel 2019: 4). For the most part, Asia is not included as part of Indigenous studies with the recent exceptions of Palestine and Kashmir. I am specifically referring to the academic discipline of Indigenous studies here. I recognize and acknowledge that Indigenous nations in Asia are important contemporary political actors within states, on the continent of Asia, and globally. As previously mentioned, Indigeneity is most often studied within settler colonial contexts and geographically bound to the Americas, Oceania, Scandinavia, the Arctic, and Russia. I understand and recognize that Indigenous scholars in these locations were and are writing and thinking about the meaning of Indigeneity and colonialism from their particular experiences with white settlers in these specific geographical contexts, especially noting that Indigenous theorization is place-based. But what about when settlers are not white but uphold or emulate their occupation and settlement of Indigenous lands on the model of white supremacy, in the form of ethnonationalist supremacy, to build their states? What about when these settlers are *given* Indigenous land to make states that serve the interests of white colonial powers? These are the kinds of questions and interventions Assyrian Indigeneity brings to Indigenous studies, globalizing and pluralizing our conceptualizations of Indigeneities and colonialisms.

Joyce Green (Ktunaxa, English, Cree-Scottish Métis) writes, "Indigenous peoples generally share similar experiences of colonialism, despite different expressions of it among settler states and despite specific Indigenous cultures" (Green 2009: 40). She adds that the terms that make "Aboriginality relevant arise only in conditions of colonial occupation, in relation to those who colonize, settle, and appropriate the territory of Indigenous nations" (Green 2009: 40). Similarly, Taiaiake Alfred (Kahnawake Mohawk) and Jeff Corntassel (Cherokee) provide a provisional definition of Indigeneity, stating,

> Indigenousness is an identity constructed, shaped, and lived in the politicized context of contemporary colonialism. The communities, clans, nations, and tribes we call *Indigenous peoples* are just that: Indigenous to lands they inhabit, in contrast to and in contention with the colonial societies and states that have spread out from Europe *and other centres of empire*. It is this oppositional, place-based existence, along with the consciousness of being in struggle against the dispossessing and demeaning fact of colonization by foreign peoples, that fundamentally distinguishes Indigenous peoples from other peoples of the world. (Alfred and Corntassel 2005: 597; emphasis added)

Green, Alfred, and Corntassel are placing emphasis on the experience of coloniality as it has meant the physical removal of Indigenous peoples from

lands they traditionally inhabit, in relation to that of the settler or occupying people (power). Alfred and Corntassel are also acknowledging that
there are multiple centers of empire that have constructed, shaped, and
politicized Indigenous identity. Finally, all these scholars emphasize that
Indigeneity is place- or land-based and oppositional to the settler/occupier.
I see these definitions as opportunities, opening the space for Assyrian
Indigeneity, which helps explicate the ways in which colonial modernity
has operated across the globe (Georgis and Lugosi-Schimpf 2021). Assyrians, the majority of whom do not speak English (unless they are in the
diaspora) and who, since 609 BCE, have been living under the rule of others
like the Persians, the Ottomans, the Arabs, and more recently the Kurds,
have maintained their presence on their homeland and their identity
despite various campaigns to eradicate them (Georgis and Lugosi-Schimpf
2021). While Assyrians in the homeland and the diaspora do not use terms
like *Aboriginal*, they do understand themselves as being Assyrian in relation
to those who have conquered, colonized, and settled their territories. They
have a word they use to refer to themselves in the context of the modern
states of Iraq, Syria, Turkey, and Iran: *Aslayeh*, which means "Native" or
"root." So, they have always understood themselves to be the original
inhabitants of this land that was stolen, even if their adoption of the
English word *Indigenous* is new. They understand their relationship with the
now Kurdish-governed north of Iraq as occupation and describe the extralegal mechanisms the Kurdistan Regional Government and its apparatuses
employ to illegally usurp Assyrian land as *zabtanta d'aratha*.[9] This is especially notable in rural villages, which have seen the continual and unop-
posed encroachment on and theft of their lands (Hanna and Barber 2017).

In her examination of the role of Muslims in aspects of European racist
and colonial epistemology in its encounters with the "New World," Muslim
feminist scholar Shaista Patel (2019: 4) calls for a "commitment to a relational understanding of transnational workings of colonialism across the
continents of Asia, North and South America, and Africa while holding
onto the multiplicity of coloniality across these seemingly disparate and
differently colonized spaces." Expanding the geographical boundaries
of Indigenous studies to look at the processes through which Indigenous
peoples in the Global South have experienced interrelated forms of colonialism, including dispossession, conquest, and settlement can reveal how
colonial modernity has operated globally (Georgis and Lugosi-Schimpf
2021). This also means thinking about non-Western empires and

conquerors; specifically, the various conquests of Beth-Nahrain, including Arab, Persian, and Turko-Kurdish invasions, and settlement of Assyrian territories (Travis 2010; Aboona 2008). These empires have not had the extensive global reach of Western powers and themselves have been conquered and subjected to Western colonialism and neocolonial processes. However, I contend that the hegemony of Western colonialism does not negate the non-Western conquest, colonization, and dispossession of Assyrians from their homeland. Rather, I am proposing that it is important to complicate these conceptualizations of colonialism and Indigeneities because it renders visible the intertwined colonial experiences of Indigenous groups in the Global South. Non-Western conquest of the Assyrian homeland by Arabs, Turks, Persians, and Kurds paved the way for Western colonialism as nation-states were created in the making of the Middle East, solidifying and entrenching Assyrian dispossession across modern borders. It also shows the extent to which the colonial global order has influenced and shaped the making and building of states in the Global South, even if these states were made by Western as well as non-Western powers.

Iraq is understood as a postcolonial state; most literature on Iraq tells us it was carved out of three Ottoman provinces by Western colonial powers, much like the rest of the region known today as the Middle East, through a series of agreements such as the Sykes-Picot Agreement, the Treaty of Sèvres, and the Treaty of Lausanne. This story operates through and because of a critical omission: the myriad levels of ongoing coloniality at play in the state of Iraq (Georgis 2017), which I am using Indigenous feminism to untangle. The Iraqi state and, prior to that, the Ottoman provinces are taken as givens in the literature, despite their configuration on the land of Assyrians, who were divided across the artificial state borders of modern Iraq, Syria, Turkey, and Iran in the making of this region, turning them simultaneously into a transnational and a numerical minority in the newly created states. Put more vividly, European colonial powers divided Assyrian land, which had already been occupied by foreign entities, the Persians, Ottomans, and Kurds, and *gave* this land to Arabs, whose rule they found to be in their best interests. Under the tutelage of the British Mandate, the "modern" state of Iraq set out to build an Arab nation with institutions modeling Britain's. It is not surprising that the first act of the independent state of Iraq in 1933 was to massacre between three and six thousand Assyrians and raze over sixty Assyrian villages (Donabed 2015). This event marked the beginning of what Sargon Donabed (2015) has called the "political unimagining" of the Assyrian identity from the fabric of Iraqi society and politics. Similarly, the remnants of the land that was considered (taken for granted) as the Ottoman Empire were then made into modern-day Turkey. The well-documented genocide against the Assyrians (as well as Armenians and Greeks) emptied southeastern Turkey of its Indigenous inhabitants (Gaunt, Atto, and Barthoma 2017). The political reverberations of this genocide are important today; it is the process through which southeastern Turkey was settled demographically by Kurds, who were the Young Turks' coconspirators in the genocide. Assyrian survivors were assimilated as Kurdish and identify as such today (Atto 2011). Modern-day Turkey and the now-majority Kurds have been fighting over this land while Indigenous Assyrians are caught in the middle, their lands seized through the Turkish legal system, and their numbers dwindle even further.[10]

The invaluable work on Kashmir identifying India as a colonizing and occupying expansionary state (Osuri 2017; Ahmed 2020; Junaid 2020; Zia 2020) is generative in terms of thinking about non-white settlers and "postcolonial" states adopting colonial mechanisms (learned through their own colonization) to construct their nationalisms and build their states. My intention here is not to dismiss the calls to hold these states accountable for their violent practices and policies by the people on the ground. But we can speak of the interconnectedness of coloniality, where colonial mechanisms are specific, formed within their current political and social contexts, and racial (caste/sectarian) hierarchies, and where European colonial legacies play a role. Assyrian Indigeneity makes a geographical shift to southwest Asia, allowing for an analysis of the ways in which Iraq, Syria, Turkey, and Iran, and the lands claimed by a greater Kurdistan in the region, operate in colonial ways despite "postcolonial" status. Specifically, it is important to map how these states, or quasi states in the case of the KRI, use similar mechanisms in their exercise of expansionary sovereignty, which recurrently comes at the cost of Assyrians' sovereignty on their territory. It is at this juncture where I see an opening to make space for and learn from Indigenous feminisms to look at the displacement and dispossession of the Assyrian population across and within borders due to violent expulsion via state- and nation-building practices. Specifically, I draw on the work of Mishuana Goeman (Tonawanda Band of Seneca) in *Mark My Words* (2013) to remap the historical context of the colonial division of the Assyrian homeland across the modern borders of the Iraqi, Syrian,

Turkish, and Iranian states. The alternative spatialities that Goeman (2013: 6) examines in her work "imagine that many histories and ways of seeing and mapping the world can occur at the same time, and most importantly that our spatialities were and continue to be in process." Using this lens, I want to focus on the contemporary KRI and its drive for independence. It is important to complicate and disrupt the narrative of Kurdish self-determination from Arab rule by bringing in the question of Assyrian Indigenous claims to this land and their assertions of their political and cultural sovereignty within both Iraq and the KRI. This assertion is pivotal in this moment as the Kurdistan Regional Government's latest bid for statehood in the long Kurdish struggle for self-determination from Arab rule (i.e., the central government in Baghdad) has resulted in the ongoing dispossession, displacement, cultural appropriation, and social, political, and economic marginalization of Assyrians on their traditional homeland.

Despite this reality, there has been significant international attention and support for Kurdish independence in post-2003 Iraq. Decolonization requires an exploration of the expansionary and colonial projects of postcolonial states through their sovereign use of imperial and colonial techniques of power. In this case, Kurdish independence and sovereignty materialize at the expense of Assyrian sovereignty on their ancestral homeland. The KRI narrative tells the story of a Kurdish project to reclaim self-determination rights as part of a long historical struggle against Arabs (and Turks and Persians). The Kurdish Regional Government tells us that they are different than their Arab counterparts; that they celebrate ethnic, linguistic, and religious diversity, that they are democratic. Audra Simpson (Kahnawake Mohawk) argues that Canada requires the death of Indigenous women to secure its sovereignty, and this in turn requires us to rethink the ways we imagine nations, states, and governance (A. Simpson 2016: 1). She writes that underpinning these arguments is a central premise to the story Canada tells about itself: "In spite of the innocence of the story that Canada likes to tell about itself, that it is a place of immigrant and settler founding, that in this, it is a place that somehow escapes the ugliness of history, that it is a place that is not like the place below it, across that border," the evidence suggests that Canada is a "settler society whose multicultural, liberal and democratic structure and performance of governance seeks an ongoing 'settling' of this land" (A. Simpson 2016: 2). I argue that this premise can also underpin the arguments I am making about the KRI because it also tells a story about how it is a place that somehow

escapes the ugliness of history, that it is a place unlike the places that sur-
round it, which have no respect for human rights or democracy. It is, after
all, a place that wishes Assyrians a happy new year; but despite these per-
formative gestures, the KRI is a project that seeks an ongoing settling of
this land, which, Audra Simpson (2016: 2) reminds us, is "not innocent—it
is dispossession." Simpson (2016: 3) also tells us the settler colonial state
seeks to destroy what it is not; it does so with a death drive to eliminate,
contain, hide, and in other ways "disappear" what fundamentally challenges its legitimacy: Indigenous political orders. Simpson tells us that
Indigenous political orders exist prior to founding, to settling, and as such
continue to point in their persistence and vigor to the failure of the settler
project to eliminate them. While they are subjects of dispossession, of
removal, their politics serve as alternative forms of legitimacy and alternative sovereignties to those of the settler state (A. Simpson 2016: 3). In every
official capacity, Assyrians are referred to as "Christian," relegating them
to a religious minority within larger societies bounded by the newly and
colonially created "borders" of the KRI (and Iraq, Syria, Turkey, and Iran).
Assyrians are further divided along denominational lines. Simply put, their
existence as Assyrian, a continuation of ancient Assyrians from this land,
points to the failure of the Kurdish (and Arab, Turkish, and Iranian) projects to eliminate them in the formation of the KRI (and the states of Iraq,
Syria, Turkey, and Iran). Even as they are removed and dispossessed,
Assyrians' continued existence as a political entity serves as an alternative
form of legitimacy and sovereignty to that of these states. This is the basis
for settler anxieties and the drive for Kurdification, Arabization, and Turkification policies toward Assyrians in those states that make up the
Assyrian traditional homeland. Alternatively, but with similar intentions,
the Iranian state has "included" Assyrians—albeit divided them into
Assyrians and Chaldeans (Assyrian Catholics)—in the governing structure
of the state as a way to subsume them into a greater "Iranian" identity and
deter them from making Indigenous claims.

## Concluding Remarks

Ancient Assyrians have been and continue to be studied in every major
university across the Global North, mostly by non-Assyrians. With very few
exceptions (Parpola 2004), ancient Assyrians are studied in the past, as if
they no longer exist. Assyrian historical artifacts can be found in every
major museum in Europe and the United States, displayed as "ancient history" as if these Assyrians are all dead. This article is an exercise in tracing

the invisibility of Assyrians in contemporary politics through the examination of two academic disciplines—political science and Middle East studies—and their subfields, international relations and Iraqi studies. In this way, this article is also a critical reflection of the ways in which the Assyrian story is unknowable or unintelligible within these fields. Using an Indigenous feminist lens and calling for the globalization of Indigenous studies and conceptualizations of Indigeneities, it is my intention to bring Assyrians into conversation with these fields and with scholarship on colonialism, decolonization, and race. In doing so, I am challenging the ways in which Assyrians have been invisible in the academy and within solidarity struggles across the globe. Assyrians continue to inhabit locations of marginality such that their survival is at the forefront of their national activities, limiting their abilities as well as inclinations to engage in academic pursuits.[11] Despite their limited engagement in the academy, Assyrians have been historically and actively engaged nationally and internationally in the struggle for recognition and self-governance rights through policy work and advocacy (see Zaya 2019, 2020).

The existence of Assyrians as Indigenous presents a direct challenge to the Iraqi, Syrian, Turkish, and Iranian nation-states, and the project for an ethno-nationalist Kurdish state. In this work, I am also situating Assyrian struggles for their homeland as the missing, invisibilized, political actor in contemporary Iraq by extending the concept of Indigeneity to the southwest Asian context. I am using Indigeneity as a lens to make comparisons to Arab and Kurdish forms of colonial erasures, appropriation of Assyrian heritage, and occupation of Assyrian land in the north of present-day Iraq, which is the contemporary Kurdistan Region. In this way, by centering Assyrian sovereignty and nationhood, I challenge accounts of Iraq as a site of struggle between an Arab majority Orientally characterized by sectarian violence (Shia and Sunni) and a Kurdish "minority." Assyrian Indigeneity has political ramifications as Assyrian claims and sovereignty over their land, their resources, and their political futures unravel the state projects of Iraq, Syria, Turkey, Iran, and more recently, the KRI. Despite its narrow geographical boundaries, I see the field of Indigenous studies, and especially Indigenous feminisms, as a pathway for potentially visibilizing Assyrian Indigeneity. Making Assyrians visible tells us something about these disciplines but also about the interconnectivity of colonialism globally, forging new pathways for global decolonization. Specifically, the Assyrian story can potentially serve as a site from which to Indigenize the fields of political science and Middle East studies and their subfields of

international relations and Iraqi studies ontologically and epistemologically. It can also help us truly globalize and pluralize Indigeneities while
maintaining local, cultural, and historical specificity.

.........................................................................................

**Mariam Georgis** is assistant professor of global Indigeneity in the Department of
Gender, Sexuality and Women's Studies at Simon Fraser University. She is Assyrian,
Indigenous to present-day Iraq and currently living on and sustained by the unceded
traditional territories of the Coast Salish Peoples, including the Tsleil-Waututh,
Kwikwetlem, Squamish, and Musqueam Nations. Grounded in embodied decolonial
feminist epistemologies, her scholarship is located at the nexus of global politics,
critical Indigenous studies, and Middle East studies. Her research interests include
issues of global security; intersecting structures of global colonialism(s), racial capitalism, and patriarchy; global Indigeneities and decolonization; and politics of
southwest Asia.

### Notes

I am immensly grateful to Joyce Green for her thoughtful and generative interventions to a first iteration of the article. Earlier versions of this article were also
presented at the Canadian Political Science Association Meeting (2021) and at a
Mamawipawin: Indigenous Governance and Community Based Research Space
workshop (2022). I thank these audiences for their engagement with my work.

1   There have been works on Indigeneity in relation to Palestine (Salaita 2016,
    2017; Sheehi and Sheehi 2020, 2021; Shalhoub-Kevorkian, Otman, and Abdel-
    nabi 2021). There have also been works referring to Assyrians as Indigenous in
    the modern context within scholarship on religious studies in the Middle East
    (Atto 2017); religion and diaspora studies (Hartney and Tower 2016); and cul-
    tural and intellectual property (Travis 2009). While important, these works
    remain on the margins of the discipline of Middle East studies (MES). More-
    over, as a discipline, MES has not seriously engaged with the theoretical, epis-
    temological, or methodological orientations of Indigenous studies.

2   Southwest Asia is a more accurate and anticolonial label for this region. Geo-
    graphically, it refers to its location in the world and not merely its distance
    from Europe. Politically, it can encompass the heterogeneity of this region
    since the Middle East has become synonymous with Arab and/or Islam.

3   While I currently live on Coast Salish Lands, my family and I have spent the
    majority of our life in Canada on the traditional territories of the Michi Saagiig
    Nishnaabeg and Haudenosaunee. This confederacy territory stretches from
    western Quebec through southern central and parts of southwestern northern
    Ontario, central and southern Manitoba down to much of Wisconsin, Minne-
    sota, and parts of Michigan. I would like to acknowledge my friend and col-
    league, Assistant Professor (UTSC, Political Science) Chad Cowie who is Michi
    Saagiig Nishnaabeg, for having many conversations with me about his peoples'

history. These conversations about the people whose lands have sustained my family and I, have given me historical and ongoing knowledges of this territory.

4  The confusion regarding the names used to refer to this nation can in part be attributed to different European missionaries, conquest, colonialism, and scholars who have studied this nation but are either not Assyrian or have not consulted Assyrians. Relatedly, like any other nation, there have been internal debates and divisions and varying responses by distinct segments of the community during different periods to these historical and ongoing experiences of colonialism, which has also further complicated the name issue. I recognize the fragmentation of the contemporary Assyrian identity along denominational lines, but I argue it is important to contextualize this fragmentation as an effect of historical and ongoing colonial modernity and the sectarianization of the region in general. For more on this, see Donabed 2012.

5  For more on historicizing the Assyrian identity and directly linking this modern Assyrian identity to ancient Assyria and *Beth Nahrain* (Mesopotamia), see Benjamen 2022; Donabed 2015, 2018; Aboona 2008; Travis 2010; Cetrez, Donabed, and Makko 2012.

6  Shilliam is referring to Persaud and Walker 2001, and before this Doty 1993; Krishna 1993; Henderson 1995; Grovogui 1996; Persaud 1997; Vitalis 2000.

7  I have made this argument about Iraqi Studies elsewhere in more detail. See Georgis 2017.

8  I have discussed the appropriation of Mesopotamian heritage in the making of modern Iraq in previous work. See Georgis 2017.

9  In Assyrian, the word is ܪ‍ܚ‍ܠ‍ܢ. This phrase and the process it refers to were substantiated by a conversation with Michael Youash, the former project director of the Iraq Sustainable Democracy Project and Assyrian policy analyst; he has intimate and long-standing links to Assyrian policymakers on the ground.

10  For more on the impact on Assyrians of the conflict between the state of Turkey and the PKK (Kurdistan Worker's Party), see Youhana, Hanna, and Ishaya 2021.

11  See Kassem and Jackson 2020 on cultural trauma and its impact on the Iraqi Assyrian experience of identity with respect to elitist pursuits like those of the academy.

## Works Cited

Aboona, Hirmis. 2008. *Assyrians, Kurds, and Ottomans: Intercommunal Relations on the Periphery of the Ottoman Empire*. New York: Cambria Press.

Achcar, Gilbert. 2013. *The People Want: A Radical Exploration of the Arab Uprising*. Berkeley: University of California Press.

Ahmed, Binish. 2020. "Sites of Power Differentials in Kashmir: Self-Determination as Anti-colonial Resistance under Un-/polic/e/y-ed Genocidal Colonial Social Order." *Indigenous Policy Journal* 31, no. 3. http://www.indigenouspolicy.org/index.php/ipj/article/view/736/703.

Alfred, Taiaiake, and Jeff Corntassel. 2005. "Being Indigenous: Resurgences against Contemporary Colonialism." *Government and Opposition* 40, no. 4: 597–614.

Atto, Naures. 2011. *Hostages in the Homeland, Orphans in the Diaspora: Identity Discourses among the Assyrian/Syriac Elites in the European Diaspora.* Leiden: Leiden University Press.

Atto, Naures. 2017. "The Death Throes of Indigenous Christians in the Middle East: Assyrians Living under the Islamic State." In *Relocating World Christianity,* edited by Joel Cabrita, David Maxwell, and Emma Wild-Wood, 281–301. Leiden: Brill.

Beier, Marshall. 2005. *International Relations in Uncommon Places: Indigeneity, Cosmology, and the Limits of International Theory.* New York: Palgrave MacMillan.

Benjamen, Alda. 2018. "Minoritization and Pluralism in the Modern Middle East." *International Journal of Middle East Studies* 50, no. 4: 781–85.

Benjamen, Alda. 2019. "The Assyrians, between the State and the Opposition." Interview by Andrew Breiner. *Insights* (blog), Library of Congress, September 26. https://blogs.loc.gov/kluge/2019/09/the-assyrians-between-the-state-and-the -opposition/#:~:text=The%20role%20of%20Assyrians%20within,promised %20cultural%20and%20social%20rights.

Benjamen, Alda. 2022. *Assyrians in Modern Iraq: Negotiating Political and Cultural Space.* Cambridge: Cambridge University Press.

Byrd, Jodie. 2011. *Transit of Empire: Indigenous Critiques of Colonialism.* Minneapolis: University of Minnesota Press.

Cetrez, Onver, Sargon Donabed, and Aryo Makko, eds. *The Assyrian Heritage: Threads of Continuity and Influence.* Uppsala: Acta Universitatis Upsaliensis.

Coulthard, Glen. 2014. *Red Skin, White Masks: Rejecting the Colonial Politics of Recognition.* Minneapolis: University of Minnesota Press.

Donabed, Sargon. 2012. "Rethinking Nationalism and an Appellative Conundrum: Historiography and Politics in Iraq." *National Identities* 14, no. 4: 407–31.

Donabed, Sargon. 2015. *Reforging a Forgotten History: Iraq and the Assyrians in the Twentieth Century.* Edinburgh: Edinburgh University Press.

Donabed, Sargon. 2018. "Persistent Perseverance: A Trajectory of Assyrian History in the Modern Age." In *Routledge Handbook of Minorities in the Middle East,* edited by Paul S. Rowe, 115–31. New York: Routledge.

Doty, Roxanne Lynn. 1993. "The Bounds of 'Race' in International Relations." *Millennium* 22, no. 3: 443–61.

Gaunt, David, Naures Atto, and Soner O. Barthoma, eds. 2017. *Let Them Not Return: Sayfo; The Genocide against the Assyrian, Syriac, and Chaldean Christians in the Ottoman Empire.* Vol. 26. New York: Berghahn Books.

Georgis, Mariam. 2017. "Nation and Identity Construction in Modern Iraq: (Re)inserting the Assyrians." In *Unsettling Colonial Modernity in Islamicate Contexts,* edited by Siavash Saffari, Roxana Akhbari, Kara Abdolmaleki, and Evelyn Hamdon, 67–87. Newcastle upon Tyne, U.K.: Cambridge Scholars Publishing.

Georgis, Mariam, and Nicole Lugosi-Schimpf. 2021. "Indigenising International Relations: Insights from Centring Indigeneity in Canada and Iraq." *Millennium: Journal of International Studies* 50, no. 1: 174–98.

Goeman, Mishuana. 2013. *Mark My Words: Native Women Mapping Our Nations.* Minneapolis: University of Minnesota Press.

Green, Joyce. 1995. "Towards a Détente with History: Confronting Canada's Colonial Legacy." *International Journal of Canadian Studies* 12 (Fall): 85–105.

Green, Joyce. 2009. "The Complexity of Indigenous Identity Formation and Politics in Canada: Self-Determination and Decolonization." *International Journal of Critical Indigenous Studies* 2, no. 2: 36–46.

Green, Joyce. 2017. "The Impossibility of Citizenship Liberation for Indigenous People." In *Citizenship in Transnational Perspective: Australia, Canada, and New Zealand*, edited by Jatinder Mann, 175–88. New York: Palgrave MacMillan.

Green, Joyce. 2019. "Enacting Reconciliation." In *Visions of the Heart: Issues Involving Indigenous Peoples in Canada*, edited by Gina Starblanket, David Long, and Olive Patricia Dickason, 239–52. Oxford: Oxford University Press.

Grovogui, Siba. 1996. *Sovereigns, Quasi Sovereigns, and Africans: Race and Self Determination in International Law*. Minneapolis: University of Minnesota Press.

Hanna, Reine, and Matthew Barber. 2017. "Erasing Assyrians: How the KRG Abuses Human Rights, Undermines Democracy, and Conquers Minority Homelands." Brussels: Assyrian Confederation of Europe. https://docs.wixstatic.com/ugd /4ec518_18285c91d7924250aa1c52b0b4c7da9f.pdf.

Hartney, Christopher, and Daniel Tower, eds. 2016. *Religious Categories under the Construction of the Indigenous*. Leiden: Brill.

Henderson, Errol A. 1995. *Afrocentrism and World Politics: Towards a New Paradigm*. Westport, CT: Praeger.

Isakhan, Benjamin. 2012. "The Assyrians." In *The Edinburgh Companion to the History of Democracy*, edited by Benjamin Isakhan and Stephen Stockwell, 40–49. Edinburgh: Edinburgh University Press.

Junaid, Mohamad. 2020. "Counter-maps of the Ordinary: Occupation, Subjectivity, and Walking under Curfew in Kashmir." *Identities* 27, no. 3: 302–20.

Kassem, Niveen, and Mark Jackson. 2020. "Cultural Trauma and Its Impact on the Iraqi Assyrian Experience of Identity." *Social Identities* 26, no. 3: 388–402.

Krishna, Sankaran. 1993. "The Importance of Being Ironic: A Postcolonial View on Critical International Relations Theory." *Alternatives: Global, Local Political* 18, no. 3: 385–417.

Kuokkanen, Rauna. 2019. *Restructuring Relations: Indigenous Self-Determination, Governance, and Gender*. Oxford: Oxford University Press.

Mahdavi, Mojtaba, and Andy Knight, eds. 2012. *Towards the Dignity of Difference? Neither "End of History" nor "Clash of Civilizations."* New York: Routledge.

Moreton-Robinson, Aileen. 2015. *The White Possessive: Property, Power, and Indigenous Sovereignty*. Minneapolis: University of Minnesota Press.

Nayak, Meghana, and Eric Selbin. 2013. *Decentering International Relations*. New York: Zed Books.

Osuri, Goldie. 2017. "Imperialism, Colonialism, and Sovereignty in the (Post)colony: India and Kashmir." *Third World Quarterly* 38, no. 11: 2428–43.

Ouahes, Idir. 2018. *Syria and Lebanon under the French Mandate: Cultural Imperialism and the Workings of Empire*. New York: I. B. Tauris.

Parpola, Simo. 2004. "National and Ethnic Identity in the Neo-Assyrian Empire and Assyrian Identity in Post-empire Times." *Journal of Assyrian Academic Studies* 18, no. 2: 5–22.

Patel, Shaista. 2019. "The 'Indian Queen' of the Four Continents: Tracing the 'Undifferentiated Indian' through Europe's encounters with Muslims, anti-Blackness, and Conquest of the 'New World.'" *Cultural Studies* 33, no. 3: 414–36.

Patel, Shaista, and Nisha Nath. 2022. "What Can 'Settler of Colour' Teach Us? A Conversation of the Complexities of Decolonization in White Universities." In *White Benevolence: Racism and Colonial Violence in the Helping Professions*, edited by Amanda Gebhard, Sheelah McLean, and Verna St. Denis, 146–62. Halifax, NS: Fernwood.

Persaud, Randolph. 1997. "Frantz Fanon, Race and World Order." In *Innovation and Transformation in International Studies*, edited by S. Gill and J. G. Mittleman, 170–84. Cambridge: Cambridge University Press.

Persaud, Randolph, and R. B. J. Walker. 2001. "Apertura: Race in International Relations." *Alternatives*, October.

Petrosian, Vahram. 2006. "Assyrians in Iraq." *Iran and the Caucasus* 10, no. 1: 113–47.

Rowe, Paul S., ed. 2018. *Routledge Handbook of Minorities in the Middle East*. New York: Routledge.

Said, Edward. 2014. *Orientalism*. New York: Routledge.

Salaita, Steven. 2016. *Inter/nationalism: Decolonizing Native America and Palestine*. Minneapolis: University of Minnesota Press.

Salaita, Steven. 2017. "American Indian Studies and Palestine Solidarity: The Importance of Impetuous Definitions." *Decolonization: Indigeneity, Education, and Society* 6, no. 1: 1–28.

Shalhoub-Kevorkian, Nadera, Abeer Otman, and Rasmieyh Abdelnabi. 2021. "Secret Penetrabilities: Embodied Coloniality, Gendered Violence, and the Racialized Policing of Affects." *Studies in Gender and Sexuality* 22, no. 4: 266–77.

Shaw, Karena. 2002. "Indigeneity and the International." *Millennium: Journal of International Studies* 31, no. 1: 55–81.

Sheehi, Stephen, and Lara Sheehi. 2020. "The Settlers' Town Is a Strongly Built Town: Fanon in Palestine." *International Journal of Applied Psychoanalytic Studies* 17, no. 2: 183–92.

Sheehi, Stephen, and Lara Sheehi. 2021. *Psychoanalysis under Occupation: Practicing Resistance in Palestine*. New York: Routledge.

Shilliam, Robbie. 2020. "Race and Racism in International Relations: Retrieving a Scholarly Inheritance." *International Politics Reviews* 8, no. 2: 152–95.

Simpson, Audra. 2016. "The State Is a Man: Theresa Spence, Loretta Saunders, and the Gender of Settler Sovereignty." *Theory and Event* 19, no. 4. muse.jhu.edu /article/633280.

Smith, Linda Tuhiwai. 2016. *Decolonizing Methodologies: Research and Indigenous Peoples*. London: Zed Books.

Taneja, Preti. 2007. "Assimilation, Exodus, Eradication: Iraq's Minority Communities since 2003." *Minority Rights Group International*. London: Minority Rights Group International.

Travis, Hannibal. 2009. "After Regime Change: United States Law and Policy Regarding Iraqi Refugees, 2003–2008." *Wayne Law Review* 55, no. 2: 1007–60.

Travis, Hannibal. 2010. *Genocide in the Middle East: The Ottoman Empire, Iraq, and Sudan.* Durham, NC: Carolina Academic Press.

Tuck, Eve, and K. Wayne Yang. 2012. "Decolonization Is Not a Metaphor." *Decolonization: Indigeneity, Education, and Society* 1, no. 1: 1–40.

Vitalis, Robert. 2000. "The Graceful and Generous Liberal Gesture: Making Racism Invisible in American International Relations." *Millennium* 29, no. 2: 331–56.

White, Benjamin Thomas. 2012. *Emergence of Minorities in the Middle East.* Edinburgh: Edinburgh University Press.

Youash, Michael. 2008. "Iraq's Minority Crisis and U.S. National Security: Protecting Minority Rights in Iraq." *American University International Law Review* 24: 341–76.

Youhana, Rosemary, Reine Hanna, and Maryam Ishaya. 2021. "Caught in the Cross-fire: Assyrians and the Turkey-PKK Conflict in Iraq." Assyrian Policy Institute.

Zabad, Ibrahim. 2017. *Middle Eastern Minorities: The Impact of the Arab Spring.* New York: Routledge.

Zaya, R. S. 2019. "What Ancient Stones Still Mean to the Assyrian People Today." *Hyperallergic,* November 1. https://hyperallergic.com/524967/what-ancient-stones-still-mean-to-the-assyrian-people-today/.

Zaya, R. S. 2020. "Iraq's Indigenous Peoples Can't Face Another Conflict." *Foreign Policy,* August 7. https://foreignpolicy.com/2020/08/07/iraq-assyrian-indigenous-peoples-another-conflict-nineveh-plains-iran-backed-militia/.

Zia, Ather. 2020. "The Haunting Specter of Hindu Ethnonationalist-Neocolonial Development in the Indian Occupied Kashmir." *Development* 63, no. 1: 60–66.

Yurika Tamura

......................................................................................

# Rehumanizing Ainu
Performance of Desubjectification and a Politics
of Singularity

*Abstract:* This article argues that many contemporary female Ainu
performance-activists from the Ainu community of Japan, including a
performance scene led by Ainu *huci* (female elders) at an Ainu cultural education center in Sapporo, Japan, engage in performance of desubjectification, which emphasizes the sameness of their humanity with the dominant
Japanese rather than arguing for Ainu ethnic difference or their colonial history. At first glance, their performance and iterations seem detached from
the discourse of Indigenous resistance. However, this article demonstrates
how such iteration of singularity—sameness—derives from a particular
Ainu colonial history and argues that their performance critically eschews
colonial and imperial ideas of authenticity, ethnic difference, and the universal human. In doing so, the Ainu performance scene in this article presents itself as a theoretical performance activism against the Western (and
Japanese imperial) notion of Indigenous peoples as less-than-human. By
using bodies, sound, and sensations, these performers define Ainu Indigeneity in their own terms, and achieve an Ainu Indigenous critique of the
"human," the concept that is built on exclusion and marginalization of ethnic minorities and colonized subjects.

The Japanese government's recent acknowledgment of the Ainu as the
Indigenous people of Japan has set the stage for a growing Ainu cultural
industry. With increasing media and scholarly attention on Ainu Culture
(with a capital *C*), popular cultural products created by Ainu artists or that
feature Ainu people as a subject circulate globally today. Such celebratory

MERIDIANS · feminism, race, transnationalism 23:1 April 2024
DOI: 10.1215/15366936-10926952 © 2024 Smith College

movement is criticized by some members of the Ainu community for its risk of eclipsing their colonial history. In fact, the New Ainu Promotion Act launched by the Japanese government in 2019 pledges to preserve and foster Ainu cultural traditions, which are specified as Ainu language, song, dance, crafts, and festivals. Narrowly defining Ainu culture without mentioning colonial history raises concerns among Ainu people as their ongoing struggles against oppression and efforts to uncover the history of colonial violence may be obfuscated, and runs the risk of reducing Ainu Indigeneity to a superficial entertainment service to be consumed by the Japanese public (Higashimura 2019; Ichikawa 2019). Yet some Ainu artists and activists, many of whom are female, continue to view Ainu music and dance performance events as occasions for autonomous self-representations as Ainu. At such performance scenes, the performers often iterate their primary political message: Ainu are human. Instead of highlighting a distinct Ainu culture or history, such statements often emphasize the commonality of Ainu and non-Ainu Japanese, a sameness iterated in the singular category of the "human."

At a historical moment when the Ainu have been finally recognized as Indigenous after many decades of struggle, why would many leading Ainu performers and artists advance such an argument that may be interpreted as assimilatory, or that may diffuse Ainu ethnic specificity? This article considers the contemporary and postcolonial Ainu politics of sameness enacted in various modes of performance and iterations as a profoundly theoretical and specifically Ainu-Indigenous decolonial project—even as it risks diminishing Ainu Indigenous difference and specificity. The terms *Indigenous* and *Indigeneity* are indeed contested words. This article demonstrates how, in their culturally and historically specific positionality, Ainu performance-activists contest Japanese colonial racism and the marginalization of the Ainu by reclaiming the terms *Indigeneity, Indigenous*, and *Ainu*. As their statement about human singularity responds to the modern Japanese notion of the colonized Indigenous (less-than-human) subject, their politics of sameness can also be understood as a subversive desubjectification, a reformulation of their identity defined on their own terms. Thus, this article argues that Ainu performance-activism conceptualizes Indigeneity, subversion, and resistance differently from common forms of identity politics activism, and instead asks for much more than mere visibility: it demands autonomy that challenges the existing racial formations of Japan, contests the subjectification of Indigenous Ainu, and even more, criticizes the Western liberal notion of the *subject*. In doing so, Ainu performer-activists demand a radical inclusion as Ainu and Indigenous, and at the same time, as a non-subject (refusing to be a subject) and singular with other humans.

In order to argue for such intricate Ainu engagement with their identity and representation, the sections below provide my own positionality vis-à-vis Ainu identity; a brief summary of the history of Ainu representation and the struggles that informed the modern Japanese perception of Indigeneity (even though such historical discourse is precisely what these Ainu performers evade in their message of Ainu sameness); and an analysis of two media performances by contemporary female Ainu performers and an interactive performance scene by Ainu *huci* (female elders) at a facility called Sapporo Pirka Kotan.

## Notes on the Author's Positionality

One of the major theoretical contributions of transnational feminism and Indigenous feminism is that they open a critique of Eurocentric liberal feminist notions of Indigenous women and women in the Global South as Other. In Indigenous and feminist ethnography, a researcher's positionality—questions such as who speaks from what position and what are the implications of speaking, describing, and making the subject—must be made clear for more ethical and equitable scholarly conduct. Especially since there have been many cases of scholars misrepresenting their ethnicity recently, making an effort to clarify one's relation to the community one is writing about has become crucial.[1] At the same time, many transnational, diasporic, and reconnecting scholars and activists also take this practice at face value, listing their affiliations as diasporic and Indigenous in the West or the Pacific and neglect to mention that they themselves are also settlers in the Indigenous land of the Americas and/or even in their homeland, or that as a reconnector, they lack shared subjectivity experienced by their estranged Indigenous community. In other words, they may claim their Indigenous affiliation, but the Indigenous community may not claim them. This statement can be problematic in the context of Ainu politics, as Ainu communities are diverse in locations and experiences, and many famous artists and activists in this standard are "unclaimed" by some Ainu communities. Yet, I mention this standard because, recently, there are some artists and musicians in the United States who promote their art through claiming their Ainu heritage without an effort to substantiate their claims. Their narratives may be useful for developing Ainu diaspora studies, but also risk cultural appropriation as some commercialize their art or music with overtly mystified Ainu cultural elements and false narratives to profit in the New Age industry.[2] Indeed the layers of diaspora and colonial forces make it difficult for Ainu descendants to validate their family history, and this is especially the case for the Karafuto-Sakhalin and Kuril Ainu. While such experience of diaspora and estrangement are no fault of such reconnectors, it also seems that more political and theoretical considerations in claiming one's ethnic affiliations are necessary, as is more caution against easily claiming the position of an inside speaker who shares the same subjectivity as their listed communities. My attempt at a self-reflection of my own positionality, mindful of the factors above, is the following.

In Japan, to qualify as Ainu, one must either have an Ainu lineage confirmed in their *koseki* (family registry, a system that functions as birth certificate, identification, social security number, and genealogical records), or be married or adopted into an Ainu family.[3] These identification criteria apparently derived from a particular Japanese racial ideology and population management strategy, and should not be confused with the U.S. blood quantum policy of Native American tribes, although they share similar elements. Also, political location of Ainu ethnicity (what it means to be Ainu) in Japanese society is different from Native American identity struggles in the United States, although both are complex and do share some elements. For instance, if a Japanese person discovers their Ainu heritage that was most carefully hidden from the person by their family, such a discovery would have radically different political and social ramifications than, say, popular white reconnector narratives in the United States.[4] My story of locating my own Ainu heritage is similar to that of many young Ainu descendants in Japan, which began with silence and oblique insinuations among relatives that led me to inquire about my ancestry.[5] Years prior to the Pirka Kotan event in this article, I obtained our family's *koseki* documents to verify our Ainu lineage.[6]

For many Ainu descendants, colonialism, displacement, financial hardship, intermarriage with non-Ainu colonial subjects, divorce, adoption, and other personal and familial situations can sever them from their Indigenous heritage at many levels and with in-depth complications.[7] Like many contemporary Ainu figures, I was not "raised as Ainu," nor did my family members who lived as Japanese in the recent generations directly acknowledge our lineage to me. In addition, my father's side is Zainichi Korean, which was another secret in my family. If there was any Ainu cultural knowledge and practice my maternal grandmother's community in the rural Sapporo/Chitose areas may have retained, they were passed down through private, familial, and mundane situations and experiences, without any acknowledgment about our lineage and without differentiating which part of the culture we practiced was Ainu or Japanese. Such cultural knowledge would be difficult to classify as "heritage."

Thus, my visit to Pirka Kotan took place in a nuanced situation. I was not a total stranger nor an old-time community member; it was neither purely intellectual field research by a visiting American scholar nor the community participation of a local member. The visit was part of my, an expatriate's, reconnection project that involved my mother, although this concept of "reconnector" is problematic. With familial and historical layers of separation and complications from multiple lineages, I consider my position as that of a settler and diasporic at multiple levels; as a transnational and interracial Ainu descendant and a reconnector to Ainu heritage (which is a description of my position according to Western scholarship); and as a person with Ainu lineage (which defines me as an Ainu according to the incomplete definition set by the Japanese government and the Ainu Association of Hokkaido, and more aptly as a *Silent Ainu* according to Ishihara [2021])[8]; whose formal training is in U.S. feminist and Native American and Indigenous studies; whose liminal position to the Ainu and the Japanese troubles the labels "insider informant," "outside observer," and "we."

## We Are All Human: The Discourse of Sameness and a Brief History of Ainu Representations

According to a *huci* (a female Ainu elder), "You are an Ainu, everyone is Ainu, and Ainu means human." She stated this message at the end of a dance performance that took place in 2009 at an Ainu cultural facility, Pirka Kotan, in Sapporo, Japan. The huci emphasized that, in this notion of human, everyone (including the audiences attending the performance) is included. At first glance, this notion that everyone is Ainu is alarmingly problematic, especially to the Western audience, as it seems to negate a specific Indigenous history, identity, and difference, all of which are important entities for the anticolonial efforts of Indigenous peoples.[9] Yet examples of similar statements are multiple. Ten years after the huci's message, in March 2019, a female Ainu singer, Mayunkiki, was invited to the conference

"Hokkaidō 150: Settler Colonialism and Indigeneity in Modern Japan and Beyond" (2019) at the University of British Columbia. At the opening performance, Mayunkiki charmed a full auditorium with her performance of Ainu songs. Then, the next day, she attended a panel as a speaker and claimed, "Indigeneity is a nuisance (*jama*, obstacle)."[10] Ainu music should be evaluated by its quality alone like any other music, without characterizing it as "Indigenous," she explained to the audience, who chuckled awkwardly at her "nuisance" comment. This generously funded conference discussed the colonization of Hokkaido and the Ainu people at the sesquicentennial mark of the 1869 incorporation of Ezo, today's Hokkaido, into imperial Japanese territory. The year 2019 marked a special occasion for the Ainu people, as it was the year that the "New Ainu Legislation" (or the Ainu Promotion Act, which legally recognized the Ainu as Indigenous people of Japan) became effective. One would imagine that, when combating historical erasure, Ainu artists would promote historical awareness and the particularity of their Indigenous identity. Adding to the dismissal of Ainu difference, many activists contest the way the concept of authenticity appeared in Ainu identity discourse. The Ainu scholar and performer Uzawa Kanako, who performed her interpretation of Ainu dance at the opening ceremony of the Sámi National Day in Norway, asked, "What does it mean to be authentically Ainu? I don't know if anyone can really answer that." She followed this comment with her response to "Ainu studies," that such a field "should be completely eradicated" (Kanako 2014: 90–91), criticizing the idea that someone can assume authority to determine authentic Ainuness. Many other Ainu people also reject the genre of "Ainu studies" as it may reinstate Ainu difference in a colonial way by differentiating them from the dominant Japanese while exoticizing the Ainu (Onodera 2009).[11] Another prominent young female Ainu figure, the Ainu language show host Sekine Maya, voiced her wish to be seen as "someone who is *not different* from any other Japanese person" (Yuasa 2019; emphasis mine). This sentiment resonates in many Ainu-led performances, surveys, and interviews. These statements collectively assert that the Ainu are no different from any other humans and should be treated as such. They indict the long colonial tradition of Indigenization and racialization of Ainu, a process in which Ainu subjectivity was determined by the discourse of the savage Other.

This concept of the singularity of Ainu and non-Ainu seems paradoxical to any projects of tribal self-reclamation, and perhaps even detrimental to global Indigenous sovereignty movements, yet similar narratives can be heard in many Indigenous communities outside of Japan. For instance, the U.S. sitcom *Rutherford Falls* aimed to show Native Americans "just like any regular people," which was a move that was politically "revolutionary" to the producer Sierra Teller Ornelas (2021). The comedy was a success in bringing out Native characters as regular people beyond stereotypes. The success of Ornelas's *Rutherford Falls* was overdue as it arrived in an era in which the American film and TV industry undervalued Native talents and maintained colonial stereotypes of Native Americans (Vassar 2021). Indigenous peoples are constantly dealing with the aftermath of colonial dehumanization in the realm of representation. Their visibility is subjected to racist attacks, stereotyping, caricatures, fetishization, and exoticism, followed by the tangible social and economic effects of such significations. On the one hand, Indigenous and other minority populations must struggle for recognition and historical awareness. On the other, they must resist tokenization, criminalization, and other damages that emanate from the realm of representation and recognition that influence their lived experiences. In the case of Ainu, the realm of representation has been one of the main sites of colonial violence.

Ainu are Indigenous people whose traditional territory (*Ainu Mosir*) in the northwest Pacific Ocean includes Hokkaido, the Kuril Islands, Sakhalin, and many more islands around and north of Hokkaido. In the old days, the Ainu's original territory expanded to the Kamchatka Peninsula, the northern mainland of Japan, and their maritime skills and trade enterprise allowed the Ainu to develop connections and conflicts with other tribes and empires, as far as Mongolia and China. Such fluid and significant Ainu presence is recorded as early as the twelfth century; however, Russian and Japanese settler colonialism that accelerated around the seventeenth century threatened and minimized traditional Ainu territory. In 1869, following the Meiji Restoration, Hokkaido became part of the imperial territory of Japan, and Sakhalin was claimed by Russia around the same time. Later, southern Sakhalin was annexed by Japan in 1905. Over Ainu Mosir, where vibrant and expansive Ainu lives proliferated, new borders imagined by those nation-states were drawn. In addition, the Russo-Japanese border conflicts and wars throughout the mid-twentieth century (which involved Western nations as well) displaced the Ainu and neighboring Indigenous peoples (Uiltas, Nivkhs, and Evenks, to name a few) southward from northern contested lands, and eventually many were relocated to Hokkaido and others were scattered into Russian territory. Hence the term *Ainu Mosir* today connotes mainly Hokkaido, but it can also refer to a geographical area the Ainu used to inhabit as well as an imagination of Ainu sovereign land. In Russia today, the Ainu and their language are officially categorized as extinct, despite the present Ainu people lobbying for their recognition.[12] In Japan, the colonial violence of genocide, slavery, sexual exploitation, and the dismantling of families was followed by the cultural genocide of banning Ainu language, hunting, fishing, and religion, as well as other cultural practices, including songs, dance, and tattoos. The Ainu and neighboring tribes experienced continuous colonization under the name of Dojin (土人, the word also connotes savages and barbarians), as seen in Karafuto Dojin (Sakhalin Aborigines) or in the Hokkaido Former Aborigine (kyū dojin) Protection Law (1899–1997).

Japanese reeducation and modernization programs for the Ainu people emulated North American colonial practices and worked in tandem with Japan's nation-building efforts since the mid-nineteenth century. The biopolitical control of Ainu was aided by the scrutiny of anthropological studies conducted by both Japanese and Western scholars. Anthropologists from imperial nations such as Germany, Japan, the United Kingdom, and the United States targeted the Ainu as a tool for building their ethnonationalist empires. The "Vanishing Race" is how Western and Japanese anthropologists characterized the Ainu (Strong and Chiri 2011; Hirano, Veracini, and Roy 2018). The censuses, maps, and ethnographic studies they produced in the early twentieth century were efforts to support this claim. Japan's attention to the "vanishing savages" also supplemented fierce colonial racism against Ainu people. With the legacy of colonial racism (i.e., difficulties in marriage, education, or obtaining jobs), dehumanization of Ainu persists, represented by the recent appearance in a nationwide morning show of a racial slur that equates the Ainu people with dogs (BPO 2021).[13]

In the 1960s, Ainu activists in Tokyo and Hokkaido gathered to begin political activism against their marginalization, discrimination, and socioeconomic deprivations. The urgency of such issues necessitated that the activists prioritize their battles. Sovereignty, land rights, and colonial history disclosures yielded to causes that are more directly related to the daily survival of Ainu households. This does not mean that Ainu activism did not address rights and policy issues. In fact, since the 1980s, the Ainu have disputed many colonial policies and administrations, such as the aforementioned Former Aborigines Protection Act, the Niptani (Nibutani in Japanese) dam case, prohibitions against hunting and fishing, as well as the large-scale theft of ancestral remains by universities and museums (Levin 1999).[14] While those disputes continue, Ainu performance activists also maintain their signature demand—radical shifts in cultural paradigms so that they might emerge as Ainu, human, and Indigenous. The activism that entailed some visibility of the Ainu in the 1960s was a phenomenal move, considering the degree of stigma around Ainu identity which had led a majority of Ainu people not to acknowledge their heritage. Today, the recorded population of the Ainu people in Japan—between twenty-four and fifty thousand (Tsunemoto 1999: 366) and sometimes much less and varying, depending on censuses—is estimated by some to be only 10 percent of the actual Ainu population (Onodera 2009). Many Ainu descendants remain unaware of their Ainu heritage as a result of silence and concealment within families (Ishihara 2021).

Ainu sovereignty and community-building efforts throughout the twentieth century suffered under Japan's self-identification as an ethnically and linguistically "homogenous nation," a discourse that denied both the presence and Indigeneity of the Ainu people. The Ainu were unrecognized as Indigenous or deemed nonexistent in Japan. An exception to this notion was the case of one local lawsuit in Hokkaido, the aforementioned Niptani dam case, whereby local Ainu members contested a dam construction project that would submerge their farmland and sacred sites in Niptani. While the dam construction was not suspended, the lawsuit was classified as a "pursuit of Indigenous rights to the land" by the Sapporo court in 1997 (Fusagawa 1999), which was the only occasion in which Ainu were acknowledged as Indigenous until the Japanese government's decision to officially acknowledge them in 2008.

In 2007, when the United Nations issued the U.N. Declaration on the Rights of Indigenous Peoples, the Japanese government endorsed this declaration enthusiastically, but with the premise that Japan itself had no Indigenous peoples. If there were any, they had all been assimilated to the point that there was no distinction between them and the Japanese, the government claimed, with a further argument that there existed no distinct languages, customs, or religious beliefs that would indicate a presence of any Indigenous people in Japan (U.N. Human Rights Committee 1989). However, Ainu representatives attended the declaration ceremony at the United Nations, insisting on their existence. Ainu activism for the recognition of their Indigeneity became publicly noticeable in the early 2000s, mobilizing international pressure, and in 2008, the Japanese government finally acknowledged the Ainu as the Indigenous people of Japan. At least

two centuries of colonization had passed by then, and it would take
another eleven years before this acknowledgment came into official effect
through the New Ainu Promotion Act in 2019.

Still, many Ainu activists are highly skeptical about the New Ainu Promotion Act, which promises to promote Ainu culture as defined by the
Japanese government and whose major contribution through the act is the
construction of Upopoy, the National Ainu Museum, in Shiraoi, Hokkaido
(Higashimura 2019). The exhibitions at the museum are framed as
multicultural-educational, promoting harmonious coexistence of diverse
people, but clearly circumvent Ainu colonial history. Performance events,
restaurants, and gift shops in the facility seem to offer a depoliticized and
commercialized version of Ainu cultural elements that is distanced from
the reality of daily socioeconomic struggles for Ainu people. Yet this facility
is the only visible and spatial contribution of the new act, supported by the
state acknowledgment of the Ainu, and a major official (and physical)
platform of Ainu cultural visibility. At a moment when Japan does not
engage in discussion about their colonial violence, multicultural education and performance venues are important media for Ainu activists,
even if they do not represent the actual (as in "offstage") lives of contemporary Ainu people, running the risk of leaving their colonial history
unacknowledged and portraying Ainu as only happily engaging in cultural
performance.

One of the reasons why it remains difficult to envision Ainu sovereignty
today, more than a decade after the state's official acknowledgment, may
be the current political climate in Japan, in which far-right activists and
municipal officials, who openly allege Ainu history as a political hoax and
any minority struggle as anti-state or anti-Japan resistance, aggressively
slander Ainu and other minorities in the media. With Japan's recent move
toward historical revisionism, it has become difficult to successfully
engage in decolonial education or activism in Japan. No doubt this political
culture has shaped contemporary modes of Ainu expression, which often
formulate their Indigenous and anticolonial activism in a nonconfronta-
tional form as educational multiculturalism.

### Ainu Media Performance—Discourse of Singularity and Desubjectification

With her aforementioned comment, "Indigeneity is a nuisance," the Ainu
singer Mayunkiki seems to defy the framework of exoticized Indigenous
visibility in all senses. "Animism, ecology, and diversity—enough already,

sick of them" Mayunkiki tweeted, refusing the way people continuously contextualize her art and life in the narrative of the noble savage and as a token for diversity (@marewrew_m, August 4, 2021). Mayunkiki negates and mocks the consumers of Ainu arts, who themselves are consumed by a colonial romanticism, seeking their exotic Ainu. Mayunkiki could qualify as an active Ainu cultural revivalist: she engages in Ainu traditional *upopo* singing and restores and preserves the art of Ainu tattoos—a custom that was no longer practiced until Mayunkiki took it up—by tattooing herself in the traditional Ainu method. However, she insists that Ainu music should be valued solely for its musical quality and not its colonial subtexts, and that Ainu women's tattoos should also be viewed outside the context of mystified and exoticized aboriginal customs. "The Ainu women wore tattoos simply as fashion, desiring to look pretty. I want society to accept Ainu women's aesthetics not in the context of exoticism but as mundane adornment and beauty" (Asahara 2018). Part research, part activism, and part performance, another project of Mayunkiki is an experiment with photography, where she dresses in traditional Ainu regalia and hands her camera to random passersby, asking them to photograph her in the way they wish to capture a figure of an Ainu woman. Some request her to "stand by the tree and pray," which to her proves how the Japanese relate Ainu women with nature, religion, superstition, and piety. "No one has told me yet that I just look nice"—which shows that it is still difficult for the Japanese to imagine Ainu as regular people in a mundane scene, she surmises. Through the photography experiment, Mayunkiki envisions a future in which Ainu women in their Ainu fashion can casually walk in public spaces and not be seen as deviant, savage, or outsider, nor equated with colonial stigma. Her insistence on diffusing Ainu specificity seems to argue that, if *stigma* is a negative visibility (widely known as a mark or brand of shame or pain in Latin) that marks the modern Ainu subject, then desubjectifying Ainu representations to the point of achieving a singularity with the colonizers can be an act of decolonization.

Working in a similar theoretical approach to present Ainu culture "as any other human," Sekine Maya is a young media personality who began broadcasting Ainu language lessons as a college student (Yuasa 2019). Sekine presents Ainu culture in a way that enables young people to encounter it without stigma. Rather than beginning with colonial history, Sekine engages with her audience as a person of no racial stigma, who happened to grow up in her own (Ainu) community as any other person in

Japan. Sekine asserts that she did not experience racism growing up, as she had been told that "Ainu means human" and did not think of the Ainu as any different from others. However, gradually becoming aware of the deep racism and discrimination faced by the Ainu people in Japan, in college she began producing an Ainu language lesson show on the radio, and also a casual and comical YouTube channel that introduces Ainu culture in a manner that is highly relatable for a general, young audience.[15] Her self-presentation with contemporary clothing assumes no colonial trauma, nor does she mention colonial history or current racism, but instead, she presents herself as someone who happily shares the interesting cultural knowledge she possesses. Her homemade videos, mostly shot in a cozy domestic space, show Sekine and her friends in casual attire introducing Ainu songs, phrases, and musical instruments like *mukkuri*. The show features Sekine as an instructor and her friends as her novices. They employ banter, jokes, and comically inserted captions and animations. The result is an image of an approachable Ainu cultural ambassador and patient teacher, friend, sister, and girl next door. The social media format of these videos may not sound novel, but in the context of the fierce colonial stigma of Ainu identity, which still discourages many people from disclosing their Ainu heritage, Sekine's casual and nonchalant communication about her Ainu identity without a narrative of stigma is as revolutionary as Mayunki-ki's statement about her annoyance at the Japanese framework of Indige-neity. That very stance of evading traditionally conceived Indigenous sub-jectivity and eschewing the definition of Ainu Indigeneity, I argue, is their methodology of Ainu Indigenous articulation and *aesthetics*—which is, by Jacques Rancière's definition, an enactment of politics through corporeal sensations.[16]

While some elders in the Ainu community worry about the lack of dis-cussion of colonial histories in such depoliticized performances, these women prioritize their encounters with the dominant non-Ainu Japanese from the position of their shared, singular humanness. They downplay any Ainu difference in an exoticized colonial imagination, foregrounding Ainu cultural elements as something that can be sensed and related to by any human. Such autonomous definition and reinvention of Ainuness is enacted in many Ainu performance sites, making such performance nar-ratives into a decolonial pedagogical material. In a moment when concepts such as diversity, multiculturalism, and coexistence (*kyōsei*) became a municipal buzzword in Japan (Shiobara and Suzuki 2020: 264), Mayunkiki and Sekine's approaches are well calculated and acutely effective in achieving a subversion of colonial Ainu stereotypes. Instead of demanding reparative actions, and without discussing the colonial past, these performers demand much more—to be heard and sensed as any other human whose lives inhabit the here and now. With such presence and contemporaneity ("here and now"), Ainu would no longer be marginalized, but instead become singular with other humans. This does not mean that their specific cultural elements are erased. In fact, the sophistication of this theoretical approach is that both performers assert such statements from their position as young Ainu women, while asserting that their difference and particularity of identity does not need to subscribe to Japanese dominance (a paradigm that defines Ainu as a stigmatized diversion). In asking for such a paradigm shift, what they really demand is a radical inclusion, a shift in how Ainu identity is conceived, in how Ainu arrive at and emerge as Ainu, and yet also as human in postcolonial Japan.

### Everyone Is Ainu: Pirka Kotan and the Huci's Performance

This message of Ainu humanity singular with the dominant subject is most acutely expressed in many Ainu performance sites that are hosted by Ainu community members. Sapporo Pirka Kotan (Beautiful Village): Ainu Cultural-Interaction Center is located in the outskirts of Sapporo, Hokkaido, Japan.[17] The facility was established in 2003 by the Sapporo municipal government. Pirka Kotan holds an indoor and outdoor museum section, lecture halls, and event spaces. The outdoor museum section exhibits reconstructed traditional-style Ainu houses, in which Ainu volunteers in ceremonial regalia lead singing events. The indoor museum exhibits a small collection of crafts, tools, and musical instruments, some of which the visitors can touch. Entirely run by community staff, Pirka Kotan clearly aims to facilitate positive receptions of Ainu culture through their hospitable interactions with the visitors, and thus ostensibly negative historical discourses appear to be absent. Behind the entrance is the administrative office, where local Ainu volunteers gather in fellowship, including children.

The establishment of this facility five years prior to Japan's acknowledgment of the Ainu as Indigenous was considered rather generous of Sapporo City at that time, although according to a volunteer member in Pirka Kotan, the establishment was "overdue and the location is in the middle of nowhere" (interview by author, July 25, 2008). In the process of designing the Kotan project, many volunteers who were living around Sapporo requested that the facility be opened in downtown Sapporo. "The middle of nowhere is the place they like to imagine Ainu to be," one elderly volunteer staff member murmured. Built next to hot spring spa hotels in the mountain scene of Jōzankei, Pirka Kotan is not so easy to access for many local Sapporo citizens, unless they intentionally plan a visit to the hot spring spa next door. However, Pirka Kotan became one of the major tourist spots in the area after incorporating group bus tours and school trips. Because the postwar tourism industry in Hokkaido featured Ainu culture as an attraction, even today, some insist on classifying Ainu museums as entertainment facilities. Some use this notion of entertainment to argue that there are no Indigenous Ainu, but just people with fraudulent intentions, who use forged Indigenous history for their economic gain. Such allegations are extensions of ongoing cultural genocide, a colonial legacy manifesting in contemporary debates about municipal budgets.

Against such a scathing discourse of erasure, the Ainu volunteers at Pirka Kotan provide evidence of a vibrant Ainu culture. The facility consists of hands-on, sensorial experiences: food sampling, trying out musical instruments, sing-alongs, and paper crafts to learn Ainu embroidery patterns, for example. In the summer, Pirka Kotan holds bimonthly festivals. Unlike traditional Ainu festivals, these festivals are museum events for visitors to learn about Ainu culture by interacting with Ainu volunteers. The event consists of half-day activities involving food, music, games, and crafts. Then, it culminates in a stage performance by the volunteer staff, showcasing *upopo* (songs) and *rimse* (dance). Most volunteers were elderly women, huci of the community, and others were their daughters and a few grandchildren, all donning Ainu regalia in different shades of distinctive dark blue accentuated by shades of white, yellow, or tan, and adorned with intricate embroidery patterns, all handmade by the huci themselves. Unlike the biased image held by many Ainu enthusiasts in Europe and the United States, Ainu do not live in a premodern and preindustrial (or worse, prehistoric) manner, but are contemporary urbanites in Japan like any other Japanese (Roth 2005). Wearing ceremonial regalia and singing and dancing by reconstructed huts is their way of offering Ainu cultural education to the visitors, preserving their heritage, and promoting visibility. In this sense, their regalia takes on a role as a stage costume as much as a cultural artifact of their heritage.

In July 2009, Pirka Kotan welcomed a moderate volume of visitors to their festival. A tour of the facility included participatory activities such as story time, group singing in a hut, trials of musical instruments, and crafts in the museum section. In the end, the audience was gathered in the auditorium for dance performances by the volunteer hosts. After the performance of several dance numbers, for the finale, visitors were invited to join the dance circle. Some of the audience put down their cameras and video recorders, leaving their seats to stand on the same stage among the volunteers. Many were shy and hesitant at first, exchanging awkward grins and headshakes. But soon we began to timidly follow the huci's steps, and eventually the bodies became coordinated in their movements. The steps themselves are not complicated, but they require physical force, and the most difficult part for the participants seemed to be getting into the groove. The volunteer staff sang louder, clapped, and ululated to add to the vibes. With all the audience pulled into the dance team, the circle spilled over the stage and took over the whole auditorium. With laughter and movement, the circle picked up speed and moved faster and faster. The auditorium turned into a vibrant and intense soundscape.

It was at this moment when affective performance involving Ainu regalia took place. As the rhythm was set and the audience synced in with the grooves, the huci stopped the circle, took their gowns off, and placed them on the visitors. The regalia are made from thick, layered cotton, and thus are fairly weighty. As a new song started, the Ainu gowns that once marked Ainu ethnicity now came close to the audience members' own skin and covered their bodies, weighing down their shoulders and arms, and moving with them as they followed the huci's steps. The audience was made to learn what it was like to move with the robes on. The circle picked up speed once again, with the sound ringing vibrantly with song, steps, laughter, and ululation. The sweat, songs, beats, breaths, and vibrations in the lungs as well as the slap of the hair on the forehead and shoulders—the soundscape felt as if it were a growing whirlwind of sound-vibes that was emerging out of the circle. This dance event ended in a large circle with everyone in it, all turning inward, which is a typical choreographic move for many Ainu cultural events. After the final beat, while everyone was bursting with laughter, still out of breath with hearts beating fast, the leading huci gave a short conclusive remark:

"In the Ainu language, the word Ainu means human."

*Everyone* in this auditorium is Ainu, she emphasized, gesturing a large circle above everyone's head. Then she continued,

> Look at us. Now that you have worn Ainu clothes and danced in a circle
> together with us, you have all become Ainu. But Ainu means human,
> as we all are. Now that you have experienced the feeling of sameness
> (*issho* 一緒, tied in one bundle or by one sash, togetherness), instead of
> being strangers, let us carry on this way, coexisting as one circle (*wa* 輪
> or circle, community).

There are many rhetorical and theoretical moves in the huci's closing
statement, including the unsaid elements of this message. On the
one hand, idealistically speaking, the dance circle may achieve what
Augusto Boal (1985) called a rehearsal of revolution and social justice. A
performance-scape or soundscape makes bodies a tool for a temporary and
transitory actualization—rehearsal—of a different relationship between
bodies. With somatic involvement and the products of synchronized
heartbeats, affect, and sensations, the result of moving together is a mate-
rialization of sensing-together. Indeed, much of the festival was not about
understanding Ainu history or culture, but simply participating in the
sensation of a shared scene and becoming one in a singular collective of
bodies. Other than the closing speech, the overall festival was centered
around singing, tasting, and dancing, where sensing was the primary
means and aim of the experience. The multisensorial soundscape, as
soundscapes always are, reproduced the bodies as a collective yet singular
material for the transmission of affect, intensity. To Diana Taylor (2003:
xvii), performance as a communal, embodied practice achieves certain
political functions, as an embodied but "nonarchival" record and memory:
a repertoire. For the audience of Pirka Kotan, by taking part in these
embodied records of Ainu dance and songs, their bodies can also become
transmitters of new perspectives, new knowledge, and, by extension, even
new politics. If politics is indeed about sensation and feelings, as Jacques
Rancière argues, then new kinetic movements taking place alongside new
soundwaves could trigger new sensations, which may open space for an
alternative political perspective.

Indeed, dancing evokes a new bodily consciousness for the audience as
they become participants. The garment is weighty, and because the large
sleeves wrap loosely around one's arms and the hem hangs below the
knees, it requires some adjustments to the wearers' movements: the kinet-
ics of dance, of jumping and turning, which are movements outside of
mundane postures and gestures in our daily routines. Donning the robe in

the dance circle then requires many adjustments in corporeal movements and attitudes. The participants who used to be viewers must learn to reorient themselves and move in the robe and allow their bodies to emulate and articulate the movements dictated by the Ainu huci in the constraints of their garb. Diana Taylor (2003: 32) points out that colonial performance requires participants' "internalization" of colonial ideology. In the same logic, perhaps this performance mobilizes an internalization of the Ainu decolonial narrative of sameness, through visual and kinetic identifications, and through the embodiment of others enabled by the robe. Once the audience steps out of their seats and moves with the huci, a certain new feeling-thinking paradigm is achieved: the rehearsal of a new order.

On the other hand, the huci's statement that "Ainu means human" achieves some level of nuanced critique. In this Ainu cultural facility, the fact that they must underscore the humanity of Ainu people already implies the colonial dehumanization that took place in the past, although this is not explicitly mentioned. Just like in other Ainu cultural facilities today, who and what caused the Ainu to articulate this evident statement was not explained. But like the Black Lives Matter slogan demonstrates, if an evident fact is mundane reality, then no proclamation should be necessary. The proclamation becomes necessary because what should be a true statement is not aligned with a real social condition (Butler and Yancy 2015). Without explaining any colonial history, the statement that "Ainu means human," framed as a revelation and epiphany, expresses a performance of postcolonial critique.

Another, rather cynical interpretation of this performance situation would suggest that, in an implicit way, the performance deploys a mocking effect—the audience came to meet the ethnic and exotic Ainu, but instead they find that they traveled to see just "humans" like themselves. The performance cleverly achieves this switching of identities by shifting Ainu as human, and the dominant non-Ainu bodies into the Ainu, by adorning them with Ainu robes and making them dance to Ainu songs.

The switch is enabled by the viewers' donning of Ainu regalia. An action that may be condemned as cultural appropriation in the West—playing Indian, fetishizing and appropriating one's cultural heritage and adornment—is actually encouraged here, and this is also what sets Ainu activism apart from many other anticolonial and Indigenous resistance movements in the West. Instead of refusing the dominant gaze on the particularity of Ainu culture—which can also be achieved productively, as

Audra Simpson (2014) argues—they mobilize it to yield positive shifts in the reception and visibility of Ainu people: Ainu who are here and now, proudly Indigenous, autonomous, and who, in fact, possess rich culture.

While all are identified as *human* in this process, this performance allows a transformation of the meaning of the word *Ainu*. The huci's claim, which was embedded in the performance, corporeally implicates the audience and makes them accomplices to the political message. With their smiles and sweat on their foreheads, and their breath and heartbeats fast from the dance, who could disagree that they were already a part of the complete circle? Who would question that they themselves are human if they assume the position of the dominant subject, visiting the cultural center to encounter Indigenous others? That they "have become Ainu," as the huci points out, plays on a double meaning: they have become the body that they came to view (an identification through an embodiment that was materialized by the robes), which makes it impossible for the wearers to *Other* the Ainu; and they must also acknowledge the fact that Ainu and human exist in singularity, or at least that Ainu difference should not be evoked to dehumanize. In the dance circle, the robed audience is corporeally implicated in these political statements. The huci's performance thus obfuscates and deconstructs the subject-object positions and critiques the Western liberal notion of the universal human, from which Indigenous people have been excluded. Reclaiming the original meaning of the word *Ainu* as a discursive signifier of all enfleshed humans, the performance achieved a distinct posthumanist statement.

As politically innovative as the huci's statement is, it also contains many risks. For those who are working for tangible Ainu sovereignty issues (reclamation of land and hunting and fishing rights, and recovering the stolen remains of the ancestors), this all-are-human-and-Ainu discourse could be depoliticizing, devoid of discussions of the colonial past. Moreover, recent discussions in the United States and Canada about cultural appropriation and ethnic cross-dressing raise a question: What if the dominant non-Ainu claim that they too can be Ainu, based on this narrative of costume switching? And what if they (dominant non-Ainu) try to qualify for government funding for Ainu culture via the recently launched Ainu Promotion Acts (2019)?[18] Such anxiety informs the recent cases, as in businesses or even in academia, where Indigenous cultures were fetishized and sought after by White settlers for their own gain. In the Ainu's case, with the history of intensive stigma, such a narrative was not imaginable in 2009, although this is changing. The recent global popularity of Ainu pop culture, music, and performance representations has somewhat shifted the negative image of Ainu (exactly what the Ainu performers aim at) and with it came a risk of fetishization. Mayunkiki troublingly reports that a Japanese fan approached her to tell her that she "wants to become Ainu" herself.[19]

The narrative of sameness and singularity can also be misused as an assimilatory tool. In fact, at this festival, one middle-aged male visitor asked a question of a huci: "How do the Ainu conduct funerals?" (In Japan, people usually conduct funerals according to the Buddhist temple they are registered to.)[20] "If the Ainu are really a different ethnic group and have their own religion, then how can you bury the dead in the current system?" When the huci curtly answered, "We conduct it like the Japanese, with Buddhist temples," the man snarked and said, "Then the Ainu are just the same as the Japanese, no different culture or religion, all assimilated as Japanese, correct?" Obviously, the Japanese colonial logic of national singularity premised on Ainu disappearance and assimilation of northern Indigenous populations is different from the Ainu activists' insistence on sameness as equality and justice in recognition of the humanity in all bodies. This incident gives a glimpse of the Japanese imperial and patriarchal attitude against Ainu. The man openly interrupted the elderly female Ainu staff to insert his negation of Ainu culture and their Indigenous heritage, exhibiting his sense of entitlement. According to his version of sameness, the two groups may be the same, but are not equal, which was also a typical ideological formation in Japan's colonial scheme. Imperial Japan promised singularity of all its citizens, Japanese or otherwise, in the letter of the law, yet colonial others never achieved equality in such incorporation. Assimilation under the facade of "protection" was indeed the primary objective of Japan's Ainu policy in colonial Hokkaido, in which Ainu rights over land, language, hunting, and fishing—the basis of Indigenous sovereignty and autonomy—were set against the Ainu in exchange for their (partial) humanization, a reward of citizenship in modern Japan. Hence Mayunkiki's statement, "*Indigeneity* is an obstacle" formulates an appropriate political critique, which also echoes Frantz Fanon's ([1952] 1986: 56) exasperation that led him to wish to "be like any other man."

Furthermore, to the man's comment, the huci responded that "it means that things are complicated for us." Indeed, this conversation illuminates the complications and dilemmas existing within the performance-statement. While Ainu singularity with all humans asserts Ainu humanity and purchases some recognition, it also inadvertently leaves room for erasure and assimilation narratives. This is a risk that arises from the politically productive ambivalence of this discourse. The corporeal and sensorial dance circle, at least for that moment, achieved a temporary Ainu sovereignty as it was set according to the Ainu's terms; rhythm, lyrics, and choreography were determined by the Ainu performers in their once forbidden, and now reclaimed, language, singing, and dance moves. A few minutes after the conversation, the man who asked the question was made to dance to Ainu song with the other tourists, as *everyone* was made to participate. While he reserved his recalcitrant idea that the Ainu do not exist except within the colonial narrative of assimilation, his body donned Ainu robes, and his steps had to follow the huci's steps and move with the dance circle. His heartbeats had to synchronize with the rhythm in the Ainu soundscape. While he may not have identified with the perspectives about Ainu history and identity, his body was incorporated as a tool for the huci's political message.

What is most potent about this dance circle, then, may not so much be critique of the colonial gaze or reversal of the robes (and roles), but the way that audience members' bodies are made into a collective mass of materials for the dance circle, like *any other* flesh in the space. Diana Taylor (1997: 25) discusses the notion of being "caught in spectacle" to qualify the viewership as an act of witness at a minority performance and the consecutive moral responsibility of such witnessing. In this case of Ainu interactive performance, bodies do more than witness; they become physical instruments of the performance scene. The claim of human singularity is made poignant (or rather, felt) as the bodies of the audience were ontologically made to evidence such a claim. This performance-scape, in which Ainu colonial subjectivity dissipates and bodies vibrantly resonate, achieves a corporeal and ontological (even if momentary) singularity, and perhaps enables a radical decoloniality: a recognition of Ainu as human, an acknowledgment of their Indigenous history, culture, and identity, and even the creation of Ainu Indigenous representations that do not derive from colonial narratives or subscribe to the dynamics of the Self/Subject versus the Other. Precisely because of such an achievement, these Ainu performances are more than minority identity politics. Beyond a narrative of recognition, the Ainu reclamation of "human" resists the notion of minority performance and overcomes their minoritization through their performance.

In his manifesto-inspired advocation for the somatic assemblages of Black lives, Alexander Weheliye (2014: 2) asks, "Why are formations of the oppressed deemed liberatory only if they resist hegemony and/or exhibit the full agency of the oppressed?" The above performance sites echo this question by bringing forth their own expressions of Indigenous autonomy, their disidentificatory self-determination. Their performance hijacks the notion of universal humanity to make them singular with the non-Ainu bodies (or rather, make the non-Ainu singular with the Ainu). In so doing, it is proudly and sensorially Indigenous, as the performers reinvent Indigeneity as more than a subjectivity or source of ethnic pride, but as a force of decolonial subversion. In such dynamic formations, Ainu activists literally and figuratively materialize the beginning of an Ainu decolonial turn.

........................................................................................

**Yurika Tamura** is assistant professor in the Department of Asian and Middle Eastern Studies at the University of North Carolina at Chapel Hill. Her forthcoming book, *Vibration of Others: Resonation and Corporeal Ethics of Transnational Indigenous Soundscapes*, uses New Materialism and sound studies to understand how Ainu artists and activists curate transnational Indigenous soundscapes and address racism and environmental crises, both of which are results of multinational imperial operations. Her articles on sexuality, ethnicity, and immigration in Japan have been published in several feminist journals, such as *Feminist Formations* and *Frontiers: A Journal of Women Studies*.

## Notes

1   Rachel Dolezal and Andrea Smith are famous examples. The list is growing as I revise this article.

2   Diasporic individuals, who are attempting to reconnect with their Ainu identity, should not be a victim of gatekeeping; however, when some artists mobilize Ainu costumes, makeup, and carelessly adopted linguistic phrases and their Orientalist imagination of Ainu spirituality and shamanism for economic gains, claiming their Ainu heritage without making an effort to verify their lineage or to learn the language and struggles of the Ainu people, such actions seem to be cultural appropriation. Depending on situations, there may be a fine line between reconnecting and cultural appropriation; however, if we criticize a white person who claims unvalidatable Native American ancestry to justify their sudden "playing Indian" to promote their products, I wonder if the same standard should be applied to Ainu heritage.

3   These criteria, albeit incomplete and problematic, are the same for Indigenous peoples of Taiwan, a former Japanese colony. For more on the koseki system, see Krogness 2014.

4   Also impostors and "Indian certificates" to falsely and celebratorily claim one's Native American heritage (like the "Cherokee princess" lineage narrative) mark the gap between different struggles of romanticized Native American identity and stigmatized Ainu identity.

5   The stories like mine are ubiquitous among Ainu performers, activists, scholars, and more. See, for instance, Kadowaki Kozue, whose Ainu lineage was invisible to her until she was informed by her Japanese husband. See Akibe et al. 2017.

6   Tracing one's own family ancestry with *koseki* documents, especially if this is to trace one's maternal line, is extremely tedious time and money consuming process. If one's Ainu lineage is outside of Hokkaido where it is no longer Japan's territory, this process becomes almost impossible. Many Karafuto Ainu today struggle to validate their heritage. See Tazawa, Mamoru, "The 5th Conference Report," *Citizens' Alliance for the Examination of Ainu Policy*. Sapporo, Japan: Citizens' Alliance for the Examination of Ainu Policy, June 18, 2017.

7   For more information about being/becoming Ainu in Japan, see Ishihara 2021 and lewallen 2016.

8   Ishihara (2021) defines the Silent Ainu as those who do not possess a clear and articulatable belonging but carry many deconstructive narratives of representations and identities.

9   My definition of *Western* borrows from Chandra Mohanty (1988, 2003), who defined the position not as a race or location but a certain Eurocentric political attitude in feminist scholarship.

10  https://meijiat150.arts.ubc.ca/panel-2-artists-conversation/.

11  One participant even suggests that "the fact that this kind of survey is conducted demonstrates the Ainu are discriminated against and seen differently from the Japanese."

12  This transnational division of Ainu populations is due to the Russo-Japanese territorial contest. As the political climates between the two nations shift, the position of the Ainu as Indigenous people in either country is also volatile.

13  See also the Hokkaido Prefectorial Government's surveys; https://www.pref.hokkaido.lg.jp/ks/ass/new_jittai.html.

14  See also http://www.kaijiken.sakura.ne.jp/newsletter/newsletterindex.html for the history of Ainu activism and issues.

15  *Sito Channel* by Sekine Maya. https://www.youtube.com/@user-sg7qz4sh8p

16  Here, I refer to Jacques Rancière's understanding of "aesthetics," which defines politics as composed of feelings ("distribution of sensibles.") In such aesthetic understanding of sensation, art which generates and modifies feelings (sensation) is a power political tool.

17  The latest website link: https://www.sapporo.travel/en/spot/facility/sapporo-pirka-kotan/ (accessed May 10, 2022).

18  I thank Michael J. Ioannides for this second question.

19  This is still new and somewhat rare, but definitely follows the Western trend of fetishization of Indigenous peoples.

20  The funeral customs depend on regions, but the common understanding is that the vast majority of Japanese conduct their funeral and burial procedures with their registered Buddhist temples who oversees their graves, although this trend may be changing.

## Works Cited

Akibe, Hideo, et al. 2017. *Irankarapte: Ainu Minzoku wo Shitteimasuka?* イランカラプテアイヌ民族を知っていますか? (*Irankarapte: Do You Know the Ainu People?*), 161–63. Tokyo, Japan: Akashi Shoten.

Asahara Hirohisa. 2018. "Ainu no onnatoshite kireini naritai" アイヌの女としてきれいになりたい ("To Be Beautiful as an Ainu Woman"). *Vice*, March 26. https://www.vice.com/ja/article/59kg4x/ainu-of-tatoo-culture.

Boal, Augusto. 1985. *Theatre of the Oppressed*. New York: Theatre Communications Group.

BPO Broadcasting Ethics and Program Improvement Organization Japan. 2021. "Nihonterebi Sukkiri Ainuminzoku Sabetsuhatsugen ni Kansuru Iken" 日本テレビ『スッキリ』アイヌ民族差別発言に関する意見 ("The Decision by the BPO Investigation Committee on the Racially Discriminatory term in Nihon TV's 'Sukkuri'"). Vol. 41. July 21.

Butler, Judith, and George Yancy. 2015. "What's Wrong with All Lives Matter?" *New York Times*, January 12. https://opinionator.blogs.nytimes.com/2015/01/12/whats-wrong-with-all-lives-matter/.

Fanon, Frantz. (1952) 1986. *Black Skin, White Masks*. Translated by Charles Lam Markmann. London: Pluto Press.

Fusagawa, Kiyoshi. 1999. "Ainu Minzoku no Shōsūsenjūminsei ni Kansuru Kōsatsu" アイヌ民族の「少数先住民族」性に関する考察 ("Notes on the Indigeneity of the Ainu"). *Hokkaido University Law Studies Junior Research Journal* 6: 245–72.

Higashimura, Takeshi. 2019. "Ima naze Ainu shinpou nanoka: Nihongata senjūmin seisaku no yukue" 今なぜアイヌ新法なのか("Why New Ainu Promotion Acts Now?") *Nippon.com*, April 1. https://www.nippon.com/ja/in-depth/d00479/.

Hirano, Katsuya, Lorenzo Veracini, and Toulouse-Antonin Roy. 2018. "Vanishing Natives and Taiwan's Settler-Colonial Unconsciousness." *Critical Asian Studies* 50, no. 2: 196–218.

"Hokkaidō 150: Settler Colonialism and Indigeneity in Modern Japan and Beyond." 2019. University of British Columbia. https://meijiat150.arts.ubc.ca/hokkaido150/.

Ichikawa, Morihiro. 2019. "Senjūken naki Ainu Shinpō dewa naku" 先住権なきアイヌ新法ではなく ("Not the New Ainu Promotion Acts without Indigenous Rights"). *Jichitai Mondai Kenkyūjo*, August 30. https://www.jichiken.jp/article/0125/.

Ishihara, Mai. 2021. *Chinmoku no Ōtoethnography sairento Ainu no itami to kyūsai no monogatari* 沈黙の自伝的民族誌オートエスノグラフィー 痛みと救済の物語 (*Autoethnography of "Silence": The Story of the Pain of Silent Ainu and Their Care*). Sapporo, Japan: Hokkaido University Press.

Kanako, Uzawa. 2014 "Charanke." In *Beyond Ainu Studies: Changing Academic and Public Perspectives*, edited by Mark Hudson, ann-elise lewallen, and Mark K. Watson. Honolulu: University of Hawai'i Press.

Krogness, Karl Jakob. 2014. "Jus Koseki: Household Registration and Japanese Citizenship." *Asian Pacific Journal Japan Focus*, August 29. https://apjjf.org/2014/12/35/Karl-Jakob-Krogness/4171/article.html.

Levin, Mark A. 1999. "Japan: Kayano et al. v. Hokkaido Expropriation Committee." *International Legal Materials* 38, no. 2: 394–429.

lewallen, ann-elise. 2016. *The Fabric of Indigeneity*. Albuquerque, NM: University of New Mexico Press.

Mayun (@marewrew_m). 2021. "アミニズムもサスティナブルもダイバーシティももううんざり。" *Twitter*, August 4. https://twitter.com/marewrew_m/status /1422916293703831558?s=20.

Mohanty, Chandra. 1988. "Under Western Eyes: Feminist Scholarship and Colonial Discourses." *Feminist Review* 30, no. 1: 61–88.

Mohanty, Chandra Talpade. 2003. "'Under Western Eyes' Revisited: Feminist Solidarity through Anticapitalist Struggles." *Signs: Journal of Women in Culture and Society* 28, no. 2: 499–535.

Onodera, Rika. 2009. "Ainu to Jendā, Hokkaido Ainu Minzoku Seikatsu Jittai Chōsa Hōkokusho" アイヌとジェンダー。北海道アイヌ民族生活実態調査報告書 ("Ainu and Gender: Report of Hokkaido Ainu People's Lifestyle"). Edited by Tōru Koyama. *Ainu Report* 2: 61–93.

Ornelas, Sierra Teller. 2021. "*Rutherford Falls* Creators on Finding Humor in America's 'Messy' History." Interview by Audie Cornish. NPR, April 28. https://www.npr .org/2021/04/28/991691409/rutherford-falls-creators-on-finding-humor-in -americas-messy-history.

Roth, Joshua. 2005. "Political and Cultural Perspectives on Japan's Insider Minorities." *Asia-Pacific Journal Japan Focus*, April 27.

Shiobara, Yoshikazu, and Mikako Suzuki. 2020. "A Theoretical Perspective for Overcoming Exclusionism." In *Cultural and Social Division in Contemporary Japan: Rethinking Discourses of Inclusion and Exclusion*. Edited by Shiobara, Yoshikazu, Kohei Kawabata, and Joel Matthews New York: Routledge, 259–72.

Simpson, Audra. 2014. *Mohawk Interruptus: Political Life across the Borders of Settler States*. Durham, NC: Duke University Press.

Strong, Sarah Mehlhop, and Yukie Chiri. 2011. *Ainu Spirits Singing: The Living World of Chiri Yukie's Ainu Shin'yōshū*. Honolulu: University of Hawai'i Press.

Taylor, Diana. 1997. *Disappearing Acts: Spectacles of Gender and Nationalism in Argentina's "Dirty War."* Durham, NC: Duke University Press.

Taylor, Diana. 2003. *The Archive and the Repertoire: Performing Cultural Memory in the Americas*. Durham, NC: Duke University Press.

Tsunemoto, Teruki. 1999. "The Ainu Shinpo: A New Beginning." In *Ainu: Spirit of a Northern People*, edited by William W. Fitzhugh and Chisato O. Dubreuil. Washington, DC: Arctic Studies Center, National Museum of Natural History, Smithsonian Institution, in association with University of Washington Press, 366–68.

U.N. Human Rights Committee. 1989. *Yearbook of the Human Rights Committee, Documents of the Eleventh to Sixteenth sessions (20 October 1980–30 July 1982) including the reports of the Committee to the General Assembly, 1981–1982*. Vol. 2. New York: United Nations.

Vassar, Shea. 2021. "*Rutherford Falls* Creator on Shattering Native Stereotypes White People Don't Even Know Exist." *Slate*, May 19. https://slate.com/culture/2021/05 /rutherford-falls-interview-showrunner-sierra-teller-ornelas.html.

Weheliye, Alexander G. 2014. *Habeas Viscus: Racializing Assemblages, Biopolitics, and Black Feminist Theories of the Human*. Durham, NC: Duke University Press.

Yuasa, Yuko. 2019. "Watashiwa Kyōkashono nakano Hitodewanai" 私は「教科書の中の人」ではない ("I Am Not 'a Figure in the Textbook'"). *Huffpost Japan*, April 22. https://www.huffingtonpost.jp/entry/storyainusekinesan_jp_5cbd5998e4b032 e7ceba12d.

Ruby Hembrom and Priti Narayan

.......................................................................................

# What It Takes to Be Counted

## An Interview with Ruby Hembrom

Abstract: In this interview, the publisher and author Ruby Hembrom speaks about being invisibilized and erased as an Adivasi, which led her to set up adivaani ("the first voices"), the first Indigenous-run platform for publishing and documenting Adivasi voices in English in India, in 2012. With a focus on both the ideological and practical aspects of running what Hembrom calls a "dependie" initiative, this interview explores adivaani's—and Hembrom's—journey in creating an Indigenous archive; the politics of knowledge production, language, and translation; and the platform's role in landscapes marked by the cultural and material dispossession of Adivasis in India. Hembrom also provides insight into some of her publishing choices, the global platforms and collaborations she and adivaani have been part of, and her visions for Adivasi feminism and solidarities.

## Introduction

For Ruby Hembrom, publishing came from a necessity to combat the invisibility of Adivasis—the original, Indigenous tribal inhabitants of parts of India—in cultural and literary spaces, rather than from entrepreneurial or commercial ambition. She started adivaani ("the first voices"), the first Indigenous-run publishing house in English in India, in 2012, out of her rented apartment in Kolkata. Although the practical circumstances of her publishing career have not changed much in a decade, adivaani is a small but vital force in India's publishing landscape today. In this time period, the publishing outfit has produced nineteen books, including

MERIDIANS · feminism, race, transnationalism   23:1  April 2024
DOI: 10.1215/15366936-10927000 © 2024 Smith College

*Disaibon Hul*, a children's book on the Santal Rebellion of 1855–57 cocreated by Hembrom and illustrator Saheb Ram Tudu; *A Girl Swallowed by a Tree: Lotha Naga Tales Retold* by Nzanmongi Jasmine Patton; and *Becoming Me* by Rejina Marandi.

Terming adivaani a communitarian venture, Hembrom has chosen to center Adivasi tellings in Adivasi voices, as a way to challenge colonial and mainstream representations. The road has, unsurprisingly, not been easy, with adivaani repeatedly coming up against gatekeepers and patronizing attitudes from printers and distributors, with authors being told their work is not good enough. But Hembrom and adivaani have soldiered on, staying true to her vision, fiercely defending her authors and publishing choices, and producing books out of small budgets in the same apartment with a volunteer colleague. While mainstream publishers have termed her "elitist" for publishing in English, she also finds herself at mainstream events and panels in the country as the "niche" or "alternative" publisher, asked to explain what she does to mainstream audiences (see Usawa Literary Review n.d.; Mitra, 2019). Hembrom is actively building collaborations with local and international institutions and thinkers to bring attention to Indigenous loss and reclamation.

When I received the opportunity to interview Hembrom, I was filled with both excitement and trepidation. Was I, yet another dominant-caste female academic, the right person to take this on? Given my own ethnographic work on and with dispossessed urban residents, even if as part of a women's social movement, I have continually questioned my own position as a knowledge producer and attempted to move toward more collaborative research methods and writing practices. After a conversation with one of the editors of this special issue where I learned that I was not among the first choices for the assignment, I took this as an opportunity to simply platform Hembrom's thinking in the format of an interview. Another interviewer would have perhaps elicited other insights, but Hembrom's own pathbreaking work and the encouragement of anonymous reviewers have allowed this interview to center the ongoing material and cultural dispossession of Adivasi worlds by colonial and Brahminical forces. In my formative years in India, I did not need to contend with this reality. But now, as I live and work in Canada where there is some visibility and discourse about ongoing Indigenous dispossession, Hembrom's words are a necessary reminder that it is the same Brahminical hegemony over knowledge production that makes my own career possible, and Hembrom's work so challenging and important to undertake. This interview has been a timely and humbling learning opportunity as I continue to try to write and teach about coloniality in knowledge production.

When this interview started, Hembrom was residing in the United Kingdom, completing a master of science in inequalities and social science at the London School of Economics as part of the Atlantic Fellows for Social and Economic Equity program, 2021–22. Between mismatched semester schedules, deadlines, ill-timed COVID bouts and personal challenges, we spoke to each other over email about our respective lives, and on a Word file on the contents of the interview. Her words leaped out at me from the page, as they might for anyone thinking critically about the politics of representation, language, and translation, as well as the practicalities of knowledge production. For Hembrom, publishing in English is necessary for Adivasi literature to be taken seriously, even as there is inevitable change, perhaps even attrition in expression while assimilating with mainstream language and literary expectations. "Translation is transmission" for her, but without a need to guarantee that the mainstream reader will understand. In what could be of immense value for academics and activists alike, Hembrom also weighs in on what an Adivasi feminism could look like, and what her imagination for solidarity is. As a publisher working with great constraints since well before the pandemic, it is no wonder that her idea of solidarity is largely and necessarily pragmatic, enacted with others also invested in the idea of Indigenous resurgence rather than monetary gains. Hembrom's vision for adivaani is also expansive, one that is interested in capacity building as much as in documentation. It spans beyond publishing to imagining international Indigenous solidarities and bridging opportunity gaps faced by Adivasis through multimedia formats while also adapting to their everyday material realities. Her thinking is a much-needed contribution to a global consideration of Indigenous resurgence.

You've had such an interesting career so far, having obtained a degree in law and worked in information technology before becoming a publisher. When and how did adivaani emerge in your own personal journey?

The becoming of adivaani is the becoming of me. adivaani was born as the result of a threshold I had reached in my lived experience of exclusion and discrimination as an Adivasi. However, my own experience is only a microscopic reflection of the scales and dimensions these take in the everyday lives of Adivasis, in addition to governmental neglect, state- and corporate-sponsored crimes against us.

As Adivasis, our faces, features, and bodies are the landscape of our lived experiences, identities, and struggles. I spent my schooling years hiding from people and places because I became the personification of the inferiority that I was made to feel, internalizing the inadequacies I was made to believe I had. I could not break through the external impressions of who I was to others to assert that there was more to me. My formative years were clearly the unmaking of me.

As a second-generation formally educated Adivasi born to first-generation migrants in the city of Kolkata, I held on to the promise of a life within the possibilities and limits of a newly acquired mainstream education. One's experience in attaining that education is what informs one's personhood—then what good is an education if the path to it is riddled with disdain, mockery, and humiliation because of your Indigenous identity? After finishing an undergraduate degree in law, I could not break through into what was a hierarchical, dynastic profession due to our family's lack of social capital. The path to pursuing a vocation directly aligned with my education ended right there.

My identity positioned me uniquely, but not advantageously, wherever I went, and all I was confronted with were perceived inadequacies—our languages were "unintelligible sounds," and our knowledge systems, not just inferior but inconsequential. The only way for us to be "civilized" was to adopt the ways of the "masters." While my English education and college degree allowed me entry into spaces not accustomed to having us nor traditionally open to us, my lone presence in classrooms, school, college, and workplaces was marked by the absence of other Adivasis.

That invisibility came to a head in April 2012, when, between jobs, I attended a publishing course. The first month was set aside for meeting industry experts, and yet again there was no Adivasi specialist on that list. Despite our tradition of orality and a relatively shorter writing history, we do write—in our native languages or adopted regional languages, and mostly self-publish, but that wasn't adequate to make the cut. That invisibility and erasure became the tipping point for the creation of adivaani, a platform for Indigenous expression and assertion. I wanted the Adivasi voice to be counted. The adivaani idea was born out of the audacity to say "enough is enough," to not being represented, to others speaking for us, to being labeled as unintelligent and non-thinking people, to being denied a place in history and literature, to the Adivasi voice being silenced and suppressed. The question that drives what I do is: How will we recognize that we are Indigenous, Adivasi, when everything that makes us so is taken from us or lost? adivaani is a response to this ever-compounding question.

You mentioned that Adivasi writers were self-publishing. Could you say a bit more about what the publishing landscape was like for Adivasi voices in India when you started adivaani in 2012? Would you say that it has changed since, particularly with regard to the presence of Adivasi women in publishing?

Adivasi authors have been traditionally self-publishing, either in our native languages or in borrowed regional dominant languages. Produced books often looked like photocopied pages, which tended to be sold along with rice or meat in village or local markets.

But the scope and impact of publications was limited.

Most people assume I publish because I love books or grew up reading books, but the truth is that ours was a family that didn't read. My parents didn't grow up with books, or a culture of reading for pleasure: they were very much immersed in our orality. Their public schooling experience was marked by teacher absenteeism, with mainstream teachers who hated to be in villages with unmotorable roads or no running water or electricity, and sporadic classes. When my sisters and I went to school, we went with incomplete homework, as my parents didn't know what homework was. I had no relationship with books and reading but for an imposed mainstream education. Books started to have an impact on me only when I began adivaani.

Your father ran a newsletter when you were young, didn't he?

Yes. When my parents arrived in Kolkata in 1977, my pastor-theologian father took over as one of the first Santal ministers of the Santali congregation (Church of North India). In the city, they met first- and second-generation Santals, working in various government services like the income tax department, the railways, and telecom services. My parents soon joined a group of Santals who wanted to remain connected to their language and roots, and decided to start a monthly newsletter, on a subscription model, called *Jug Sirijol* (*New Era*), in (Roman) Santali. The newsletter made its way to Santal homes in Assam, Jharkhand, Bihar, Odisha, and West Bengal. Weekly meetings were held in our house, where there were many animated discussions about the contents of each issue . . .

there was singing, with the playing of Santal musical instruments. None of these contributors were trained writers but they began writing: news pieces, cultural commentary, political opinions, poetry, lyrics, and recipes. This group also funded its upkeep and circulation. My father wrote under several pseudonyms depending on what he was saying, and sometimes all of them featured in a single issue. The group also met at a small office-storage space of the printed newsletter in the by-lanes of central Kolkata. My mother was the treasurer, receiving India Post money orders and recording sender addresses. My sisters and I were very young. Sometimes we'd greet the guests in the Santal way (*dobok'-johar*) and help Mom with serving tea and snacks, but mostly, we would just run out to play. Ours was a home that had guests from Santal Parganas all the time, even people not known to us, who would come for medical treatment or wedding shopping or just to see the big city Kolkata. Knowing of a Santal family in the city, they'd come knocking, and our family always accommodated everyone. So, we grew up around a lot of Santals and Santali, including the *Jug Sirijol* group, who immersed us in traditional food, language, stories, discussions, even if we did not actively participate in them.

The people who started and kept *Jug Sirijol* going for nearly forty years have passed on, and it has now been temporarily suspended. The enormity of *Jug Sirijol*'s influence and impact dawns on me now. This is a testimony to the phenomenal effort of city-based Santals, who'd spent half their years in the village, and were spending the rest of their lives in Kolkata, and who'd return to their villages post-retirement. Through their lives, their ways of living remained connected to their culture and ancestry. *Jug Sirijol* is an invaluable archive through the eyes, convictions, and experiences of a changing demography of Santals, who were committed to their Indigeneity, and to Adivasi discourse.

So even since before adivaani, there has been a continuous stream of production by Adivasi authors, albeit in small numbers. But this work doesn't count as representative, because in India, one has to publish in English to be paid attention to. So, that's what I chose to do as both a strategy and an act of defiance: whether we know English or not, we'll publish in English, if that's what it takes to be counted. adivaani became the first Indigenous-run publishing house publishing in English.

Up until 2012, we had a handful of tribal women authors from Northeast India, the authors Mamang Dai, Easterine Kire, Temsüla Ao, for instance, publishing in English, and by known independent publishers like Zubaan located in New Delhi, but almost none from peninsular India.

One might have found the occasional Adivasi in academic publishing and academic anthologies, such as Virginius Xaxa, but the landscape was pretty much bare.

The needle has moved very little, unfortunately, but I guess we should celebrate it moving nonetheless. About 70 percent of adivaani's authors, both solo authors and contributors to anthologies, are women, but that only amounts to about ten authors.

Might you say that "feminism" is a useful framework to describe the orientation of your work? What does an Adivasi feminism look like to you?

One of adivaani's works in progress is an inquiry into and discovery of the articulation of Adivasi feminism through an anthology. Confronted with having to define Adivasi feminism, we couldn't really frame it in explicit terms, and ended up writing about our own experiences and negotiations with discrimination, subjugation, and exclusion. This autoethnographic and ethnographic biography approach will lead us to the formulation of what we think Adivasi feminism is, or not. This also happens to be my master's thesis topic.

Adivasi feminism as a framing paradigm is one that is still in the making. What Adivasi feminism is doing is to Indigenize mainstream feminism to make room for articulation. This does not imply that "feminism" as a practice or the agency of Adivasi women to exercise control over their lives didn't or doesn't already exist. It did and does, through negotiations with systemic powers that subjugate, both within and outside the community. Indigenous feminists of the Western world name the systemic oppression as emergent from a patriarchy that is "inseparable from colonialism" (Gilio-Whitaker 2020).

Adivasi feminism responds to patriarchy entrenched in both colonialism and Brahminical coloniality: the encroachment by outsiders, both British and Indian upper-caste and -class landlords, on lands Adivasis made habitable; enslavement on these very ancestral lands; militarization, state excesses, and mass dispossession in the name of extractive development. The unending violence visited upon Adivasi peoples and lands is a direct attack on the cultures and traditions that shape our feminism. One's identity as a woman does not supersede her multiple identities as expected by mainstream feminism, be it Western or Brahminical upper-caste and -class. It is through this nuance that the Adivasi woman's articulation of feminism from the land diverges from other feminisms.

The promise of Indigenous feminism in India lies in the connection of self and community. There is a dire need for the collective curation and protection of the nuanced lifeways and practices of Adivasi women, which is only possible through the Indigenization of feminism.

adivaani's goal is "to document every Adivasi narrative, record oral traditions, stories, folklores, sagas and literatures that may be forgotten or lost in the wake of modernity." I am thinking about the conversation we have had so far: could you speak a bit more specifically about modernity, how you are responding to its impacts and finding ways to work in the face of loss?

Large-scale "development" or "conservation" projects imposed on Adivasis amount to an invasion and dispossession of our land and traditional culture. Being stripped of our land is a severance from ancestral lifeways and practices, often leading to mass exodus into the unknown, dominant spaces where to survive we have to adopt those ways, their ways. Losing our land brings the death of all that we value, everything that makes us Indigenous, Adivasi, tribal, and is a direct threat to our identity. How will we continue to remain Indigenous when the various, layered systems fundamental to our culture and identity are effectively destroyed as we're dispossessed of our land? This pushes us into a poverty of identity, culture, language, and food diversity.

We take pride in being self-sufficient for most of our needs: cultivating food, building houses, creating our own hunting and farming tools, sourcing medicine from the forest, and so on. Indigenous knowledge has been learned experientially and passed on to the next generation in a natural, informal way, through stories, values, skills, music, dance, healing, crafts, toolmaking, hunting and gathering, cooking, feeding, and feasting. This tradition of teaching and learning, both for adults and children, has existed for millennia and has sustained our environment and us in an organic manner for this long. A separation from our lands entails losing all this. Adivasis have also paid the price for demanding their right to life and livelihood: by losing our identity.

Our work is positioned around issues of loss and retrieval, but also in understanding that the writing on and documentation of Adivasi life has been done by non-Adivasis, outsiders including colonial figures and mainstream Indians, primarily Hindu upper caste and class. Our ability to read and write now enables us to question and contest these accounts and set records straight. That is one way in which modernity allows us to participate in the repossession of our knowledges, histories, and identities.

Resilience is the ever-renewing energy emerging from our struggles in the face of dispossession and Hindutva ultranationalism, drawing from the struggles of our ancestors. Our knowledge systems are kept alive through singers, storytellers, and family who, in their oration and singing, preserve and recreate their community's idea of itself. The essential quality and strength of oral traditions lie in the ability to survive through the power of collective memory and renew themselves by incorporating new elements. That remains with us as we begin to inhabit writing worlds. Beginning to write ourselves is a way to supplement our oral knowledge systems, but it's not that simple or straightforward. The influx of dominant cultures and uprootings places us in new spaces and systems and positions us in an unequal equation where to survive, we imbibe and imitate the dominant ways and languages. This cultural encroachment and takeover by dominant cultures, languages, and modes of communication further marginalizes Indigenous ways and effectively displaces culture.

Writing and literature then become the tools to resist cultural displacement and loss of traditional ways of being, thinking, and expression that varying existences, both imposed and circumstantial, have set us up for. Even if and when we are displaced, we are still the owners and carriers of our stories. We are the ones able to retell them in unconventional ways given what mainstream writing cultures expect or are habituated to. But there is an urgency to undertake this enormous task and that is what adivaani is responding to: the urgency to record and document our stories, before our elders, who hold them like our ancestors did, pass on.

We are seeing the mushrooming of small-scale, Adivasi-led ventures that are driven by the same goals as us. Adivasi Resurgence, Adivaasi Dhrishyam, and The Adivasi Post are all examples.[1]

Are you concerned about the appropriation of Adivasi stories? Surely this is something you have faced . . .

The necessity and idea of seeking to tell every Adivasi story is to salvage, capture, retell, shield, and express ourselves. We are having to navigate a rapidly changing world, where the demands of changing lifestyles and the pressures of making a living in competitive, contemporary ways have taken over time that was dedicated to the passing on of oral traditions. The death of an elder is a loss of a knowledge system, lifeways, lived wisdom, and traditions. It is a link to our ancestors wiped off. It is that link that we're trying to protect, not necessarily for worldwide dissemination or for negotiating processes of Adivasi rejection and ethnographic refusal (Hembrom 2022; Simpson 2007). It is to remind ourselves that we have access to this knowledge, and to make meaning for ourselves. Yet, we are a long way from even creating that archive.

I used to speak freely about my ideas, about insider experiences of Adivasi traditions, which I want to publish or document in multiform ways, to non-Adivasi researchers, cultural consultants working on Adivasi issues, NGO workers, and journalists. I realized in no time that these ideas became projects. Their social and commercial capital and networks enabled them to get a head start and have the means to work on these ideas immediately, while I was limited by both support and capacity. I have had researchers and cultural consultants send me documents asking me to develop the ideas I spoke of, asking me to review a proposal for a grant. They've even sent me a government call for funding on Adivasi issues and asked me to provide them ideas. This entitled expectation, with my role not being clearly defined, is not just unpaid, unacknowledged labor and intellectual property. It is also based on the assumption that what they're doing is service to the community, and therefore it is our moral duty to readily comply. The thing is, even if compensation was offered, there are many things we will refuse to do. We won't participate in the appropriation and commercialization of our own ideas and stories.

Once, I was approached to feature in a documentary film about Santal art, culture, and traditions. This was in the early years of adivaani, so I said yes, and shot my part. Soon after, I received a congratulatory message from a Santal filmmaker for bagging a government grant for a documentary film. I was shocked and told him I had not applied for such a thing. I then go onto the funding website, and see my name listed as codirector of the documentary. I was to be a subject of the documentary, not a director; I had never consented to that. When I confronted the filmmaker, he feigned ignorance on how that happened. I asked to have my name removed as codirector, failing which I would pull out of the interview. He refused to make a single change. Then I began receiving emails from the funding agency about updates on the film which was getting delayed! The onus of completing the film was also on me somehow! I was made accountable for something my Adivasi name was used for, duplicitously and without my consent.

Images from our picture books are routinely lifted without permission or attribution and made into book covers or posters for events. Once, I noticed three books at the Kolkata Book Fair with images from *Disaibon Hul* as book covers. A lawyer friend sent legal notices to the publishers, but we received no response. To follow up would require bandwidth I can ill afford. adivaani not being acknowledged, I can make my peace with. But an Adivasi artist going unacknowledged is not acceptable, especially as they are already facing so many difficulties breaking into mainstream creative circles. Often, my candid email responses refusing to participate in an invitation to "collaborate" or to be part of research themselves become research material. I have now stopped providing explanations or attempting to educate people, and use the lack of time as the pretext to prevent any engagement. My experience with appropriation and exploitation has been varied and has taken several forms.

To speak to the question of production, reproduction, and appropriation of literary works, I discuss in *Cohabiting a Textualized World: Elbow Room and Adivasi Resurgence*:

> Who writes and who publishes is not what we're negotiating with, because we can't stop anyone from doing so. Who has written and who has published can tellingly point to the vacuum in the body of our narratives—that it has not been us telling our stories until very recently. We can't stop anybody from telling our stories, but that someone would want to stop us, can, and does, tells us more about those others' insecurities and fragilities in indigenous knowledge production—not forgetting the immense power, control, and possibilities of manipulation they also hold. Anyone can tell our stories, but can they love them? When we tell and retell our stories it's from knowing our own existence is at stake, it's from the realization of being on the brink of disappearance—and the emotions this evokes is an anticipatory grief that is personal. That's what no outsider can own or appropriate: our stories run through the fabric of our collective life like blood made out of time, dreams, and hope. (Hembrom 2022)

To speak more about your publishing choices: in your attempt to document every Adivasi narrative, how did you decide what to start publishing? What are some of the choices you have made to build what promises to be a formidable archive?

Our books are a result of curating, commissioning, and writing ourselves too. I use the first-person plural as Adivasis tend to speak in inclusive ways. I consider adivaani a communitarian venture.

When we started off, we had the vision, the name, and the outfit registered as a nonprofit, but we had no manuscripts. We were a publishing venture with no books. So, we began looking for stories in our immediate circles, those we could write or collate ourselves, and those from authors with ready manuscripts. A monetary transaction was never contracted, was never a consideration, given that we didn't have the financial means or seed funding. Authors also looked at it as their contribution to building an Adivasi discourse and a collective resurgence.

Being Santal, it was only natural that we first sought out stories in Santali and of Santal origin. My father was incidentally our first author. He was going to self-publish the (Roman) Santali translation of his English book about the Santals, their lifestyle and belief systems. We proposed to professionally produce the book, and he bit the bait. I sweet-talked him into paying for the printing of the book too.

We then went into wider circles and asked our academic and activist friends: some of our books emerged from those connections. Others were through chance encounters at events, or through scouring social media to see what Adivasis were writing and illustrating . . . that's how we discovered some of our authors, poets, and artist collaborators. Some of the works that emerged thus include the activist Gladson Dungdung's *Whose Country Is It Anyway* and *Crossfire*, and Jacinta Kerketta's poetry collection *Angor*.

I took to writing because it was the desperate need of the hour. I was reading my father's out-of-print English book on the Santals and discovered the Santal creation stories there. I felt cheated of an important part of my identity because I hadn't heard these stories until then. The thought that these stories are not being told in families anymore worried me; it signaled the fading of our oral tradition. I wanted to retell the mythical Santal creation stories in an illustrated format, as a way to initiate young readers into engaging with their roots. But who would do the writing? We didn't have the money to commission an author, so I filled those shoes. I took the creative liberty to recast the text for a three-part series on the

Santal Creation Stories with parts one (*We Come from the Geese*) and two
(*Earth Rests on a Tortoise*) out in the market now (both illustrated by Boski
Jain).

While publishing in English, what are the some of the considerations you,
your authors and translators make to preserve the essence of the original
work? More broadly, what are the key considerations in representing a
rich, multimodal literary culture and history in particular ways?

Thus far, most of our manuscripts have been submitted in English or in
already translated bilingual versions, like *Angor* [Hindi-English] and *Soso-
bonga* by Ram Dayal Munda and Ratan Singh Manki [Mundari-English].
While the negotiations around language certainly play a big part in Adivasi
publishing—and English is as foreign to us as Hindi—it is the spectrum
of genres our books cover, from fiction to nonfiction, children's literature,
poetry, academic work and the themes of folklore, Adivasi epistemology,
tangible and intangible memory, loss, romance, art and culture, feminism,
displacement, land grab, extractivism, governmental neglect, state- and
corporate-sponsored crimes, identity, human and Indigenous rights, that
encapsulate our rich, multimodal literary culture and history.

Translation is transmission for us, fueled by the desire and need to be
heard, known, and understood worldwide. As Indigenous peoples, we
release our material to translation with the belief that if you don't understand me, I'll tell it to you in your language. However, I cannot guarantee
that you will understand.

Our literature may be distinctive from others that reading cultures have
encountered, and in many cases, it will require some extra effort, imagination, and graciousness from readers to appreciate it. We may feel burdened
or imprisoned by standards of language and be forced to simplify our text.
But how much is too much? The politics of language and its nuances in
translation and publication of tribal literature is something we continue
to grapple with. I've had to defend one of our Adivasi authors who (also)
writes in English, having learned the language in the last five years of his
adulthood. I was told that his writing "is so basic, very everyday blog material." As his publisher and editor, I have the liberty to change the language
to suit and meet so-called erudite standards; but then that would not be
him anymore, that would be me. My responsibility is toward the author,
and his authorship whose simplicity in a foreign language doesn't take

away from the impact of his stories and narratives. This is who we are, and how we write, and we have to take pride in it. I am often ambushed by this arrogance in language, and it is no easy experience. As a publisher who's also going to undertake translation as a tool to promote tribal literature, I'd also like to push for translation in the other direction, where what are considered universally acclaimed texts will be translated for Adivasis to read in their native tongues. Adivasis are expected to write about themselves and their tribal ways. Why should we not have the liberty to write about whatever, whoever, or wherever we want? I'd also like to publish the Adivasi view of the changing world. We have an opinion on worldviews too, why should it not matter? Whichever means of documentation or visualization is used, at the core of it lies language—spoken, written, or signed—to express that knowledge. For a book publisher, this knowledge is displayed in the printed form, in a script that mirrors the language. However, all languages are constantly evolving; particularly with Adivasi ones, they are imbibing new words and expressions from dominant regional and global languages, losing more complex and specific Native words as a way of leveling the ground of language barriers and comprehensibility. The process of mainstreaming and the assimilation of Indigenous peoples with "organized" and "civilized" society, both enforced and self-initiated, has pushed us to adopt the more urbane languages and allowed them to influence our own Native tongue. This is a reality. With the change and dilution in language, thought processes and meanings change. The knowledge, lifeways, and literature that were once exclusive to a people are now becoming generic and common. That may not necessarily be a bad thing or immediately spell doom, but we need to question how, in preserving Indigenous knowledge as authors, writers, scholars, translators, and publishers, we have used language. Have we modified our syntax and expressions in language so that the nontribal world relates to what we have to say? Have we simplified our language to ensure conformity and acceptability in the established academic and literary world? Or have we retained what is unique and exclusive to us as Indigenous people unapologetically and left it for the world to apply itself to understand us and our ways? Reclamation of the lost entails acknowledging and respecting the liberty and responsibility of knowledge producers. It also entails asking whether we're handing down and preserving for our next generation, publications which reflect an adulterated version of who we are as Indigenous peoples.

The question of who our audience is, and how many Adivasis or Santals use or can use our books in English, has a direct correlation to the tribal/ Adivasi literacy rates, access to English education, circulation of cultural and literary products, and purchasing power. As an Adivasi publisher coming from a tradition of orality who publishes in English, how was I going to build an Adivasi writing canon, in the context of us not being a literate society, when we still have first-generation learners and those who never go to school? If we have a chance at formal education, it is not in our native languages; so how do we write or read in them? What does publishing in English even mean for Adivasis?

The last census of 2011 records India's literacy rate at 73 percent, and tribal literacy at 59 percent (Census India 2011). The Santal literacy rate is not known as the data is not disaggregated. The Population by Mother Tongue shows the total number of Santali speakers at 73,68,192 (Census Digital Library 2011). What we know is that there is a considerable population of Santals across the states of Assam, Bihar, Jharkhand, Odisha, and West Bengal in India, and Bangladesh and Nepal outside, who speak Santali.

Santali is one of the two Adivasi/tribal languages in the Eighth Schedule of the Indian Constitution included in 2003, along with Bodo. The landscape of Santali speakers is, in a way, expansive, but how that translates to an English-language readership, or a readership of adivaani books is quite another matter. We have a print run of one thousand copies and nineteen titles in ten years. In the last five years or so, the stock of five of our earliest titles began running out. We still have fourteen titles with more than 50 percent still in stock. We have fewer than five independent bookstores, and two online portals carrying our books: that is the circulation lifecycle of our books and readership.

My choice to publish in English, as I mentioned, is to give us universal reach and legitimacy. English-language publishing was a gap in Adivasi publishing by Adivasis. While I recognize that the number or percentage of Santals or Adivasis being able to access English writing is trifling, that shouldn't deter us from producing in English because we need to exist in all languages. All material produced in every language will never be irrelevant as it is the link to our identities and ancestries.

In addition to books by Indigenous authors in India, adivaani has published Leanne Betasamosake Simpson's *Dancing on Our Turtle's Back*. What can we learn from diverse Indigenous experiences from both across the world, and within India? What were some of the particular learnings from this collaboration?

We discovered Leanne Betasamosake Simpson while following the Idle No More movement in Canada. On hearing her expound on the idea of resurgence, we knew an Indian version would be crucial to build solidarity among Indigenous populations across geographies by sharing Indigenous knowledge and experiences with and among them. By starting to write ourselves, we are starting a movement of decolonization and resurgence, and the book reaffirmed why we needed to begin engaging with ideas across Indigenous lands, across different histories of struggles.

A special introductory section for the Indian edition titled "Because We Belong to the Land" makes clear what Indigenous peoples worldwide have in common, an environmental consciousness in the face of state-facilitated environmental devastation, alongside an infinite array of differences. In Canada, Idle No More has produced potent political waves, challenging past takeovers of Indigenous lands. In India, thousands of Indigenous communities, often against massive odds, struggle just to hold on to their lands against a massive wave of corporate invasions.

Simpson's book constructs a new and vital bridge between Indigenous communities in Canada and India's Adivasis. Indigenous communities in the Americas have a longer history of standing up against the colonizing, industrializing impulse that came from Western Europe. In India, confrontations have been delayed and mediated by a long history of Adivasis living alongside mainstream societies. British colonizers did not try to displace or "develop" Adivasis. However, India's rapid takeover of Adivasi land and resources in the name of "development" resonates with the history of takeovers and escalating assaults on the environment faced by Indigenous peoples such as the Ojibwe people whose tradition this book comes out of.

The book affords glimpses into traditions and thought processes both very distant and very close to living Adivasi traditions, whose wealth is rapidly eroding in the rush for change. *Dancing on Our Turtle's Back* gently invokes Indigenous consciousness, with great sensitivity toward issues of child-rearing and female identity.

An intriguing choice you have made is to publish a volume based on the illustrations of Walter Stanhope Sherwill, a British Empire functionary in the Indian subcontinent. I would love to hear more about how that came to be. What does the book tell us about colonial representations of Indigenous people?

adivaani started its imprint "One of Us" in 2014, in order to include selected non-Adivasis' writing on Adivasi issues. The first work we published under this imprint was *Sylvan Tales: Stories from the Munda Country* by Samar Bosu Mullick, a Jharkhand-based activist who lives and works among Adivasis. He had been close to some of our Adivasi leaders who have long since passed away. Even though our commitment was to publish only Adivasis, we had to make room for some voices and narratives like these.

The art historian Ngaire Gardner, the great-great-granddaughter of Walter Stanhope Sherwill, got in touch with us about unpublished material she inherited, which also included notes and illustrations of the Santal Rebellion (Hul) in 1855. There is no visual art created by Adivasis from that period of tribal rebellions and uprisings. Writing, of course, was out of the question.

All that we have from that time are depictions from the British Revenue officer W. S. Sherwill published in the *Illustrated London News*, 1855–56. Accompanying these is a wood engraving apparently made from a sketch by Sherwill of Sidhu Murmu, one of the leaders of the rebellion, after his capture. Sidhu and his brothers, all of whom were sentenced to death by the British, are still highly revered by the Santal people. Because this portrait is the only recorded likeness of Sidhu, it has remained the most significant representation of the rebellion and is used for the assertion of our identity even within today's political framework.

The earliest maps of the Bengal Presidency were Sherwill's handiwork. Because he knew the region like the back of his hand, he was asked to help with hunting out the Santals from their hiding places in that difficult, forested terrain. During this time, Sherwill was appointed deputy assistant quartermaster general under Major General G. W. A. Lloyd. On July 29, 1855, Sherwill and Lieutenant Gordon led the Fortieth Native Infantry regiment in a battle at Munkatora.

The only images of the rebellion are Sherwill's illustrations, including new material that Gardner was offering. Sherwill is said to have excused himself from work during the rebellion, probably because he couldn't take what guns and arms were doing to bows and arrows. Despite his

contentious history with the rebellion and our people, we decided to do
the book because our history needed to be made public. The writing demonstrates Sherwill's culturally superior attitude, reflecting his background
and the politics of those times. His views are racist and offensive but hiding them will not make them go away. Our ability to read them now is our
chance to defend and counter those narratives.

Legacies are complex. Gardner was looking for a way to honor her great-
great-grandfather, and in many ways, this work links us to our great-
grandfathers and -mothers as well. This controversial account is possibly
the only window to that time, and to the lives of our ancestors. By publishing this book, we have enabled our Adivasi brethren to reengage with their
ancestries and histories and make peace with colonial legacies.

How might you locate your work on a global stage, contending with colonialisms as well as reclaiming space at multiple scales? I am thinking
about your collaboration on the *Another India: Explorations and Expressions
of Indigenous South Asia* exhibition at Cambridge's Museum of Archaeology
and Anthropology (MAA) a few years ago. Tell us about your experience,
and what you learned from curating Indigenous history there.

Dr. Mark Elliott proposed the research project and exhibition to me as an
opportunity to highlight Adivasi India on the occasion of India's Seventieth
Year of Independence, engaging with material that had never been exhibited before.

Our involvement in the project involved facilitating and supporting the
commissioning of new artworks for MAA, participating with artisans
from Adivasi (Santal and Gond) communities in India at workshops, and
copublishing the catalog of the exhibition for sale and distribution within
India and the United Kingdom. adivaani's work mostly entailed facilitating
contributions from the central Indian tribes.

This was mostly an opportunity to reengage with cultural heritage for
all Adivasis involved. The precommissioning workshops allowed us
access to art and culture stashed away in faraway lands, via photos of our
lands and our people from over a century ago that were never exhibited
before.

We worked with a group of artists, most of whom were accustomed to
selling what they had created, or fulfilling orders for artifacts being placed
with specific requirements, or being asked to assist in construction work

such as building doors, windows, and pillars. These traditional artists had almost never attended a workshop, where a deliberation would decide the outcome of what they'd create.

We didn't know what the photos would evoke. If nothing else, I just hoped for us to bear witness to the familiar and unfamiliar in the display, in many ways linking us to our ancestors. I was keen to see how the traditional artists would respond to the objects displayed because many of the objects are perhaps crafted by the artists regularly, for everyday or special use, and are themselves original works. When Mark showcased the photographs, reactions of awe and familiarity filled the room. The Gonds and Santals instinctively moved to the areas where photos from their respective region were displayed. I caught snatches of excited voices recognizing an object or a sigh acknowledging some exquisite craftsmanship. Then as groups crossed over to displays from "other regions," there were whispers of "we have this too." The Santal artist and adivaani illustrator Saheb Ram Tudu remarked, "Look at the sophistication of the objects, the technique and intricacy in design—and they call us uncultured and backward!"

Objects only make sense when people make sense of them. In Saheb, they elicited the need to assert that we're not backward as the stereotype suggests. Both Santal artist Som Murmu and Gond artist Pandi Ram's responses to almost every object was "I can make that." It was not a display of arrogance, but a genuine self-assessment of their abilities. Their unassuming confidence was both endearing and empowering.

The lessons from this were that Adivasis not only share an experience and memory of marginalization and discrimination, but that we share the burden of knowing that we continue to live invisible lives. One way of being visible, then, is becoming a museum artifact, sometimes even at the cost of tokenism. Being a museum artifact or being displayed is a validation of existence: the existence of a people who created, or inspired others to create and utilize the creation. It shatters typecasts of an unintelligent, "backward" people incapable of culture, creativity, or utility. Museum artifacts help set some records straight, provide agency, and certainly elicit an acknowledgment from observers of an assertion of a people's ethnicity and identity.

*Another India* allowed us Adivasi creative collaborators the opportunity to debut our works internationally, adding a much-valued boost to our careers. Crucially, it also enabled us to imagine an effective approach to art creation and exhibition to supplement our traditional ways of living, thinking, and practicing art. Coproduction of the catalog, which was designed and printed in Kolkata, was adivaani's first foray into museum and heritage publication. Our collaboration on *Another India* led directly to a partnership with the curators Simon Chambers, Alpa Shah, and Jens Lerche to produce the catalog for their exhibition *Behind the Indian Boom: Inequality and Resistance at the Heart of Economic Growth*, at the Brunei Gallery, SOAS, University of London in late 2017.

I have also taken my work to other global events that had an India Focus, where the Indian partners involved looked to include marginalized voices. The Literature Forum India at Villigst, Germany in May 2016, and the Literaturhaus Zürich—Days of Indian Literature in February 2018, are among them. My presence in the global is in irregular, unpredictable bursts, through connections and networks that care about Adivasi issues. At every event I have been to, I've spoken not just about knowledge production, reproduction, loss, and revitalization, but also about Adivasi issues and rights.

In January of 2016, I was fortunate to meet Anna Moulton, CEO of Magabala Books, Australia, which has been producing Aboriginal material for thirty years now. We have remained in contact, following each other's work, and trying to formalize copublication of a picture book.

Apart from that, my work is heavily informed by the global Indigenous scene, where I actively keep myself updated on what is happening in Indigenous publishing and movements.

What have your recent experiences in academia, now outside of India, been like? Academia is a critical site of knowledge production and is arguably more dominated and gatekept by white and dominant-caste researchers, perspectives, and framings than popular press publishing. What have learning, critique, and resistance looked like in academic spaces?

I was returning to formal education after twenty years and was intimidated by the prospect. It was a change compared to where I came from, where being quiet and unquestioning was a virtue for a student. Here, we were expected to and prodded to speak candidly. Yet, the space was unsettling, because I was confronted yet again in lectures and presentations on inequalities in India. There I was, an Adivasi in the room; yet I was also relegated to being an inanimate object on graphs and charts, a statistic, a data point. The feeling of being researched was familiar. There may have been truth in the figures, yet there was a dissonance of being there, seated there.

The first and only time I encountered a direct reference to Santals was in an assigned reading. I was taken aback by the inaccuracies in a reductive analysis by an upper-caste Savarna academic, which was in turn cited by a Southeast Asian scholar on Indigenous issues. While I could voice my objection in the discussion, I was speaking to those for whom the context of Adivasi India was new, and so the impact of my rebuttal remained limited.

Here was a text that I had not known existed until this chance reading. There are tasks to be undertaken: reading everything written on Adivasis—acknowledging, assenting, defending, and challenging them when necessary, but how do we find the time and capacity, especially when there are so few of us doing this work, already pulled in so many directions?

I began writing what I wanted to read, centering Adivasi issues and lived experiences, into every question posed in assignments, which were the only openings to write during such an intense program. It was both cathartic and empowering to be able to produce Adivasi thought, arguments, and analyses, even if the professors didn't always get it. I do plan to develop and publish those writings someday, contributing to the making of an Adivasi discourse, regardless of whether they receive white and dominant-caste academic acknowledgment or inclusion.

What are the sorts of solidarities you have and imagine for adivaani, at the regional and global scales?

Solidarity is a no-holds-barred, lifelong, intergenerational commitment. Our Adivasi authors, artists, and musicians continue to invest their creativity and human ingenuity in adivaani, with complete understanding of our nontraditional, noncommercial operations. They expect no monetary returns for what they think is their contribution to resurgence.

For instance, we pay our authors in books instead of royalties. The usual royalty in India is 10 percent of the retail costs of books. But we keep retail costs very reasonable so Adivasis can buy our books, so we give the authors 10 percent of the print run, which is usually a thousand copies, so they get a hundred books. This is a deal our Adivasi authors accept, as their motivation is to contribute to the larger project of documentation. We would like to be able to pay our authors in monetary royalties, but that means we need to build long-term funding support, including a corpus fund.

While I'm known as an indie publisher, I call myself a "dependie" one, because we have to depend on so many factors to be in circulation. Our best allies have been the small, independent bookstores that keep us in circulation, and the social development workers and activists who not only contribute to our work as authors but also take along our books to every event they organize or speak at. Most importantly, it's been our printers who have given us a "pay when you can" option without compromising on quality, which ensures the continuous production of our printed material.

Our collaboration with Tribal Intellectual Collective India (TICI), a network of Indigenous scholars, to produce online journals is another example of solidarity. When they decided to go to print, they were considering starting a publishing house until someone told them about adivaani. One phone call later, we became allies. Not only did we realize that this academic movement needed to be freed from the shackles of mainstreaming and appropriation, but also that we have a voice that needed to be heard. After a few conversations, we realized that we were not just looking to publish Indigenous knowledge and worldviews but needed to start organizing people to discuss what issues needed to be written about. That's when the idea of holding annual congresses happened. The first National Congress of TICI took place in September 2016, at which we released the first book of the collective too. We're committed to producing more academic work promoting our own knowledges.

I wish funding were not such a struggle though: solidarities to support the logistics of our work are crucial to us. I'm a publisher who hasn't been able to publish in five years. A large part of my time goes into writing funding proposals for adivaani and myself (people do find an English-speaking Adivasi person an attractive proposition to fund through fellowships, which I then channel back into work), facing constant rejections, but continuing to keep at it.

Pitching Indigenous knowledge as something worth sponsoring can be tough because of the limitations of showcasing it as a large-scale, life-changing outcome. That, for example, does not happen when you seek funds to sponsor health or relief initiatives like cataract operations, artificial limbs, food, shelter, or blankets for the needy. Positioning books as a medium to preserve entire Indigenous communities from extinction and cultural genocide is not an easy sell.

However, we are not just interested in books. We want to document and disseminate the tangible and intangible cultural facets of Adivasis in English, using diverse multimedia channels accessible to Adivasis. These include books, documentary films, musicology, and exhibitions. To do this, we have to build human capacity, perhaps by creating a resource center where training in the English language, revival of dying traditional skills and artistry, and instruction on the process of using modern technology for preservation can all be housed. We want to bridge the opportunity gaps for Adivasis in the modern world due to educational and linguistic barriers. For this, we need to adopt adaptable and flexible methods that can be customized for the realities of Indigenous communities bereft of electricity, internet, gadgets, or printers.

**Ruby Hembrom** is an Indigenous cultural practitioner, documentarian, writer, and publisher. Her work addresses and challenges issues of nonrepresentation, suppression, and appropriation of Indigenous cultures. She is the founder of adivaani, the first Indigenous-run platform for publishing and documenting Adivasi voices in English in India. Ruby has written three books for children, including two on the Santal creation story, as well as the prizewinning *Disaibon Hul* (*Let's Remember the Rebellion*), on the Santal uprising of 1855 against the oppressive forces of Indian landlords and the British Empire. She holds a law degree from Calcutta University and a master of science in inequalities and social science from the London School of Economics and Political Science.

**Priti Narayan** is assistant professor in the Department of Geography, University of British Columbia. Her primary research and teaching interests center around urban processes and politics, particularly in India. Using ethnographic and archival methods, she investigates how residents preserve citizenship in urban landscapes marked by violent, large-scale slum evictions. Her academic work is largely informed by her long-term association with and learning from Pennurimai Iyakkam (Women's Rights Movement), a forty-year-old organization that mobilizes female residents of urban poor settlements around the rights to land and housing and access to basic services in Tamil Nadu, India.

### Note

1   Adivasi Resurgence is a platform to "produce knowledge through people's subjective experiences and history" ("About Us," https://adivasiresurgence.com /about-us/ [accessed June 17, 2022]). *Adivaasi Dhrishyam* is a Youtube channel and webinar platform showcasing the knowledge systems of Adivasi communities. A feature on the founder Eugene Soreng was published by the *New Indian Express* edex live on Sept 25, 2020 (https://www.edexlive.com/40-under-40/2020 /sep/25/eugene-soreng-14706.html). The *Adivasi Post* hosts dialogue on Adivasi issues on Facebook and Instagram.

**Works Cited**

Census Digital Library. 2011. "C-16: Population by Mother Tongue, India—2011." Office of the Registrar General and Census Commissioner, India (ORGI). https://censusindia.gov.in/nada/index.php/catalog/10191.

Census India. 2011. *Provisional Population Totals Paper 1 of 2011 India Series 1.* New Delhi: Office of Registrar General and Census Commissioner.

Gilio-Whitaker, Dina. 2020. "The Indigenous Roots of Modern Feminism." *As Long as Grass Grows: The Indigenous Fight for Environmental Justice from Colonization to Standing Rock.* Boston: Beacon Broadside.

Hembrom, Ruby. 2022. "Cohabiting a Textualized World: Elbow Room and Adivasi Resurgence." *Modern Asian Studies* 56, no. 5: 1464–88. http://doi.org/10.1017/S0026749X22000117.

Mitra, Ipshita. 2019. "Ruby Hembrom: 'We Never Needed to Write Because We Were Living Documents.'" *The Hindu Businessline,* September 6. https://www.thehindubusinessline.com/blink/know/ruby-hembrom-we-never-needed-to-write-because-we-were-living-documents/article29350425.ece.

Simpson, Audra. 2007. "On Ethnographic Refusal: Indigeneity, 'Voice,' and Colonial Citizenship." *Junctures,* no. 9: 67–80.

Usawa Literary Review. n.d. "Interview—Ruby Hembrom." https://www.usawa.in/issue-3/interview/interview-with-ruby-hembrom.html (accessed June 17, 2022).

Marilyn James
Introductory Note by Lori Barkley
Transcription by Sarah Beauchamp

......................................................................

# The Contemporary Origins of Smum'iem
# Matriarchy in Sinixt Təmxʷúlaʔxʷ

Transcribed from recordings with Marilyn James,
Sinixt Smum'iem Matriarch

## Introduction

Marilyn James was appointed by Matriarchs as spokesperson for the Sinixt
Nation in Canada in the 1990s. Sinixt təmxʷúlaʔxʷ (homeland) is crossed by
the Canada-U.S. border, with 80 percent of Sinixt traditional territory in
what is now called British Columbia, Canada. The Canadian government
deemed Sinixt "extinct for purposes of the Indian Act" in 1956, an official
designation that persists to this day. Sinixt in the United States are recognized as one of twelve Colville Confederated Tribes in Washington State.

As spokesperson for Sinixt in Canada, Marilyn repatriated sixty-four
ancestral remains from museums and collections back to Sinixt təmxʷúlaʔxʷ.
To this day, she continues her work as Sinixt Smum'iem Matriarch and
knowledge keeper. Marilyn is also an accomplished storyteller of traditional
and contemporary Sinixt stories, as well as the coauthor of Not Extinct: Keep-
ing the Sinixt Way (2021). In addition, Marilyn holds a master of education and
works extensively in educating all ages. Marilyn is an ardent and powerful
advocate for her ancestors, Sinixt təmxʷúlaʔxʷ and all that it contains.

This text and audio are from "Maps of My World," a graphic and digital
memoir project by and about Marilyn James. As a lifelong Indigenous rights

MERIDIANS · feminism, race, transnationalism   23:1 April 2024
DOI: 10.1215/15366936-10926928  © 2024 Smith College

activist and now a Sinixt elder and Matriarch, her memoir includes snapshots from her life as well as Sinixt philosophy and history. The project aims to create a "book" which is based primarily in audio and visual representations with some textual support. The paper and online versions of *Maps of My World: The Life Stories of Marilyn James* are slated for release in 2024.

In this particular piece, Marilyn discusses Smum'iem, which is the traditional matriarchal governing body of the Sinixt Peoples. She discusses deciding to embrace the role of Smum'iem Matriarch for Sinixt Peoples. In this elder-appointed role, Marilyn is responsible for upholding traditional protocols and laws in the Sinixt təmxʷúlaʔxʷ under the laws of whuplak'n and Smum'iem. *Smum'iem* translates as "belongs to the women," meaning that everything in the təmxʷúlaʔxʷ also belongs to the women—good and bad. There are two laws of Smum'iem: (1) take care of your own stuff first, and (2) be of service. The "old gals" Marilyn refers to are the Matriarchs, including Eva Orr and Alvina Lum, who brought Sinixt interests back to the northern part of their traditional territory in Canada in the late 1980s and passed the mantle onto Marilyn before they "dropped their robes" (died).

—Lori Barkley

### Transcribed from recordings with Marilyn James, Sinixt Smum'iem Matriarch

> I saw that it clearly was time,
> and clearly still is the time,
> and it was time before that,
> and that time probably should have come before the old gals
> > dropped their robes, but this claiming of my actual role and
> > function of Matriarch
> was really all based on Smum'iem.
> The example that I got from the old gals of what being a Matriarch
> > is,
> what upholding the responsibilities of Smum'iem are,
> what that law really entailed,
> which the old gals demonstrated in such a community-minded way
> was that we do have an obligation to educate,
> we do have an obligation to engage,
> but we no longer have an obligation to carry the lie.
> We no longer have an obligation to hide the power of the
> > matriarchy

or what the matrilineality and matriarchy of our culture has
    achieved
for our survival.
And if we want to carry this forward,
not just as survival of the Sinixt
but as survival of humanity, of human beings, of skilxʷ,
we have to re-engage the matriarchy in an active aspect
of living our lives
and supporting what is going to make our sustainability
and our ability to survive,
a reality.
And that's when I finally said publicly—and I got a lot of flak
    about this too—
I am no longer the Sinixt spokesperson.
I am now the Matriarch of Smum'iem for the Autonomous Sinixt.
Stepping into that role and identifying myself as the Matriarch
has really opened me up as a target for many people because,
you know, the patriarchy is alive and well.
And it's not just the men who want to stab ya,
it's the women who want to stab ya too and take you down,
but that's the patterning of patriarchy that has been so clearly
    suffocating humanity,
suffocating the reality of how humanity should function.
We should be functioning with empathy,
with compassion,
with consciousness,
with honor,
with integrity,
with respect.
With all of those things—
with concern and responsibility for everything,
not just your own self and your own pocketbook.
And, you know that matriarchal war is raging,
it's raging alive, it's a firestorm.
Slowly, very, very slowly, there are some young women stepping
into their woman-ness,
dipping their big toe and going,
"Oh, that resonates with me. I do hold the responsibility.

*Yes! I should be of service.*

*How do I do that?*

*Oh, I don't have to ask a man . . . "*

*That encourages me that the matriarchy is coming back to life.*

. . . . . . . . . . . . . . . . . . . . . . . . . . . . . . . . . . . . . . . . . . . . . . . . . . . . . . . . . . . . . . . . . . . . . . . . . . . . . . . . . . . . . . .

**Lori Barkley** is a settler, political anthropologist, educator, and activist supporting the work of Sinixt resurgence in Canada. She volunteers for the matriarchy and tries her best to live by their laws.

**Sarah Beauchamp** is Métis-Anishinnabbe from Treaty Two lands, and an award-winning author, supporting the work of Autonomous Sinixt Matriarchy.

Esther Oluwashina Ajayi-Lowo

..................................................................................

# Safe Motherhood Initiative
## Whither African Indigenous Birthing Knowledge?

Abstract: In the quest to create global maternal health care protocols, African Indigenous birthing epistemologies are often overlooked in research, policy, and advocacy aiming to improve maternal health and reduce the maternal mortality ratio (MMR). The global maternal health strategy, the Safe Motherhood Initiative (SMI), excludes Indigenous birthing knowledge by requiring all childbirth to be attended by only birth attendants trained in the Western medical paradigm. This forms the bedrock of the assumed authoritative expertise of the Western medical birthing approach. Despite the campaign for sole reliance on SMI, Africa's MMR remains the highest compared to other regions. Nigeria, Africa's most populous country, also has the third-highest MMR in the world as of 2020. This failure of SMI to reduce MMR for Nigeria and Africa more broadly calls for the inclusion of marginalized Indigenous birthing knowledge for its epistemological and practical significance. Using Nigeria as a case study, with a transnational connection with the United States, the article argues that excluding African birthing knowledge and methods in SMI promotes epistemic and obstetric violence. Adopting the reproductive justice framework as a decolonial tool, the article asserts that African Indigenous birthing knowledge is simultaneously valid and valuable for holistic approaches to maternal health.

## Introduction

The Safe Motherhood Initiative, the globalized maternal health strategy developed for making motherhood safer, promotes Western medical maternal health as the sole approach for improving maternal health and reducing maternal mortality. Regardless of the global health intentions,

MERIDIANS · feminism, race, transnationalism   23:1 April 2024
DOI: 10.1215/15366936-10926960 © 2024 Smith College

exclusive reliance on the Safe Motherhood Initiative has the perhaps unintended consequence of delegitimizing African Indigenous knowledge[1] and methods. Given its aim to reduce global maternal deaths, the Safe Motherhood Initiative has been popularly adopted in developing regions,[2] especially the continent of Africa, where the maternal mortality ratio[3] is highest. The Safe Motherhood Initiative stipulates that all births be attended by a "skilled" health provider, defined in the initiative as Western–medically trained personnel like nurses, midwives, and obstetric gynecologists. By extolling Western medical approaches as the authoritative maternal health strategy, the Safe Motherhood Initiative marginalizes all birth attendants adopting Indigenous knowledge and practices by implicitly categorizing them as unskilled. Through these specific reproductive and childbirth health strategies, Indigenous knowledge is further silenced, marginalized, and driven far afield. Notably, Indigenous birthing knowledge is an aspect of the local knowledge system that generally relates to pregnancy and childbirth. Like other Indigenous ways of knowing and doing, it existed prior to the contact and influence of the colonizers on the continent of Africa (Hunt 1999; Tabobondung 2017; van Tol 2007). I contend that all aspects of African Indigenous knowledge—including African medicine, beliefs, worldviews, and practices relating to pregnancy and childbirth— are epistemologically valid. Hence, excluding African Indigenous birthing knowledge from the global maternal health strategy constitutes epistemic violence. Further, ignoring the potential of African Indigenous birthing knowledge for improving maternal health and reducing maternal mortality is tantamount to obstetrical violence. Ultimately, the argument that epistemic and obstetrical violence results from the exclusion of African birthing methods from the global maternal strategy rests on the evident failure to reduce the rate of maternal death on the continent.

The historical and practical significance of African Indigenous birthing knowledge has received minimal research attention, although a few scholars document the history of Indigenous midwifery in certain African countries (Hunt 1999; van Tol 2007). Some noted the need to incorporate traditional birth attendants[4] to supplement Nigeria's scarcely available maternal healthcare services (Ohaja and Murphy-Lawless 2017; Mathole, Lindmark, and Ahlberg 2005). The validity of African Indigenous birthing knowledge in and of itself, however, is hardly highlighted. While Indigenous birthing knowledge is being explored and reclaimed in Native American communities in the Global North, including the United States, such efforts have not extended to the African continent. The marginalization of African Indigenous birthing knowledge is yet to be considered a part of the ongoing neocolonial framework reinforcing reproductive injustice. Thus, I ask, How significant are Indigenous epistemologies in the quest to improve maternal health and reduce maternal mortality in Africa, and in Nigeria specifically? Do Indigenous midwives possess any non-Western medical birthing knowledge or skills that are valid on their own terms and also beneficial for safe childbirth? Should engagement with Indigenous midwives on maternal health exist within a binary of either training them in Western methods or totally discarding them? These questions are particularly relevant as the African region bears the highest burden of global maternal mortality, and Nigeria, the most populous African country, has the third-highest maternal mortality ratio on the continent (World Health Organization 2023a). These questions are also crucial as African countries face the dilemma of situating intergenerational Indigenous birthing knowledge within a global maternal health paradigm that prioritizes Western medicalized childbirth.

I write this article as a Nigerian mother of four children,[5] in her mid-forties, who grew up in one of the government-underserved communities in Lagos, Nigeria, and whose parents did not have Western formal education. Growing up, I witnessed women in my family and community give birth to their children at home, either unattended, with the assistance of other women in the community, or with the help of Indigenous midwives. However, my Western education made me refuse the birthing wisdom of my mothers, foremothers, and most women without Western education in my community. My feminist activism for reproductive health and human rights in Nigeria hinged only on making Western maternal healthcare available, accessible, and affordable for women. It took my personal experience with the reality of Nigeria's maternal healthcare system to rethink the need for a more multipronged approach to maternal health than is outlined by the Safe Motherhood Initiative. In 2007, I lost my baby due to medical negligence and the public hospital's lack of facilities for an emergency C-section that I eventually needed. The prenatal clinics I visited were also rife with stories of avoidable maternal and infant deaths.

On the one hand, in my prenatal care, which is modeled on the Western medical approach and the neglect of the birthing wisdom of my mothers, I was promised the best maternal and infant outcome. On the other hand, I was ultimately confronted with the failure of that promise. As a feminist activist, I had advocated for Nigerian women to have each childbirth attended by a "skilled" birth attendant. In practice, I experienced the critical shortcomings of that strategy. The irony of the great promise—and consistent failure—of absolute reliance on Western birthing framework in Indigenous communities is what Barbara Gurr (2015: 68–87) describes as "double discourse." It took my infant loss and near–maternal death in 2007 to put the consequences of neglecting Indigenous birthing into proper perspective for me. This experience was my turning point toward remembering the importance of African Indigenous knowledge and practice. My near-deadly maternal experience led me to ask how this experience could have been different had I considered the validity of Indigenous birthing knowledge. What difference would it make if my Western education and narrow feminist activism had not both reinforced the ideological authority of Western medical birthing approaches over African Indigenous birthing knowledge and practice? Since that experience, I have researched the perspectives of Indigenous midwives and the birthing persons who use their services in Lagos, Nigeria (Ajayi-Lowo 2021).

While this article is influenced by the findings from my dissertation research study with Indigenous midwives and birthing women's experiences in Nigeria, I do not attempt to explore the expertise of African Indigenous midwives and the experiences of birthers who use their pregnancy and childbirth services per se. Rather, in this article I argue for the epistemic validity of African Indigenous birthing knowledge in and of itself, using Nigeria as an example. I adopt a reproductive justice theoretical framework, which incorporates a feminist standpoint and decolonial theories, and argue that African Indigenous birthing knowledge is valid and, therefore, should be considered significant in maternal health paradigms on the continent. In elaborating on the stringent meshwork of reproductive justice theory, I place this article in conversation with the discourse on reclaiming traditional and Indigenous birthing knowledge in the Global North, the United States in particular. I critique the Safe Motherhood Initiative's exclusion of Indigenous birthing knowledge and its overall influence on existing maternal health research, policy, and advocacy in Nigeria. Additionally, I provide evidence for my argument supporting the epistemic and practical significance of African Indigenous knowledge. I conclude this article by reasserting the need to connect the discourse on African Indigenous knowledge with other reproductive justice efforts at reclaiming Indigenous birthing knowledge and practice.

## A Critique of the Safe Motherhood Initiative

Launched in 1987 and funded by global development organizations, including the World Health Organization and the World Bank, the Safe Motherhood Initiative ultimately became the dominant global maternal health strategy, especially in "developing" regions. The initiative originally adopted multiple maternal health strategies for holistic maternal healthcare, including partnerships with local communities and collaborations with traditional birth attendants (Starrs 2006; Weil and Fernandez 1999). Apparently, the Safe Motherhood Initiative, in its initial iteration, attempted to incorporate diverse approaches for improving global maternal health. However, its exclusion of Indigenous birthing methods seems to have crept in subtly but surely. From the 1950s to the 1980s, the World Health Organization considered traditional birth attendants instrumental in reducing maternal mortality and intensified training for them. However, this stance changed in 1997. The World Health Organization excluded traditional birth attendants from the Safe Motherhood Initiative by claiming that there was no evidence to substantiate their contribution to reducing the maternal mortality ratio and requiring all births to be attended by Western–medically skilled birth attendants alone (Kruske and Barclay 2004; Sibley and Sipe 2006; World Health Organization 2008). Using the Western medical model as the yardstick for expertise in child deliveries, the World Health Organization regarded non-Western-medical birth attendants as unskilled, stating that "short trainings were not adequate to teach an otherwise unqualified person the critical thinking and decision-making skills needed to practice" child delivery (World Health Organization 2008: 3). In a departure from the emphasis on community-based efforts to promote reproductive health and maternal health in particular, the twenty-first-century iteration of the Safe Motherhood Initiative symbolizes a radical shift in prioritizing Western medical methods for preventing maternal mortality and morbidity over Indigenous birthing paradigms.

The exclusion of Indigenous birth approaches from the Safe Motherhood Initiative results in a contradiction between the Safe Motherhood Initiative and the application of global human rights to health principles. One of the goals of the United Nations' global human rights to health framework is to make all approaches to health culturally appropriate and locally sustainable (OHCHR 2000). Drawing from the United Nations' rights to health frameworks, the World Health Organization's human rights-based approach also calls for healthcare that is culturally appropriate, people-centered, gender-sensitive, and involves meaningful participation of all stakeholders (World Health Organization 2017). Human rights approaches to maternal health also require making maternal health available, accessible, acceptable, and of good quality (OHCHR 2000). To meet the acceptability clause, maternal healthcare must align with women's cultures and incorporate plans to respect women's views about their bodies and health. However, the Safe Motherhood Initiative's requirement that all births to be attended by birth attendants deemed "skilled" by Western norms implicitly and explicitly excludes traditional birth attendants, who adopt Indigenous methods in providing prenatal and childbirth services. Therefore, the Safe Motherhood Initiative, which is the global maternal health strategy designed to correspond to the United Nations human rights framework, falls short of the human rights to health policy goals. This contradiction poses a challenge for making maternal health culturally appropriate, locally sustainable, respectful, and participatory for birthers, especially in "developing" countries. Rather than act as the vehicle to deliver the promise of human rights to maternal health, the initiative infringes on the right of participation of Indigenous birth attendants and fails to respect Indigenous birthing standpoints.

Simply stated, the Safe Motherhood Initiative reifies a colonial conception of what qualifies as birthing skills. The exclusion of Indigenous midwives' knowledges and practices from the maternal health parlance about what constitutes "skilled" birth attendants implies that Indigenous midwives are either unskilled or not skilled enough for safe pregnancy care and child delivery. This assumption automatically establishes the Western medical birthing approach as the authoritative birthing method. The binary notion of "skilled" and "unskilled" birth attendants forms the baseline for the World Health Organization's engagement with maternal health in "developing" countries (Kruske and Barclay 2004; Sibley and Sipe 2006). Since Indigenous midwives are by definition "unskilled," they easily become the target of blame for poor maternal health and high maternal mortality ratios. At the same time, there is less interrogation of the maternal and birth outcomes of birthers under the care of "skilled" birth attendants. Research studies on traditional birth attendants sometimes simply move from an assumed lack of skill by traditional birth attendants to the foregone conclusion on their threat to maternal health. Working with an assumed premise of unskilled traditional birth attendants and without adequate empirical evidentiary support for their conclusion, several research studies blame the high burden of maternal death in Nigeria and other "developing" countries on traditional birth attendants (Ayede 2012: 22; Maduka and Ogu 2020). To attain an in-depth analysis of traditional birth attendants' skills and their contribution to maternal health, birthing "skills" must be broadly defined to include the generational birthing skills that do not fit the Western biomedical archetype.

The call to either ban or Western–medically train traditional birth attendants in Africa is also premised on the assumption that traditional attendants are unskilled. Based on the Western medicalized paradigm of the Safe Motherhood Initiative, some researchers conclude that traditional birth attendants should be entirely banned as they are incapable of being trained (Harrison 2011; Maduka and Ogu 2020). In terms of policy, some states in Nigeria work to ban traditional birth attendants entirely. For example, Governor Mimiko of Ondo State in 2013 accused traditional birth attendants of increasing maternal mortality and argued that they are of no use in the maternal healthcare system (Johnson 2013). This conclusion results from the conflation of skilled birthing knowledge with Western forms of education. In some instances, education is viewed as synonymous with fluency in the English language and with Western technical and bio-medical training. In a complete denial of the traditional birth attendants' ability to acquire any birthing skills, the researcher Ana Joseph argues that traditional birth attendants are illiterate, cannot speak the English lan-guage, and also are "too old and therefore too set in their ways to adapt to modern healthcare methods" (Harrison 2011: 1341). Emphasizing formal, institutionalized education and training for traditional birth attendants does not acknowledge that they possess valid birthing knowledge attained via apprenticeship and intergenerational knowledge transfers.

Additionally, the superficial acknowledgment of traditional birth atten-dants' potential benefit for maternal health overlooks their ability to receive and use modern biomedical birthing methods as complementary to their traditional practices. Some research studies show that traditional birth attendants can be trained to refer complicated maternal cases to healthcare facilities (Campbell, Graham, and LMSSSG 2006; Prata et al. 2013; Wilson et al. 2011; Sibley and Sipe 2006). These studies emphasize traditional birth attendants' capacity for medicalized training and poten-tial for incorporation into the Western medical maternal health sector. Influenced by the Safe Motherhood Initiative, these researchers measure traditional birth attendants' activities vis-à-vis Western medical standards, prioritize only biomedicalized birthing approaches, and aim to fit all birth attendants into that mold. Likewise, some government policies in different states in Nigeria promote Western medical training for traditional birth attendants as a potential strategy for improving maternal health. The Lagos State government, for example, commits to training traditional medicine practitioners, including traditional birth attendants, to improve the skills of attendants during childbirth and to reduce mother-to-child transmission of HIV during child delivery (Lagos State Government 2019; Olasunkanmi 2020; Omotayo and Udosen 2020). The Brown Button Foundation, a nongovernmental organization, has also trained a total of 5,200 traditional birth attendants across the country in Western medical skills (Iwenwanne 2019). These training projects might be a worthy cause on their own, and the initiators might genuinely aim at improving maternal health care and averting maternal mortality.

However, simply calling for traditional birth attendants to be trained in Western biomedical method connotes that traditional birth attendants do not possess any initial or unique Indigenous birthing knowledge that would likewise be useful to Western medical practitioners and systems. Magdalena Ohaja and Jo Murphy-Lawless (2017) argue that aiming to medicalize traditional birth attendants through training is a one-sided collaboration that deprives maternal medicalized experts of learning from the traditional birth attendants, as well. It denies the opportunity for a reciprocal exchange of knowledge between Western–medically trained birth attendants and traditional birth attendants. While offering Western medical training to traditional birth attendants is a laudable project, it is also important to understand traditional birth attendants' Indigenous birthing knowledge and what lessons it holds for maternal health policy-makers and medical experts. Hence, recognizing Indigenous birthing knowledge as valid on its own would also offer an opportunity to engage Indigenous midwives in training and collaborations. The incorporation of traditional birth attendants' Indigenous birthing knowledge and the perspectives of their clients must move beyond training, banning, or simple "inclusion" of traditional birth attendants into the medical paradigm. It must entail an epistemological exploration of what traditional birth attendants' knowledge and methods are, as well as the birthing standpoints of birthers who use their services.

Although the World Health Organization acknowledges that "evidence can come from many sources," including "ethnographic observations of community involvement in health programming" (World Health

Organization 2013), evidence-based approaches in the Safe Motherhood Initiative prioritize medical and numerical evidence for measuring countries' progress in reducing maternal mortality (Storeng and Béhague 2014). The conception of what counts as evidence in the Safe Motherhood Initiative is restricted to the numerically quantifiable. Statistical value is preferred to the broader spectrum of subjective evidence. As Katerine T. Storeng and Dominique P. Béhague (2014: 265) note, the Safe Motherhood Initiative currently centers the use of "numbers," "measurement," and "quantitative health indicators," and is entangled in the "measurement trap." Owing to this reliance on statistical and quantitative indicators, the multiple and complex sociocultural factors that affect maternal health in "developing" countries receive less attention. Using an evidence-based approach might be convenient for global maternal health experts and funders, who rely on numbers and statistics for measuring funding outcomes, but it limits engagement with sociocultural intricacies of childbirth and clouds our understanding of Indigenous birthing knowledge, as well as birthers' meaning-making of childbirth.

Evidence-based methods that rely solely on numbers are also insufficient for measuring the complexities of maternal health and birthing or measuring the progress of reducing maternal mortality in "developing" countries because of the lack of accurate data recording and management systems, which raises questions on the reliability of statistical evidence relating to childbirth and maternal health (Oleribe and Taylor-Robinson 2016; Alkema et al. 2017). Furthermore, a higher percentage of Nigeria's maternal mortality cases have been reported in hospitals than in nonhospital births (Ronsmans, Graham, and LMSSSG 2006; Okonofua et al. 2017; Ntoimo et al. 2018). This dispels the underlying assumption in the Safe Motherhood Initiative that birthing with "skilled" birth attendants in medical facilities is the only effective approach to improving maternal health and reducing maternal mortality ratio. Given this disparity and lack of credible numerical data, evidence-based analysis about where, when, and how often maternal deaths occur remains open to doubt. Hence, there are further reasons to be skeptical about a complete reliance on numbers as the sole evidence of the state of maternal health and maternal mortality. What counts as evidence must include local and cultural maternal health intricacies that cannot necessarily be enumerated.

If there is one crucial reason to expand beyond the box of the Safe Motherhood Initiative to incorporate African Indigenous birthing approaches, it would be because the Safe Motherhood Initiative fails to reduce maternal mortality in Africa more broadly, and in Nigeria in particular. Rather than decreasing under the initiative, maternal mortality in Nigeria and "sub-Saharan"[6] African regions has, in fact, been increasing. As an operational strategy for promoting the Safe Motherhood Initiative, Target 5 of the United Nations' Millennium Development Goals (MDG 5) aimed at reducing the global maternal mortality ratio by 75 percent between 2000 and 2015. However, at the end of the MDG's fifteen-year time span, Nigeria had the fourth-highest maternal mortality ratio, "sub-Saharan" African countries accounted for 66 percent of global maternal deaths, and 99 percent of global maternal deaths occurred in the "developing" regions (World Health Organization 2015). Similarly, Target 3c of the Sustainable Development Goals (SDG 3c), which succeeded MDG 5 in 2015, aims to reduce the global maternal mortality ratio to less than seventy by the year 2030. Five years into the SDGs, the rate of maternal mortality for Nigeria and the "sub-Saharan" African countries at large is increasing, compared to the MDG 2015 record (World Health Organization 2023a). As of 2020, Nigeria has become the country with the third-highest maternal mortality ratio, and "sub-Saharan" African countries now account for 70 percent of global maternal deaths (World Health Organization 2023a). Considering these data, it is clear that achieving the promise of a "better" Western childbirth paradigm that will reduce maternal and infant mortality is a promise that keeps failing to be kept.

Not only has the Safe Motherhood Initiative failed to reduce the maternal mortality ratio in Africa, but it has also failed to guarantee good quality maternal healthcare. Additionally, it is questionable if birthers' overall maternal health experience has improved with the reliance on Western medical birth attendants only. Nigerian birthers who receive Western medicalized care during childbirth are often not satisfied by the quality of maternal healthcare, and their childbirth experiences are, overall, poor, regardless of the maternal and infant outcome (Ajayi-Lowo 2018; CRR and WARDC 2008). Other African countries are seeing the effects of this failure, in addition to Nigeria. In African countries, there has been a gradual increase in the over-medicalization of childbirth, including the rising number of unnecessary Cesarean sections (C-sections) with resultant worse maternal and infant outcomes (Maanvi 2019; Yaya et al. 2018). The Safe Motherhood Initiative's failure to deliver on its promise to ameliorate the maternal mortality ratio questions its very premise as the "authoritative" maternal health approach as well as its effectiveness as a global maternal health strategy. It reveals the need to reconsider the place of an African Indigenous birthing paradigm within a holistic maternal health approach.

The Safe Motherhood Initiative guidelines determine much of the national maternal healthcare policies in African countries and also have regional implications. In Nigeria, for instance, where opinions on the roles of traditional birth attendants in pregnancy and childbirth remain divided among health policymakers, there is no national consensus on appropriate policy. In the race to meet the MDGs, for example, the Agbebiye program in Ondo State requires traditional birth attendants to refer all clients that seek their services to healthcare facilities, for which they receive a financial reward of 2000 naira (about $5) per referral (Mimiko 2017; Muanya 2016). In other words, Ondo State's implementation of the Safe Motherhood Initiative seeks to completely stop traditional birth attendants from attending any births. In Lagos State, however, the government's maternal health and prevention of mother-to-child transmission (PMTCT) programs include training of and collaborations with traditional birth attendants (Premium Times 2014). The contradictory strategies adopted by Ondo State and Lagos State reflect the lack of a coherent national plan to engage traditional birth attendants outside the limitations set by the dictates of global maternal health strategy.

On the continental level, the adoption of the Safe Motherhood Initiative is also leading to conflicting policies on the place of Indigenous birthing knowledge. In 2007, Malawi's president banned traditional birth attendants from attending births but lifted the ban in 2010 when it was discovered that more childbirths continue to take place outside of healthcare facilities (Relief Web 2010). Also, traditional birth attendants have been either completely banned or restricted from attending childbirth in several African countries, including Burundi, Uganda, Sierra Leone, and Somalia, as governments seek to comply with the global maternal health goal of having all births attended by "skilled" birth attendants (Chi and Urdal 2018). Global maternal health strategies also entail focusing on training the traditional birth attendants, having them refer all the patients to "skilled" birth attendants, or repositioning them to work as nonmedical staff at healthcare facilities (UNFPA 2006: 36, 50). Offering financial incentives to traditional birth attendants to refer all their clients to healthcare facilities is becoming a trend in Nigeria and other African countries as they seek to meet the Safe Motherhood Initiative guidelines (Chukwuma et al. 2019; Oyebola et al. 2014; Pyone et al. 2014). While encouraging birthers to seek prenatal, childbirth, and postnatal services at healthcare facilities when necessary is a good practice in itself, the attempt to foreclose the possibility of birthers choosing the services of traditional birth attendants or the location of their labored delivery ultimately attempts to eliminate African generational Indigenous birthing standpoints.

This quantitative data-driven model of maternal health also influences the level of attention paid by the Nigerian government toward improving maternal health and reducing maternal mortality ratio. Hiding under the evidence-based statistical paradigm, the Nigerian government simply plays what Storeng and Béhague (2014) call "the number game," as it strives merely to meet the quantifiable goals set in global maternal strategy, without attention to women's holistic childbirth experiences. This is evident in the discrepancy between the World Health Organization's reporting and that of the Nigerian government after the MDGs in 2015. While the WHO's (2015) MDG lists Nigeria's maternal mortality ratio as 814 per 100,000 live births, the Nigerian government reports a maternal mortality ratio of 243 per 100,000 live births for the same period (OSSAPMDG 2015). The very broad numeric goal of reducing maternal mortality set in MDG 5 and its relatively new successor, SDG 3c, therefore, might not translate into the realities of birthing persons in Nigeria.

Reliance on the Safe Motherhood Initiative for improving maternal health and reducing maternal mortality ratio in Nigeria has also influenced women's health advocacy by nongovernmental organizations. Maternal health as a human right in Nigeria has been mainly championed by nongovernmental organizations that hold the Nigerian government accountable for increasing access to "skilled" birth attendants (CRR and WARDC 2008). This strategy has yielded minimal progress because, as Rebecca Cook (2013) argues, it is difficult to ensure that sovereign states fulfill their commitment to the human right to health, even when they are signatories to it. Despite the impunity with which countries like Nigeria contravene the global legal framework on the right to health, and maternal health specifically, sanctions for such violations are rarely enforced given the complexities of applying international human rights laws in each sovereign state party (Dunn et al. 2017). While Nigeria has a duty under international law to protect and promote maternal health as a human right, there is little hope that holding the Nigerian government accountable to the international human rights approach to health can reduce maternal mortality.

Leveraging effective local maternal health strategies is, therefore, necessary and timely, even as scholars and activists continue holding the Nigerian government accountable for their commitment to a human rights-based approach to maternal healthcare. These advocacy efforts are steps in the right direction. However, we must also look deeply into the perspectives of Indigenous birthing knowledge and approaches, as improving maternal healthcare and reducing the maternal mortality ratio in a country like Nigeria cannot be restricted to the colonial Western medical model. Since advocacy for better maternal healthcare aims at improving the birthing person's experience and outcome, what if we listen to and validate the perspectives of those who prefer Indigenous birthing approaches? Also, the human rights–based approach to health care mandates that maternal healthcare must be appropriate, sensitive, and respectful about gender and culture. What if we listen to and incorporate the cultural perspectives of Indigenous midwives in the maternal health discourse?

**The Global Application of Reproductive Justice**
In highlighting the significance of African Indigenous birthing knowledge, I ground my analysis on the scholar-activist framework of reproductive justice. Fundamentally, reproductive justice theory delineates an individual's right to have children, to not have children, and to raise their children in safe and culturally sustainable environments (Ross et al. 2017; Ross and Solinger 2017). Reproductive justice includes a struggle for bodily and epistemological autonomy that is necessary for holistic reproductive health and rights. In seeking holistic justice relating to all issues of reproduction, reproductive justice centers marginalized Indigenous perspectives on pregnancy- and childbirth-related issues. In their analysis of feminist standpoint theory, Patricia Hill Collins (2000) and Uma Narayan (2004) argue that the embodied experience of the marginalized needs to be prioritized as epistemologically valid. In their articulation of reproductive justice as a theory, Loretta Ross and Rickie Solinger (2017: 72) explicitly affirm that reproductive justice "incorporates standpoint theory." The epistemological frame of reproductive justice, therefore, allows for centering not only the individual's reproductive health and rights but also their knowledge systems and worldviews on reproduction. Rather than relying solely on Western medical and statistical approaches to reproduction, reproductive justice centers subjective experiences and Indigenous birthing knowledge as equally valid and reliable data for holistic solutions to reproductive health.

Though developed by women of color in the United States, reproductive justice has a global reach for demarginalizing the reproductive epistemologies of people of color, which are suppressed under Western paradigms and rhetoric, by analyzing pregnancy- and childbirth-related oppression beyond health indices and social determinants of health. Scholars in the Global North are already adopting reproductive justice to center the subjugated Indigenous birthing perspectives of motherhood and childbirth. For instance, in Native North American communities, reproductive justice accommodates critique of the marginalization of Indigenous peoples' birthing knowledge and the resultant poor maternal and infant outcomes (Gurr 2015; Tabobondung 2017). Additionally, in Western Europe, specifically in Germany, scholars argue for a reconstructed concept of motherhood (Heffernan and Stone 2020). Maternal health discourse on the continent of Africa also entails epistemological discourse to demarginalize Indigenous birthing experiences and knowledge. One example is Meredith Reiches (2019), who, in her critique of the oppressive prioritization of prenatal supplementation in the Gambia, also discusses the importance of reproductive justice for the already racially and economically marginalized.

While the global application of reproductive justice relates to a broader range of discourse on reproduction and the sustenance of a community, this article focuses specifically on the reclaiming of epistemology around pregnancy and childbirth. As a framework that seeks to center birthers' embodied experiences during pregnancy, labor, childbirth, and postpartum, reproductive justice is essential for critiquing the exclusion of Indigenous birthing epistemologies and birthers' standpoints in the Safe Motherhood Initiative. For African Americans, it involves Black birthing persons' rights to use doulas and granny midwives for childbirth, if they so desire (Oparah and Bonaparte 2015). For Native North Americans, it enables the struggle against the assimilation of Indigenous birthing methods and rituals into colonizers' medicalized birthing paradigms that do not save the lives of birthers and their babies (Pember 2018; Gurr 2015). Overall, the reproductive justice movement entails the struggle to retain Indigenous birthing methods in resistance to medicalized birth that overlooks birthers' meaning of unmedicated childbirth. Reproductive justice zooms in on the importance of Indigenous birthing knowledge for improving maternal health outcomes for birthers of color.

A reproductive justice perspective enables a decolonial approach to maternal health practices and policies. By "decolonial approach to reproductive justice," I refer to an epistemological shift that is critical of colonial influences on the birthing process—a shift that validates African birthers' ways of knowing and being relating to childbirth. A decolonial approach is essential for analyzing the maternal health landscape, given that African ways of knowing remain subsumed in the hegemonic Euro–North American epistemology that continues to invalidate African epistemology, despite political independence (Ndlovu-Gatsheni 2013a, 2013b, 2015). Reproductive justice is a helpful framework from which to examine maternal health and birthing in Nigeria from a holistic perspective not limited to the adoption of global strategies and policies. It not only adopts a human rights framework, but also emphasizes the choices, voices, and cultures of birthing persons in the struggle for reproductive health and rights. Beyond holding governments primarily responsible for protecting, promoting, and fulfilling human rights to maternal health, the reproductive justice perspective strives to empower each person to take agency in her reproductive life. More broadly, this lens allows for a transnational interrogation of the high maternal mortality rate for Black birthing people globally, while exploring the similarities and differences in local history and culture.

Using a reproductive justice framework for reclaiming African Indigenous birthing knowledge into maternal health discourse, beyond the stipulations of the Safe Motherhood Initiative, is a decolonial act. As a decolonial approach, reproductive justice is relevant as a remembrance framework of Africa's historical birthing epistemologies and as a resistance tool for unshackling Africans' birthing skill sets that have been submerged in Western knowledge paradigms. María Lugones (2010: 745) noted that even after colonization, coloniality continues in the form of colonization of memory, reality, and identity, requiring the uprooting of colonized thoughts and identity. Although the colonial interlopers are no longer physically present on the continent of Africa, they maintain an incessant colonial grasp on the continent through a system of coloniality (Ndlovu-Gatsheni 2013b:). The denial of the cultural and spiritual significance of Indigenous midwives' maternal services is associated with the colonial belief that the Indigenous spiritual knowledge of the traditional birth attendants is deficient when compared to Western medical and scientific knowledge. The exclusion of African Indigenous knowledge reflects a colonial tendency in the Safe Motherhood Initiative framework, which requires the decolonial critique that reproductive justice enables.

The connection between reproductive justice and standpoint theory is significant for the decolonial project of reclaiming Indigenous birthing knowledge submerged under colonial and neocolonial frameworks. Notably, the subjugation of precolonial birthing epistemology is common to Black and Indigenous communities across borders. Rather than being confined within any specific geographical boundaries, reproductive justice allows for an overarching analysis of the interconnectedness of white supremacist oppression of reproduction in Indigenous communities and communities of color (Smith 2005; Gurr 2015). It allows for reclaiming Indigenous knowledge that existed during the precolonial periods while paying attention to and synergizing the postcolonial dynamics of maternal care. Against the backdrop of the precolonial birthing paradigms that birthers continue to find useful, reproductive justice theory allows for an analysis of Nigerian birthers' navigation of and resistance to global maternal health's compulsory use of "skilled" birth attendants. It allows for exploring African Indigenous birthing knowledge that Indigenous midwives possess. As a decolonial approach prioritizing birthing standpoints for holistic maternal and infant outcomes, reproductive justice also includes the birthing person's access to all forms of birthing options, including the Western medical alternatives when necessary for complications and emergencies or simply when preferred by the birthing person.

**From Safe Motherhood to Reproductive Justice**

A historical remembering is needed to fully understand the colonial dismissal of African Indigenous birthing knowledge in the Safe Motherhood Initiative. The exclusion of Indigenous midwives from the World Health Organization's list of skilled birth attendants is rooted in the imposition of "modern" medical birthing methods on African countries during the colonial era, at which juncture African Indigenous birthing methods were criticized, condemned, and demonized (van Tol 2007: 16). Childbirth was one of the arenas in which the colonizers reinforced their epistemologies and methods as superior to the colonized. In fact, Nancy Hunt (1999: 11) has described childbirth as "an arena of colonial bargaining and strife" during the colonization of African countries. The distinction drawn in the global Safe Motherhood Initiative between birthing with Western medical attendants as the only safe and acceptable birth method, and the portrayal of traditional birth attendants as dangerous and risky, thus reinforces the colonial rhetoric of Western perspectives and practices as better than

Indigenous perspectives and practices. While researching the archive of the British Annual Medical Reports on infant and maternal welfare services in Nigeria between 1925 and 1945, Deanne van Tol (2007) finds the reduction of infant and maternal mortality amplified as the justification for displacing Indigenous birthing knowledge for "modern" methods. It serves as the cover-up for other underlying cultural and racial motives driving the suppression of Indigenous ways of knowing and doing. As the menace of maternal mortality continues to ravage African countries, the rationale for displacing Indigenous birthing methods remains the same in the current global maternal health strategy as in the colonial era.

The world needs to remember that precolonial African Indigenous birthing systems were not crude and dirty as popularly portrayed, but innovative and solution oriented. Historically, not only were Africans of earlier generations able to attend successful vaginal deliveries, but they were also using Indigenous birthing methods for performing successful surgical procedures when necessary. Successful C-sections were carried out in African countries such as Uganda and Rwanda well before Western surgical childbirth methods were introduced to Africa (NIH 2013). For example, Robert Felkin (1884) reports a successful C-section he witnessed in Kahura, Uganda, where Indigenous substances such as "banana wine," "iron needles," and "paste prepared from roots" were used to save the lives of the mother and child (NIH 2013). In fact, American gynecology owes a great deal to the immense contribution of Indigenous birthing knowledge enslaved women brought with them from the continent of Africa to the Western Hemisphere (Owens 2017; Oparah and Bonaparte 2015; Turner 2015). The history of medicine in the United States provides evidence that traditional birth attendants hold valid birthing knowledge and skills and offered effective material health strategies. Hence, the exclusion of African intergenerational Indigenous birthing knowledge and approaches by the Safe Motherhood Initiative disregards both the historical success of Indigenous birthing knowledge and its current relevance and potential.

Moreover, the binary and hierarchical categorization of traditional/ Indigenous versus modern biomedical/scientific birthing knowledge reifies a colonial conception of what counts as science. African Indigenous knowledge in and of itself is valid science. For example, in his philosophy of "Native science," Gregory Cajete (2000: 2) argued that Indigenous ways of knowing or doing are "a metaphor for a wide range of tribal processes of perceiving, thinking, acting and 'coming to know' that have evolved through human experience with the natural world." Indigenous midwives' ways of birthing, which fall under the category of what Cajete described as Native science, have been developed through generations of observing and aiding the natural process of birthing. While traditional midwives' birthing experience has been excluded from the modern medical birthing process because it is presumed to be unscientific, it falls under what Cajete (2000: 3) described as Native science that is already "inclusive of modern science." The notion of what is scientific in general and in relation to childbirth specifically must also include non-Western intergenerational birthing epistemologies. Seeing African Indigenous knowledge as scientifically valid in and of itself disrupts the colonial assumption of the superiority of Western medical science to Indigenous birthing approaches. It helps deconstruct the binary of "traditional" versus "medical/scientific," the "skilled" versus "unskilled" approach to maternal health policies and strategies that continues to harm maternal and infant outcomes for people of African descent.

Not only does the colonial denial of African Indigenous birthing knowledge constitute epistemic violence, but hampering its practical potential for improving maternal care and outcomes also constitutes obstetric violence. Western medical facilities and personnel are not sufficiently available, accessible, affordable, or of good quality in a country like Nigeria. Hence, in practical terms, restricting the birthing care of Indigenous midwives in a country with inadequate Western biomedical resources and personnel results in obstetrical violence. For instance, the minimum number of required "skilled" birth attendants is 5.9 health workers per 1,000 people (World Health Organization 2016). Nigeria, however, has only 0.4 physicians per 1,000 people, and only 1.179 nurses and midwives per 1,000 people (World Bank 2020). While there is no global standard for hospital bed density—number of hospital beds per 1,000 population—Nigeria's 0.5 density is lower than the world average of 2.7 and less than 0.8, which is the average for "low- and middle-income countries" (World Bank 2023). Additionally, there are only 34,423 healthcare facilities in Nigeria, the majority of which are concentrated in the southern states, the state capitals, and major cities, leaving the few facilities in the rural and remote locations overextended (Makinde et al. 2018). Since the population of Nigeria stands at over two hundred million (World Bank 2021) and the numbers of healthcare workers, facilities, and equipment are insufficient, the solution to improving maternal health and reducing maternal mortality cannot solely rely on the approach of the Safe Motherhood Initiative.

Despite being one of the countries of the world with wealth from petroleum, the Nigerian government continuously fails to fund healthcare in
general and maternal care in particular. At the 2001 African Union Abuja
Declaration, Nigeria committed at least 15 percent of the budget to healthcare (Organisation of African Unity 2001). But the country's healthcare
budgets were only 5.1 percent, 3.9 percent, and 4.1 percent of the total
annual budgets in 2017, 2018, and 2019, respectively (Ojetun 2019). This
low budget for healthcare puts higher financial burden on women seeking
Western medical maternal health. Even in states where maternal healthcare is declared partially or totally free, women are still charged several out-
of-pocket fees, and most of them are unable to access the National Health
Insurance Scheme, which is only currently available for persons employed
in the formal sector (Nnamuchi et al. 2018). The poor funding of healthcare
also negatively impacts the overall quality of Western maternal healthcare
in Nigeria. Tertiary hospitals in Nigeria that need to provide healthcare in
cases of emergency lack sufficient medical personnel and equipment due to
poor funding (Alkali and Bello 2020). The scene at most Nigeria public
hospitals is one of long queues at prenatal clinics, overcrowded shared
labor wards (rooms), and personnel who are underpaid and overextended
(CRC and WARDC 2008). Hence, even as the Western medical maternal
health framework is made to appear superior to the Indigenous maternal
health framework, the promise of a "better" Western medical framework
merely raises false hopes. It does not align with local birthing realities and,
therefore, is not locally sustainable. It shifts attention away from Indigenous birthing practices without a workable replacement and literally end-
angers the lives of birthing persons and their infants.

The emphasis placed by global maternal health strategy on the use of
Western medical birth attendants for all childbirths in developing countries hinders the attainment of culturally appropriate maternal health
needed to reduce maternal mortality. Even if it were possible for Nigeria
and other African countries to make Western biomedical maternal healthcare adequately available, accessible, and of good quality, restricting African Indigenous birthing approaches from birthing people who prefer it is
unacceptable. In general, the high rate of Nigerian birthing women's use
of traditional midwives is often assumed to be synonymous with lack of
access to the Western biomedical framework. The cultural and spiritual
significance of Indigenous birthing is often ignored or downplayed. However, as valid science, African Indigenous knowledge and practice has cultural and spiritual contributions to the childbirth experience (Aziato and

Omeyo 2018; Izugbara, Ezeh, and Fotso 2009; Mathole, Lindmark, and Ahlberg 2005). Further, African birthers' preference for Indigenous birthing approaches is a continuum of the popular use of traditional medicine for healthcare in Nigeria (Oluwadare et al. 2018). Significantly, while the global coverage of biomedically trained birth attendants at childbirth increased from 61 percent in 2000 to 78 percent in 2016, they attended only half of all live births in African countries in 2016 (World Health Organization 2021). Despite the voracious global and local campaign for birthing with "skilled" birth attendants (Gayawan 2014), Nigerian women's use of Western medical birth attendants decreased over time, as 23 percent were found "less likely to utilize skilled delivery services in 2013 compared to 2003" (Atuoye et al. 2015: 728). Notably, of the 63 percent of women in Nigeria who do not hire "skilled" birth attendants as of 2013 (NPC and ICF International 2014), 29 percent consider birthing with "skilled" birth attendants as unnecessary/uncustomary, and 22 percent specifically hire traditional birthing attendants (National Population and ICF 2014). The preference of some Nigerian women for traditional midwives, as opposed to the "skilled" birth attendants, questions the cultural appropriateness and sustainability of the global maternal health strategy that compels the use of Western medical birth attendants for childbirth.

As the recent coronavirus pandemic has shown, depending strictly on the Western medical healing paradigm, in general, cannot be our sole maternal health approach. COVID-19 did not impact the African continent as negatively as it did other regions, but it has revealed the unsustainability of the continent's reliance on the Western medical framework for healthcare, including maternal care. Nigeria, as a country, relies on importing basic healthcare equipment, such as masks, ventilators, and other essential medications and medical appliances that became unavailable during the peak of the pandemic (Akande-Sholabi and Adebisi 2020). Nigerians were forced to start to look inward for local and herbal ways of attacking the COVID-19 menace and other diseases (Mutethya 2020). Ironically, the World Health Organization became receptive to scientifically proven traditional medicinal cures for COVID-19 and endorsed protocols for COVID-19 herbal medicine clinical trials (WHO Regional Office for Africa 2020). While traditional birth attendants are being banned or restricted from attending childbirth in African countries for lack of medico-statistical "evidence" of their expertise (Chi and Urdal 2018), U.N. bodies—including UNESCO and the WHO—are exploring the potential of African traditional medicine for curing COVID-19 (UNESCO 2020). Considering the resurgent hope in traditional medicine for curing COVID-19 in the context of trial and error of Western medicine, there is a strong need to reconsider the assumed superiority of the Western medicalized healing paradigm over Indigenous healing approaches. What would a country such as Nigeria be like during a time of COVID-19, if all pregnancy care and child delivery were attended by only Western medical birth attendants or took place only at healthcare facilities? Or, more bluntly, how terrible would it have been for the women and children of Nigeria during the pandemic if traditional birth attendants using Indigenous birthing paradigms were not available to remove significant strain from the overwhelmed medical system? Childbirth within the context of the coronavirus pandemic demonstrated the inadequacy of the Western medical model for solving Nigerian problems, including its maternal healthcare problems.

Adopting a reproductive justice approach for reclaiming African Indigenous birthing knowledge and practices enhances the understanding of the connection between and among Black maternal birthing issues across borders. The strict focus on access to medical maternal healthcare for improving maternal health or reducing the maternal mortality ratio has not only proven ineffective in a developing country like Nigeria, it is also failing in a developed economy like the United States, where most birthers give birth with skilled birth attendants in well-equipped health care facilities (Gold and Starrs 2017; Novack 2017). Despite the relatively higher access that Black birthers in the United States have to Western medical maternal healthcare than birthers in Nigeria, the maternal mortality ratio is also significantly higher for Black birthers in the United States than for their white counterparts. In the United States, the maternal mortality ratio for non-Hispanic Black birthers is 47.1 percent, compared to 13.4 percent for their non-Hispanic white counterparts between 2014 and 2017 (Centers for Disease Control and Prevention 2020). Beyond the United States, birthers of African descent across geographical borders experience a high maternal mortality ratio (Small, Allen, and Brown 2017). Black birthers' high maternal mortality rates globally show that there is a connection between global and racial health disparities and that solutions cannot only be medical but need to include Indigenous approaches.

Additionally, the increasing rate of maternal death among Black birthers in a developed region such as the United States, where there is relatively higher access to skilled birth attendants, calls for a rethinking of the hopes of better maternal outcomes from medicalized birth through strategies such as the Safe Motherhood Initiative. The use of midwives and doulas in the Global North is gradually receiving comparatively popular scholar-activist attention as a form of resistance to the overmedicalization of birth and a reclaiming of Indigenous birthing practices (Apfel 2016; Gumbs, Martens, and Williams 2016; Pember 2018; Oparah and Bonaparte 2015). On the other hand, birthers' use of traditional birth attendants in developing countries is still largely represented in research as more of a savage practice contravening the global maternal strategy and the compulsory use of "skilled" birth attendants for all childbirth (Okonofua and Ogu 2014). Without conflating Black midwives and doulas in the United States with African Indigenous midwives, a fundamental connection exists requiring a reproductive justice approach that validates non-Western medical birthing approaches. There is a need for a global critique of compulsory medicalization and/or overmedicalization of birth and the neglect of the sociocultural and spiritual birthing standpoints of already marginalized minorities. More importantly, given that only half of birthers in African countries use "skilled" birth attendants for child deliveries, the use of Indigenous birthing approaches in this region also deserves critical scholarly attention that is not framed in purely Western medical and quantitative terms.

## Conclusion

As I have argued in this essay, the sole reliance on the Western biomedical birthing model represents a colonial marginalization of African Indigenous birthing knowledge. The globalized, one-size-fits-all Safe Motherhood Initiative has not been adequate for improving maternal health and reducing the maternal mortality ratio in the African region. There is, therefore, a need to reconsider both the epistemological and practical significance of Indigenous birthing paradigms. The significance of Indigenous midwives cannot be limited to the numerical ends of the statistical reduction of maternal mortality regardless of the importance of such. The epistemological, cultural, and spiritual expertise that Indigenous midwives hold is equally important knowledge. While considering any medical training for traditional birth attendants, there is a need to reexamine and reconsider the sociocultural significance of traditional birth attendants' prior Indigenous knowledge. There is a need for open-mindedness to investigate and learn from the attraction that Indigenous birthing holds for birthers. For any engagement with Indigenous midwives to be effective, it must respectfully acknowledge the validity of Indigenous birthing knowledge and approaches. Hence, this essay has called out and critiqued the assumed authoritative expertise of the Western medial birthing framework as colonial. It has challenged the assumed inferiority and consequent marginalization of African Indigenous knowledge, using Nigeria as a case study.

The failure of global maternal health strategies and policies to deliver holistic maternal health and reduce maternal mortality as expected by global experts reiterates the need for more inclusive strategies. If a country such as Nigeria is expected to make the desired progress in maternal health, the desired strategy cannot simply be a blanket global approach compelling childbirth with only Western medicalized birth attendants. The sole reliance on Western medical birth attendants to deliver the promises of "safe motherhood" consistently leaves Nigeria and the entire African continent at the bottom rung of maternal outcomes. Nigeria, like most African countries, lags behind in ensuring adequate personnel, facilities, equipment, and funding needed to facilitate the Safe Motherhood Initiative and the prescribed childbirth with "skilled" birth attendants. Hence, while scholarly and advocacy efforts to improve access to Western medical approaches are essential for birthing persons who desire or require them, the potentials of Indigenous birthing knowledge in maternal health cannot be overemphasized.

As I have also argued, the place of Indigenous knowledge cannot be a mere stopgap to be ultimately submerged or discarded for the "skilled" birth attendants. It must be engaged with as a significant and intrinsic part of maternal health discourse and practice. As the maternal landscape of Black birthing persons in the United States has shown, the sole reliance on a Western medical birthing framework has not proven to reduce the maternal mortality ratio for Black birthers, even where there is relatively higher access to Western medical facilities. In line with the reproductive justice approach, Indigenous birthing standpoints need to be prioritized. Rather than an argument for a complete return of all birthers to Indigenous midwives for pregnancy- and childbirth-related services, reproductive justice allows a both/and inclusive approach. It provides birthers with the option to access their desired birth attendants, including "skilled" birth attendants when necessary. It seeks a two-way collaboration where both traditional birth attendants' Indigenous birthing knowledge and "skilled" birth attendants' Western medical expertise are simultaneously valued and allowed to supplement one another for more effective results in maternal healthcare. Using a reproductive justice framework in maternal health discourse allows us to engage with Indigenous birthing knowledge as an option that is simultaneously valid and useful.

**Esther Oluwashina Ajayi-Lowo** is assistant professor of comparative women's studies at Spelman College in Atlanta, Georgia. She holds a PhD and MA in multicultural women's and gender studies from Texas Woman's University. Her research interests include African feminisms, transnational feminism, Indigenous birthing epistemologies, Black maternal health, and global reproductive health/rights/justice. As a scholar-activist-teacher, Ajayi-Lowo's passion lies at the intersection of gender, race, healthcare, and social justice.

## Notes

1   *Local and Indigenous knowledge* refers to the understandings, skills, and philosophies developed by societies with long histories of interaction with their natural surroundings (UNESCO 2021: paras. 1–3). For rural and Indigenous peoples, local knowledge informs decision-making about fundamental aspects of day-to-day life. This knowledge is integral to a cultural complex that also encompasses language, systems of classification, resource-use practices, social interactions, ritual, and spirituality.

2   I have reservations using the term *developing regions* because it connotes a judgment that some regions of the world are more developed than the others. However, the World Health Organization still uses the terms *developed/developing/ least developed regions* for development indicators. I retain the terms *developing countries* and *developing regions* as used by the World Health Organization, since I am examining maternal health and using mostly WHO data and references in my critique and analysis. It does not reflect my opinion about countries of the world.

3   The World Health Organization defines maternal mortality ratio as "the number of maternal deaths during a given time period per 100,000 live births during the same time period" (World Health Organization 2023b: para. 2).

4   *Traditional birth attendants* as a term originates from the World Health Organization's categories for traditional and Indigenous midwives. In 1992, the WHO defined a traditional birth attendant as "a person who assists the mother during childbirth and initially acquired her skills by delivering babies herself or through apprenticeship to other traditional birth attendants" (World Health Organization 1992: 4). In 2004, the WHO further defined traditional birth attendants as those who are "traditional, independent (of the health system), non-formally trained and community-based providers of care during pregnancy, childbirth, and the postnatal period" (World Health Organization 2004: 8). While I retain the term *traditional birth attendants* in my analysis of global maternal health, I argue that the term does a disservice to midwives whose birthing skills are rooted in intergenerational beliefs that are strongly connected to Native language, culture, and general ethnolinguistic and metaphysical worldviews of diverse Indigenous peoples. Hence, I replaced the term with *Indigenous midwives* when highlighting the significance of the birth attendants who possess African Indigenous birthing knowledge and skills.

5   My four children include my three living children and my dead infant, Iremide, who became one of the statistics of avoidable infant mortality connected to poor and negligent maternal health care during pregnancy and childbirth.

6   The term *sub-Saharan Africa* has been critiqued for reinforcing colonial and racial classification with no geographical justifications (Mashanda 2017). However, the U.N. agencies and other international development organizations continue to use the term *sub-Saharan African* to describe African countries with Black populations, excluding other African countries considered "close to whiteness." While I use this term to discuss the global classification of the maternal mortality ratio, I put it in scare quotes each time I use it to problematize such classification.

**Works Cited**

Ajayi-Lowo, Esther O. 2018. "Perception of Hospital Birth in Nigeria: Through Women's Stories." ANTH 5032: Ethnographic Research paper, University of North Texas.

Ajayi-Lowo, Esther O. 2021. "Decolonizing Childbirth: Women, Traditional Birth Attendants, and Reproductive Justice in Nigeria." PhD diss., Texas Woman's University.

Akande-Sholabi, Wuraola, and Yusuff Adebayo Adebisi. 2020. "The Impact of COVID-19 Pandemic on Medicine Security in Africa: Nigeria as a Case Study." *Pan African Medical Journal* 35, no. 2: 73. http://doi.org/10.11604/pamj.supp.2020.35.2.23671.

Alkali, Nura H., and Mohammed R. Bello. 2020. "Tertiary Hospital Standards in Nigeria: A Review of Current Status." *Annals of African Medical Research* 3, no. 1: 28–32. https://doi.org/10.4081/aamr.2020.108.

Alkema, Leontine, Sanqian Zhang, Doris Chou, Alison Gemmill, Ann-Beth Moller, Doris Ma Fat, Lale Say, Colin Mathers, and Daniel Hogan. 2017. "A Bayesian Approach to the Global Estimation of Maternal Mortality." *Annals of Applied Statistics* 11, no. 3: 1245–74. https://doi.org/10.1214/16-AOAS1014.

Apfel, Alana. 2016. *Birth Work as Care Work: Stories from Activist Birth Communities.* Oakland, CA: PM Press.

Atuoye, Kilian Nasung, Jenna Dixon, Andrea Rishworth, Sylvester Zackaria Galaa, Sheila A. Boamah, and Isaac Luginaah. 2015. "Can She Make It? Transportation Barriers to Accessing Maternal and Child Health Care Services in Rural Ghana." *BMC Health Services Research* 15, no. 1: 1–10. https://doi.org/10.1186/s12913-015-1005-y.

Ayede, A. I. 2012. "Persistent Mission Home Delivery in Ibadan: Attractive Role of Traditional Birth Attendants." *Annals of Ibadan Postgraduate Medicine* 10, no. 2: 22–27.

Aziato, Lydia, and Cephas N. Omenyo. 2018. "Initiation of Traditional Birth Attendants and Their Traditional and Spiritual Practices during Pregnancy and Childbirth in Ghana." *BMC Pregnancy and Childbirth* 18, no. 1: 1–10.

Cajete, Gregory. 2000. *Native Science: Natural Laws of Interdependence.* Santa Fe, NM: Clear Light.

Campbell, Oona M. R., Wendy J. Graham, and LMSSSG (Lancet Maternal Survival Series Steering Group). 2006. "Strategies for Reducing Maternal Mortality:

Getting on with What Works." *Lancet* 368, no. 9543: 1284–99. https://doi.org/10
.1016/S0140-6736(06)69381-1.

Centers for Disease Control and Prevention. 2020. *Pregnancy Mortality Surveillance System.* https://www.cdc.gov/reproductivehealth/maternal-mortality/pregnancy
-mortality-surveillance-system.htm?CDC.

Chi, Primus Che, and Henrik Urdal. 2018. "The Evolving Role of Traditional Birth
Attendants in Maternal Health in Post-conflict Africa: A Qualitative Study of
Burundi and Northern Uganda." *Sage Open Medicine* 6: 1–8. https://doi.org/10.1177
/2050312117753631.

Chukwuma, Adanna, Chinyere Mbachu, Margaret Mcconnell, Thomas J. Bossert, and
Jessica Cohen. 2019. "The Impact of Monetary Incentives on Referrals by Traditional Birth Attendants for Postnatal Care in Nigeria." *BMC Pregnancy and Childbirth* 19, no. 1: 150.

Collins, Patricia Hill. 2000. *Black Feminist Thought: Knowledge, Consciousness, and the Politics of Empowerment.* New York: Routledge.

Cook, Rebecca J. 2013. "Human Rights and Maternal Health: Exploring the Effectiveness of the Alyne Decision." *Journal of Law, Medicine, and Ethics* 41, no. 1: 103–23.
https://doi.org/10.1111/jlme.12008.

CRR (Center for Reproductive Rights) and WARDC (Women Advocates Research
and Documentation Center). 2008. "Broken Promises: Human Rights, Accountability, and Maternal Death in Nigeria." https://www.reproductiverights.org
/document/broken-promises.

Dunn, Jennifer Templeton et al. 2017. "The Role of Human Rights Litigation in
Improving Access to Reproductive Health Care and Achieving Reductions in
Maternal Mortality." *BMC Pregnancy and Childbirth* 17, no. 2: 71–83.

Felkin, Robert W. 1884. "Meeting III.—January 9, 1884: Notes on Labour in Central
Africa." *Transactions, Edinburgh Obstetrical Society* 9: 28–39.

Gayawan, Ezra. 2014. "Spatial Analysis of Choice of Place of Delivery in Nigeria."
*Sexual and Reproductive Healthcare* 5, no. 2: 59–67. https://doi.org/10.1016/j.srhc
.2014.01.004.

Gold, Rachel Benson, and Ann M. Starrs. 2017. "U.S. Reproductive Health and
Rights: Beyond the Global Gag Rule." *Lancet Public Health* 2, no. 3: e122–23.

Gumbs, Alexis Pauline, China Martens, and Mai'a Williams, eds. 2016. *Revolutionary
Mothering: Love on the Front Lines.* Oakland, CA: PM Press.

Gurr, Barbara. 2015. *Reproductive Justice: The Politics of Health Care for Native American
Women.* New Brunswick, NJ: Rutgers University Press.

Harrison, Kelsey A. 2011. "Are Traditional Birth Attendants Good for Improving
Maternal and Perinatal Health? No." *BMJ* 342: d3308. https://doi.org/10.1136/bmj
.d3308.

Heffernan, Valerie, and Katherine Stone. 2021. "Regretting Motherhood in Germany:
Feminism, Motherhood, and Culture." *Signs: Journal of Women in Culture and Society*
46, no. 2: 337–60. https://doi.org/10.1086/710807.

Hunt, Nancy Rose. 1999. *A Colonial Lexicon: Of Birth Ritual, Medicalization, and Mobility in
the Congo.* Durham, NC: Duke University Press.

Iwenwanne, Valentine. 2019. "Training for Quality Delivery: Brown Button's Drive to Improve TBAs Skills in Lagos." *Nigeria Health Watch.* https://nigeriahealthwatch .com/training-for-quality-delivery-brown-buttons-drive-to-improve-tbas-skills -in-lagos/.

Izugbara, Chimaraoke, Alex Ezeh, and Jean-Christophe Fotso. 2009. "The Persistence and Challenges of Homebirths: Perspectives of Traditional Birth Attendants in Urban Kenya." *Health Policy and Planning* 24, no. 1: 36–45. https://doi.org/10.1093 /heapol/czn042.

Johnson, Dayo. 2013. "My Problem with Killer-Birth Attendants." *Vanguard,* December 29. https://www.vanguardngr.com/2013/12/problem-killer-birth-attendants -mimiko/.

Kruske, Sue, and Lesley Barclay. 2004. "Effect of Shifting Policies on Traditional Birth Attendant Training." *Journal of Midwifery and Women's Health* 49, no. 4: 306–11. https://doi.org/10.1016/j.jmwh.2004.01.005.

Lagos State Government. 2019. "LASG Trains Traditional Medicine Practitioners for Improved Healthcare Delivery." *Traditional Medicine.* https://traditionalmedicine .lagosstate.gov.ng/2019/02/06/lasg-trains-traditional-medicine-practitioners-for -improved-healthcare-delivery/.

Lugones, María. 2010. "Toward a Decolonial Feminism." *Hypatia* 25, no. 4: 742–59. https://doi.org/10.1111/j.1527-2001.2010.01137.x.

Maanvi, Singh. 2019. "The Risks of a Cesarean Section." NPR, March 17. https://www .npr.org/sections/goatsandsoda/2019/03/17/703759288/the-risks-of-a-cesarean -section.

Maduka, Omosivie, and Rosemary Ogu. 2020. "Preventing Maternal Mortality during Childbirth: The Scourge of Delivery with Unskilled Birth Attendants." In *Childbirth,* edited by Miljana Z. Jovandaric and Svetlana J. Milenkovic. IntechOpen. http://doi.org/10.5772/intechopen.90463.

Makinde, Olusesan Ayodeji, Abayomi Sule, Olayinka Ayankogbe, and David Boone. 2018. "Distribution of Health Facilities in Nigeria: Implications and Options for Universal Health Coverage." *International Journal of Health Planning and Management* 33, no. 4: e1179–92. https://doi.org/10.1002/hpm.2603.

Mashanda, Tadenda. 2017. "Rethinking the Term Sub-Saharan Africa." *The Herald.* https://www.herald.co.zw/rethinking-the-term-sub-saharan-africa/.

Mathole, Thubelihle, Gunilla Lindmark, and Beth Maina Ahlberg. 2005. "Competing Knowledge Claims in the Provision of Antenatal Care: A Qualitative Study of Traditional Birth Attendants in Rural Zimbabwe." *Health Care for Women International* 26, no. 10: 937–56. https://doi.org/10.1080/07399330500301796.

Mimiko, Olusegun. 2017. "Experiences with Universal Health Coverage of Maternal Health Care in Ondo State, Nigeria, 2009–2017." *African Journal of Reproductive Health* 21, no. 3: 9–26. https://hdl.handle.net/10520/EJC-b459ba0fc.

Muanya, Chukwuma. 2016. "Ondo Records 75% Reduction in Maternal Deaths." *Guardian,* February 25. https://guardian.ng/news/ondo-records-75-reduction-in -maternal-deaths/.

Mutethya, E. 2020. *Nigeria Seeks Local Remedy for COVID-19*. ChinaDaily. https://www
.chinadaily.com.cn/a/202005/29/WS5ed0d672a310a8b241159896.html.

Narayan, Uma. 2004. "The Project of Feminist Epistemology: From a Nonwestern
Feminist." In *The Feminist Standpoint Theory Reader: Intellectual and Political Controver-
sies*, edited by S. Harding, 213–24. New York: Routledge.

Ndlovu-Gatsheni, Sabelo J. 2013a. *Empire, Global Coloniality, and African Subjectivity*.
New York: Berghahn Books.

Ndlovu-Gatsheni, Sabelo J. 2013b. "Why Decoloniality in the Twenty-First Century?"
*Thinker for Thought Leaders* 48: 10–15. https://hdl.handle.net/10210/470999.

Ndlovu-Gatsheni, Sabelo J. 2015. "Decoloniality as the Future of Africa." *History Com-
pass* 13, no. 10: 485–96. https://doi.org/10.1111/hic3.12264.

NIH (National Institutes of Health). 2013. "History of Medicine: Cesarean Section—
A Brief History." https://www.nlm.nih.gov/exhibition/cesarean/part2.html.

Nnamuchi, Obiajulu, Samuel Nwatu, Miriam Anozie, and Emmanuel Onyeabor.
2018. "Nigeria's National Health Act, National Health Insurance Scheme Act,
and National Health Policy: A Recipe for Universal Health Coverage or What?"
*Medicine and Law* 37: 645–82.

Novack, Sophie. 2017. "Texas' Maternal Mortality Rate: Worst in Developed World,
Shrugged off by Lawmakers." *Texas Observer*, June 5. https://www.texasobserver.org
/texas-worst-maternal-mortality-rate-developed-world-lawmakers-priorities/.

NPC (National Population Commission) and ICF International. 2014. *Nigeria Demographic and Health Survey, 2013*. https://dhsprogram.com/pubs/pdf/FR293/FR293.pdf.

Ntoimo, Lorretta F. et al. 2018. "Prevalence and Risk Factors for Maternal Mortality in
Referral Hospitals in Nigeria: A Multicenter Study." *International Journal of Women's
Health* 10: 69–76. http://dx.doi.org/10.2147/IJWH.S151784.

Ohaja, Magdalena, and Jo Murphy-Lawless. 2017. "Unilateral Collaboration: The
Practices and Understandings of Traditional Birth Attendants in Southeastern
Nigeria." *Women and Birth* 30, no. 4: e165–71. https://doi.org/10.1016/j.wombi
.2016.11.004.

OHCHR (Office of the High Commissioner for Human Rights). 2000. "CESCR Gen-
eral comment No. 14: The Right to the Highest Attainable Standard of Health
(Art. 12)." http://www.ohchr.org/Documents/Issues/Women/WRGS/Health
/GC14.pdf.

Ojetun, Damilola. 2019. "Nigeria Remains Perpetual Defaulter of the 'Abuja Declaration' on Health Funding." International Centre for Investigative Reporting, January 1. https://www.icirnigeria.org/nigeria-remains-perpetual-defaulter-of-the
-abuja-declaration-on-health-funding/.

Okonofua, Friday, and Rosemary Ogu. 2014. "Traditional versus Birth Attendants in
Provision of Maternity Care: Call for Paradigm Shift." *African Journal of Reproductive
Health* 18, no. 1: 11–12. https://hdl.handle.net/10520/EJC150482.

Okonofua, F., Imosemi, D., Igboin, B., Adeyemi, A., Chibuko, C., Idowu, A., and
Imongan, W. 2017. "Maternal Death Review and Outcomes: An Assessment in
Lagos State, Nigeria." *PloS One* 12, no. 12: e0188392. https://doi.org/10.1371
/journal.pone.0188392.

Olasunkanmi, O. 2020. *LSACA Trains Traditional Birth Attendants*. Lagos State Government, June 30. https://lagosstate.gov.ng/blog/2020/06/30/lsaca-trains-traditional -birth-attendants/.

Oleribe, Obinna Ositadimma, and Simon David Taylor-Robinson. 2016. "Before Sustainable Development Goals (SDG): Why Nigeria Failed to Achieve the Millennium Development Goals (MDGs)." *Pan African Medical Journal* 24, no. 156: 1–4. https://doi.org/10.11604%2Fpamj.2016.24.156.8447.

Oluwadare, C. T., A. A. Dada, B. I. Oluwadare, and S. AlHassan. 2018. "Women Health Seeking and Utilization of Indigenous Medicine in Urban Ekiti State, Nigeria." *Journal of Contemporary Politics* 4, no. 1.

Omotayo, O., and A. Udosen. 2020. "How Lagos State Is Tackling the Challenge of Alternative Birth Methods." *Medium*, May 26. https://nigeriahealthwatch.medium .com/how-lagos-state-is-tackling-the-challenge-of-alternative-birth-methods -d003f256ae3d.

Oparah, Julia Chinyere, and Alicia D. Bonaparte. 2015. *Birthing Justice: Black Women, Pregnancy, and Childbirth*. New York: Routledge.

Organisation of African Unity. 2001. "Abuja Declaration on HIV/AIDS, Tuberculosis, and Other Related Infectious Diseases (OAU/SPS/ABUJA/3)." African Summit on HIV/AIDS, Tuberculosis, and Other Related Infectious Diseases. https://au.int /sites/default/files/pages/32894-file-2001-abuja-declaration.pdf.

OSSAPMDG (Office of the Senior Special Assistant to the President on Millennium Development Goals). 2015. *Millennium Development Goals: End-Point Report, 2015*. https://www.undp.org/nigeria/publications/nigeria-mdgs-end-point-report-2015.

Owens, Deirdre Cooper. 2017. *Medical Bondage: Race, Gender, and the Origins of American Gynecology*. Athens: University of Georgia Press.

Oyebola, Bolanle C., Fatima Muhammad, Allen Otunomeruke, and Abare Galadima. 2014. "Effect of Performance-Based Incentives for Traditional Birth Attendants on Access to Maternal and Newborn Health-Care Facilities in Gombe State, Nigeria: A Pilot Study." *Lancet* 384: S10. https://doi.org/10.1016/S0140-6736(14) 61873-0.

Pember, Mary Annette. 2018. "The Midwives' Resistance: How Native Women Are Reclaiming Birth on Their Terms." *Rewire.News*, January 5. https://rewirenews group.com/2018/01/05/midwives-resistance-native-women-reclaiming-birth -terms/.

Prata, Ndola, Paige Passano, Suzanne Bell, Tami Rowen, and Malcolm Potts. 2013. "New Hope: Community-Based Misoprostol Use to Prevent Postpartum Haemorrhage." *Health Policy and Planning* 28, no. 4: 339–46. https://doi.org/10.1093/heapol /czs068.

Premium Times. 2014. "Lagos Moves to Reduce Maternal, Infant Mortality." June 11. https://www.premiumtimesng.com/news/162614-lagos-moves-reduce-maternal -infant-mortality.html.

Pyone, Thidar, Sunday Adaji, Barbara Madaj, Tadesse Woldetsadik, and Nynke Van Den Broek. 2014. "Changing the Role of the Traditional Birth Attendant in Somaliland." *International Journal of Gynecology and Obstetrics* 127, no. 1: 41–46. https://doi .org/10.1016/j.ijgo.2014.04.009.

Rai, N. 2015. "Attending to Traditional Birth Attendants: Incentives and Responses in Western Kenya" (Publishing no. 3700166). PhD diss., Georgetown University. ProQuest Dissertations Publishing.

Reiches, Meredith. 2019. "Reproductive Justice and the History of Prenatal Supplementation: Ethics, Birth Spacing, and the 'Priority Infant' Model in The Gambia: Winner of the 2019 Catharine Stimpson Prize for Outstanding Feminist Scholarship." *Signs: Journal of Women in Culture and Society* 45, no. 1: 3–26. https://doi.org /10.1086/703493.

Relief Web. 2010. "Malawi: President Lifts Ban on Traditional Birth Assistants." October 11. https://reliefweb.int/report/malawi/malawi-president-lifts-ban -traditional-birth-assistants.

Ronsmans, Carine, Wendy J. Graham, and LMSSSG (Lancet Maternal Survival Series Steering Group). 2006. "Maternal Mortality: Who, When, Where, and Why." *Lancet* 368, no. 9542: 1189–1200. https://doi.org/10.1016/S0140-6736(06)69380-X.

Ross, Loretta, Erika Derkas, Whitney Peoples, Lynn Roberts, and Pamela Bridgewater, eds. 2017. *Radical Reproductive Justice: Foundation, Theory, Practice, Critique.* New York: Feminist Press.

Ross, Loretta, and Rickie Solinger. 2017. *Reproductive Justice: An Introduction.* Berkeley: University of California Press.

Sibley, Lynn M., and Theresa Ann Sipe. 2006. "Transition to Skilled Birth Attendance: Is There a Future Role for Trained Traditional Birth Attendants?" *Journal of Health, Population, and Nutrition* 24, no. 4: 472–78. https://www.ncbi.nlm.nih.gov /pmc/articles/PMC3001151/.

Small, Maria J., Terrence K. Allen, and Haywood L. Brown. 2017. "Global Disparities in Maternal Morbidity and Mortality." *Seminars in Perinatology* 41, no. 5: 318–22. https://doi.org/10.1053/j.semperi.2017.04.009.

Smith, Andrea. 2005. "Beyond Pro-Choice Versus Pro-Life: Women of Color and Reproductive Justice." *NWSA Journal* 17, no. 1 (Spring): 119–40.

Starrs, Ann M. 2006. "Safe Motherhood Initiative: Twenty Years and Counting." *Lancet* 368, no. 9542: 1130–32. https://doi.org/10.1016/S0140-6736(06)69385-9.

Storeng, Katerini T., and Dominique P. Béhague. 2014. "'Playing the Numbers Game': Evidence-Based Advocacy and the Technocratic Narrowing of the Safe Motherhood Initiative." *Medical Anthropology Quarterly* 28, no. 2: 260–79. https:// doi.org/10.1111/maq.12072.

Tabobondung, Rebeka. 2017. "Revitalizing Traditional Indigenous Birth Knowledge." In *Indigenous Experiences of Pregnancy and Birth*, edited by Hannah Tait Neufeld and Jaime Cidro, 129–43. Ontario: Demeter Press.

Turner, Darline. 2015. "Queen Elizabeth Perry Turner: Granny Midwife, 1931–1956." In Oparah and Bonaparte 2015: 31–33.

UNESCO (United Nations Educational, Scientific, and Cultural Organization). 2020. *The Place of African Traditional Medicine in Response to COVID-19 and Beyond.* United Nations, March 12. https://en.unesco.org/news/place-african-traditional -medicine-response-covid-19-and-beyond.

UNESCO (United Nations Educational, Scientific, and Cultural Organization). 2021. *Local and Indigenous Knowledge Systems (LINKS)*. United Nations. https://en.unesco.org/links.

UNFPA (United Nations Population Fund). 2006. *UNFPA Maternal Mortality Update, 2006: Expectation and Delivery; Investing in Midwives and Others with Midwifery Skills*. United Nations. https://www.unfpa.org/sites/default/files/pub-pdf/mm_update06_eng.pdf.

van Tol, Deanne. 2007. "Mothers, Babies, and the Colonial State: The Introduction of Maternal and Infant Welfare Services in Nigeria, 1925–1945." *Spontaneous Generations: A Journal for the History and Philosophy of Science* 1, no. 1: 110–31. https://doi.org/10.4245/sponge.v1i1.1761.

Weil, Olivier, and Hervé Fernandez. 1999. "Is Safe Motherhood an Orphan Initiative?" *Lancet* 354, no. 9182: 940–43. https://doi.org/10.1016/S0140-6736(99)02369-7.

Wilson, Amie, Ioannis D. Gallos, Nieves Plana, David Lissauer, Khalid S. Khan, Javier Zamora, Christine MacArthur, and Arri Coomarasamy. 2011. "Effectiveness of Strategies Incorporating Training and Support of Traditional Birth Attendants on Perinatal and Maternal Mortality: Meta-Analysis." *BMJ* 343: 1–10. https://doi.org/10.1136/bmj.d7102.

World Bank. 2020. *Global Health Workforce Statistics, OECD, Supplemented by Country Data*. https://data.worldbank.org/indicator/SH.MED.PHYS.ZS?locations=NG.

World Bank. 2021. "Population, Total—Nigeria." https://data.worldbank.org/indicator/SP.POP.TOTL?locations=NG.

World Bank. 2023. "Hospital Beds (per One Thousand People)." https://data.worldbank.org/indicator/SH.MED.BEDS.ZS.

World Health Organization. 1992. "Traditional Birth Attendants: A Joint WHO/UNFPA/UNICEF Statement." https://apps.who.int/iris/handle/10665/38994.

World Health Organization. 2004. "Making Pregnancy Safer: The Critical Role of the Skilled Attendant." https://apps.who.int/iris/bitstream/handle/10665/42955/9241591692.pdf;jsessionid=05D3136F6F87B579354293860EF68B8F?sequence=1.

World Health Organization. 2008. "Skilled Birth Attendants." Factsheet WHO/MPS/08.11.

World Health Organization. 2013. "Women's and Children's Health: Evidence of Impact of Human Rights." https://apps.who.int/iris/bitstream/handle/10665/84203/9789241505420_eng.pdf.

World Health Organization. 2015. "Trends in Maternal Mortality: 1990 to 2015 Estimates by WHO, UNICEF, UNFPA, World Bank Group and the United Nations Population Division." http://apps.who.int/iris/bitstream/10665/194254/1/9789241565141_eng.pdf?ua=1.

World Health Organization. 2016. *Health Workforce Requirements for Universal Health Coverage and the Sustainable Development Goals*. Health Resources for Health Observer Series 17, no. 1. https://apps.who.int/iris/bitstream/handle/10665/250330/9789241511407-?sequence=1.

World Health Organization. 2017. "Human Rights and Health: Key Facts." December 29. https://www.who.int/news-room/fact-sheets/detail/human-rights-and-health.

World Health Organization. 2019. *Trends in Maternal Mortality, 2000 to 2017: Estimates by WHO, UNICEF, UNFPA, World Bank Group, and the United Nations Population Division.* https://www.unfpa.org/sites/default/files/pub-pdf/Maternal_mortality_report .pdf.

World Health Organization. 2021. "Births Attended by Skilled Health Personnel (%)." Global Health Observatory. https://www.who.int/data/gho/data/indicators /indicator-details/GHO/births-attended-by-skilled-health-personnel-(-).

World Health Organization. 2023a. "Maternal Mortality Ratio (per 100,000 Live Births)." Global Health Observatory. https://www.who.int/data/gho/indicator -metadata-registry/imr-details/26.

World Health Organization. 2023b. *Trends in Maternal Mortality, 2000 to 2020: Estimates by WHO, UNICEF, UNFPA, World Bank Group and the United Nations Population Division.* https://www.who.int/publications/i/item/9789240068759.

WHO (World Health Organization) Regional Office for Africa. 2020. "WHO Supports Scientifically-Proven Traditional Medicine." May 4. https://www.afro.who.int /news/who-supports-scientifically-proven-traditional-medicine.

Yaya, Sanni, Olalekan A. Uthman, Agbessi Amouzou, and Ghose Bishwajit. 2018. "Disparities in Caesarean Section Prevalence and Determinants across Sub-Saharan Africa Countries." *Global Health Research and Policy* 3, no. 1: 1–9.

Dana Barqawi

....................................................................................

# About the Artwork "Woman Digging Thorns out of Field"

This artwork is a collaboration between the artist Dana Barqawi and the Palestinian/Lebanese writer, Hind Shoufani, on the Relation to the Land.

The artistic collaboration process centers on a poem by Samih al-Qasim, a resistance poet and an outspoken opponent of racism and oppression in the Middle East. Hind was inspired to write about "the Land," and Dana visualized the poem in color.

The artwork is adorned with gold leaf, thread, and newspaper clippings, and is a commentary on the politics of land and the colonization of the Indigenous body. It incorporates verses from Samih's poem titled "Sadder Than Water."

....................................................................................

**Dana Barqawi** is a multidisciplinary artist and urban planner based in Amman, Jordan. She holds a bachelor of science in architecture and a double master of science in international cooperation, urban development, and emergency architecture.

For Dana, the act of artistic creation is inseparable from notions of the real world. In times where sociopolitical changes compose an inherent part of our reality, Dana chooses to reflect the context within her work, consequently creating politically and socially engaged art. Dana's work challenges colonial narratives while exploring Indigenous identities and aspects of womanhood and community. This approach unfolded as a result of her years of work with INGOs and government bodies and her international training spanning Europe, Africa, and the Middle East, which focused on community participation and development.

MERIDIANS · feminism, race, transnationalism   23:1 April 2024
DOI: 10.1215/15366936-10935417 © 2024 Smith College

Growing up with women who painted, sewed, designed, and made art, Dana extends herself through artistry and has a long-standing fascination with detail. Working from a studio in Amman, her work involves experimenting with material and is constantly evolving.

She participated in exhibitions in Amman, Washington DC, Connecticut, and Seoul, and she curated an exhibition in collaboration with an academic entity. Dana's work has been published in *World Literature Today* and *Discontent* magazines.

# 2024 Paula J. Giddings Best Article Award

## *Winner*

Zeynep K. Korkman for her article
"(Mis)Translations of the Critiques of
Anti-Muslim Racism and the Repercussions
for Transnational Feminist Solidarities"
*Meridians* 22:2

*Bio:* Zeynep K. Korkman is assistant professor of gender studies at University of California, Los Angeles. Her research explores the gendered relationships between affect, labor, religion, and feminist politics, with a focus on Turkey. Her book, Gendered Fortunes: Divination, Precarity, and Affect in Postsecular Turkey, was published in 2023 by Duke University Press.

*Abstract:* As critiques of anti-Muslim racism travel transnationally, they get translated in relation to complex histories of imperialism, colonialism, postcolonialism, and nationalism. These (mis)translations produce unexpected uses and abuses of anti-Muslim racism as an academic and political concept, with significant consequences for transnational feminist solidarity. This article explores, as a case in point, the emergence of a "Black Turk" identity in millennial Turkey where pious Muslim identity, once marginalized under a secularist state, has reasserted itself by deploying an analogy of Black to pious Muslim. Obscuring the nuances of local power relations, the pious Muslim/secular fault line was oversimplified and mistranslated into the resonant American idiom of the Black/white binary. This analogy and the progressive critiques of anti-Black and especially anti-Muslim racisms were then instrumentalized by an increasingly authoritarian and gender-conservative Islamist Turkish government to legitimize its repressive agendas, even succeeding to garner unexpected sympathy from some feminist politicians and academics in the United States. Naive confidence that such dichotomous racial/religious categories and familiar political vocabularies can guide feminist analyses and politics risks employing a seemingly transnationalist and anti-imperialist but in truth U.S.-centric understanding of non-U.S. struggles for social justice and thwarting potential transnational feminist solidarities.

*Read the article:* https://read.dukeupress
.edu/meridians/article/22/2/267/382324/
Mis-Translations-of-the-Critiques-of-Anti-Muslim

# 2024 Paula J. Giddings Best Article Award

## *Honorable Mention*

Grace L. Sanders Johnson for her article
"Picturing Herself in Africa: Haiti, Diaspora,
and the Visual Folkloric" *Meridians* 22:2

*Bio:* Grace L. Sanders Johnson is assistant professor of Africana studies at the University of Pennsylvania. She received her PhD in history and women's studies at the University of Michigan where she specialized in modern Caribbean and Latin American history, transnational feminisms, oral history, and African diasporic studies.

*Abstract:* This essay explores the relationship between imaging, archival cataloging, and African diasporic belonging through the developed and undeveloped photography of Haitian anthropologist Suzanne Comhaire- Sylvain. Using her family correspondences and research on folklore to contextualize her image-based archive on Haiti, the Belgian Congo, and Nigeria, the author proposes that Comhaire-Sylvain's visual catalog is rendered legible through her undeveloped images taken in Africa. Tracing Comhaire-Sylvain's contortions in front of and behind the camera, the author shows that her undeveloped and unpublished imaging practices of play and experimentation exemplify a medium of scholarly and personal reflexivity that troubled the authority of her professional research practice and enlivened the range of her diasporic expression. With particular attention given to photos taken during her time in the Belgian Congo between 1943 and 1945 and her long-stay return to Haiti in 1957, the author argues that Comhaire-Sylvain's imaging catalog is most provocatively read as an assemblage bound by her use of folklore as a unique technology for crafting meaning between overlapping sites of diasporic belonging and intellectual inquiry.

*Read the article:* https://read.dukepress
.edu/meridians/article/22/2/348/382327
/Picturing- Herself-in-AfricaHaiti-Diaspora-and-the

# 2024 Paula J. Giddings Best Article Award

## Honorable Mention

Dia Da Costa for her article "Writing Castelessly: Brahminical Supremacy in Education, Feminist Knowledge, and Research" *Meridians* 22:2

*Bio:* Dia Da Costa is professor of social justice and international studies in education at the University of Alberta. She is the author of Politicizing Creative Economy: Activism and a Hunger Called Theatre (2016) and Development Dramas: Reimagining Rural Political Action in Eastern India (2009). Her current research focuses on the relationship of caste, multiple colonialisms, and the reproduction of Brahminical domination within transnational feminism, higher education, and development.

*Abstract:* This article combines historical and life-writing approaches to demonstrate how caste is made invisible in histories and structures of education, canonical knowledge, and research. As a dominant-caste (savarna) Bengali academic, the author follows caste-oppressed feminists to offer a methodological intervention that challenges several ways in which castelessness is reproduced in feminist scholarship. The author asks why savarna write castelessly. "Writing castelessly," wherein caste reflexivity is absented from analysis, solidarity, and teaching, is one manifestation of savarna feminists' historical-material relation to caste. Narrating regional caste histories of savarna Bengalis, the author shows that her practice of writing castelessly is founded on material structures of power—historically claimed monopolies over culture and education, land, labor, and political representation. Relatedly, another reason savarna write castelessly is that disciplinary training in social sciences in higher education taught the author to think, feel, read, and write castelessly. Finally, the author traces the reproduction of these disciplinary structures in her scholarship. Ultimately, this self-critique grounded in historical and material relations of caste seeks a feminist readership invested in public accountability and denaturalizing Brahminical merit in academia.

*Read the article:* https://read.dukeupress.edu
/meridians/article/22/2/297/382318/Writing-Castelessly
Brahminical-Supremacy-in

Printed and bound by CPI Group (UK) Ltd, Croydon, CR0 4YY

13/04/2025

14656482-0001